Family Theories

Family Theories

Foundations and Applications

Katherine R. Allen and Angela C. Henderson

WILEY Blackwell

This edition first published 2017

Registered Office
John Wiley & Sons Ltd, The Atrium, Southern Gate, Chichester, West Sussex, PO19 8SQ, UK

Editorial Offices
350 Main Street, Malden, MA 02148-5020, USA
9600 Garsington Road, Oxford, OX4 2DQ, UK
The Atrium, Southern Gate, Chichester, West Sussex, PO19 8SQ, UK

For details of our global editorial offices, for customer services, and for information about how to apply for permission to reuse the copyright material in this book please see our website at www.wiley.com/wiley-blackwell.

Library of Congress Cataloging-in-Publication data applied for.

9780470673409 [paperback]

A catalogue record for this book is available from the British Library.

Cover image: Gettyimages / © Jorg Greuel

Set in 10/12pt Bembo by Aptara Inc., New Delhi, India

SKY10020372_081020

To Katherine's family of origin: Jack, Betty, Beth, John, Dan, and Doug

and

To Angie's family of origin: Bev, LaVerne, Brad, and Chris

Contents

Acknowledgments

This book has been a pleasure to write. Our shared passion for theory has developed into a seamless collaboration, where our strengths and interests enhance one another. We also share a passion for guiding students in the discovery process of linking theory, research, and application as family scholars and practitioners. Our goal is to reveal how understanding theory and being able to theorize are essential qualities for a life well lived. Surely, we have benefited from this journey in theory, and we sincerely hope that readers will as well.

Speaking of our readers, we acknowledge that we wrote this book by keeping in the forefront the thousands of students we have taught in our collective 30-plus years as educators. Our students have taught us many lessons about the value of theory in the scientific enterprise and the excitement in learning to understand and use it effectively. We have also kept in mind our peers who teach students about theory and theorizing. It is encouraging to know that there are many other educators who share our interest in theory and our commitment to sharing this knowledge with students.

We have many individuals to thank for their scholarly and editorial contributions to this book. First, Brandy Renee McCann, who initially was one of the authors of this book until family responsibilities required her attention, was instrumental in developing the proposal for the book and drafting one of the early chapters. We thank Brandy for generously sharing her expertise in the development of the project. Second, several undergraduate and graduate students at Virginia Tech provided insightful feedback about the initial chapters we wrote: Emma Potter, Katie Barrow, and Lauren Byrd. In the later stages of completing the book, Erin Lavender-Stott was our trusted reader. Erin read every chapter and all of the supplemental materials, diligently offering her excellent assistance. Third, we humbly thank our anonymous reviewers for their invaluable comments and critiques of the manuscript, each of which helped make this book better. We especially thank Fiona Tasker for her many helpful suggestions. Fourth, the Wiley editorial teams with whom we have worked have been a wonderful resource for the book. From the very beginning, when Julia Teweles invited us to write the book and shepherded the work through its first stages, we have felt we are in expert hands. We have also benefited from the thoughtful feedback and timely editorial advice we have received from Deirdre Ilkson, Julia Kirk, Haze Humbert, Mark Graney, and Sue Leigh. Ann Bone and Allison Kostka, in particular, have guided us through the final stages with such patience and skill. We are grateful to all of these individuals who have helped us along the way.

The process of learning to utilize theory began with our own family theory teachers. Robert Pickett and Colleen Johnson ignited Katherine's passion for family theory in graduate school at Syracuse University. Charlotte Dunham and Jill Suitor both fueled Angie's interests in family theories during her graduate coursework and writing her dissertation.

Finally, we thank our families, Jeff Burr and Matt Special, and Jimmy, Owen, Cameron and Cora Henderson, who enrich our lives and provide the private testing ground for theorizing about intimate life. We thank them beyond measure for walking with us on this journey every step of the way.

About the Website

www.wiley.com/go/allen

The *Family Theories: Foundations and Applications* companion website features instructor resources created by the authors to help you use this book in college and university courses.

- Criteria for Evaluating Family Theories
- Sample Syllabus for Family Theories Course
- Sample Syllabus for Sociology of Family Course (Online)
- Test Bank: Multiple Choice and Essay Questions
- Test Bank: Answers to Multiple Choice Questions
- Glossary

1

What Is Theory?

You are probably familiar with Apple's phrase "There's an app for that!" – it is one we use often in modern society to refer to the ways in which our smartphones, tablets, and other electronic devices can help us be more efficient, more creative, and *better* at what we do. "Apps" help us problem solve, help us think in different ways about our everyday lives, our friends, our families, and our social calendars. They help us put it all into a manageable, knowable format that provides a framework for understanding our daily lives.

You may ask yourself why we are beginning our theory text with a discussion of electronic applications. A **theory** – or a set of ideas – serves as a framework for understanding the world around us. The social science theories that we describe in this text can be applied, tested, and even revised over time in order to fit the changing social world. This text presents you with 10 theories of family; 10 unique ways to look at the world, to help you, as a student, better understand how to look at and solve problems that you will face in your profession someday. As a practitioner, how will you make sense of the dynamics of the families you are serving? How will you make an informed decision about how to provide services, inform policy, or conduct research on changing family dynamics? As an example, consider that you are charged with developing state policies to make the Family and Medical Leave Act of 1993 (2006) more accessible to very diverse working- and middle-class families. As a policymaker, you will need to know the demographic trends that show just how diverse families are in modern society: there are blended families, single parents, same-sex partnerships, grandparents raising grandchildren, and many more variations. Contemporary society tends to be **pluralistic**, which means we have a heterogeneous population made up of different genders, racial-ethnic groups, religions, sexual orientations, and social classes. You need to be aware of how each of these characteristics intersects to create advantage or disadvantage for your clients. You need to be aware of barriers that prevent working-class families from using family policies because they cannot afford to. You need to be aware of historical data, so you can consider what has and has not worked. You need to be able to think outside the box – question the status quo – so that you can develop new, innovative policies for today's changing families. In sum, you need an "app" for that.

Theory – as we present it in this text – is your app. Theories help you be a problem solver, an informed researcher, an effective educator, program director, nurse, social worker, or therapist with a unique perspective to be able to work through problems and solve them with forethought that will set you apart. We want your theoretical mind to be actively engaged at all times, so that when you are tasked with problem solving in your profession, you are able to tackle the problem with the applicability that theory offers to your profession.

When it comes time for you to utilize your theoretical knowledge in the everyday world, we want you to be able to say "There's a theory for that!" – a theory that will help you look at the problem through a critical lens. Knowing theory means you are able to access multiple data points – you are familiar with larger trends and patterns that help explain social institutions and social injustice. Theoretical minds are also familiar with how the theory has informed research;

Family Theories: Foundations and Applications, First Edition. Katherine R. Allen and Angela C. Henderson.

for instance, we are able to study families on a **macro-level** by analyzing larger patterns in society, such as rates of marriage, fertility, and divorce. Using a macro-level of analysis, we can examine patterns of behavior on a large scale: How is socioeconomic status (SES) related to marital patterns, fertility, and divorce? Do middle- and upper-class individuals wait to get married until they are older, compared to working-class individuals? In addition, studying families through a theoretical lens can also be done at the *micro-level*, by analyzing phenomena more closely, in smaller doses. For example, a **micro-level** of analysis would frame questions about social class and marriage much differently: instead of large-scale patterns, we would be interested in finding out what the meaning of marriage is for individuals from different social class backgrounds. We could also explore each partner's perceptions of what an "ideal" spouse is, based on their SES. Has the "ideal" changed over time? Does the description of an ideal spouse depend on gender? What about whether or not the partnership is lesbian, gay, or heterosexual? Theories give us a framework for understanding each and every one of those intersecting factors – on multiple levels – as we work with and study families.

Case Study

Bo-Meh, the subject of our case study, is a first-generation college student who has only been living in the United States for five years. She entered the country with refugee status, along with her mother and three younger siblings, after living in a refugee camp in Thailand for eight years. After graduating from high school in America, she enrolled in college with the hopes of becoming a social worker so she can someday pay back the many services she benefited from as a newcomer to the US. She has three younger siblings, all of whom have depended on her for care since her mother works 12-hour shifts at her job.

As Bo-Meh sits through her first "Theories of Family" course as a family studies major, she wonders about her classmates. The professor put the students into groups of five for a class project, which requires them to work together to answer a research question using various theories of family. Her group members are very diverse. Maggie is a 41-year-old mother of three who put off college to raise her children, and she is majoring in nursing. Seneca is a 22-year-old media studies major who wants to develop television programming for children. Natalie is a 20-year-old elementary education major, and Curtis is a middle-aged war veteran who wants to go into marriage and family therapy. Given how diverse the group members are, Bo-Meh wonders how well they will work together, and how they will find anything in common to be able to accomplish the tasks for the semester. Will they be able to find times to meet outside of class, given their conflicting schedules and outside responsibilities? Will they be able to agree on a theoretical framework to answer the research questions, given how different their majors and career goals are?

Like other students taking a family theory course, these budding professionals (e.g., social worker, nurse, television programming developer, elementary school teacher, and family therapist) all have to take family dynamics into account as a part of their coursework. Yet, their interactions with and perceptions of families will differ greatly, possibly creating rough patches when it comes to completing their project. Finally, how will each classmate's own family upbringing affect how they view families? In this chapter, we explore **epistemologies** – or, one's orientation to answering questions about the world – as they relate to the study of families. Your epistemology provides a framework for how you approach answering questions, such as "Why do people get divorced?" Think about how different people may answer that question, depending on their life experiences and beliefs. If you have grown up in a family that has experienced divorce, you may feel that poor communication skills or financial strain lead to divorce. Another classmate may see divorce as a blessing, given how much his parents verbally abused one another. Yet another classmate may suggest that divorce is not even on his radar, since his two fathers fought most of his life for the right to be legally recognized as a married couple in his home state of Minnesota. Each of these different life experiences contribute to one's view of families. In addition, each student's major or career trajectory will influence how they perceive issues of the family as well. While Bo-Meh may see these differences

Box 1.1 At a Glance: Theory Is …

- "The word *theory* sends a glaze over the eyes of most people. This is somewhat ironic because the word theory comes from the Greek *theoria*, which means "a looking at." … A theory is simply one's understanding of how something works" (Shoemaker, Tankard, and Lasorsa, 2004, pp. 5–6).
- "Theorizing is like being presented with a puzzle where only some of the pieces are visible or seem to fit together. Fitting the pieces together is fun, though often frustrating, particularly when the overall picture is vague or elusive" (Bengtson et al., 2005, p. 5).
- "In everyday family life, there are many activities that take up considerable time, energy, and attention but that are poorly represented in our theorizing about families … The result is that family life tends to be viewed in terms of averages around measures of central tendency, rather than in the diversity and complexity of shared meanings and interrelated perceptions" (Daly, 2003, p. 772).
- "No one group possesses the theory or methodology that allows it to discover the absolute 'truth' or, worse yet, proclaim its theories and methodologies as the universal norm evaluating other groups' experiences. Given that groups are unequal in power in making themselves heard, dominant groups have a vested interest in suppressing the knowledge produced by subordinate groups" (Collins, 1990, p. 235).

as barriers to her group coming to consensus on a theory to explain family dynamics, it is important to instead consider them as valuable differences. With each person's experience and academic focus comes a new lens – or, epistemology – that can help others in different professions view the family in a new way.

Theory Building Blocks: Epistemologies, Assumptions, Concepts, and Propositions

In order to understand theories, we first need to understand how they are used to explain ideas. Scientific theories consist of epistemologies, assumptions, concepts, and propositions. These building blocks of theory are important to both build *and* deconstruct theory. Figure 1.1 shows how to think of each layer of theory building as a pyramid; beginning with the bottom layer (epistemologies), each layer builds on the previous one. In order to understand how a theory explains families, we can remove the blocks and analyze each layer.

Epistemologies

At the foundation of the pyramid are epistemologies. Epistemologies are the overall frame of reference that a theorist brings to the study of families. They answer the questions: (a) What is knowing? (b) How do we know what we think we know? And (c) How useful is what we think we know? (Bengtson et al., 2005). All theorists have an epistemology that guides their thinking.

For example, a **positivist epistemology** presumes that there is an objective truth that we can discover

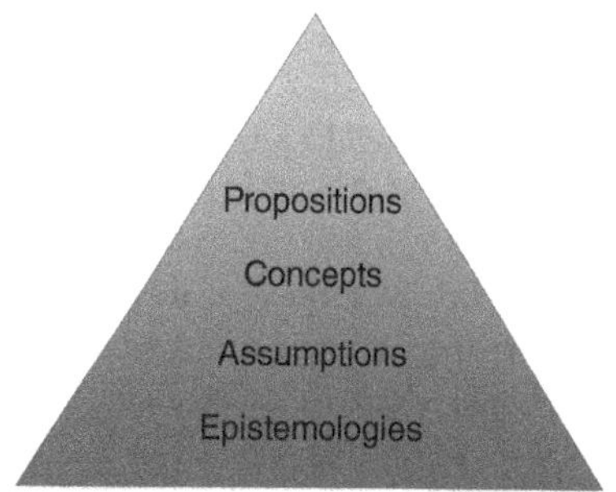

Figure 1.1 Building blocks of theory

about families through systematic research procedures. Positivism guides the scientific method and presents knowledge as value-neutral or value-free. When studying families, a positivist would approach the study of divorce by examining perhaps length of marriage, age at first marriage, and variables such as the race/ethnicity of the couple, the region of the country in which they marry, and perhaps their religious identity. From a positivist view, a family researcher is able to explain the *who*, *what*, and *where* of divorce, but not necessarily the *why*. Positivist theories are useful for predicting and explaining phenomena on a large scale.

On the other hand, an **interpretive epistemology** views knowledge as subjective, with the goal of understanding how families make meaning of their own experiences. Family scholars with this epistemological orientation differ from positivists because they are interested more in the *why* of explaining family dynamics. That is, instead of being interested in facts and statistics about divorce, the interpretivist would want to know what divorce means to families. Divorce could mean very different things to families, depending on the situation. In some families, divorce could signify the end of an abusive and unhealthy relationship. In others, it could symbolize a mutually agreed-upon move in a new direction for both partners. Therefore, an interpretive epistemology allows researchers and theorists a way to conceptualize "truth" as something that is changing and not the same for all parties. This orientation allows for multiple truths to hold for each family, and each family member, being studied. Interpretivist theories are useful for understanding multiple dimensions of family, and being empathetic with different lived realities for each.

A **critical epistemology** holds that what gets to count as knowledge is defined by those who are in power, and thus, the powerful members of society impose their definitions onto others. This orientation is critical of what is held to be true about families; that is, the assumption that all families should procreate. That perspective, however, is not a "truth" for all members of society wishing to call themselves families. Critical theorists also examine what are referred to as **social constructions of reality**. A social construction is something that was defined as important and valuable by powerful members of society. Often, socially constructed truths serve the purpose of reifying the social structure and inequality that exists. For example, if divorce rates increase, powerful members of that society may start disseminating **rhetoric**, which refers to messages that are aimed at persuading the audience. Anti-divorce rhetoric would suggest that the "American family is on the decline" and "the future of America is at stake" unless the increase in divorce rates is stopped. The rhetoric is based on a social construction that suggests divorce is always harmful, not only to the individuals involved, but to society as a whole. Critical theorists examine these messages as social constructions of reality that are not true for all families. Critical theory is useful for breaking down ideologies and suggesting that it is important to give voice to those with marginalized power and status in society.

Assumptions

Given how different these epistemologies are, each theory will have certain assumptions about how the world works. **Assumptions** are the ideas that scholars believe to be true about families. They are the starting point for a theory – the taken-for-granted ideas that lay the groundwork for theory building. Assumptions are unique to each theory – they provide an orientation to studying the social world that is specific. For example, functionalist theory (Chapter 2) assumes that families are functional for all members. This assumption overlooks a stark reality for families – that some interactions are harmful for family members. Other theories, such as conflict theory (Chapter 3), assume that conflict is an inherent part of both the social world we live in, and inevitable within families as well. These two theories have very different assumptions, which will shape how the theory is applied and how it is used to explain family forms and family dynamics.

The way that social scientists view and theorize families inevitably changes over time, as norms change and society evolves. How assumptions have shifted over time is evident when we examine perceptions of women in families and in the legal profession throughout the past century. For example, in the latter half of the nineteenth century, women tried to enter the legal profession, which prompted responses not only from law school administrators, but also from state and Supreme Court justices in the United States. Based on the dominant gender and family ideologies of the time, women were denied both entrance into law school and licenses to practice law. Three concurring Supreme Court justices wrote in 1869:

> Man is, or should be, woman's protector and defender. The natural and proper timidity and delicacy which belongs to the female sex evidently unfits it for many of the occupations of civil life. The constitution of the family organization, which is founded in the divine ordinance, as well as in the nature of things, indicates the domestic sphere as that which properly belongs to the domain and functions of womanhood ... The paramount destiny and mission of woman are to fulfill the noble and benign offices of wife and mother. (Weisberg, 1977, p. 492)

In 1875, the Wisconsin Supreme Court agreed, writing that any woman who attempted to become a lawyer was "committing 'treason' against 'the order of nature'" (Weisberg, 1977, p. 493). This view of women was not only widely accepted in the legal profession, but also among other professionals. A Harvard University physician argued that women should not even be allowed to study law because it posed a threat to women's health (and therefore the future of America) because women would become unable to reproduce: "[It is] dangerous for women to engage in strenuous intellectual activity, [which would] divert energy from female reproductive organs to the brain, harming the health of women and their children" (Clarke, 1873, p. 126).

Some men supported letting women into law school, but with certain stipulations. A graduate of Yale Law School wrote to the admissions office that he supported allowing women to study law, "provided they are ugly" (Morello, 1982, p. 625).

Clearly, these views are no longer a part of our orientation to studying families. Yet, perhaps some of the views remain, such as the perception that women are better suited to care for children. This is called **cultural lag**, where society evolves but facets of culture, such as beliefs and values, take longer to change. What do you think? Do we still view women differently than men, when it comes to families? What are your own personal assumptions about studying gender and families?

Concepts

Concepts are terms and definitions used to explain the theory's framework based on the assumptions. Concepts are integral to explaining theories: they provide the building blocks used to create the theory. For example, structural-functionalist theorists use the term "roles" to describe a set of expectations associated with each family member. The head of household – typically assumed to be the husband in functionalist theory (Chapter 2) – performs *instrumental* roles in the family, or the tasks needed to ensure the family's basic survival (Parsons, 1970). Based on the assumption that families are functional for all members, the husband makes important decisions, gives orders, and exerts power over other family members. The *concepts* used in this example are "role" and "instrumental." They are derived from the *assumptions* that functionalist theorists hold to be true about families.

There are many important concepts used in family theories. Sometimes the same term is defined in different ways by different theories. For example, the concept of "conflict" is defined as inevitable in conflict theory (Chapter 3), but as deviant in functionalist theory (Chapter 2). In order to understand how theorists "see" the world and explain family dynamics, we need to be familiar with the concepts and their definitions, as they are used in various theories. Once we can explain the assumptions behind a theory, and define the concepts, we can then apply, test, and refine the theory in family practice and research.

Propositions

Propositions are statements based on both assumptions and concepts that we use when we "apply" theory to the study of families (Bengtson et al., 2005). For example, a proposition derived from social exchange theory (Chapter 7) is that a husband's income level is related to the probability of divorce. Propositions are operationalized as hypotheses; that is, hypotheses restate the proposition in a way that can be tested in research (Babbie, 2013). The proposition that a husband's income level is related to the probability of divorce can be restated to test in a research study as: Men with higher incomes than average have lower divorce rates than average (Nye, 1979). Hypotheses, which reformulate propositions into their empirical version, specify the direction of change the researcher expects will occur. Propositions, then, can be upheld based on the findings in a research study, or they can be refuted, or deemed inapplicable, depending on the family to which we are applying the propositions.

Propositions are the pinnacle of the theory; propositions allow us to tell whether the theory is still relevant 50 years after its creation, or perhaps that it needs to be updated to reflect, for example, changing demographics and marital patterns in society. Thus, theory informs research, and research informs theory (Klein, 2005; Wallace, 1971). Science is a process of going from induction (beginning with observations and moving on to theory) to deduction (beginning with theory and moving on to observations) in repetitious fashion (see Figure 1.2). One way to think about this cycle of knowledge building is to imagine theory building as a "cycle." Theoretical propositions contribute to scientific inquiry (hypotheses and data collection), and those results then contribute to a broader body of knowledge about the topic. Then, the theory is either confirmed, or updated and modified depending on the results.

Propositions make theories testable; what this means is that each theory has statements about how the world works – or in this case, how families work. When you are using the theory, whether it is for data collection as a researcher, or interpreting a case as a social worker, you will be applying the propositions to the families you are working with or studying. Depending upon the result of applying a proposition, you will either confirm or refute the proposition, and thus further refine the theory. To build on our example using functionalist theory (Chapter 2), one of this theory's propositions is that when a family member deviates from their role expectations, dysfunction may occur. Then, in order for the family to properly function again as a whole, the family member must figure out a way to conform to the role expectations set forth by the family. Functionalists view the family as a human body – when the brain is compromised, so are other parts of the human body. The brain sends messages to the heart, lungs, and other vital organs. If the brain is injured, functionalists argue that in order for equilibrium to be reached, repairs need to be made to allow the brain to continue fulfilling its role expectations. Similarly, according to this theory, a husband, or head-of-household, must fulfill instrumental role expectations in order for everyone else in the family to know what to do, when to do it, and how to do it.

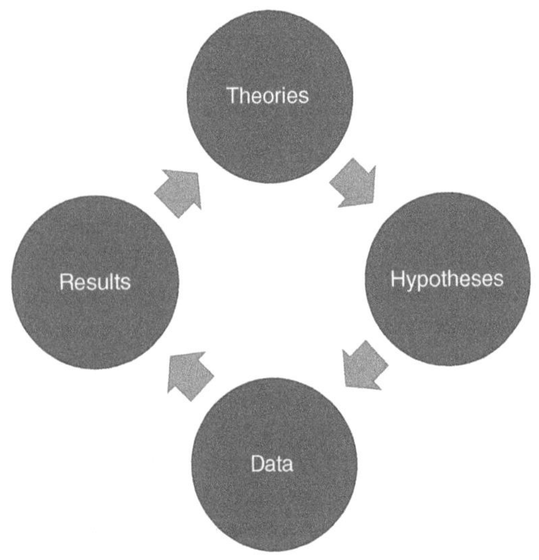

Figure 1.2 The scientific process and theory building

What Is a *Family* Theory? Common Assumptions across All Theories

Although this is a book about different types of family theories, there are several assumptions made about families that are embedded in all of the theories we cover in this book. These assumptions reveal what the community of scholars, that is, the researchers, theorists, and practitioners, in the family field perceive about the inner workings of families and the broader structures that constrain their lives.

Developmental assumption: families change over time

The incorporation of time into the family life course is one of the most important contributions of family theory. Families consist of interdependent lives that continually change over time. Conceptualizing both the individual life course and the family life cycle is critical to family theorizing. Your own life course, for example, begins with your birth and ends with your death. In that sense, the life course is linear. However, the life course of families is cyclical, in that family roles and relationships at each stage are eventually occupied by new members. As a person moves through time, he or she occupies various positions in the life course (e.g., child, sibling, partner, parent, widow), but the cycle of the family spirals on, beyond any one person's life course. Think back to our case study; Bo-Meh is in the life course stage of young adulthood, and her group member Maggie is in the middle of her life course, having raised children before attending college. Each person has an individual life course (i.e., young adulthood versus mid-life) as well as a family life cycle. Bo-Meh has cared for her younger siblings in the absence of her working mother, which situates her a little farther along – in terms of the family life cycle – than her peers. In fact, she and Maggie share child-rearing in common, even though they are at different stages of the life course. Each of these intersecting experiences is important to take into account when thinking about families and development.

Diversity assumption: families vary in their composition and structure

As we explain below, there is no singular type of family. Families differ in multiple ways, according to the intersections of each individual's race, class, gender, sexual orientation, age, nationality, and other characteristics. Families also differ across these divisions (e.g., Black families; families where the parents are lesbian, gay, bisexual, transgender or queer (LGBTQ); childless families; extended families; single-adult families). There are many structural variations in families as well. For example, families include intragenerational relationships (e.g., married couples; adult sibling relationships) and intergenerational relationships (e.g., parent–child; aunt–nephew; grandparent–grandchild). Families also differ by household structure: members of families, even nuclear ones characterized by two parents and their children, can live in different households; examples include (a) a young adult who lives in an apartment "away from home" during college; (b) a married couple who "live together apart" by occupying two households, often due to working in separate locations; and (c) a binational family, in which a mother goes to work in a country with greater economic opportunities, while her children stay back in the home country and are cared for by relatives. This "diversity" assumption is an important one; before family theorists adopted the assumption that families were not "one-size-fits-all", theories were developed based on one standard model, which does not fit for families in contemporary society.

Systemic assumption: families are systems

Families are more than a collection of individuals related to each other. Families consist of interrelated parts, where lives are connected through communication (process) and composition (structure). When some event occurs in one person's life, all the members of the family system are impacted. If a father gets a new job, the whole family could move to a different state, possibly disrupting the children's lives by having to change schools and find new friends. The parents could experience stress at work, and that stress may spill over into family life. What happens to one family member may affect the entire family system, and therefore, the whole of the family is greater than the sum of its parts. An example of this systemic assumption is Curtis, the middle-aged veteran from our case study. Curtis put off attending college until after he served in the military, including a two-year deployment in Afghanistan. During his time in Afghanistan, an explosion close to him injured Curtis, and damaged his nervous system. Three years after the explosion, Curtis married his high school sweetheart and they had a daughter within their first few years of marriage. Unfortunately, the damage to his nervous system from the explosion started to cause seizures, one of which resulted in hospitalization and Curtis being unable to drive for six months (until he could be retested and evaluated). Therefore, every weekday morning at 5 a.m., his wife Donna has to wake up their infant daughter and drive Curtis to the train station for his commute into work and his night classes, and then pick him up every night after his classes are done at 9 p.m. This is a perfect example of how one family member's well-being affects the entire family system.

Processual assumption: families are dynamic

At the micro-level of analysis, families are an emotional domain (Daly, 2007). Family members constantly communicate with one another in visible and invisible ways. Sometimes there is harmony, sometimes there is conflict, and sometimes harmony and conflict are simultaneous. For example, families are often a site of tension between the dynamics of caring for one another and the competing needs that arise in fulfilling caregiving responsibilities while also taking care of oneself (Dressel and Clark, 1990). Bo-Meh is a good example of completing the developmental tasks of emerging from adolescence to adulthood, while at the same time, filling in as a caregiver for younger siblings because her help is needed at home. At the macro-level of analysis, families are dynamic in that they both affect and are affected by broader social systems. Families must deal with social and historical change – demographically, economically, and politically. Bo-Meh's family fled to the United States in order to escape war and persecution. Upon arriving, her family had to adapt in several ways, most notably to a new culture that was more individualized than collectivist. Refugees and immigrants alike still experience similar macro-level cultural adjustments after relocating to the US.

It is also important to note that from a macro-perspective, legal barriers prevented certain immigrants from even entering the United States. Until the mid-twentieth century, the US used the quota system, which limited the number of Asian, Latin and South American, African, and southern European immigrants coming to the US. In 1965, the Immigration and Nationality Act was passed, which opened the doors to others regardless of race or nationality (History.com, 2016). Families need to be flexible and adaptable in order to cope and/or thrive as broader social forces create new challenges and opportunities.

Popular media provide relevant examples to understand the assumptions made by family theorists. As shown in Box 1.2, the television program *Modern Family* demonstrates the key assumptions we just identified: families change over time; families vary in their composition and structure; families are systems; and families are dynamic.

Box 1.2 Family Theory in Pop Culture: *Modern Family*

A scene from *Modern Family*, 2009, cr. Christopher Lloyd and Steven Levitan, 20th Century Fox Television

Modern Family is an American sitcom based on the lives of three families, tied together by the patriarch, Jay. In the show, Jay is married for the second time to a Latina woman (Gloria) who has a 14-year-old son (Manny) from a previous relationship. Jay and Gloria have another child together, a son (Joe). This nuclear family is a good example of a blended family.

Jay's daughter, Claire, has a nuclear family that most closely resembles the traditional family in US society. Claire is married to Phil Dunphy, and they have three children (Haley, Alex, and Luke). Claire is a homemaker for the majority of the show (although she does run for local political office in one episode), and she fulfills fairly traditional feminine gender expectations.

Jay's son, Mitchell, is partnered with Cameron, and together they adopted a Vietnamese daughter, Lily. Their gay-father family is an example of pluralistic American society; modern families vary and a one-size-fits-all model is rare.

This television series also is a good example of both micro- and macro-levels of analysis. In the second season, the show was heavily criticized from the LGBT community for not portraying physical affection between the gay couple, Cameron and Mitchell. This is indicative of a larger, macro-level trend; Americans were not only comfortable with a gay couple on television, they now wanted physical affection – namely, kissing – to be a part of the cultural landscape. The producers of the show responded with just that in an episode titled "The Kiss".

Family dynamics illustrating a micro-level of analysis are replete throughout the show. Jay is at first uncomfortable with his son's homosexuality, which strains their relationship. There are also examples of how Mitchell and Cameron negotiate expectations as both partners and fathers; their interactions show the importance of meaning and communication styles.

Finally, it is interesting to note that the two leading women in the series are stay-at-home mothers; this arrangement rarely creates friction between Jay and Gloria, but often presents issues the Dunphy family has to work through. There are times when Phil feels emasculated, and when it is clear that Claire "wears the pants" in the family. On the surface, it appears that Phil is the head of household. This alludes to the cultural dialogue that occurs within modern families; sometimes role negotiations are ongoing, emotionally charged, and a far cry from what they appear to be on the surface.

"The Family" versus Families: The Normative Family and the Diversity of Families

From the beginning of theorizing about families, scholars were more concerned with the similarity across all families, rather than with the variation among families. The search for "what is normal" provided a starting point and a baseline for family theorists, researchers, and practitioners to understand how the typical family functions. Beginning with the average or the typical family also gives scholars a shortcut in studying and understanding families. This shortcut allows us focus only on **The Family**. Focusing on family with a "capital F" makes it easier to theorize about families as a system that operates among many other macro-systems in the social structure (e.g., the economic system, the religious system, the political system; the criminal justice system).

Assumptions about the normative family are rooted in the nineteenth-century concept of separate spheres for women (inside the home tending to family members' emotions) and men (outside the home, in the world of work and politics). In the language of functionalist theory (Chapter 2), which was one of the earliest family theories to dominate the field, women fulfilled the expressive roles within families and men fulfilled the instrumental roles, and this separation was deemed both efficient and natural. This normative model was based on what family researchers now refer to as the **Standard North American Family** (SNAF) (Smith, 1993) and reflected the experiences of White, middle-class Americans with married, heterosexual parents. Assumptions about the family against which all other families should be judged included (a) families need a "head-of-household" with centralized power in order to function effectively, (b) males should fulfill that role, and (c) roles and expectations are static, and unchanging, over the life course.

As the saying goes, one size does not fit all. The SNAF model excluded variations such as single-parent families, LGBTQ-parent families, families without children, grandparent-headed families, aging parents and their adult children, families formed with chosen or fictive kin who are not biologically related to one another, among many other family forms (Allen, 2000). Coontz (1992) and others have critiqued this model as being outdated and a product of what she refers to as the "nostalgia trap" that we fall into when we romanticize the 1950s as the "Golden Era." Her critique is based on the fact that during that time period, the post–World War II economy was booming. Most families had enough economic stability to only need one breadwinner (the male). Mothers stayed at home; the Civil Rights Movement had not yet occurred, so women of color were overrepresented in domestic work, working for White families. Federal assistance programs such as the G.I. Bill and low-interest housing loans were tailored to help young *middle-class* families become homeowners.

Today, in contrast, most families need two paychecks to maintain economic stability. In addition, the most common family "form" today is a **blended family**; one that includes children from a previous marriage (Sweeney, 2010). Today, scholars recognize that families are very diverse and the roles of partners are not as strict as they once were (Cherlin, 2004; Demo, Allen, and Fine, 2000). Therefore, families are inevitably affected by historical and social forces. When society changes, theories must also change in order to remain effective and timely. An example of such social change is legalizing same-sex civil unions. When such a macro-level change occurs, it inevitably affects protections for and perceptions of LGBTQ individuals. It also affects micro-level factors such as meanings associated with marriage, divorce, partnerships, and roles. Each of these dynamics affects the explanatory power theories have: a theory based on the SNAF model would not be appropriate in explaining family dynamics for all.

On balance, despite the fact that the normative model has been critiqued in recent decades, it is still very entrenched in family theory and research as well as popular culture (Allen, 2000; Bahr and Bahr, 2001; Cheal, 1991). In other words, assumptions about what is normal, ideal, and how families should be, as opposed to how they really are, are very resistant to change. Social norms about the ideal that all families should strive for, and against which all families are judged, are still influential. As Pittman (1993) explains, the normative model may be down, but it certainly isn't out. It is important, then, to understand how this norm developed and why we cannot discount it altogether. As current trends reveal, the SNAF model does not fit all, or most, families; but its influence still lingers.

Although the SNAF model was useful for developing theories of family early on, its description is limited to individualistic cultures, as in North America (e.g., the US and Canada) and Northern Europe (e.g., England). However, as we emphasize in this book, social norms vary from culture to culture, and they also change over time, mostly because ideas and behaviors change. Another important concept related to SNAF is Beck and Beck-Gernsheim's (2001) idea of the "post-familial family" caused by, in part, the global transition from collectivist concerns of the responsibility to take care of others to individualist concerns, where personal freedoms take precedence in everyday life. That is, there is a major societal trend where "living for others" has evolved into "living a life of one's own." This gradual process of "individualization" means that the decisions individuals make for themselves affect the possibilities of forming and maintaining families. What should come first: one's responsibility to oneself, or one's responsibility to a spouse, children, aging parents, and others who have traditionally relied on family members for instrumental and expressive support? Thus, the critique of the nuclear family structure as the normative way in which people should live is a phenomenon that is occurring in North America, Western Europe, Australia, and now, throughout the globe.

How Theory Informs Practice in Global Perspective

There are several ways in which educators, practitioners, and family policy makers can apply theory in their work with individuals and families. First and foremost, it is our hope that after reading this text and utilizing theory as your "app," you will view the world in a multidimensional way. That is, when you notice family dynamics in your own life, or in television and films, your "app" will automatically turn on and you will better understand what you see because you have a trained theoretical mind. In this way, theory informs the practice of *every* professional; no matter where your studies or career take you, your theory app will be with you and will help you see the world and family issues from a variety of different theoretical perspectives. This is vital because one of the most important contributions you can make as a professional who works with and studies families is

Box 1.3 Global Comparisons of the Legal Definitions of Marriage and Family

There are variations from country to country about how marriage, divorce, parenthood, sex, and gender are defined. Consider these examples of current laws in five different countries:

Brazil Members of the same sex can be legally married. (www.pewforum.org)

Germany Gender does not have to be assigned at birth. (www.wsj.com)

Pakistan A man may be married to more than one woman. (www.refworld.org)

Philippines Divorce is illegal. (www.npr.org)

South Africa Same-sex couples are allowed to jointly adopt a child. (www.adoption.laws.com)

being flexible. By applying your theoretical app, you will be able to think outside the box to tackle a problem by taking into account both historical data (e.g., what has and has not worked in particular contexts) as well as contemporary shifts in the changing family landscape.

Therefore, for each chapter in this book, we make specific suggestions for how each theory can be used in a practical setting. Some theories may be helpful for informing policy, such as feminist theory (Chapter 8), family ecological theory (Chapter 10), and family stress and resilience theory (Chapter 11). Others, like family systems theory (Chapter 6) and symbolic interactionist theory (Chapter 4), are useful for understanding how families communicate in order to help teachers, nurses, social workers, or therapists work more effectively with students, clients, and patients. Other theories, such as life course theory (Chapter 9) and family developmental theory (Chapter 5), are useful for understanding a family's development through different life stages, including the needs of caregivers or grandparents raising grandchildren.

In addition, theory frames problems we will encounter in our everyday lives and professions from both a micro- and macro-perspective. That is, we can understand family dynamics by gauging macro-level influences as well as micro-level interactions within the family. A good example of this would be socioeconomic status; when a family's income and wealth situate them in the working class, the wage earners (i.e., parents) may not have access to a solid retirement plan because it is not likely to be included as a part of their benefits package at work. Therefore, over time, they realize the only stability they will have access to after a certain age is Social Security income. This could likely create strain not only among the wage earners but also among the children in the family, because the children may be faced with supporting their parents in their later years. Over time, the power dynamic in the family shifts (micro-level interactions) and the parents, once in a powerful position in the family, are now depending on their children for financial support. These dynamics are influenced by larger forces at play – macro-level structures in society – that are often out of the family's control. Having a solid theoretical foundation – an "app" for problem solving – will help you better serve the needs of your clients, students, and patients. Ideally, a strong theory app will also inform how policies are written and developed to meet the needs of modern families.

Applying Theory: The Case of Transnational Carework

One of the ways that students learn theories is by applying each new theory to the same social issue. Below, we evaluate a contemporary family issue – transnational carework – using the theoretical concepts and assumptions for a few theories. This should provide you with a tangible, internationally relevant example that is applicable to several different theoretical perspectives.

Transnational carework is the term used to describe migrant women working as live-in or live-out domestic workers for families in wealthy nations

(Lutz, 2011). Domestic workers can be hired to care for children or older adults, for housekeeping maintenance or specific duties such as cooking meals or running errands. The reason this is a "transnational" issue is because the majority of domestic workers are migrant women, which means that they come from developing nations, particularly the Philippines, Sri Lanka, India, and throughout the Caribbean and Africa, to live and work in more affluent places such as the United States, Hong Kong, Taiwan, Israel, and Middle Eastern countries. Careworkers leave their homes, their families of origin, and their spouses and children, to migrate to another country to work as a domestic servant, nanny, or elder caregiver. This creates complex new family forms that challenge western ideas of what it means to be a mother, a father, or even a family (Mahalingam, Balan, and Molina, 2009).

From a theoretical standpoint, how would we evaluate this issue? How would we begin to evaluate which theory would be a good fit for understanding transnational carework? First, we would have to decide whether we were going to examine the issue from a micro- or macro-perspective. If we are assessing the ways in which transnational careworkers become so integrated into their employers' families that they are *considered* to be kin, we would be analyzing the issue from a micro-level perspective. From this perspective, we could examine how many hours a day the careworker spends with the family's children versus how many hours the parents, who are employing her, spend with their children, and assess the strength and bonds of the different types of relationships. A family systems perspective (Chapter 6) would be an appropriate theory to use for this type of analysis. We could ask how careworkers frame their domestic caring labor, and how they maintain connection to their own children and family members in their home countries.

On the other hand, if we were to consider the macro-level processes that have led to this phenomenon of transnational carework, we would try to frame our analysis using conflict theory (Chapter 3). The second wave of feminism enabled more women (in wealthy countries) to be able to pursue professional careers that were previously unheard of. However, the capitalist nature of wealthy societies creates advantage for some, and oppression for others. Feminist theorists (Chapter 8) critique carework for the disadvantage it creates for migrant women who work for wealthy families, sending home every paycheck to provide economically for their own children, tens of thousands of miles away (Ungerson, 2006).

Yet another macro-level perspective, functionalist theory (Chapter 2), might suggest that as long as careworkers help family systems and social systems maintain equilibrium, scholars should not be concerned with transnational carework as a social problem. That is, each part of the system needs to contribute to the overall functioning of the whole; careworkers fulfill the expressive duties within the employers' home, and they, in turn, have someone in their home countries caring for their own children and families. Every member of the system has a purpose, and each does their part to keep the system running smoothly.

You can see from the example of transnational carework how each theory applied above has a different epistemology (e.g., positivism, interpretivism, critical), which leads to certain assumptions. A positivist epistemology, which undergirds functionalist theory (Chapter 2), would be interested in whether or not each part of the system worked, not necessarily what having a careworker *means* to the employer's family or the worker's family of origin. Therefore, a functionalist would make the assumption that if each role is fulfilled and the systems are working smoothly, then the arrangement is functional for all members. This is very different from a conflict theory perspective (Chapter 3), which takes a critical epistemology and questions the dominant paradigm represented by a positivist epistemology. For example, conflict theorists would question the capitalist structure that necessitates the role of paid careworkers in the first place. Feminist theorists (Chapter 8) would also examine how such arrangements can be harmful to societies and families, both the privileged and oppressed groups. For example, why is it assumed that carework should be performed by women? Does this social construction of gender roles prevent men from feeling as though they can fully participate in their children's caregiving? Furthermore, why is it that in some European countries (e.g., France), men's gender roles are more fluid and flexible than they are in other countries, like the United States and Mexico? After reading this text, answering questions like these will come easier, using theory as your "app." Likewise, your eyes will be opened to the different epistemologies, concepts, assumptions, and propositions that make up family theories. You will also be able to see how theory can be used by a number of different professions that work with and study families – so that, like Bo-Meh and her group members, you can capitalize on differences and learn even more in the process of theorizing.

Our Definition of Theory

As we have shown in this chapter, we recognize that there are many ways to define theory, and those definitions of what theory means change over time. Keeping that in mind, our definition of theory includes the following points: A theory is a strategy to describe, interpret, and/or explain a phenomenon. A theory helps us address questions that need answers such as: Why do people do what they do under certain conditions? For example, researchers studying sibling relationships might use a theory to describe "How do parents show favoritism to different children in their family?" or they might try to explain "Why do parents show favoritism when they report that they do not?" (Suitor, Gilligan, and Pillemer, 2013). To **theorize** is the process that we work through in creating or refining a theory. Theory, in our view, must also be relevant to practice; that is, theory is a way of understanding the problems that people experience in daily life and offering relevant options for addressing those constraints. A theory, then, offers a compelling storyline that helps us interpret the how and why of a situation or experience where we need to know more. As we said at the beginning of the chapter, a theory is the "app" we use to help us organize, manage, and make sense of the people, processes, and relationships that comprise our social world.

Criteria for Evaluating Family Theories

Just as there are many ways to define theory, there are also many ways to evaluate the strengths and weaknesses of theory. Theory evaluation is a process; it must begin by situating the theory into the historical context in which it emerged and gained popularity in the field. Once the theory is placed in context, we can better understand its clarity, logic, relevance, and practical application. Below are some of the key criteria that we have found useful in evaluating theory (see also Bengtson et al., 2005; Doherty et al., 1993; Gubrium and Holstein, 1990; Sprey, 1990 and 2013; White, 2013). In evaluating a family theory, you can ask yourself questions such as:

1 *Is the theory relevant?* This criterion refers to the applicability the theory has for the group(s) you are studying and/or serving. Is the theory adaptable to your population? Does the theory make assumptions about families that are not true for *your* family? Was this theory grounded in an epistemological orientation that is limiting (e.g., is it positivist in nature, when you need it to be interpretivist)?
2 *Is the theory practical?* Family theories must be able to be translated into practice. The scholarly, or academic side of studying families must directly benefit families through policy, intervention, therapy, education, health care, or advocacy. Without practical implications, theories often are criticized for living only in the "ivory tower" of academia, far removed from families' every day realities.
3 *Is the theory logical?* Theories of family must be coherent. This means that the assumptions, concepts, and propositions must logically build on one another and fit together well into an explanatory model that makes sense.
4 *Is the theory explicit?* Components of a theory are explicit when they are stated clearly, specifically, and leaving nothing implied. When evaluating whether or not a theory is explicit, consider how thorough and detailed it is: Are the concepts precisely defined? Or, on the contrary, are there implicit (underlying or unstated) components of the theory?
5 *Is the theory systematic?* Components of a theory need to be systematic, or formulated as a coherent set of assumptions, concepts, and propositions. This means that the theory can be applied repeatedly to the study of families with the reassurance that because of the theory's systematic nature, application of the theory should produce reliable results.
6 *Is the theory contextual?* When evaluating this criterion, pay attention to the cultural context in which

the theory was developed for; not every theory fits every family. Can the theory be used in different contexts, or adapted to fit a new context? For example, is the theory relevant to the study of native-born *and* immigrant families in the US?

Text Organization

This textbook presents 10 theories of the family, in the general chronological order in which they emerged within the disciplines of human development and family studies, psychology, and sociology. Most of the theories were developed in social science disciplines before they were utilized to study the family, and we note this throughout the text.

Each chapter begins with a case study, which is designed to set the stage so that our readers can apply the theory in a meaningful way. The case study's characters are used to illustrate key concepts throughout each chapter. We also provide a brief history of each theory so that the theories are located in a sociohistorical context, which helps us understand why the assumptions of the theories are so important. For example, the structural-functionalism of Parsons (1970) was a very popular theoretical approach in sociology in the mid-twentieth century. It was based on assumptions that most families could conform to societal standards of the SNAF model. It is important to note that the 1950s was a unique period in American history (as we discussed earlier in this chapter), which contributed to structural-functionalism's popularity. Later, this theory was criticized for its inability to deal with change during a time when the Civil Rights Movement and the Women's Liberation Movement of the 1960s were gaining momentum. The history and origins section of each chapter details these types of sociohistorical shifts and how they contributed to each theory's assumptions and framework.

Each chapter also presents key assumptions, concepts, and propositions (if applicable). A highlight of this text is the use of examples; we provide detailed descriptions of how family theories can be applied to popular culture, as well as supplementary content designed to challenge students to think about how the theory is applicable to their own lives. Each theory is also discussed with respect to its strengths, weaknesses, and alternate applications. Further, we provide global comparisons to illustrate that family theories are relevant beyond the US.

Another highlight of this text is the inclusion of the "trifecta" (that is, attaining three important achievements) of detailed connections we draw between theorizing, research, and practice. Each chapter includes a section on current theorizing, which provides a cutting-edge look at how the theory is in the process of changing, formulating new ways of expanding the theory and applying it to changing demographics of individuals and families in society. This is followed by an example of an empirical study illustrating the theory to draw a closer link between theory and research. Each study included is given a detailed description, highlighting research terms and concepts and their usefulness in informing theoretical propositions. Finally, we draw links between the theory and its applicability to practice, encouraging practitioners who work with families to consider ways in which the theories can make them better human service workers, researchers, program directors, teachers, health care providers, and students of family science. We end each chapter with questions and resources for students to reflect further on the material, including suggestions for further reading as well as several multimedia suggestions (e.g., websites, films, and television shows depicting family theories) that help bring the material home for readers. (All websites referred to were current as of early 2016.)

Before you delve into this text on family theories, it is important to note that your "app" will take time and patience to develop. Unlike how applications work in modern technology, you will not become a seasoned family theorist overnight. Your theoretical mind will take time to develop, but once you get the hang of it, you will be well on your way to seeing family theories everywhere you look! This text will provide the groundwork for developing your "app", and by the time you reach the end, you will have a good understanding of how to navigate the "theory map" we present in Chapter 12. It is our hope that the way we have organized and presented material in this text will help you to be a strong theoretical thinker, who is able to see theory as an exciting, applicable guide for understanding, serving, and studying families no matter what your profession.

Multimedia Suggestions

www.stephaniecoontz.com

This is the website of author Stephanie Coontz, a professor at Evergreen State College in Olympia, WA. She is a well-known historian and speaker who focuses on contemporary families. She has a multitude of media appearances.

Activate your theory app: Peruse Coontz's website and consider which theoretical framework she might best identify with. Additionally, would Coontz be best described as a practitioner, teacher, or researcher? Think about the intersection of those identities for Coontz, as well as for your own career aspirations. How do they compare and contrast for you?

www.ncfr.org

This is the website for the premier professional association in family sciences, the National Council on Family Relations (NCFR), headquartered in Minneapolis. NCFR publishes three major journals, all of which include the most current and rigorous ideas about family theory, research, and practice: *Journal of Marriage and Family*; *Family Relations*; and *Journal of Family Theory and Review*. NCFR hosts an annual conference that includes a Theory Construction and Research Methodology (TCRM) workshop; certification in family life education; professional resources about jobs in family science; statewide and student chapters; and many other resources to theorize about and study families.

Activate your theory app: Look through the Professional Resources tab on this website and familiarize yourself with the jobs center and career resources. Where are the majority of positions? What level of degree is required? How do these options match your own career interests? Add this website to your "favorites" list – you will need these resources before you know it!

Stories We Tell (2013)

This is an award-winning documentary film by Canadian director and actor Sarah Polley. The film utilizes staged home-movies, and actual memoirs, obtained through interviews with family members and friends that Polley conducted in order to explore a complex web of family secrets. Each person tells their own "story" about the marriages, extramarital affairs, biological and nonbiological parent–child ties, sibling ties, deaths, and intricate, ambivalent relationships across the generations. One of the more powerful messages is that, like different family theories, different family members have their own unique perspectives on similar events.

A scene from *Stories We Tell*, 2012, dir. Sarah Polley, National Film Board of Canada

Activate your theory app: What would your own "home movie" look like if it were included in this documentary? Throughout the rest of this book, you will undoubtedly think about how the material explains your own family experiences and relationships. Consider whether or not your own story would change, depending on who tells it.

Vantage Point (2008)

This action film – told from eight different perspectives – is about an attempt to assassinate a US President. The reason this film is useful for studying family theories is because it illustrates how different vantage points – or, different theoretical perspectives – can help paint a more holistic picture of what is really going on. No one perspective can tell "the whole story." All of these perspectives, including that of the President, the television producer, the secret service agents, the bystanders, and the terrorist, provide a partial version of the events that took place but collectively, a more complete version once all of the perspectives are revealed.

A scene from *Vantage Point*, 2008, dir. Peter Travis, Relativity Media

Activate your theory app: Similar to *Stories We Tell*, this movie offers different perspectives on the same story. Select one or two characters and identify their assumptions and epistemologies. How do their orientations to explaining the world around them compare and contrast, based on their unique perspective?

Further Reading

Bengtson, V. L., Acock, A. C., Allen, K. R., Dilworth-Anderson, P., and Klein, D. M. (eds), *Sourcebook of family theory and research* (Thousand Oaks, CA: Sage, 2005). About every 10 to 15 years, the National Council on Family Relations (described above) updates and revises the authoritative reference work on family theories. This is a joint effort of NCFR's Theory Construction and Research Methodology workshop, and the Research and Theory section. The 2005 version of the *Sourcebook* takes a unique approach to family scholarship by demonstrating how theories are embedded in research studies and clinical practice. This edition offers chapters on substantive topics, such as "Theorizing about Marriage," "Theorizing about Aggression between Intimates," and "Theorizing and Studying Sibling Ties in Adulthood," and demonstrates how theory, research, and practice work together to understand families from different perspectives.

Boss, P. G., Doherty, W. J., LaRossa, R., Schumm, W. R., and Steinmetz, S. K. (eds), *Sourcebook of family theories and methods: A contextual approach* (New York: Plenum, 1993). Often called the "green bible", this 1993 version of the *Sourcebook* is an important reference that examines the classic and emerging theories used to explain family phenomena. Organized chronologically from when the various theories were first introduced in the family field, this edited collection allows readers to see the evolving nature of family theories and the building blocks that family scholars use to test and refine theories over time. Each chapter includes an application to how the theory is used in research or has been revised to reflect changing demographics and trends in families in the modern day. The *Sourcebook* is an excellent reference for more in-depth coverage of family theories, and its chapters can be used to supplement the explanations supplied in our introductory text.

Coontz, S., *The way we really are: Coming to terms with America's changing families* (New York: Basic Books, 1997). In this text, Coontz elaborates on her critique of America's romanticization of the 1950s "traditional" family by detailing what family life looks like in the modern era. Coontz claims that while in the mid-twentieth century families experienced economic security at unprecedented levels, today's families are living in a very different sociocultural context, which makes it difficult, if not impossible, to model families after that era. Coontz points out both the positive and negative changes the family has experienced since the 1950s and

1960s, making the argument that we should be careful to not fall into a "nostalgia trap," focusing instead on a more historically informed view of families.

Flyvbjerg. B., *Making social science matter: Why social inquiry fails and how it can succeed again* (New York: Cambridge University Press, 2001). Flyvbjerg addresses three ways of knowing, based on Aristotle's ideas. The three ways are episteme (analytical, scientific knowledge), techne (technical knowledge, know-how), and phronesis (practical wisdom, prudence). He explains how all three of these are needed for scientific inquiry. He claims that the scientific method is based mostly on episteme and techne, to the exclusion of phronesis. He also critiques the human and social sciences (such as family science, sociology, and the like) for modeling their work strictly on the natural (or so called "hard") sciences. He suggests phronesis is essential in the human sciences, where we must use our intuition and practical knowledge to understand the nature of human beings (in all of their variability and complexity) and to help them solve their problems and improve their lives.

Sarkisian, N., and Gerstel, N., *Nuclear family values, extended family lives: The power of race, class and gender* (New York: Routledge, 2012). In this brief text, the authors utilize both classic and current versions of family theory to describe how families actually live, communicate, and change in response to demographic developments, social problems, and cultural transformations. Sarkisian and Gerstel critique the Standard North American Family (SNAF) model that continues to permeate family research, and they show that families are much more varied than a nuclear structure of heterosexual marriage and parent–child relations. For most individuals, daily life is comprised of extended family relationships, including aging parents, adult children, siblings, aunts, uncles, cousins, grandparents, and fictive kin. Extended family and community ties are an essential survival strategy, especially for those families who face racial, class, gender, and sexual orientation prejudice. This book demonstrates how important it is to go beyond "marriage" and "parenthood" to examine the range of family structures and ties that proactively address social problems and help families survive and thrive.

Questions for Students

Discussion Questions

1 Why are theories important to individuals who work with, and study, families?
2 How have your views of theory changed after reading the first chapter?
3 Compare and contrast the different types of epistemologies described in this chapter: positivist, interpretive, and critical. Consider how research would be conducted using a theory app. How would we devise research questions, or construct surveys to measure them, without guidance from a theory?
4 How does research inform theory? Do family scholars revise and develop new theories as a result of research? How do you think that process works?
5 Consider how practitioners use theory; is it realistic to think that theory better prepares us to understand our roles as practitioners serving families? Why/why not?
6 How do *you* define "theory"? What definition would you add to the definitions we have included in this chapter?

Your Turn!

Find an article that has used *any* theory as a framework for its empirical research on families. What aspects of the theory did the research utilize? Now reread the article, leaving theory out; just skip over it entirely whenever it is mentioned. Does the article make as much sense without it? Does the theory enhance the research? Why/why not?

Personal Reflection Questions

1 Write down five reasons why you think people get divorced. You can use personal experience or anecdotal insights for this. Save your five reasons,

and return to them as you read through each chapter of this book. By the time you are finished, you will be able to attach a theory to your previous knowledge and experiences. (Because, yes, "there's a theory for that!")

2 How does your family compare to the SNAF? What about families you know well? Compare and contrast your own experiences with the assumptions about SNAF and also about other forms and nationalities of families.

3 What assumptions do you personally hold about family? Based on those assumptions, how would you explain the way families interact and operate? Write down your orientation to the study of families, and like question #1, save it. Return to your assumptions about family as you read through each chapter of this book. By the time you are finished, you may be able to write your own theory of family!

4 Think about the family you have grown up in. Now think about the family you have created or wish to create in the future (with a partner, with children, etc.). How does broader social change influence your perception of being in a family of origin, compared to a family of creation?

5 What is your favorite book, TV program, or movie? What theories have the writers used to explain the actions of the characters?

6 How do you use the word "theory" in your daily life?

References

Allen, K. R. (2000). A conscious and inclusive family studies. *Journal of Marriage and the Family, 62*, 4–17. doi:10.1111/j.1741-3737.2000.00911.x.

Babbie, E. (2013). *The practice of social research* (13th edn). Belmont, CA: Wadsworth.

Bahr, H., and Bahr, K. S. (2001). Families and self-sacrifice: Alternative models and meanings for family theory. *Social Forces, 79*, 1231–1258. doi:10.1353/sof.2001.0030.

Beck, U., and Beck-Gernsheim, E. (2001). *Individualization: Institutionalized individualism and its social and political consequences*. London: Sage.

Bengtson, V. L., Acock, A. C., Allen, K. R., Dilworth-Anderson, P., and Klein, D. M. (2005). Theory and theorizing in family research: Puzzle building and puzzle solving. In V. L. Bengtson, A. C. Acock, K. R. Allen, P. Dilworth-Anderson, and D. M. Klein (eds), *Sourcebook of family theory and research* (pp. 3–33). Thousand Oaks, CA: Sage.

Cheal, D. (1991). *Family and the state of theory*. Toronto: University of Toronto Press.

Cherlin, A. J. (2004). The deinstitutionalization of American marriage. *Journal of Marriage and Family, 66*, 848–861. doi:10.1111/j.0022-2445.2004.00058.x.

Clarke, E. H. (1873). *Sex in education: Or a fair chance for the girls*. Boston: Houghton Mifflin.

Collins, P. H. (1990). *Black feminist thought: Knowledge, consciousness, and the politics of empowerment*. Boston: Unwin Hyman.

Coontz, S. (1992). *The way we never were: American families and the nostalgia trap*. New York: Basic Books.

Daly, K. J. (2003). Family theory versus the theories families live by. *Journal of Marriage and Family, 65*, 771–784. doi:10.1111/j.1741-3737.2003.00771.x.

Daly, K. J. (2007). *Qualitative methods for family studies and human development*. Thousand Oaks, CA: Sage.

Demo, D. H., Allen, K. R., and Fine, M. A. (eds) (2000). *Handbook of family diversity*. New York: Oxford University Press.

Doherty, W. J., Boss, P. G., LaRossa, R., Schumm, W. R., and Steinmetz, S. K. (1993). Family theories and methods: A contextual approach. In P. Boss, W. Doherty, R. LaRossa, W. Schumm, and S. Steinmetz (eds), *Sourcebook of family theories and methods: A contextual approach* (pp. 3–30). New York: Plenum Press.

Dressel, P., and Clark, A. (1990). A critical look at family care. *Journal of Marriage and the Family, 52*, 769–782. doi:10.2307/352941.

Family and Medical Leave Act of 1993, 29 U.S.C. § 2601–2654 (2006).

Gubrium, J. F., and Holstein, J. A. (1990). *What is family?* Mountain View, CA: Mayfield.

History.com (2016). *U.S. Immigration since 1965*. At www.history.com/topics/us-immigration-since-1965.

Klein, D. M. (2005). The cyclical process of science. In V. L. Bengtson, A. C. Acock, K. R. Allen, P. Dilworth-Anderson, and D. M. Klein (eds), *Sourcebook of family theory and research* (pp. 17–18). Thousand Oaks, CA: Sage.

Lutz, H. (2011). *The new maids: Transnational women and the care economy*. New York: Zed Books.

Mahalingam, R., Balan, S., and Molina, K. M. (2009). Transnational intersectionality: A critical framework for theorizing motherhood. In S. A. Lloyd, A. L. Few, and K. R. Allen (eds), *Handbook of feminist family studies* (pp. 69–80). Thousand Oaks, CA: Sage.

Morello, K. B. (1982). Women's entry into the legal profession. *American University Law Review, 32*, 623–626.

Nye, F. I. (1979). Choice, exchange, and the family. In W. R. Burr, R. Hill, F. I. Nye, and I. L. Reiss (eds), *Contemporary theories about the family: General theories/theoretical orientations* (vol. 2, pp. 1–41). New York: Free Press.

Parsons, T. (1970). *Social structure and personality*. New York: Free Press.

Pittman, J. F. (1993). Functionalism may be down, but it surely is not out: Another point of view for family therapists and policy analysts. In P. Boss, W. Doherty, R. LaRossa, W. Schumm, and S. Steinmetz (eds), *Sourcebook of family theories and methods: A contextual approach* (pp. 218–221). New York: Plenum Press.

Schoemaker, P. J., Tankard, J. W., Jr, and Lasorsa, D. L. (2004). *How to build social science theories.* Thousand Oaks, CA: Sage.

Smith, D. E. (1993). The Standard North American Family: SNAF as an ideological code. *Journal of Family Issues, 14*, 50–65. doi:10.1177/0192513X93014001005.

Sprey, J. (ed.) (1990). *Fashioning family theory: New approaches*. Newbury Park, CA: Sage.

Sprey, J. (2013). Extending the range of questioning in family studies through ideas from the exact sciences. *Journal of Family Theory and Review, 5*, 51–61. doi:10.1111/jftr.12002.

Suitor, J. J., Gilligan, M., and Pillemer, K. (2013). Continuity and change in mothers' favoritism toward offspring in adulthood. *Journal of Marriage and Family, 75*, 1229–1247. doi:10.1111/jomf.12067.

Sweeney, M. M. (2010). Remarriage and stepfamilies: Strategic sites for family scholarship in the 21st century. *Journal of Marriage and Family, 72*, 667–684. doi:10.1111/j.1741-3737.2010.00724.x.

Ungerson, C. (2006). Gender, care, and the welfare state. In K. Davis, M. Evans, and J. Lorber (eds), *Handbook of gender and women's studies* (pp. 272–286). Thousand Oaks, CA: Sage.

Wallace, W. L. (1971). *The logic of science in sociology*. Piscataway, NJ: Aldine Transaction.

Weisberg, D. K. (1977). Barred from the bar: Women and legal education in the United States 1870–1890. *Journal of Legal Education, 28*, 485–507.

White, J. M. (2013). The current status of theorizing about families. In G. W. Peterson and K. R. Bush (eds), *Handbook of marriage and the family* (3rd edn, pp. 11–37). New York: Springer.

2

Functionalist Theory

Have you ever had to go a day, or even a few hours, without your mobile phone? Perhaps you dropped it in the tub, cracked the screen to the point of no repair, or maybe it just refuses to turn on. What are the consequences when you are without your mobile phone? Think about your close friends or family, who may have sent you important text messages that you do not have access to. How will you stay in touch with them? How long could you really stand to be without your phone? Imagine the updates, photos, and events you might miss if you had to go – shudder at the thought – one week without your phone. What other options do you have for contacting someone? How would you stay integrated, or connected, into your social circles?

Functionalist theory, as it is often called, helps us understand what happens when one part of a larger whole or system stops working. Functionalism, one of the founding theories in social science, is based on the analogy that society is like a living organism, and when one part of it stops working, other parts are affected. If your lungs do not receive enough oxygen, your body reacts, and you might feel lightheaded, dizzy, or nauseous. The entire system is affected by the functionality of just one piece of the whole. In addition, functionalism helps us understand how healthy levels of social integration are important to normal functioning in society. This theory considers how individuals within families need to maintain healthy levels of social integration, promoting and reinforcing societal norms for "citizens-in-training." This theory highlights the interplay between social norms, family functions, and how family members contribute to the equilibrium (or not) of the entire family. In addition, this perspective sheds light on the purpose the family serves beyond the four walls of the home; as a social institution, families are vital to the overall functioning of the greater society.

In this chapter, we discuss the history of functionalist theory and how the key concepts can be used to understand how families function in society. As one of the earliest theories applied to the study of families, functionalist theory has been widely influential, yet also widely critiqued (Kingsbury & Scanzoni, 1993). We will address both aspects of the theory as it has developed over time. Our treatment of functionalist theory is designed to show the continuing usefulness of this theory, despite claims that it is no longer relevant to the study of the diverse and complex families in our world today. In order to gain a fuller understanding of how functionalism works, we start with a case study that illustrates how families adapt to change, and how overall system functionality is affected by each contributing member.

Case Study

Cassie, the subject of our case study, was born two years after her parents had their first daughter, Shaila. Shaila was so excited to have a little sister – someone to play dolls and dress up with – and someone to teach new things to. Throughout their childhood, Shaila and Cassie became very close, and their parents joked that they were attached at the hip. They rarely fought because their personalities complemented one another so well. Shaila was very emotionally mature for a young child and was able to help her little sister understand her own emotions early on.

Family Theories: Foundations and Applications, First Edition. Katherine R. Allen and Angela C. Henderson.

Their parents were often impressed when they overheard Shaila explaining in detail how they would play dolls for 30 minutes, and then go outside and play soccer for 30 minutes so that each of them got to do what they wanted. Cassie usually agreed with most of Shaila's plans, because most of the time, they ended with her favorite activity – playing soccer.

Thinking back to her childhood, Cassie knew the whole time how different she was from her sister, despite their closeness. Cassie felt like a boy trapped in a girl's body, and the way that her sister insisted she "perform" her gender was the exact opposite from how she felt inside. Cassie felt like a boy. She knew she was transgender the minute she learned as an adolescent what transgender meant. She waited until she was 15 to talk to her parents and sister about it, and to Cassie's relief, they were very supportive. Her parents helped support her through psychological therapy, and assisted in her transition from a "she" to a "he" with hormone replacement therapy and a legal name change: Cassie would now be Casbah. Shaila was sad to lose her sister, and she struggled with the transition internally. The family sought support from a family counselor referred to them by good friends. Over time, Shaila became more accepting of Casbah, excited to have a brother and even more thankful that it was someone she knew all along. Her parents also learned valuable communication skills in therapy; skills that carried over into their marriage and other family relationships.

Think about Shaila and Casbah's childhood, and how Shaila helped their relationship function smoothly by fairly distributing their playtime between two very different tasks. This also contributed to a smooth "daily life" for their parents – mom and dad rarely had to intervene in their children's play time, helping the family maintain overall system functionality. Moreover, consider how valuable it was for the family to receive help from an external, trained professional and licensed counselor. How would the family have dealt with this issue without this resource?

Additionally, consider Casbah's new life as a boy in high school – what are the consequences of him now identifying as a boy? Casbah was a star player on the women's soccer team, and still wants to play the sport. Should he be allowed to participate on the men's soccer team, and use the men's locker rooms? Think even more broadly about this situation: Would this transition from being born female, but identifying as male, have been accepted a hundred years ago? Functionalism helps us understand how societies and social institutions change over time, reacting to difference and adapting in order to maintain stability. From a functionalist perspective, families both interact with larger social norms, and also serve functions inside the family for their members. Functionalists would argue that it is impossible to understand society without taking into account the functionality of all parts of a social system, and families, as one of the most important social institutions in society, are no exception.

What Is Functionalist Theory?

Functionalist theory is used by researchers to help explain processes both within families as well as how families operate in and contribute to society at large. Functionalism has a long history in the social sciences, beginning with the French scholar Émile Durkheim, considered to be the father of sociology, who identified problems associated with the rise of the modern world during the Industrial Revolution (Appelrouth and Edles, 2011). Later, American sociologist Talcott Parsons (1951), also discussed in Chapter 1, developed a model for studying society during a time of economic prosperity and conservative values which included taking large and complex social processes into account, including how families **function**, or serve a purpose, as social institutions in society, and how they react to change at the macro-level. Finally, Robert Merton (1957), who was Parsons's student, extended functionalism by taking deviance and reactions to cultural goals into account, which are useful when trying to understand how families react to difference *within* and *outside* of their families.

History and origins

In order to understand any theory, it is vital to situate it in the proper historical context. Durkheim, in his book of 1893, first introduced functionalist concepts into the study of society during the Industrial Revolution, when major social upheaval

Box 2.1 At a Glance: Functionalist Theory

Structure The composition of the unit of analysis, or the family.

Function The purpose each part of a system serves to contribute to overall operation.

Mechanical solidarity Societies held together by commonalities.

Organic solidarity Societies held together by differences.

Expressive A term used to describe feminine characteristics, such as showing love, care, concern, and support for the system.

Instrumental A term used to describe masculine characteristics, such as being a leader, making important decisions, and providing material needs for the system.

Deviance A term used to describe when behavior differs from the norm.

Cultural goals Socially accepted norms that guide behavior.

and economic change occurred in Western Europe (Durkheim, 1984). Before the Industrial Revolution, most people lived in villages and small towns, relying on the local community to provide for them. Food was produced locally, and agriculture sustained only the surrounding communities. When industrialization replaced agricultural production, people flocked to cities as a result of the changing economy; families now had to find employment to sell their labor for a wage in order to provide for their family's basic needs. Therefore, most families that were once self-sufficient, relying on agricultural production for sustenance, had to give up agriculture as a way of life and instead move into large cities to find jobs (Giddens, 2002). This had consequences not only for social life, but also for how families functioned both inside and outside the home. Families often tried to have fewer children, because the shift from an agriculture-based economy to a market-based economy meant that families no longer needed more "workers" (i.e., children) at home, tending to the land and livestock. Instead, in the new economy, families often *all* went to work in factories, until compulsory education and child labor laws were passed in industrializing countries. An example in the United States was the Fair Labor Standards Act, which set minimum ages for child laborers (16 for boys, 18 for girls) (US Senate, 1937). These macro-level historical changes undoubtedly affected families' structure and functionality in society.

You will read about industrialization in other chapters because it was such a major event in our world's history in terms of the way it shaped social interactions and families. However, you will probably notice right away how differently each theorist interprets the Industrial Revolution. Both Marx (Chapter 3) and Durkheim defined the problems associated with industrialization very differently. We start our discussion of the key concepts of functionalist theory by first outlining Durkheim's perspective of how society works.

Key concepts

Émile Durkheim's view: functionalism Émile Durkheim was concerned with the increasing **dynamic density** that occurred following the Industrial Revolution, defined as the number of people living in any given place, as well as the number of people interacting. The reason this was problematic for Durkheim was because of the accompanying shift from mechanical solidarity to organic solidarity. Solidarity is a term functionalists used to describe the processes by which societies or groups – such as families – are "held together," or put another way, what unifies members of a group into a functioning unit. **Mechanical solidarity** is found in more primitive societies, such as those that existed before the Industrial Revolution. Members of these societies were generalists, performing similar tasks with similar responsibilities. Family members could carry out nearly any task necessary to the survival not only of the family, but of the larger community as a whole. It was common for the patriarch – or father – to provide education inside the home with a family Bible, educating his wife and children on morality and other religious teachings. He also contributed to farming his land (and most likely also that of his landowner, from whom he rented farmland), and probably also helped with the construction of buildings in the community as well as on his own property. Most women and children also worked at home, but not in the sense we think about today. Before industrialization, women and children had contributed to the overall functioning of the family unit by farming the land, gathering water and firewood, and tending to livestock (Appelrouth and Edles, 2011). Most members of these societies were what we could call "jacks of all trades." Societies had a repressive law in place, in which punishments for deviants were swift and harsh. Lawbreakers were held accountable to the entire society because any deviation from the law was a threat to group cohesiveness or solidarity. At the same time, members of societies like this contributed to a **collective conscience**, which is a common sense of morality that all community members believed in and upheld (Durkheim, 1984 [1893]). This kept members of a society accountable and provided a set of rules and regulations, guided by morality, for all to follow.

After the Industrial Revolution, societies were characterized by **organic solidarity**, a term used to describe societies with a well-specified division of labor. This meant that people went from being generalists to specialists, responsible for a very specific aspect of work both within the family as well as outside of it, in the larger community (Durkheim, 1984 [1893]). This shift occurred in sync with the increase in dynamic density. With a very large number of individuals interacting, there was a major social shift away from similar people having shared experiences to people with different tasks, more isolated from one another, having very different experiences. In contrast to mechanical solidarity, where societal members were cooperative for the benefit of the greater good, these more industrialized societies were more competitive in nature. Competition increased because of the sheer number of people in any given society, or city. Additionally, competition increased because there was not a shared sense of morality among all members of the group; it was virtually impossible for all residents of a city, for example, to subscribe to the same worldview or religion. Therefore, the collectivist aspects of society that characterized preindustrial societies were replaced by competition and difference. People depended on one another because they did need each other – a machinist did not do the job of a transporter or a miner. Their jobs were very specialized, which, according to Durkheim, was part of what held this new type of society together.

Consider the structure of a family in either type of society: In an agriculture-based society, family members are likely focused on the needs of the entire family, working toward providing for siblings, helping parents, and caring for their land. In an industrialized society, family members are much more scattered in terms of where they likely spend their waking hours: the father is at work as a manufacturer, the mother is at work as a weaver, and the children as chimneysweeps or domestic workers (most children did not attend elementary school until after child labor laws were passed). This type of familial structure inevitably has an impact on the functionality of the home and family. Each family member is likely concerned with their wages making a meaningful contribution to the family, but their daily lived experiences are vastly different from one another, compared to preindustrial family life.

This macro-level shift in how society and families operated altered the social norms and social integration of all members of society. Instead of being held together by a common sense of morality like in agricultural societies, Durkheim suggested that **moral individualism** – an outlook on life based on what is good for oneself – replaced collective consciousness. That is, when dynamic density and the division of labor both increased, no solidifying conscience increased along with it. This, in turn, affected levels of **social integration**, or the degree to which people are tied to their social groups. According to functionalism, you can experience normal levels of social integration, levels that are too high, or levels that are too low. Social integration is best described using a continuum (see Figure 2.1).

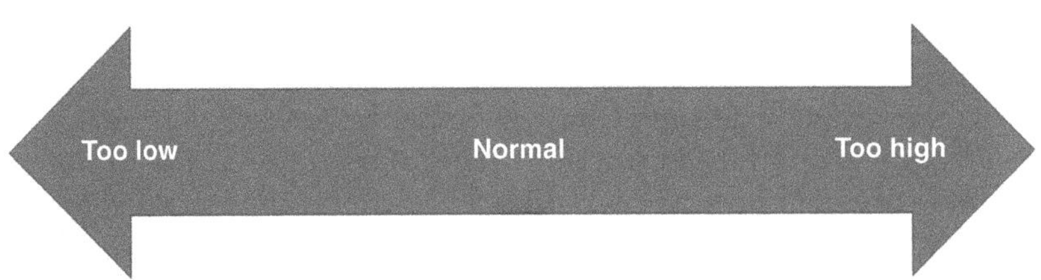

Figure 2.1 A continuum of social integration

Normal social integration for everyone is ideal, but sometimes individuals become too highly integrated into a group, losing sight of the norms that govern behavior in the greater society. An example of this would be a religious cult; cult members might idealize their cult leader as a "god," putting the needs of the group ahead of their own individual needs, and definitely ahead of the goals of greater society. On the other hand, individuals who are not members of any social groups and live in a secluded area, removed from society, are at danger of experiencing extremely low levels of social integration, vulnerable to acting on human impulses or violence against others. Unfortunately, there are examples of this type of behavior in our society when we consider those who perform school shootings. Often we wonder about the shooter's background, how his family could have overlooked the heavy weaponry hidden under his bed, or the painful experiences the shooter had being bullied in his school. In asking these questions, we are inadvertently using functionalist theory, because we are trying to identify the **dysfunction**, or the part of the whole that broke down. What happened in the shooter's life that led to this event? We hypothesize about the level of social integration, by asking if the student was a "loner," without proper guidance and/or healthy social ties. We ask about his family upbringing, his church family, his extended family. Most of us – without even knowing it – already view the world from a functionalist perspective!

While Durkheim is considered to be the "father" of functionalist theory, other theorists who came after him adapted his theoretical framework to apply to a more modernized society (i.e., long after the Industrial Revolution had occurred). Next, we discuss two more modern theorists, Talcott Parsons and Robert Merton, and their adaptations of functionalist theory, the new concepts they introduced, and how each perspective adds to the study of the family.

Parsons's view: structural functionalism In contrast to Durkheim's level of analysis, which often included functions inside the family, Talcott Parsons (1951) based many of his theoretical ideas on how society functioned at the macro-level. That is, his model of functionalism took into account both societal *structure* and function, or how social systems produced shared moral codes and norms and how those trickled down to social actors. In this way, he extended Durkheim's model by suggesting that several large-scale systems – the cultural, social, and personality systems – are interdependent and help to maintain stability. Thus, his model is best described as **structural functionalism**. However, before we discuss those systems in detail, it is important to provide historical context to help understand how these theoretical ideas emerged.

From the 1930s through the 1970s, structural functionalism was a very popular theoretical perspective in American social sciences (Appelrouth and Edles, 2011), and had a significant impact on the field of family studies. You might remember from Chapter 1 that the time period of the 1950s was often referred to as the "Golden Era," when the post–World War II economy was booming and most families only needed one breadwinner (Coontz, 1992). The cultural norm in America was for mothers to stay at home with children, and federal assistance programs such as low-interest housing loans significantly helped young families maintain economic stability. Therefore, Parsons's model was situated in a historical time and place where social institutions seemingly functioned "well" for the White, middle-class American family, or what we referred to in Chapter 1 as the Standard North American Family (SNAF) (Smith, 1993). The Civil

Rights Movement for Black Americans was on the horizon, but for the most part, adhering to the "norm" was achievable for some families, or at least for the families that Parsons wrote about.

Therefore, it is not surprising that Parsons's (1951) model is based on the idea that shared norms and values are the key to a smoothly functioning society. However, in contrast to Durkheim, who described what holds societies together before, during, and after rapid social change, Parsons instead attempted to explain how individuals "fit" within larger social systems (in abstract terms) and how those systems are interdependent. Parsons identified how individuals fit within preexisting systems, and how, by them fitting in, society functions in an orderly way. Let's analyze each of those systems in turn.

The first, and arguably the most overarching, is the cultural system. The **cultural system** is made up of the "values, norms, and symbols which guide the choices made by actors and which limit the type of interaction which may occur among actors" (Parsons and Shils, 1951, p. 55). Think of this system as the taken-for-granted norms and ideas about how things work in the world; this includes the range of acceptable behaviors, ideas, and beliefs that govern society (Parsons et al., 1965). According to Parsons, our culture determines every social institution that exists in our society, and every role we are allowed to fulfill, the choices we are allowed to make, and even the preferences and tastes we have! Think about your own decisions – what you decide to wear every day, what kind of mobile phone you buy, where you chose to go to college – all of these are part of the cultural system, which suggests that we should dress fashionably (according to whichever subculture you identify with), that we should each have our own mobile phones, and that we assume most young adults will go to college. Each of these norms is often taken for granted, assumed to be the "way of life" for most people in our culture. It is those norms that make up our cultural system, and as long as we "fit" into these ideals and conform to the preexisting system, society functions in a predictable and orderly way. The cultural system, then, works down on the other two systems, the personality and social systems. To show the relationships among the three systems, see Figure 2.2.

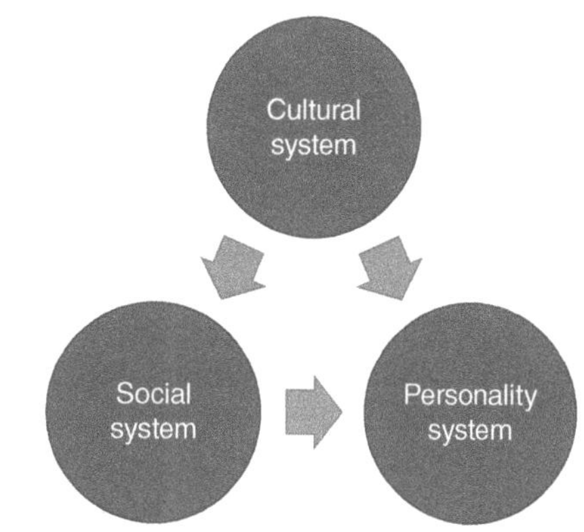

Figure 2.2 Parsons's systems

It is important to point out here that Parsons's framework is often critiqued for suggesting that the goal of society is complete institutionalization of and conformity to norms and values (Appelrouth and Edles, 2011). Though Parsons did argue that following rules benefited each system and maintained equilibrium, his model did not ignore the possibility of social change, or environmental conditions adapting and producing subsequent changes in his three systems. In fact, Parsons's model suggests that society is like a living organism, and systems are continuously in flux, adjusting and changing over time: "Complete and perfect institutionalization is an ideal; it refers to when role demands from the social system complement cultural ideals and when both, in turn, meet the needs of the personality system" (Appelrouth and Edles, 2011, p. 355).

Parsons wrote about generation gaps to illustrate this point. Often, younger generations' views and outlooks on life clash with the views and outlooks of older generations, which can create conflict within systems. These conflicts can be functional for one part of the system, but not another. Because each of the systems is comprised of various **subsystems** (e.g., larger American culture includes a sport subculture, and a hunting subculture), disagreements between subsystems is inevitable, but that does not mean they cannot be managed. Indeed, one of the functions of youth culture is to "[ease] the difficult process of adjustment from childhood emotional dependency to full 'maturity'" (Parsons, 1943, p. 189). Therefore, these disagreements can and do slowly lead to social change over time, which will affect the cultural system as well. Though Parsons did not fully develop how divergences from the norm can also contribute to the functionality of society, his student Robert Merton did. We will discuss Merton in more detail later in this chapter.

In a broad sense, then, we can apply Parsons's systems to Casbah from our case study. The cultural system during Casbah's youth is vastly different from the one his grandparents and great-grandparents experienced. Casbah is coming of age in a culture that is becoming increasingly aware and accepting of lesbian, gay, bisexual, transgender or queer (LGBTQ) persons. Until the 1970s, the American cultural system defined homosexual persons as having a diagnosable illness/disorder (Silverstein, 1991). In more contemporary societies, however, the cultural system has adapted to change, which trickles down to the other "system" levels. Transgender persons are – for the most part – no longer considered to be mentally ill or disordered. Today, you probably know someone who is transgender. It is a part of our larger culture; Hollywood films portray transgender characters, in films like *TransAmerica* (Bastian, Moran, and Dugan, 2005) and in the television series *Orange Is the New Black*, based on the book by Piper Kerman (2011). All of these indicators suggest that the cultural system has adapted to social change, which in effect dictates both the social and personality systems.

The social system is directly influenced by the cultural system. In order to understand what Parsons meant by social system, let's start with what it is *not*. Social systems do not refer to tangible, material structures or social institutions, such as churches or educational systems. The idea is more abstract, and has to be considered by imagining how we interact with one another. Parsons defined the **social system** as the level of interactions between two or more actors, where actors are aware of one another's ideas and intentions, and their interactions are governed by shared norms or expectations (Parsons and Shils, 1951). In other words, the behaviors we carry out on a daily basis are part of the social system. We understand what to do when we enter a bank – we approach a bank representative, conduct our banking business, and leave. We do not go behind the counter to make our own withdrawals, start helping other customers, or do jumping jacks while being waited on at the counter. The social interactions are predictable, and orderly, and are part of a larger social system, or set of social interaction expectations, that we adhere to, consciously or not.

The reason these interactions are considered part of a system is because they are made up of roles (Parsons and Shils, 1951). **Roles** are complementary, detailed sets of obligations for interaction. There are expectations associated with the role of "professor." Consider your professor for this course; she or he has a higher degree and most likely has areas of expertise in the family and theory, and a professor's behavior is predictable because you know she or he fulfills a specific role. You likely do not invite your professor on family vacations with your family, or ask your professor to pick up your dry cleaning. Those interactions are not part of a professor's role, and are therefore not part of the social system (we hope!).

The third system Parsons wrote about is the **personality system**, which takes individual characteristics into account. However, the personality system is still embedded in the social structure, which means that individuals' unique and distinctive sense of "self" is limited by the choices they are given by both the cultural and social systems. Therefore the personality system is organized by what Parsons refers to as **need-dispositions**, which are types of action guided by emotion and individual drive, or representations of individuals' personal uniqueness. Our daily decisions – our tastes, preferences, drives – are limited by what is available. To help us understand what that means for families, we return to Casbah.

As mentioned earlier, the cultural system makes it possible for Casbah to "come out" to his family in contemporary society. The social system is also undoubtedly affected by this larger norm. Consider how social interactions have changed since LGBTQ persons have been afforded more rights and respect. First and foremost, a word, transgender, exists for how Casbah identifies. The case study suggested that Casbah knew he was different from a very young age, and when he learned during adolescence what transgender meant, he knew that label correctly identified him. He was then able to research support groups online for others who were similar to him, and feel a sense of belonging to a community of people instead of feeling alone and as if there was something "wrong" with him. This helped make coming out easier for him, as did his parents' willingness to assist him in transitioning with hormone therapy as well as individual psychological therapy and group therapy for the family. The existence of these resources shows evidence that the cultural system has adapted to broader social change. Following the various civil rights movements of the 1960s, society began to react to and absorb new subsystems, which redefined patterns of interaction at the social and personality levels. Again, while Parsons was not writing specifically about material spaces and places, it is still worth noting that the processes that led to the establishment of "transgender" as an identity, hormone therapy as a possibility, and individual and group therapy as a solution for dealing with adjustments to family and individual identity, were all part of a set of integrated interactions. This means that as society absorbed new subcultures as an acceptable part of the cultural system, conversations and concerted efforts were made to include and support LGBTQ persons in the social system. This opened up new possibilities for inclusivity for people who were once considered to be on the "margins" of society and not acceptable to the larger cultural system.

In sum, we can see how each system worked together as Casbah moved through the next stage in his life. Eventually, his need-dispositions were met, even though his family's subsystem was disrupted in the short term. Parents, friends, and faculty and staff in Casbah's school have likely been exposed to "Safe Zone training," which was created to "develop, enhance and maintain environments in workplaces, schools and other social settings that are culturally competent and supportive to LGBTQ individuals" (Safe Zone Project, 2014). Casbah, when deciding where he will go to college, will most definitely take into account which campuses are considered to be LGBTQ-friendly and inclusive. His personal choices of what to major in, what clubs he will be a part of, and which dorm he feels most comfortable in, are all determined by the *cultural system*. The *social system* – the interactions he hopes he will experience, when the time comes, should be somewhat predictable based on his knowledge of the campus culture. Then, the *personality system*, or the unique way he will go about his daily life, who he is attracted to and who he dates, are all dependent on what is available to him. He is still unique, but the culture and social systems definitely affect his personality. He could not truly "be" Casbah had he been born 50 years earlier to different parents in a different time and place. Each of the systems has worked together to function and impact his life.

Part of what contributes to the change we see in systems is institutionalization. **Institutionalization** occurs when a part of the larger cultural system becomes part of a standard in society; a long-standing tradition that is embedded and identifiable. As an example, consider the cultural norm that exists in most of American society that two people who choose to marry can go through the legal process of becoming legally recognized as a married couple. We can see institutionalization when the cultural system works down on the social system.

Internalization, on the other hand, is when individuals adhere to the cultural norms in such a way that they become part of need-dispositions and our patterns of communication and ways of thinking. Because of the overarching cultural system, we may all adhere to the norms that guide behavior (e.g., the expectation that you should marry), but we do so differently. We make different choices based on the subculture we identify with, and soon the signs, symbols, and interactions with others in subsystems become second nature, or taken for granted, because we have internalized the cultural norms. We can see internalization when the cultural system works down on the personality system. Consider the contemporary options for marriage – some couples are choosing to integrate a "flash mob" type of dance choreography into either their wedding ceremony or reception. Couples who have participated in this new practice are still conforming to cultural norms, but they choose their own song, dance moves, and setting in order to fulfill their need-dispositions of being unique.

One of the reasons why having a "flash mob" at a wedding ceremony is acceptable is because of how we are socialized. **Socialization** occurs when individuals come to regard specific norms as binding. It occurs during the interaction of the personality and social systems. How we are raised by our parents or loved ones determines our socialization; in contemporary cultures, there are several choices parents can make when it comes to raising their children. Some parents may choose to hover over their children, a practice referred to as "helicopter parenting," where parents pay extremely close attention to their teenage and young adult children's lives, often stepping in to solve problems for their children. Researchers and other experts have criticized this model of parenting because it prevents children from ever experiencing disappointment, leading to higher rates of anxiety and depression among children of helicopter parents (LeMoyne and Buchanan, 2011; Schiffrin et al., 2014). This approach to parenting, which is part of the contemporary cultural system, is a choice for parents. Parents in contemporary culture, particularly mothers, are socialized to be "perfect" parents (Hays, 1996), which in turn determines how their children will be socialized.

Now that we have described some of Parsons's general concepts as they relate to family, we can turn to one of his most notable articles, "The kinship system of the contemporary United States." In this work, Parsons (1943) reiterates that all systems have functions, and the family's main function is to procreate and socialize children. This work is highly criticized for dictating to families that there is only "one" family form, and any deviation from the SNAF is dysfunctional. This work is also criticized for suggesting that the ideal way in which families can serve positive functions in society is by reinforcing traditional gender roles. That is, Parsons suggested that women are better suited for **expressive roles** – showing love, care, concern, and support for the system. Therefore, men are better suited to perform **instrumental roles**, such as being a leader, making important decisions, and providing material needs for the system. Essentially, if families are to function appropriately, then the family structure needs to be divided along traditional gender lines. This makes sense, given Parsons's assertion that the need-dispositions of individuals in the personality system are met within the social and cultural systems. If an individual has a need, they should turn to the social and cultural systems to make a choice about how to fulfill that need. That choice should stay within acceptable, established cultural norms in order to strive for equilibrium between and within all systems and subsystems.

Parsons's model of structural functionalism did not account for deviance, or difference. If a family did not fit an established model within the preexisting cultural system (e.g., the SNAF), then it was deemed dysfunctional. The only way for system equilibrium to be reached is for everyone to stay within acceptable boundaries that are already established by the culture. The reason for this is because Parsons believed that changes in one system (e.g., mothers leaving the home to enter the paid workforce) would inevitably affect other systems, creating dysfunction. In the example of two working parents, which other systems might be affected? From Parsons's structural-functionalist perspective, we would need to examine how childcare facilities would need to adapt to meet the need-dispositions of the mother who wants to work outside the home for pay. If a vast majority of mothers decided to enter the paid labor force, a major shift in other systems would need to occur to maintain equilibrium between systems.

Considering the historical context in which Parsons formulated his theoretical framework, his assertions make sense. Dual-earner households did not conform to the cultural system of the 1940s, when Parsons conceptualized his theoretical framework. It was not until later, after the cultural system adapted to economic and social change, that dual-earner households became part of a cultural norm, with accompanying support from external social institutions. In order to better understand how society shifted over time to allow for different family forms to still "fit" within the larger culture, even though they are different from the mainstream, we now turn to Merton's theory of structural functionalism.

Merton's view of structural functionalism Merton (1957) was studying sociology at Harvard University when Parsons was in his early years as a faculty member there. Because of this, Merton has been noted for directly expanding Parsons's abstract structural functionalism to be a more useful and applicable framework for explaining action (Appelrouth and Edles, 2011). Merton disagreed with Parsons's view that changes that are functional for one part of a system will produce changes that are dysfunctional for other parts of a system. In fact, Merton is best known for his theory of deviance, which suggests that when there is a disconnect between the cultural goals of a society and the means available for individuals to achieve cultural goals, the natural result is strain. From Merton's perspective, not all members of society have the means to achieve, for example, the "ideal family." Therefore, the systems and subsystems that Parsons identified do more than simply fulfill functions and maintain equilibrium; they often produce unintended consequences that contribute to moving society forward in a positive way.

Though Merton did not write specifically about the family like Parsons did, his theoretical contributions can most definitely be applied to the study of families. Merton suggested that each system, or social institution in society (including families), has both manifest and latent functions. **Manifest functions** describe the intended purpose of the system; as an example, the criminal justice system exists to deter crime. However, Merton acknowledged that sometimes there are latent functions embedded into our social interactions and structures as well, and these unintended consequences, or **latent functions**, still contribute to the functionality of systems. The latent function of the criminal justice system is that it creates jobs. Police officers, judges, lawyers, prison guards, parole officers, court reporters among others, all depend on individuals committing crime so that they can remain employed. Have you ever thought about what might happen if all of a sudden, one day, everyone stopped committing crime? Imagine the effect that would have on the economy!

To bring an example a little closer to the study of families, think back to Casbah. When he decided to "come out" to his family, his parents sought help in order to support their child. They discussed psychological therapy with Casbah, and together they decided that was something they wanted to pursue. The manifest function of therapy was to help the family address and adapt to changes. The latent function was that the therapy sessions taught the married couple many tools that they could use for communication in other parts of their lives. For example, they became more emotionally intelligent at work and in their interactions with friends and loved ones. The latent functions of Casbah's transformation and therapy led to *positive* change in other systems.

Another of Merton's theoretical contributions to structural functionalism is **strain theory**. Strain theory posits that societies have a set of cultural goals that all societal members are pressured to achieve, or live up to; this results in strain. However, not all members of society follow the norm when it comes to achieving those cultural goals. Merton defined these individuals as deviant, and came up with four categories that describe the nonconforming ways in which people react to cultural goals. The first category, *innovators*, are individuals who accept cultural goals, but use innovative and sometimes illegal means to achieve them. An example would be a single woman who wants to have children, and decides to have them on her own by using a sperm donor.

The second category, *ritualists*, are those who accept cultural goals, but simply "go through the motions" of achieving them. A ritualist may seem apathetic, or dispassionate. An example of this would be a parent who is married and has children, but does not *really* enjoy those roles. She or he may just go through life, day by day, trying to get through. His or her nature is not to leave the family, but to do "what's right," even if it means not truly being involved or 100 percent invested. Merton used the example of someone "being in a rut" to illustrate a ritualist (Merton, 1938).

Third, *retreaters* are individuals who reject cultural goals of a society as well as the means to achieve them. The Amish would fall under this category; they subscribe to traditionalist Christian church teachings, and generally reject modern technology for simple living and self-sufficiency. They typically seek to remain separate from mainstream culture, operating their own schools, and living a rural lifestyle characterized by manual labor and humility (LancasterPA.com, 2016).

Fourth, *rebels* are similar to retreatists, but they are active in trying to create a new social structure. This category represents a "transitional response seeking to *institutionalize* new goals and new procedures to be shared by other members of the society" (Merton, 1938, p. 44, emphasis in original). Therefore, rebels reject prevailing cultural goals in an attempt to substitute new values. This concept is a major point of divergence from Parsons's theoretical framework. While Parsons would have suggested that systems do adapt to environmental change over time, Merton details and defines the process using strain theory, and in particular, the case of rebels. Indeed, consider this: would the Civil Rights Movement have moved forward without "rebels" like Rosa Parks or Martin Luther King, Jr?

Although Merton does not view a final category – *conformists* – as deviant, we still need to mention that individuals in society do accept cultural goals and use institutionalized means to achieve them. While values do vary within cultural systems and subsystems, we could suggest that conformists are individuals who try to marry around the ages of the "average" couple, have children around the ages of the "average" family, and follow the norms of parenting that "average" families do. Individuals in this category are the ruler against which all other members of society are measured (Ganong, Coleman, and Mapes, 1990).

Evaluating Functionalist Theory

Strengths of functionalist theory

Although functionalist theory is the most widely criticized of all the family theories, it has served as the foundation for many, if not most, of the other theories, and it is still in use today, whether scholars acknowledge it or not. Indeed, functionalist theory has proven to be remarkably adaptable even to current family circumstances (Hughes, Sharrock, and Martin, 2003; White, 2013).

Box 2.2 Functionalist Theory in Pop Culture: *The Village*

A scene from *The Village*, 2004, dir. M. Night Shyamalan, Touchstone Pictures

This film is set in a small, isolated Pennsylvania village in what appears to be the early nineteenth century. The village is characterized by mechanical solidarity, where all members of society have similar beliefs and deviance is punished publicly and harshly. One of the main characters, Noah, stabs another community member and is removed from society because his deviance is a threat to the cohesiveness of the group.

Toward the end of the film, another main character, Ivy, escapes the village in order to get to the nearest town to secure medicine for her love interest, Lucius. After Ivy runs through the forest surrounding the village, she climbs over a high wall and realizes that her entire community has been lying to her and the other children all along. The village was actually founded not in the nineteenth century but in the 1970s by one of the elders, a professor whose father was murdered. He met others at a grief counseling clinic and together, they decided to purchase land inside of a wildlife preserve with the hopes of protecting their offspring from any of the dangers of the outside world. This turn of events in the film is a clear illustration of Merton's concept of retreatism, where individuals react to cultural goals by rejecting them and trying to remove themselves from society. In this case, the elders established the village to escape the horrors of losing loved ones to murder in a violent world.

Finally, we can see the concepts of manifest and latent functions. The manifest function of creating the village was to remove loved ones from experiencing pain and trauma in the modern world. However, there was no escaping the latent function of being isolated, because villagers were unable to benefit from modern medicine, which also protects humans from pain, illness, and unnecessary complications from injuries.

Families are part of a global system Functionalist theory provides the basis for understanding how families work at the macro-level. In examining the functions of family as an all-encompassing social system, the theory provides an umbrella under which family systems around the world may be analyzed. For example, every society and culture has some form of family system to specify how individuals depend upon one another for nurturance, sustenance, social support, and the regulation of sexual and reproductive behaviors. In this way, functionalism provides a common language for comparing family systems as a global structure, and therefore at the broadest level of social organization.

The institution of the family persists through major social changes Functionalist theory assumes that "the family" is one of the major institutions around which societies are organized. Other major institutions are the economic system, the political system, and the legal system. That is, every society has ways of organizing that are the most efficient way to keep that society going. Every society must also deal with sweeping changes that transform the functioning of institutions. For example, the technological revolution has created a social order in which national boundaries break down and time becomes compressed. Family members can stay connected through the internet even if they are living in different countries. Television shows made in the US are broadcast all over the world, and vice versa. The nightly news brings family life styles and intrasocietal conflicts into our homes, blurring the lines between diverse cultures. Functionalist theory allows us to examine the unique ways in which intimate lives are organized and operate compared with other institutional systems and to assess the relevance and enduring functions of family as an institution despite global transformations. Is the family still the primary institution for regulating individual decisions around reproduction, sexuality, marriage, and care of children and elders? Global communications reveal that, yes, families are still vitally important, and the disruption or loss of family ties is traumatic in the face of war and other international conflicts.

Modern adaptations of functionalism account for different family forms Modern adaptations of functionalist theory suggest that various family structures can be functional for society, accounting for changes in the sociohistorical context that lead to significant changes in the cultural system. Indeed, Merton adapted the original model to include deviant family forms, and suggested that different structures can still contribute to overall function and positive change in society. For example, the social upheaval surrounding World War II produced a need for women to leave their posts at home and enter the workforce to "fill in" for men who had been deployed abroad. The cultural system redefined, for a short time, what the normative roles were for women; day care centers emerged to care for working mothers' children; and following the war, women realized they had other options than being a stay-at-home mother. Adapting to meet the needs of major systems (e.g., the American military and manufacturing workforce) led to positive social change for families and women over time.

Weaknesses of functionalist theory

Many scholars have critiqued functionalist theory. Conflict theorists (Chapter 3) and feminist theorists (Chapter 8), in particular, have challenged the relevance of a theory that describes families as having a universal, normative structure or that divides family roles according a strict interpretation of gender differences as the naturalized social order. These critiques can be organized in the following ways.

Outdated and limited in scope In general, functionalist theory, regardless of its evolving nature, has been criticized as being "old-fashioned" for imposing a way of explaining family structures and functions as a "one size fits all" model (Cheal, 1991, p. 6). The functionalist view does a disservice to the vast diversity of how we actually enact family life; it idealizes and oversimplifies gender roles and enforces a rigid view of how men and women interact in marriage and family relationships. The basis of the functionalist view of families that was common in mid twentieth-century America cannot adequately account for the variations in how families live today. Indeed, the search for a universal definition of family is not relevant when we consider the infinite ways that individuals couple, uncouple, raise children, and care for the old throughout the world. Scanzoni and Marsiglio (1993) identified the weaknesses of traditional functionalist theory and expanded the theory to the inclusion of diverse structures. That is, it is not the "structure" of blood ties and legal marriage that make individuals a family. Instead, families are a social form of organization in which blood and marriage are only two of the ways that interpersonal commitments and caring responsibilities are expressed.

Overlooks inequalities built into social structure Functionalist theory has tended to downplay the ways in which individuals are treated differently and unequally on the basis of gender, race, class, sexual orientation, and other forms of social stratification. In her critique of functionalism, feminist sociologist Barrie Thorne challenged three of the major assumptions of functionalist theory: "The ideology of the monolithic family, beliefs that the family is natural or biological, and analyses that freeze present family ideals in a language of function and roles" (1982, p. 3). That is, the functionalist view of the family blames mothers for child problems, assigns higher status to men as the major breadwinner, and treats families from ethnic minority groups as deviant from the White, nuclear, middle-class family form.

Ignores extended family systems Family scholars who study multiple generations and intergenerational relationships have challenged Parsons's view of structural functionalism on the basis of its exclusive view of the nuclear family (e.g., two generations). As we show in the example of Vern Bengtson and his colleagues later in this chapter, generations matter in families. That is, families consist of more than parents and their children. Sibling ties remain important throughout life and the parent–child relationship does not stop when children leave home. Increasingly, families are characterized by multiple generations, and kin ties are an important source of social support (Bengtson, 2001; Sarkisian and Gerstel, 2012).

An alternative theory app: symbolic interactionism

In this chapter, we have laid out the key concepts, origins and background, and modern applications as well as the strengths and weaknesses of functionalist theory. Sometimes when learning a new theory, it is useful to compare it to another one to more easily pinpoint the differences between the two. Therefore, in each chapter we will show you how to switch your "app" at any time by offering up an additional theory that contrasts to the one you just learned.

Symbolic interactionism (Chapter 4) is a theory that is perceived as being in sharp contrast to functionalist theory. Symbolic interactionism focuses on the meaning associated with symbols, gestures, and language. For this reason, it is often used as a micro-level theory, which is the opposite of functionalism. To illustrate the differences, consider how we could analyze the case study (Casbah/Cassie) using a micro-level theory. We would focus much more on the micro-level (face-to-face) interactions Cassie had with her family before she transitioned to identifying as male, including her gender performances and the power associated with the male and female labels in modern society. Interestingly, both functionalism (utilizing a macro-perspective) and symbolic interactionism (utilizing a micro-perspective) take into account how societies change over time. Where functionalism focuses on how institutions change over time to help society function smoothly, symbolic interactionists focus more closely on how such social change allows for individuals to create and re-create new meanings and symbols because broader social movements make possible new identities, roles, and other possibilities.

Working with Functionalist Theory: Integrating Research and Practice

Now that we have described the historical origins, key concepts, and strengths and weaknesses of functionalist theory, we turn to how the theory can be used in research and practice. We then analyze an empirical study that was rooted in functionalist theory, in order to see how scholars put the theory to work in a research project. Finally, we present ideas about how the theory informs the practice of developing policies on a college campus.

Functionalist theory today

Drawing on pioneering longitudinal research on intergenerational transmission of values, social gerontologists Bengtson, Biblarz, and Roberts (2002) examine the concept of how (and if) families are important in the lives of individuals. The Longitudinal Study of Generations (LSOG) was begun by Vern Bengtson in 1970–1971 as a way to examine the linkages between the quality of intergenerational family relationships and a person's psychosocial development over time. Initially, the study surveyed more than 300 families, consisting of a total of 2,044 individuals and representing three generations from each family. Thus, it initially mirrored a structural-functionalist perspective on the family as a macro-system that is charged with meeting the social-psychological needs of its members. One of the most important early contributions of the LSOG was that it did not stop at Parsons's notion of the two-generation nuclear family, but added in a third generation (e.g., grandparents) to consider how social-historical events across the life course impacted each subsequent generation and thus affected the transmission of family values. The framing of the study is an early exemplar of how older functionalist ideas and newer ideas about the life course (Chapter 9) can be integrated to study generations.

Over time, great-grandchildren were added to the mix of family members studied. The four generations were (G1): Grandparents, born 1896 to 1911; (G2): their children, born 1916 to 1931; (G3): their grandchildren, born 1945 to 1955; and (G4): their great-grandchildren, born 1978 to 1983. Individuals were asked to report on many issues. The researchers gathered extensive demographic data over time, particularly on education, occupation, residence, income, ethnicity, marital status, and number of children. These data helped them to understand how families transmit aspirations, such as economic achievement, over time. They also assessed many aspects of social-psychological health. Self-esteem, for example, was measured by questions such as "I feel that I'm a person of worth, at least on an equal basis with others." Finally, participants were also asked to rank order their values in life, including social justice, financial security, friendship, patriotism, personal freedom, and family loyalty.

After assessing all of these areas of intergenerational transmission, Bengtson and colleagues (2002) found the remarkable persistence of values across the generations. Contrary to reports in the popular media, the members of Generation X (G4) were not disengaged from their families. Indeed, the researchers found tremendous support for the belief in family solidarity. And, although major demographic shifts were transforming families over time (e.g., the increase in the divorce rate), families were able to deal with conflict and remain connected to one another. This study shows the importance of measuring family change over time, so that what endures about families (that is, what is functional) can be uncovered.

Functionalist theory in research

Modern family scholars have built on the original principles of functionalist theory to gain a fuller understanding of how families have adapted to cultural norms over time. Researchers Kathryn Edin and Maria Kefalas investigated the norms of motherhood for poor women in the inner city. While not overtly stated as using functionalist theory, these researchers investigate the ways in which women conform to cultural goals (having children), using innovative means to reach them (foregoing marriage for motherhood).

In their book titled *Promises I can keep: Why poor women put motherhood before marriage*, Edin and Kefalas (2005) spent five years living with, working with, and interviewing poor women from various racial and ethnic backgrounds in the inner city of Philadelphia. The authors present data from 162 single mothers, illustrating how social class affects women's expectations about marriage and the importance of having children. Merton's (1938) strain theory is evident in this study because the overarching cultural goal – to have children – is accepted and sought after among women in the inner city. Indeed, many of the women readily admit that they wanted children, and were happy when they found out they were pregnant. They also reported fearing being "owned" by an authoritarian man, and some said they did not believe in divorce, which is why they had not married. The women also reported accepting the cultural goal of wanting a successful career, but they were not interested in waiting until after their career was established to have children. This pattern is in contrast to how many middle-class individuals approach family, where people are more likely to marry *in order to* have children. Therefore, the cultural goals are the same, but women in the inner city are more likely to reorder establishing a family with children, then career, then marriage. This study is a good example of how women can be innovative in order to achieve cultural goals even in the face of obstacles they face. Family educators, practitioners, and policymakers should study this text as a way to access just why poor women choose motherhood above all else.

Functionalist theory in practice

One of the most important places where family scholars can utilize functionalist theory is in the development of workplace policy (Pittman, 1993). Human resource (HR) offices exist in a multitude of settings – hospitals, universities, private for-profit companies, nongovernmental organizations, and the military, to name a few. All HR professionals have to adapt policies to protect their employees. Given the shift in cultural awareness about LGBTQ rights, it should be no surprise that some institutions offer training to help all employees maintain respect for others in the workplace.

An example of a program that has become part of the cultural mainstream is the "Safe Zone" program. In 1992, the Lesbian, Bisexual, and Gay Student Association at Ball State University (now, the LGBTQA community) developed a "safe program" to help eradicate homophobia and discrimination against LGBTQ people on college campuses (Safezone, 2016). The program is designed as a bridge between the LGBTQ community and the heterosexual community, via "Allies," a term used to describe heterosexual people who are supportive of inclusion and equality. Since 1992, the program has spread across the US and is best known for its symbol of an inverted pink triangle, which stands for alliance with gay rights, and promoting a safe, open, and respectful dialogue free from homophobia. On college campuses, HR professionals, faculty, staff, administrators, and students are educated and exposed to the symbolism of the "safe zone" or "safe space." Campus community members are encouraged to participate in the "Safe Zone" training sessions, which usually last a few hours and include eye-opening activities designed to let attendees walk awhile in an LGBTQ person's shoes. One such activity, a guided imagery to experience heterosexism, which involves participants closing their eyes and imaging what it would be like to live in a world described by a leading narrator, was introduced to the higher education community as a tool for using in college classrooms across multiple disciplines (Henderson and Murdock, 2012).

Several aspects of this evolving set of practices surrounding the rights of and respect for LGBTQ persons are applicable using functionalist theory. As previously mentioned, the cultural system has absorbed LGBTQ rights as part of the mainstream dialogue on human rights. This trickles down to the social system, redefining interactions between people (e.g., being introduced to guided imagery activities and reminded of homophobic language in the college classroom). It also opens up opportunities for individuals' need-dispositions to be met at the personality level, because ideally, one's awareness of LGBTQ issues is raised, which provides a safe space for individuals to "come out." Indeed, National Coming Out Day (October 11) was established in 1988 as an internationally observed civil awareness day to celebrate individuals who publicly identify as members of the LGBTQ community (Stein, 2004). Individuals who pioneered these causes could definitely be considered "rebels" according to Merton's strain theory, because they actively rejected old (homophobic and heterosexist) cultural norms and sought to create new social norms. The result was, and continues to be, change at the cultural level in society.

Conclusion

Functionalist theory has provided important ideas that allow researchers and practitioners to put the theory to use beyond the conceptual level. Highly critiqued as an outdated theory, and limited in application, there are many ways in which functionalist theory can still be applied to the study of families. Indeed, it is often considered to be foundational to all of the major family theories.

Additionally, it is important to highlight how functionalist theory is applicable to the study of

Box 2.3 Global Comparisons of Maternity and Paternity Leave Policies

There are variations from country to country when it comes to how much time new parents are given to take care of children (Kamerman, 2000; Ray, Gornick, and Schmitt, 2009). Consider these examples:

United States Mothers are guaranteed 12 weeks of unpaid family leave according to the Family and Medical Leave Act of 1994, which includes maternity leave.

Norway Norwegian parents receive one year of parental leave, earning 80 percent of their pay while away. Alternatively, they can take 42 weeks off at full pay. Parents can also take child-rearing leave, paid at a flat rate, until the children are two years old.

Canada Mothers are guaranteed 17 weeks of maternity leave, and 35 weeks of parental leave, which can be used by either parent or shared within the first year. Canadian parents are paid 55 percent of their regular earnings while on leave.

Japan Mothers are granted up to 58 weeks (including 26 weeks of paid leave and 32 weeks of unpaid leave). There is no paid leave granted to fathers. In Japan, one parent must take all of the family's parental leave; given income disparities, fathers have little incentive to take leave.

Poland Mothers are guaranteed full pay for 16 weeks of maternity leave for the first child, 18 weeks for subsequent births, 26 weeks for multiple births. Single parents are also accommodated with a flat rate of up to 36 months off.

families across the globe. Because access to paid or unpaid maternity and paternity leave is an important consideration for functionalist theorists and family scholars, we highlight in Box 2.3 how parental leave is encouraged and economically supported in some nations, but not others. We challenge you to consider these global applications of the theory as you move on to the discussion and reflection questions, and areas for further study, in the concluding pages of this chapter.

Multimedia Suggestions

www.feministmormonhousewives.org

This website houses a blog that covers various social issues, and the contributors to the blog all self-identify as "feminist Mormon housewives." Both the contributors to the blog and their readers find a sense of community and solidarity by discussing how their feminist views can both conflict with and complement their religion. This site is a great example of how the need-dispositions of feminist Mormon housewives are met through an online community. In addition, this site is also an example of how a typically conservative, patriarchal culture can adapt to social change over time.

Activate your theory app: After browsing through this website, compare and contrast how Durkheim, Parsons, and Merton would each explain the presence of this group. Would they agree or disagree, and why?

http://www.bountifulbaskets.org/

This is the website for Bountiful Baskets (BB), a food cooperative, which provides families with a low-cost alternative to shopping in big-box grocery stories for healthy foods. This cooperative operates weekly, and families can choose to give around $15 to the pool of money, which the BB volunteers use to purchase produce and bread directly from producers. This co-op is just one of many that families are joining to be a part of the movement to eat healthy and save money. From a functionalist perspective, shopping for food is beginning to look and function differently. Individuals who participate in this (and other) co-ops are, in Merton's terms, innovators, responding to the relatively recent cultural message to eat healthy, organic food, but not conforming to the "norm" of shopping in a chain grocery store to do it.

Activate your theory app: Find another website (or product) that offers a new way of fulfilling some of the family's main functions. How will this affect overall cultural change and family expectations? Will it shift gender norms, or intensify them?

Babies (2009)

This documentary simultaneously follows four babies around the world, and illustrates cultural differences in child-rearing during the first year of the babies' lives. Mari is raised in Tokyo, Japan by her two parents, in a very busy metropolitan area. Hattie lives in San Francisco and is raised by two very ecologically conscious, egalitarian parents. Ponijao lives in Namibia with her parents and eight older siblings. She is part of the Himba tribe and lives in a small village with other families. Bayar is raised in Mongolia on a small family farm with his brother and parents. The documentary illustrates the differences in how families "function" in varying cultural systems, from westernized cultures like Japan and the United States, to developing countries like Namibia and Mongolia.

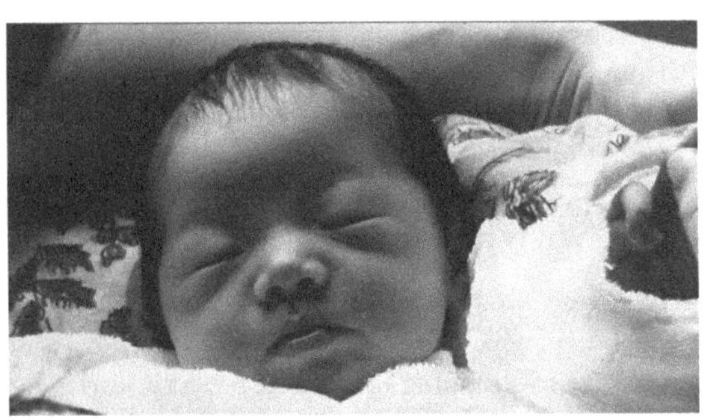

A scene from *Babies*, 2010, dir. Thomas Balmès, StudioCanal

Activate your theory app: Compare and contrast Parsons's cultural, social, and personality systems among the four different countries. How does each system affect how babies are raised around the world?

Breaking Bad (2008–13)

This American television series features a high school chemistry teacher, Walter White, who is diagnosed with inoperable lung cancer. In order to make sure his family is provided for after he dies, he turns to a life of crime by producing and selling crystal meth. This series illustrates several functionalist concepts, one of the most obvious being Walter's endeavors as an innovator. Also evident in this series is the idea of moral individualism: Walter's very specific job of making and selling meth may have honorable roots (providing for his family in the long term), but he continually operates on morally shaky ground, not always doing what is good for greater society.

A scene from *Breaking Bad*, 2008, cr. Vince Gilligan, Sony Pictures Television

Activate your theory app: See if you can find additional evidence of Merton's strain theory in this program. In addition to Walter White's clear portrayal of an "innovator," do you see examples of ritualists, rebels, retreatists, and conformists?

Further Reading

Bernard, J., "The good provider role: Its rise and fall," *American Psychologist, 36* (1981), 1–12 (doi:10.1037/0003-066X.36.1.1). Jessie Bernard, one of the leading figures in sociology, analyzed how the gendered nature of marriage makes it a very different institution for men and women. Men have experienced more economic, emotional, and health benefits from marriage, given their historically elevated position as breadwinners. Yet, with dramatic macro-level economic and global changes that have eroded manufacturing and industrial jobs employing a large number of men, men's opportunities to live up to the ideal of "the good provider" role have drastically reduced. In this classic article, Bernard analyzes the trends that have led to the undoing of the expectation that men can continue to enjoy this privileged status in families.

Cherlin, A. J., *The marriage-go-round: The state of marriage and the family in America today* (New York: Vintage, 2009). In this book, Andrew Cherlin explains the enduring importance of marriage in US society, even in the face of major demographic changes in the way that individuals partner and raise families. Despite high rates of cohabitation, divorce, and remarriage in the American context, marriage is still the idealized social status, prized by most Americans as the ultimate goal. Yet, social change has also led to restrictions on who is able or allowed to marry. Marriage is readily available to members of the middle class, who are able to delay it until they have completed education and established careers. To poor individuals, on the other hand, marriage is often not feasible, given the lack of available partners and the lack of economic resources. And, until quite recently, gay and lesbian couples have been legally barred from marriage in the US. Despite these practical and legal barriers, marriage is seen as the ultimate path to adult status and retains its importance as one of the primary functions of the family.

Durkheim, E., *Suicide: A study in sociology*, trans. J. A. Spaulding and G. Simpson (New York: Free Press, 1951). In this classic work, originally conducted in the late nineteenth century, Durkheim analyzed the occurrence of suicide as a social phenomenon. He critiqued the individualistic perspective that suicide is linked only to psychopathology (e.g., mental illness, such as depression and anxiety), and instead revealed its roots in how a society is organized. He conducted a cross-cultural analysis of suicide rates (from 1841 to 1878) in the major European countries at the time (e.g., France, Prussia, England, Denmark, Saxony, Bavaria). He found three different types of suicide, all of which are linked to social events and/or cultural factors. Anomic suicide was prevalent when a major event such as war occurred which disrupted the social fabric of individuals' lives. Egoistic suicide occurred more often according to different types of family and cultural patterns. For example, he found that Protestants were more likely to take their own lives than Catholics. Finally, altruistic suicide occurred in situations where individuals were (too) strongly tied to their families and communities as in the case where women might take their own lives upon the death of their husbands.

Hawkins, A. J., Amato, P. R., and Kinghorn, A., "Are government-supported healthy marriage initiatives affecting family demographics? A state-level analysis," *Family Relations, 62* (2013), 501–513 (doi:10.1111/fare.12009). Following changes in the federal welfare system, the US government provided funding streams under the umbrella of the Healthy Marriage Initiative to encourage marriage for economically needy couples and to reduce the rise in nonmarital pregnancies among women living in poverty. This effort has been controversial because it involves the federal government's intrusion in people's private lives by taking away economic assistance and trying to reestablish the nuclear, two-generation family ideal among those in economic need. The study reported on in this article is the first experimental evaluation of federal programs designed to create and sustain healthy heterosexual marriages. Although inconclusive, the findings reveal the potential positive effects of marriage enrichment programs. This article also provides a way to systematically assess how well governmental funding is conducted.

Pruett, K. D., *Fatherneed: Why father care is as essential as mother care for your child* (New York: Broadway,

2000). Child psychiatrist Kyle Pruett addresses the importance of father engagement in children's lives. He claims that fathers and mothers have different roles to play in the family. The role of the father is necessary to positive child development, even if fathers still believe that mothers are most important. He explains how fatherhood also contributes to the well-being of men. Although Pruett emphasizes that fathers are essential in fulfilling one of the defining functions of the family, he also recognizes that the role of father may differ from culture to culture. For example, he has criticized the misuse of his perspective about the importance of fatherhood by those who argue against gay marriage.

Questions for Students

Discussion Questions

1 Parsons's model of structural functionalism was developed in the United States during a time of economic prosperity (1950s). Consider applying his model to contemporary Chinese culture. Would it fit? Why or why not?
2 Compare and contrast how Merton and his mentor, Parsons, would view the issue of same-sex marriage. How would Parsons's explanation of gay marriage differ from Merton's? Use at least two terms from each theorist.
3 Many behaviors are defined as social problems, even deviant, including drug abuse, prostitution, and theft. In what ways would a functionalist theorist suggest that any of these behaviors could be "functional" for society?
4 We presented several examples of how countries other than the US offer maternity and paternity leave for workers. Choose a South American country to compare its policies to those we have described.
5 In recent years, the definition of heterosexual marriage as the most functional family form for raising children has changed to include other forms such as cohabiting and single-parent families. Are there additional forms that you think should also be included as functional?
6 Which other theory from this text is most similar to functionalist theory? Which is most different? Explain.

Your Turn!

Many schools across the country are now addressing the needs of transgender students. Your job, as school board president of a public school in a small rural community in Wisconsin, is to consider all aspects of the debate, and decide on a policy to bring to the school board for a vote. What are the cultural, social, and personality systems you should consider as you draft your policy? How do you deal with the fact that the school board and parents are divided on the rights and protections of transgender students? At issue are whether or not they can use the restroom and locker rooms of the gender with which they identify, and whether or not male-gendered students can participate on male sports teams, and female-gendered students on female sports teams. Find information on what other schools are doing so that you are well-informed.

Personal Reflection Questions

1 How did gender roles operate in your household? Were they traditionally divided, or did your family adapt in order to maintain equilibrium?
2 Think about times in your family when equilibrium was disrupted. What happened? Who and how was the dysfunction managed?
3 Did you grow up in a society more characterized by organic or mechanical solidarity? In what ways?
4 Describe a time when either you or someone you know has experienced low or high levels of social integration.
5 How has the cultural system you've grown up in differed from that of your parent(s), or grandparents?
6 Have you ever travelled to another country, or had a cross-cultural relationship with a friend or classmate? How did you rely on your own cultural knowledge to help you understand and appreciate the other?

References

Appelrouth, S., and Edles, L. D. (2011). *Classical and contemporary sociological theory: Text and readings.* Los Angeles: Pine Forge Press.

Bastian, R., Moran, L., and Dugan, S. (prod.), and Tucker, D. (dir.) (2005). *TransAmerica.* Motion picture. IRC Films and The Weinstein Company.

Bengtson, V. L. (2001). Beyond the nuclear family: The increasing importance of multigenerational bonds (Burgess Award Lecture). *Journal of Marriage and Family, 63,* 1–16. doi:10.1111/j.1741-3737.2001.00001.x.

Bengtson, V. L., Biblarz, T. J., and Roberts, R. E. L. (2002). *How families still matter: A longitudinal study of youth in two generations.* New York: Cambridge University Press.

Cheal, D. (1991). *Family and the state of theory.* Toronto: University of Toronto Press.

Coontz, S. (1992). *The way we never were: American families and the nostalgia trap.* New York: Basic Books.

Durkheim, E. (1984). *The division of labor in society.* New York: Free Press. (Originally published 1893.)

Edin, K., and Kefalas, M. (2005). *Promises I can keep: Why poor women put motherhood before marriage.* Los Angeles: University of California Press.

Ganong, L. H., Coleman, M., and Mapes, D. (1990). A meta-analytic review of family structure stereotypes. *Journal of Marriage and the Family, 52,* 287–297. doi:10.2307/353026.

Giddens, A. (2002). *Capitalism and modern social theory: An analysis of the writings of Marx, Durkheim and Max Weber.* New York: Cambridge University Press.

Hays, S. (1996). *The cultural contradictions of motherhood.* New Haven: Yale University Press.

Henderson, A. C., and Murdock, J. L. (2012). Getting students beyond ideologies: Using heterosexist guided imagery in the classroom. *Innovative Higher Education, 37,* 185–198. doi:10.1007/s10755-011-9198-4.

Hughes, J. A., Sharrock, W. W., and Martin, P. J. (2003). *Understanding classical sociology: Marx, Weber, Durkheim* (2nd edn). London: Sage.

Kamerman, S. B. (2000). Parental leave policies: An essential ingredient in early childhood education and care policies. *Society for Research in Child Development: Social Policy Report, 14*(2), 3–15.

Kerman, P. (2011). *Orange is the new black: My year in a women's prison.* New York: Random House.

Kingsbury, N., and Scanzoni, J. (1993). Structural-functionalism. In P. G. Boss, W. J. Doherty, R. LaRossa, W. R. Schumm, and S. K. Steinmetz (eds), *Sourcebook of family theories and methods: A contextual approach* (pp. 195–217). New York: Plenum Press.

LancasterPA.com (2016). *Amish and the plain people.* At www.LancasterPA.com/amish/.

LeMoyne, T., and Buchanan, T. (2011). Does "hovering" matter? Helicopter parenting and its effect on well-being. *Sociological Spectrum, 31,* 399–418. doi:10.1080/02732173.2011.574038.

Merton, R. K. (1938). Social structure and anomie. *American Sociological Review, 3,* 672–682. doi:10.2307/2084686.

Merton, R. K. (1957). *Social theory and social structure.* New York: Simon & Schuster.

Parsons, T. (1943). The kinship system of the contemporary United States. *American Anthropologist, 45,* 22–38. doi:10.1525/aa.1943.45.1.02a00030.

Parsons, T. (1951). *The social system.* New York: Free Press.

Parsons, T. E., and Shils, E. A. (eds) (1951). *Toward a general theory of action.* Cambridge, MA: Harvard University Press.

Parsons, T., Shils, E., Naegele, K. D., and Pitts, J. R. (eds) (1965). *Theories of society: Foundations of modern sociological theory.* New York: Free Press.

Pittman, J. F. (1993). Functionalism may be down, but it surely is not out: Another point of view for family therapists and policy analysts. In P. G. Boss, W. J. Doherty, R. LaRossa, W. R. Schumm, and S. K. Steinmetz (eds), *Sourcebook of family theories and methods: A contextual approach* (pp. 218–221). New York: Plenum Press.

Ray, R., Gornick, J. C., and Schmitt, J. (2009). *Parental leave policies in 21 countries: Assessing generosity and gender equality.* Washington, DC: Center for Economic and Policy Research. At www.cepr.net.

Safezone (2016). Safezone: Projects in support of the LGBTQA community. Ball State University. At cms.bsu.edu/campuslife/counselingcenter/additionalservices/safezone.

Safe Zone Project (2014). At www.thesafezoneproject.com.

Sarkisian, N., and Gerstel, N. (2012). *Nuclear family values, extended family lives: The power of race, class, and gender.* New York: Routledge.

Scanzoni, J., and Marsiglio, W. (1993). New action theory and contemporary families. *Journal of Family Issues, 14,* 105–132. doi:10.1177/0192513X93014001009.

Schiffrin, H. H., Liss, M., Miles-McLean, H., Geary, K. A., Erchull, M. J., and Tashner, T. (2014). Helping or hovering? The effects of helicopter parenting on college students' well-being. *Journal of Child and Family Studies, 23,* 548–557. doi:10.1007/210826-013-9716-3.

Silverstein, C. (1991). Psychological and medical treatments of homosexuality. In J. C. Gonsiorek and J. D. Weinrich (eds), *Homosexuality: Research implications for public policy* (pp. 101–114). Newbury Park, CA: Sage.

Smith, D. E. (1993). The Standard North American Family: SNAF as an ideological code. *Journal of Family Issues, 14*, 50–65. doi:10.1177/0192513X93014001005.

Stein, M. (ed.) (2004). *Encyclopedia of lesbian, gay, bisexual, and transgender history in America* (vol. 2). Farmington Hills, MI: Gale/Cengage Learning.

Thorne, B. (1982). Feminist rethinking of the family: An overview. In B. Thorne, with M. Yalom (eds), *Rethinking the family: Some feminist questions* (pp. 1–24). New York: Longman.

US Senate (1937). Committee on Education and Labor and House Committee on Labor. *Joint hearings on the Fair Labor Standards Act of 1937*. Washington, DC: Government Printing Office.

White, J. M. (2013). The current status of theorizing about families. In G. W. Peterson and K. R. Bush (eds), *Handbook of marriage and the family* (3rd edn, pp. 11–37). New York: Springer.

3

Conflict Theory

Think about when you were a child, what you wanted to be when you grew up. What did you dream of, who did you dress up as for career day at your elementary school? Most children have unlimited imaginations when it comes to this question. A little boy may want to grow up to be a professional football player, or maybe even the president of the United States. Why is it improbable that these dreams will come true for most children? Can all little boys achieve the dream of being president of the United States someday? Does social class have anything to do with where we start, where we see ourselves, and where we end up? How are our childhood dreams affected by social stratification?

Conflict theory, which is considered to be one of the founding theories in social science, provides family studies scholars with a useful framework to understand how social stratification affects families. In this chapter, we discuss the history of conflict theory and how the principles and key concepts can be used to understand challenges families face. Conflict theory helps us answer questions about how families' access to limited (or unlimited) resources can affect their ability to cope with day-to-day struggles. In order to gain a fuller understanding of how conflict theory works, we start with a case study that illustrates how a family's access to resources is important to all members of the family.

Case Study

Marie, the subject of our case study, was no different than most children with big hopes and dreams. During career day in fifth grade, Marie dressed up as Neil Armstrong, because she wanted to be an astronaut. Marie was fascinated by the fact that we were able to send humans into outer space, and she fantasized about how cool it would be to be floating around in space, looking back at the earth from so far away. Marie honestly thought that someday she could be an astronaut just like Neil Armstrong.

Throughout high school, Marie did not fully understand that having the dream of wanting to be an astronaut was so far-fetched. She spent her entire life in a very small town in rural South Dakota, where her parents owned the local hardware store. They worked six or seven days a week, 10-hour days, just to provide for Marie and her two brothers. On Thursday nights, when the freight truck would bring the weekly shipment of merchandise to her parents' store, Marie's family had to meet the truck driver at the store to unload everything. Since they did not know exactly when the truck would arrive, Marie's parents asked the truck driver to honk his horn when he drove by their house (which was on the outskirts of town) so they knew to get up out of bed – no matter how late it was – to come unload that week's shipment of merchandise. When the truck driver honked, Marie and her brothers climbed into their parents' old pickup truck and went up to the store to unload the truck. Marie's childhood memories are built around helping in the store; she loaded cases of oil onto a dolly from the truck and wheeled them into the warehouse when she was eight years old. Her whole life, Marie thought that it was normal for kids to do these things; it was what she had to do to support her parents' hardware store.

Family Theories: Foundations and Applications, First Edition. Katherine R. Allen and Angela C. Henderson.

Contrast the realities of Marie's childhood with her dream of wanting to be an astronaut. Why was that dream probably not going to come to fruition? Why is it not possible for "just anyone" to be what they want to be when they grow up? Conflict theory helps us understand differences between classes in society in competition for scarce resources, including wealth, power, and prestige. Conflict theorists argue that the way society is structured benefits a few at the expense of many, and consequently, for most of us, it is very difficult to escape the class into which we are born.

What Is Conflict Theory?

Conflict theory is used by researchers to help explain competition between the "haves" and the "have nots" in society. At its core, this theory addresses conflict between these two groups over scarce resources, which can range from families' access to wealth, power, and privilege, to the conflict within families over inheritance rights and caregiving duties. Therefore, in this chapter, we will present both micro- and macro-approaches to using conflict theory as it relates to differences between families based on social structure and access to resources, as well as differences within families when it comes to power and decision-making. Additionally, we will consider how conflict at the macro-level (i.e., structured inequalities) is reinforced by interactions at the micro-level (i.e., parenting approaches) through the transmission of different types of capital.

History and origins

Although it might be fairly easy to see conflict between the rich and the poor in modern society, conflict theory is rooted in a different time and place, arising from the Industrial Revolution when major social upheaval and economic change occurred in Western Europe (see functionalist theory, Chapter 2). Karl Marx, writing in the mid-nineteenth century and considered to be the "father" of conflict theory, saw firsthand the effects industrialization had on the workers (Marx, 1977). Families had to send men, women, and children to work long hours (sometimes between 50 and 70 hours per week) to make ends meet. Most families lived in makeshift housing in dismal sanitary conditions, without heat or light, because the population growth in cities was too rapid for the infrastructure to sustain. It was during these economic times that Marx and his collaborator Friedrich Engels developed conflict theory's theoretical model for understanding the social and economic conditions of the time. Not surprisingly, the model, published by Marx and Engels in 1848 in *The communist manifesto*, is based on economic classes and the struggle for resources.

While the conflict approach to understanding society was clearly grounded in real experiences of inequality and access to resources, conflict theory was not commonly used as a framework for understanding society, much less families, until long after Marx was gone. Sociologists who did utilize Marx's theories – referred to as **Marxists** – critiqued the effects of capitalism on racial minorities (Blank, Knowles, and Prewitt, 1970), the criminal justice system (Quinney, 1970), and families in poverty (Piven and Cloward, 1971). Marxists were deemed "radical" by many during the 1950s and 1960s, because the post–World War II economy was booming and a critique of capitalism also brought with it a critique of the revered "American social institutions and core cultural values" (Farrington and Chertok, 1993, p. 364). Because conflict theory was not widely used – and arguably did not have scientifically testable propositions – most family studies scholars did not utilize conflict theory until the late 1960s (Farrington and Chertok, 1993). At that point, family studies scholars like Jetse Sprey (1969) argued that conflict theory is a useful framework for understanding families because conflict within families is inevitable. Similar to Marx's proposition that social structure causes conflict, Sprey argued that the family itself causes conflict. Family members have different (sometimes competing) interests, which cannot be satisfied for every member of the group. Additionally, conflict arises when family members want the *same* things, but there is only a limited supply. Family scientists adapted a macro-level theory, often critiqued for being a grand theory – too big to actually apply to real, scientific study and analysis – and began applying it on a micro-level to the study of families.

Box 3.1 At a Glance: Conflict Theory

Members of society and families are in competition over scarce resources.

Macro-level competition
- Haves (capitalists) versus have-nots (workers) struggle for power
- Workers sell labor to capitalists, in return for a wage
- Workers become alienated from their labor

Types of capital families produce for members
- Economic: wealth, land, income
- Cultural: education level, tastes and preferences, verbal skills
- Social: network of contacts
- Symbolic: prestige, reputation, charisma

Micro-level competition
- Conflict within families is inevitable, but can be positive
- Family dynamics are a zero-sum game; one family member wins, another loses

Handling conflict
- Conflict management: address conflict directly
- Conflict resolution: conflict ends; solution reached
- Consensus: a state of stability (or balance between competing needs), necessary to reach resolution or management

Key concepts

According to conflict theory, society is composed of groups in competition for scarce resources. These groups, or **classes**, are defined by their relationship to the means of production. The ruling class, or **bourgeoisie** (e.g., landowners and capitalists), own the means of production, and the working class, or **proletariat**, only own their labor, which they sell to the capitalist class in return for a wage. In the example of a factory, the owner profits from it, and the laborer earns a wage from selling his or her labor to it. According to conflict theorists, this two-sided relationship to the means of production inherently creates oppression because the two sides are interdependent on one another. **Capitalists** need workers to sell their labor in order to turn a profit, and laborers have very few other choices than to join the masses working in factories in order to provide for their families.

While it may seem like both sides benefit from this relationship because laborers need wages and capitalists need workers, conflict theorists find it troubling. This is because the dichotomy of the capitalist system creates two – and only two – classes: property-owners and propertyless workers (Marx, 1977). Therefore, the worker sells his or her labor to the factory owner, and receives only a wage in return. He or she does not have the opportunity to build capital, buy property, or "move up" the social class ladder. The worker, according to Marx, is a slave to the system of capitalism. He or she only makes enough to sustain the bare minimum standard of living.

Because of the way the capitalist system works, only one side of the relationship can benefit (see Figure 3.1). The owners profit directly from the labor that the workers sell (e.g., an increase in wages decreases

Upper class (owners) profit

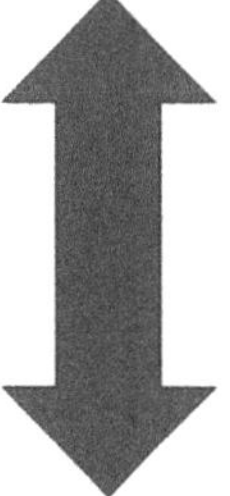

Working class (proletariat) sell their labor, see no profit

Figure 3.1 Two sides of oppression

profit, and a decrease in wages increases profits). This invisible, yet powerful force characterizes conflict theory. Conflict between groups is dependent on one side profiting, and the other being exploited.

Because of the worker's dependence on wage labor, Marx argued that alienation was inevitable. Workers became alienated from the product of their labor; they are no longer in control of the products they produce. Put this concept into historical context; Marx studied economic and social change during a time when people were leaving agriculture and moving into mass-producing goods in factories. As explained in Chapter 2, before industrialization, farmers were much more likely to feel closely tied to what they were producing – crops. They were involved in every aspect of growing corn, for instance. They planted the seeds, watered and weeded, and harvested the corn when it was ready. After industrialization, these same farmers, who likely took great joy in producing food for their loved ones and community members, were not only producing something that they might not see completed, but they were only a minor part of the overall production (Ritzer, 2010).

Let's go back to Marie's childhood. After she was old enough to get a job on her own, outside of her parents' store, she worked at a local factory for minimum wage. The summer Marie turned 13, she awoke every morning at 6:45 a.m. and rode her bike to the factory and worked for five hours on the production line. The factory made leather jackets for welders, and Marie's job was to cut 1-inch strips to reinforce the buttons that the next person on the line would put in the jackets. That is all that her job entailed – cutting 1-inch canvas strips for the jackets with a pair of metal scissors. If the factory had a big order to fulfill, Marie and her coworkers had to work harder. Marie's minimum wage did not increase because she cut more strips; the wage stayed the same. In fact, if there was a big order to fulfill in a short time, the workers all worked harder. The workers did not profit; the owner of the factory profited from their labor. The owner bought their labor for a wage, and Marie only went to work to earn that wage. She never made the jacket from start to finish by herself; she never wore one, used one, or saw one being used. Marie was alienated from her labor; she was merely an appendage of the machine according to Marx (1977). **Alienation** occurs when workers are removed from the product of their labor; that is, when workers complete tasks devoid of any redeeming human qualities. Conflict theorists are concerned with alienation because they are optimistic about human nature; they want human beings to realize their full human potential, whatever that may be. However, capitalism prevents us from doing what we are meant to do, and being what we "want to be when we grow up." Because the structure of the economy requires us to earn money through selling our labor to capitalists, we are not only unable to realize our full human potential, but we are also inevitably alienated from the products we make.

What does this have to do with families? Families are dependent on the economy to sustain a basic standard of living, at best. Additionally, family membership is involuntary; we do not choose our parents or our siblings, and we certainly do not choose which social class we are born into. Therefore, family conflict is something every individual will experience; we are all members of different social classes, with different upbringings, different family dynamics, and differential access to power and resources both inside and outside of our families.

Consider the illustration in Figure 3.2, the "inequality track." Using a macro-level of analysis, we can see how social phenomena are related to other larger social forces, such as the interaction of education and social class. Using this lens, the four lanes each represent a different rung on the social class ladder. In the image, the runner on the inside track has the advantage. Lane 1 portrays an "insider" with access to Ivy League schools and distinct economic advantages

Figure 3.2 Inequality track. *Source*: Reproduced with permission of the African Policy Forum.

that the other participants do not; in conflict theory terms, the "competition for scarce resources" will be more or less challenging depending on which lane you are in. The lanes represent the different social classes; there is a direct relationship between their capital, or resources, and their ability to win the race.

The individual in lane 1 comes from a wealthy family. He is dressed nicely and has access to a tailor, who custom makes his suits. His parents both went to Ivy League schools and own real estate throughout the northeast. He, too, graduated from an Ivy League school with a degree in business administration, and after graduation, he took a position as a manager in his father's investment firm. On the illustration, we can see that he does not even have to walk in his lane – he is on a "people mover" that moves forward for him. He is probably a member of the bourgeoisie (capitalist) class.

The individual in lane 2 is dressed in casual business attire. He probably has a bachelor's degree – perhaps working toward a master's degree – and he is engaged in a slight jog to keep his position in second place. His lane is free of obstacles, but he is carrying his briefcase with him during the race. He is probably a mid-level manager at a bank branch, hoping to someday move up the social class ladder.

The individual in lane 3 has quite a few obstacles in his lane. He is sweating, trying to dodge large rocks and holes in his lane. He has to work very hard just to make sure he does not trip and get hurt, disqualifying him from the race. He is wearing a tank top and shorts and has darker hair than the two men in lanes 1 and 2, which could signify that he belongs to a minority group with even less privilege than the dominant (White) group. His workbag is bigger than the person's in lane 2, so he may be an electrician or part of a specific trade. He is probably a member of the proletariat (working class) or lower middle class.

The individual in lane 4 has the most obstacles to get over in order to stay in the race. This person has darker skin, no briefcase or workbag at all, and has to get around barbed wire, barricades, and boulders. There is no room in this lane to jog without having to navigate an obstacle. This person has by far the most difficult time reaching the finish line, much less staying injury-free during the race. She or he is most likely a seasonal worker, hired to pick grapes or other produce in the fields. At best, she or he has a job as a maid, nanny, or domestic worker (the gendered nature of these types of jobs is discussed in detail in Chapter 8 on feminist theory). This individual is definitely a member of the proletariat (working class).

As we can see, the four lanes are separated by social class, and their access to resources either helps or harms them in the race to the finish line. However, it is also important to look at how all four lanes are related to one another. Not only are the individuals in each lane stratified, but they are also dependent on one another. The individual in lane 1 would not be successful without the man in lane 2, who manages his bank accounts. The individual in lane 3 services lane 1's "people mover." The individual in lane 4 takes care of lane 1's children, which makes it possible for lane 1's wife to be actively involved in charity events. Therefore, the inside lanes *depend on* the lanes farther out (2, 3, and 4) in order to maintain the inside track. The individual in lane 1 directly benefits from the other three individuals selling their labor to him. He becomes wealthier, better dressed, and more effective at work *because of* the structure of society. He does not have to depend on wages to stay ahead; he is a capitalist. If he became unemployed suddenly, his investments and his wealthy family would be his safety net. The other three individuals are dependent on employment – a monthly wage – in order to stay afloat. They become alienated from the product of their labor because it does not directly benefit them; it benefits only the individual in lane 1.

Thus far, we have been discussing conflict theory as it relates to families using a macro-perspective. Before we shift our focus to using a micro-perspective, we need to look a little more closely at the lanes and how they are maintained by taking a look at what is going on inside families on the track. Sometimes it is just as important to understand how privilege is reproduced by analyzing the intangible ways that inequality is transmitted within families. While at first glance, we would describe inequality using only economic means, sociologist Pierre Bourdieu (1990) suggested that sometimes the forces which reproduce inequality are invisible. According to Bourdieu, individuals in each lane have access to different types of capital that families produce for their members, which creates advantages that can be transmitted from generation to generation. These advantages can range from simply having the same family name to learning proper etiquette for formal dinner parties. The four types of capital Bourdieu outlines are economic capital, cultural capital, social capital, and symbolic capital. Each is described with respect to families below.

Economic capital refers to the material resources – wealth, land, money – that one controls or possesses (Appelrouth and Edles, 2011). This is the only type of capital that Bourdieu refers to that is tangible, or something that can be seen or touched. Economic capital is the basis for determining access to the other types of capital. As an example, money makes it possible to travel. Traveling allows one to see the world and take in diverse cultures, thereby developing one's tastes for upper-class living. Economic capital directly translates into privileges that are closely related to the other types of capital that also set people apart on the inequality track.

Cultural capital is nonmaterial – it cannot be "seen" – and it refers to aesthetic preferences, verbal skills, and levels of knowledge, expertise, and education. This is just another way of indicating what one's tastes are, and can refer to food, music, and art. Consider Marie's cultural capital, or her tastes; growing up in a lower middle-class family, she developed expertise on how to catch her own food. She remembers taking great pride in catching a big catfish for the family to fry on the weekends. An interesting way to think about social class and cultural capital is to consider what types of fish people eat – there is a vast difference depending on social class. For Marie, the only fish she is exposed to is catfish (or walleye if she gets lucky!) that her family catches in the river near her house. Catfish are clearly not a high-class food; they are readily available in rivers and are consumed mostly by individuals from families in the working and lower middle classes. Bluefin tuna, on the other hand, is not readily available in rivers and lakes. This type of fish is rare compared to catfish, and cannot be caught by the "average" American; they are caught by professional fishermen and sold in stores for a very high price. Because of this, bluefin tuna is consumed by individuals in higher social classes; the only tuna Marie had as a child came from a can, mixed into tuna casserole. As another example, think about Marie's exposure to music – growing up, she only heard country music on the radio. She never attended symphonies, knew what a viola was, or why anyone would want to listen to opera. Her tastes – her cultural capital – are vastly different from those in the inside track, or upper class. Her expertise on how to bait a hook, clean a catfish, and fry it for dinner is a far cry from those on the inside track who eat bluefin tuna prepared by gourmet chefs in high-end restaurants.

Another type of capital Bourdieu describes is social capital. **Social capital** refers to an individual or family's network of contacts and acquaintances that can be used to secure or advance one's position (Appelrouth and Edles, 2011). While we all know friends or acquaintances who may help us out on occasion, Bourdieu argued that social capital circulates within defined boundaries that reproduce the existing social structure. That is, Marie's parents' contacts would likely not be able to help her achieve the dream of becoming an astronaut. Her parents' contacts would at best help her secure her own small business, or perhaps help her become a teacher or a secretary. Had she been a member of a family with a history of engineers, public figures, or scientists, it would be much more likely that she could also follow that trajectory.

Symbolic capital refers to prestige, honor, reputation, or charisma. Individuals with symbolic capital might have credentials that make them "experts" or help them to command an audience to exert power. Something as simple as a family's last name (e.g., Kennedy, Rockefeller) can insinuate power, and the ability to command an audience. Symbolic capital is key when discussing families' access to power because children often inherit reputations that are not of their own making, such as the propensity to pick up golf as a pastime or fluency in foreign languages. Marie had no access to upper-class symbolic capital growing up, and unless she breaks out of her social class category, the chances that she will gain access to symbolic capital are slim.

As we have described in this section, families are affected by the economic structure in major ways. First, and perhaps most important, we are born into a social class that is not of our own choosing. Marie did not "choose" to grow up in a lower middle-class family. Yet, Marie's family's wealth (or lack of it) has a direct effect on her opportunities. Could she have gotten into Harvard? Probably not; Ivy League schools tend to weigh alumni status heavily when considering admissions (Kahlenberg, 2010). That is, if your relatives graduated from Harvard, you are more likely to be admitted. Utilizing conflict theory in this way is macro-sociological; this means that we are conceptualizing conflict theory in relation to greater social structures in society. What this means is that families have differential access to power, resources, and property, and also access to varying levels of social, cultural, and symbolic capital (Adams and Sydie, 2002). Where a family is situated on the inequality track limits its opportunities.

Not only does social stratification limit the choices family members have, but it also has an influence on the struggle for resources *within* the family. This is where conflict theory can be applied using a micro-level of analysis. That is, conflict theory takes into account forces both external to as well as within families, and how they might influence competition for resources. As a budding family theorist, it is important to know how conflict relates to both contexts of studying family dynamics. Therefore, theorists using conflict theory to study dynamics within families ask: Who has access to resources *inside* the family? Who has power, and who does not? While the gendered struggle for power and resources will be addressed in more detail in Chapter 8 on feminist theory, it is worth mentioning here that conflict theory helps us understand that husbands typically have more power in a marriage, which is related to husbands' and wives' marital happiness, the marital division of labor, and ownership (Bernard, 1982; Gilman, 1998 [1898]; Hochschild and Machung, 1989; Jackson et al., 2014; Sassler, 2010). Additionally, recent research on same-sex couples reveals that it is the higher-earning partner in a coupled relationship who typically has more power (Solomon, Rothblum, and Balsam, 2005). This illustrates that the link between macro-level and micro-level issues of inequality is clearly related to conflict within partnerships and families as well.

Family researchers have also built on the conflict theory framework by arguing that conflict within families is inevitable; most notable among these scholars is Jetse Sprey (1969; 1979; 1999). In this work, Sprey applies conflict theory to families by suggesting that, as is true in the greater society, family conflict occurs because of differential access to resources and power, and a lack of alternatives throughout their lives (Sprey, 1999). Those family members with the power to make decisions generally are able to maintain the social order within the family. Children do not choose their parents; the stratification within families is inevitable. In addition, membership in families is generally involuntary. Yet, children (for the most part) have to adhere to the social order of the family in order to be cared for. Think about Marie's life: Did she have a choice when it came to helping to unload the freight truck every Thursday night? No, she did not; her parents needed her help, along with her brothers, to support the family business. Once she was old enough, she was able to get a job at the factory, which increased her power in small ways. She had some economic freedom, which meant she was able to make decisions about her spending money, so she was less dependent on having to work at her family's business. However, given that they still provided food and shelter to her, the obligation toward maintaining the family business was still present.

According to Sprey, family conflict is the "state of negative interdependence between the elements of a social system" (1979, p. 134). Family dynamics, then, are dependent on one another and are a **zero-sum game**; when one member of the family gains, other family members lose. It is not possible for all members of the family to have equal access to resources; nor is it true that family members have access to resources and power consistently over the course of their life cycles. In the early stage of the family life cycle, parents have access to power; in the later stages, parents tend to lose power as they age and the power shift may create conflict. The key is to remember that even as the power dynamic shifts, conflict will remain, and family studies scholars are interested in how conflict is managed and/or resolved.

Conflict management is one way of responding to the existence of competition within the family. **Conflict management** occurs when the conflict is addressed, but it does not disappear. It acknowledges that there is conflict over access to scarce resources, and competitors should have equal access to those resources (Sprey, 1969). However, since equal access is not possible, competitors have to concede in order to manage the situation. As an example, since both of Marie's parents had to be at the hardware store on Thursday nights to unload the truck, Marie and her brothers also had to be there. They were not old enough to be left home alone so late at night. The children knew that when the oldest brother turned 12, their parents felt comfortable leaving the younger siblings under his supervision. The conflict – work–family struggle – did not disappear, as both parents still had to work. However, it was managed by bringing the entire family to the store to help unload the freight truck. The competitors (all members of the family) had to concede to this arrangement until the conflict could be directly resolved by letting them stay at home late at night once the eldest child was old enough to be trusted with that responsibility.

Conflict resolution, then, is when the conflict ends because a solution has been reached (Sprey, 1969). This is different from conflict management because in the former, the conflict does not end, it is merely managed. With conflict resolution, the issue creating conflict gets resolved. For example, Marie's mother could decide to stay at home full-time to relieve the stress (conflict) of having to bring young children to the hardware store when the freight truck comes in. Because of the stress that everyone in the family was experiencing, Marie's mother's decision would shift the breadwinner responsibility to her husband.

Consensus refers to a stable state needed to reach either conflict resolution or management (Sprey, 1969). Conflict affects all members of a family in different ways, because each family member has differential access to power within the family. However, in order for consensus to occur, a common awareness or at the very least, the ability to think in the role of the "other" is necessary given the inequitable distribution of power within families. Marie has to put on several hats for the sake of the family: she is a worker, a peacemaker, and a caregiver for her younger brother. In order to be able to come to consensus as a family, Marie had to take the role of the "other" (her mother and father) by understanding that the family business needs her parents and the care of her younger brother could be reallocated. Marie was responsible for him from sunup to sundown. She got him ready for school, she made his lunch, and she helped him with homework after school. She also vacuumed, dusted, and made dinner. She did not have a choice; there was a void in the family, and because the family relied on her, she filled that role. This is a good example of conflict from both *outside* the family and also *within* the family pressuring her to be the caregiver. Marie learned at a young age (by reaching a mutual consensus with the entire family) that she needed to step in because their family lived in the third lane; she also knew that she had no other choice than to take care of her younger brother. If she did not, no one would.

It is important to note here that the micro-level of analysis through a conflict lens can be *and often is* positive. Conflict management, resolution, and consensus are all ways in which families address inevitable disagreements, struggles, or problems. Conflict is a process; it is not inherently negative because it brings about change and adaptation that families and relationships need in order to survive and thrive. The results of conflict – addressing needs, barriers, and improved communication – promote progress and change. Conflict often reinforces solidarity and unity *within* groups. At the same time, it also challenges norms at the structural level. An example of conflict both within families as well as at the structural level is a University of Iowa student named Zach Wahls, who spoke about the strength of his family during a 2011 public forum on House Joint Resolution 6 in the Iowa House of Representatives (see multimedia suggestions at the end of the chapter). Zach has two mothers, and testified to oppose House Joint Resolution 6, which would end civil unions in Iowa. Zach's story is an example of conflict on both the micro- and the macro-levels; his grandparents would not acknowledge that his mother was pregnant with him because of their opposition to homosexuality. He said:

> I'm a sixth-generation Iowan and an engineering student at the University of Iowa, and I was raised by two women. My biological mother, Terry, told my grandparents that she was pregnant, that the artificial insemination had worked, and they wouldn't even acknowledge it. It actually wasn't until I was born and they succumbed to my infantile cuteness that they broke down and told her that they were thrilled to have another grandson.

These tensions undoubtedly created conflict between Zach's mother and her parents, which was resolved after he was born. In another example, Zach discussed how he managed conflict within the classroom at the University of Iowa when the issue of gay marriage came up:

> Being a student at the University of Iowa, the topic of same sex marriage comes up quite frequently in class discussions. The question always comes down to, "Can gays even raise kids?" And the conversation gets quiet for a moment, because most people don't really have an answer. And then I raise my hand and say, "Well actually, I was raised by a gay couple, and I'm doing pretty well." I scored in the 99th percentile on the ACT [American College Testing]. I'm an Eagle Scout. I own and operate my own small business. If I was your son, Mr. Chairman, I believe I'd make you very proud. I'm not so different from any of your children. My family really isn't so different from yours. After all, your family doesn't derive its sense of worth from being told by the state, "You're married, congratulations!" The sense of family comes with the commitment we make to each other to work through the hard times so we can enjoy the good ones. It comes from the love that binds us. That's what makes a family.

Zach manages the potential conflict by emphasizing how similar he is to other college students, raised by heterosexual parents. He uses this sameness (on a micro-level) to broaden the discussion to equal and fair treatment from the Iowa state government (on a macro-level).

> I guess the point is that my family really isn't so different from any other Iowa family. When I'm home, we go to church together. We eat dinner, we go on vacations. But, we have our hard times too; we get in fights. My mom, Terry, was diagnosed with multiple sclerosis in 2000. It is a devastating disease that put her in a wheelchair, so you know, we've had our struggles. But we're Iowans. We don't expect anyone to solve our problems for us. We'll fight our own battles. We just hope for equal and fair treatment from our government.

Additionally, as Zach alludes to above, conflict exists for his family on a macro-level. The very reason he testified is because his family's rights to marriage were threatened; the conflict in this case is between two groups in society – lesbian, gay, bisexual, transgender or queer (LGBTQ) persons and those who oppose marriage equality. Those who oppose marriage equality have power and access to resources (legal protections) that, until very recently, LGBTQ persons do not. This discrimination on a macro-level creates conflict between two groups in society. He ends his testimony by again managing the conflict on a macro-level using emotions that originate from a micro-level, saying, "Not once have I ever been confronted by an individual who realized independently that I was raised by a gay couple. And you know why? Because the sexual orientation of my parents has had zero impact on the content of my character" (Wahls, 2011).

This case is also an example of the positive aspects of conflict. Without individuals or groups challenging the norms, and advocating for their rights, social change would not occur. When groups in society have different values, conflict is inevitable. But as history has shown, fighting for equal rights eventually leads to social change and consensus, which results in conflict resolution. In this sense, individuals and families demonstrate their empowerment (see Chapter 8 on feminist theory for further ideas about empowerment).

To summarize, conflict theory can be applied to families in various ways with both positive and negative outcomes. Thinking about Marie, we can see how the family's position in the lower middle class inevitably affects conflict over resources within the family as well. Marie could not escape the obligation to help the family; the obligation existed because of structural barriers that were out of her control as a child in this working-class family. She could not move "up" a lane because she was too busy overcoming the obstacles in her own lane. Her childhood was spent helping her family dodge roadblocks, such as spending Thursday nights unloading the freight truck. Marie did not have the time to put in long hours to prepare for an engineering degree, researching schools, making connections with faculty at prestigious universities; she was responsible for her younger brother, and his well-being came first. Additionally, Marie did not have access to the cultural or social capital she needed to make her dreams a reality. Her social capital consisted of her parents' contacts, who were also working- or middle-class contacts, at best. These external barriers created conflict within the family that had to be managed, or resolved if possible.

Box 3.2 Conflict Theory in Pop Culture: *Little Miss Sunshine*

A scene from *Little Miss Sunshine*, 2006, dir. Jonathan Dayton and Valerie Faris, Fox Searchlight Pictures

While conflict theory may seem complicated, there are several examples of it in popular modern films. The 2006 film *Little Miss Sunshine* portrays a family who struggles with conflict both internally as well as externally. For example, at the beginning of the film, the audience learns that Richard, the father, is struggling to build a career as a motivational speaker and life coach. The family is solidly middle class. Additionally, the family is housing Sheryl's gay brother, Frank (after a suicide attempt), and Richard's father, Edwin (after being evicted from a retirement home for using heroin). Due to these specific family dynamics, we can already see that conflict is inevitable. Nuclear family members (parents Sheryl and Richard, and children Olive and Dwayne) have to sacrifice space in their home, food (with two more mouths to feed), among other things, to accommodate the unique needs of the extended family members.

In addition, given the risk associated with both Edwin (drug abuse) and Frank (suicidal tendencies), the entire family needs to adjust to be able to make sure both men are watched over at all times. Because of this, when the youngest child, Olive, learns that she qualified for the "Little Miss Sunshine" beauty pageant in California, the entire family must travel with her so that she can participate in the pageant. This illustrates conflict management, because the family has no other choice but to bring Edwin and Frank with them. We can also see conflict on a macro-level because the family has limited economic capital; they are in a struggle with other families for scarce resources. Because this family lives in a society characterized by capitalism, they have limited access to wealth and income. Therefore, they are "strapped" for resources and the ability to pay for things like competing in beauty pageants unless they sacrifice somewhere else along the way.

Additionally, given the financial limitations of the family, each family member is on a strict budget for every meal as they stop along their road trip. This exemplifies consensus in that the family agrees to stay within the budget for the trip, making it possible for everyone to have a little money for food, for the good of the entire group.

Finally, we can see examples of Olive's cultural capital during the beauty pageant. In preparation for the pageant, Edwin taught Olive a secretly choreographed dance to the song "Super Freak," which is atypical and definitely scandalous for a beauty pageant for little girls. This exemplifies Olive's family's cultural capital; she was not raised in an upper middle-class family like some of the other pageant contestants were. Her cultural tastes and preferences are different from the other girls; Olive is untrained in proper beauty pageant etiquette, and her appearance also identifies her cultural capital as well – she is plain looking, slightly overweight, wears large eyeglasses, and does not style her hair like most other pageant contestants. Therefore, her cultural capital shines through because it is very different from that of the subculture she is performing in.

Evaluating Conflict Theory

Strengths of conflict theory

Conflict theory is one of the earliest and most influential of all the theories applied to families. Family scholars find it useful in dealing with how individuals and families distribute power and deal with change. Conflict theory helps us to appreciate that all families have challenges and problems, and it is not the fact of having problems, but how families resolve the inevitable conflicts that arise. Thus, conflict theory has many strengths in terms of helping us understand the positive and negative dimensions of power.

Conflict can lead to positive change As conflict theory is presented in this text, it is diverse in its scope, allowing researchers to understand structural barriers families face on a macro-level, as well as power dynamics and access to resources *within* the family on a micro-level. Conflict theory frames the study of family dynamics in terms of access to resources and the struggle for equal access. Yet, it also often results in positive outcomes: marriage equality for same-sex couples, and family members facing tough problems that result in management, consensus, or resolution on issues they face every day. A major strength of conflict theory is that it addresses injustices and problems, yet often can result in positive outcomes.

Examines "invisible" processes Contemporary conflict theorists help us understand intangible processes – those we cannot easily see – in families. Intangible dynamics, such as parenting strategies, can actually work to reproduce inequality at the structural level. For instance, through the process of interaction, cultural, social, and symbolic capital are invisibly transmitted to children, helping secure their place in their parents' social class. This is vital to understanding why certain policies or programs designed to help even the playing field for families may not be effective. A parent's level of education will likely predict how they interact with authority figures in society. As an example, if a child needs to be placed in a special needs program in elementary school, parents may not know enough to reach out and advocate for their child, they may not know exactly what to say or who to ask, or have the ability to persist in making sure their child's needs are met. Alternatively, parents may not have time to take out of their workday to take on such time-intensive tasks. Therefore, another strength of conflict theory is that it takes both tangible and intangible processes into account.

Practical implications Conflict theory is not simply a way to theorize about or explain social processes. It offers practitioners tools to lead families in conflict to management, consensus, and resolution. Practitioners are able to draw from the "big picture" that conflict theory provides by taking into account structural barriers families face based on stratification. At the same time, conflict theory provides useful ways to help families work through and address conflict on the family level. This combination of both a macro- and micro-perspective in the study of families allows us to understand how those external forces create limitations *within* the family, and how families may adapt to such challenges. For example, a working-class family faces significant economic barriers when it comes to caring for older family members. They may not be able to afford the best assisted living facility for their loved ones; yet, given their extensive kin network of aunts, uncles, and cousins who live nearby, they may be able to come to consensus about sharing caregiving duties. Thus, a macro-level barrier (low economic capital) is addressed at the micro-level using social capital resources, illustrating how the family can reach consensus to manage the conflict.

Weaknesses of conflict theory

As we have established throughout this text, every theory has strengths as well as weaknesses. Conflict theory is no exception; here we discuss the weaknesses of using this approach when studying family dynamics.

Overlooks family resources and strengths One of the criticisms of conflict theory is the assumption that it places family dynamics in negative terms, assuming that conflict is destructive. Many family scholars and practitioners may argue that, on a macro-level, families are not as restricted by the "inequality track" as conflict theorists would suggest. As an example, while families in the outermost lanes of the track experience structural barriers that may lead to additional family conflict, they may also have access to resources that are atypical in upper middle-class White families. Families of color, specifically African American families – tend to have stronger kinship ties (e.g., joint residency, visiting, and the exchange of mutual aid among kin (Dilworth-Anderson, Williams, and Gibson, 2002; Heath, 1983; Lareau, 2003; Stack, 1974; Taylor et al., 2013; Ward, 1971; Wilson, 1989). In addition, families of color are traditionally more likely than White families to feel that children should help their older parents, and reciprocal obligations of help from kin are more salient among these racial and ethnic groups (AARP, 2001; Dilworth-Anderson, Williams, and Gibson, 2002; Taylor et al., 2013). Therefore, structural barriers may be mitigated by extended family networks and a culturally embedded tendency to foster and experience closer kinship relationships. Family systems theory (Chapter 6) and family stress and resilience theory (Chapter 11) may be better equipped to handle family resources and strengths.

Overlooks intersectionalities Another weakness of conflict theory is that it oversimplifies very complex social dynamics that also contribute to inequality, such as the intersections of race, gender, and sexual orientation. As an example, how might a child in the outermost lane experience discrimination for being transgender? Are there social class differences in how families would perceive LGBTQ issues? What if she or he were non-White? Conflict theory does not allow for an examination of these intersecting statuses, and therefore is arguably limited in scope. We turn to contemporary feminist theory (Chapter 8) for understanding intersectionality.

Is conflict theory relevant to modern social class distinctions? A third weakness of conflict theory is that it oversimplifies social class distinctions present in modern society. The father of conflict theory, Karl Marx, is often criticized for formulating a two-class system of only the owners and workers, when in contemporary society, there is undoubtedly a middle class and more distinctions between owners and workers. The same analysis goes for applying conflict theory to families; conflict present within a family could have several layers and origins, which can be overlooked using the dichotomy of the powerless versus the powerful.

An alternative theory app: social exchange theory

In this chapter, we have laid out the key concepts, origins and background, and modern applications as well as the strengths and weaknesses of conflict theory. As we illustrated in Chapter 2 on functionalist theory, it is useful to compare theories to more easily identify the differences between the two. In addition, it is interesting to consider that even though each of these theories focuses on the concept of *power*, their interpretations of power relations are very different. Don't worry; even though you have not read about this theory yet, we will compare it to the case study from this chapter (Marie) to continue to build on your ability to switch your theory app at any time.

As you just learned in this chapter, conflict theory can take into account power relations on both the micro-level and the macro-level. Social exchange theory (Chapter 7), on the other hand, uses the *individual* as the unit of analysis, assuming that individual family members are interested in and capable of negotiating for the "best" deal in exchanges with other family members. The exchange that takes place within families is based on both parties' desires for power and rewards that guide their decision-making. This theory assumes that individuals within families have the ability to negotiate the "best deal" for themselves, and often focuses on micro-level interactions and exchanges to better understand family dynamics. How would we explain Marie's family life using social exchange theory? First, we would most likely disregard the structural inequality that situates Marie's family lower on the social class ladder. In contrast, we would hone in on the actual exchange of resources between Marie and her family, or even between Marie's mother and her father. Social exchange theorists would ask how Marie and her parents engage in "bargaining" interactions to make sure that they are individually getting the best deal. We would focus on what resources, power, and rewards are available within the family, and analyze how individual family members negotiate for these things, weighing costs against the potential benefits. The major commonality between these two theories is the assumption that conflict over resources is inevitable within families, and that negotiations are a "zero-sum game," where one family member wins and another one loses.

Working with Conflict Theory: Integrating Research and Practice

Now that we have described the historical origins, key concepts and assumptions, and strengths and weaknesses of conflict theory, we turn our attention to how the theory can be used in research and practice. We then analyze an empirical study that was rooted in conflict theory, in order to see how scholars put the theory to work in a research project. Finally, we present ideas about how the theory informs the practice of family policy.

Conflict theory today

As we have discussed throughout this chapter, researchers using conflict theory can apply it to family studies in a number of ways, addressing power struggles both within and outside of families that create conflict. In Chapter 1, we described the changing demographics of society, such as the rising costs of health care, increased life expectancy, changes in the levels and timing of fertility, and the increase in women's labor force participation. These demographic shifts mean that there are more generations of one family alive at any given time, and each generation might be in very distinct and conflicting life course stages, which creates unprecedented demands on family caregivers (Allen, Blieszner, and Roberto, 2011; Cherlin, 2010; Silverstein and Giarrusso, 2010). It is important to understand how these factors impacting the population generate conflict and burden within families.

One current area within family science that we can see conflict theory utilized to study contemporary family issues is with intergenerational ambivalence theory (IGA) (Luescher and Pillemer, 1998). IGA theory suggests that family members can feel hate and love for another family member at the same time, especially in a caregiving relationship. Thus, simultaneous feelings of duty, love, and obligation toward caring for older adults can exist in caregiving relationships. This theory considers both the individual-level and the structural-level feelings of ambivalence, suggesting that family members experience contradictions in relationships that cannot be reconciled. This may include personal feelings of love and concern that occur on the individual level and the obligations of a career and other nuclear family duties that occur on a social-structural level. Demographically, a couple may have started their family in their mid to late thirties, which situates them on a trajectory where they could be well into their fifties when their children are graduating from high school. At the same time, their own parents could be in their seventies or eighties, needing help driving to and from doctor's appointments, and dealing with chronic or serious illness and a general loss of independence. Individuals caught between caring for their children and their parents have been referred to as members of the "sandwich generation." This group of individuals is at risk of experiencing ambivalent feelings toward the care receiver simply because the stress of managing the conflicting duties and responsibilities lends itself to simultaneous feelings of love, duty, and frustration and anger because of the additional responsibilities of caregiving (Henderson, 2013). Additionally, given a family's position on the inequality track, they may or may not have access to economic resources that would help pay for in-home health care to help alleviate the strains associated with caregiving. However, families in the outside lane may not only have an extended family depending on them, but they also are likely to have low-wage jobs, with no paid time off to care for a family member. This limits their ability to access needed resources, which exacerbates the feelings of ambivalence within the family. IGA is a useful current way of using conflict theory at both the structural and individual levels.

Conflict theory in research

Modern family scholars have built on the original principles of conflict theory to gain a fuller understanding of how inequality persists both outside of and within families. In her study, Annette Lareau (2003) suggests that societal inequalities that we see between families emanate from invisible parenting styles occurring *within* families from different social class backgrounds. Therefore, Lareau's work is an ideal example of how to link the macro-level forces to the micro-level interactions that occur within families' everyday lives. Lareau interviewed and observed 12 families and their children from middle-class, working-class, and poor families. About one half of the people in her sample were Black, and one half were White.

Lareau's methodology involved three phases of research. In phase 1, she and her research assistants conducted participant observation of two third-grade classrooms in a public school in the Midwest. After two months of observation, Lareau grouped the families of the third graders into separate racial and social class categories, and requested interviews with the mothers and fathers of the children. Ninety percent of the parents agreed to be interviewed, which is what social scientists refer to as a response rate – the percentage of participants who agree to take part in the study after being asked.

The second phase of Lareau's study involved a different data collection site, to broaden the scope of the study. For this phase, Lareau and her research assistants conducted participant observation over a 15-month period in two third-grade classrooms in the northeast region of the US. They then interviewed 17 more families of those third graders. In the third phase of the study, the researchers conducted home observations of 12 children and their families who had been previously interviewed. This meant that over the course of the three weeks, one fieldworker from the research team spent a few hours with the families, participating in their normal routines. This included at least one overnight visit, and attending events such as baseball games, church, and taking part in the normal activities of everyday life. The researchers observed, audio recorded, and took notes, which they later used to help frame their analysis. They also utilized interviews with the family members over the three weeks as well. It is also important to note that the researchers took steps to match fieldworkers with the families they were observing. For Black families with male children, the team included a Black male graduate student fieldworker, and a White male fieldworker observed the poor family with a White son. Throughout the week, the research teams met and compared notes to review the emerging analytic themes (Lareau, 2003).

The goals of this research were to produce a realistic picture of the day-to-day rhythms of families with children of elementary school age, paying special attention to what differences could be attributed to social class. The results of the study revealed two distinct approaches to parenting, coined by Lareau as concerted cultivation and the natural growth model. Concerted cultivation is promoted by middle-class parents, who enroll their children in numerous age-specific activities that dominate family life. The parents believe that the activities foster children's talents, opinions, and skills, and provide important life skills as well. These life skills include the development of reasoning and language (i.e., answering questions with questions), and encouraging children to think and talk for themselves. The natural growth model, on the other hand, is emphasized by working-class and poor families. This model is based on the idea that as long as the child's basic needs are provided for, the children will grow and thrive. These children participate in few organized activities and have more free time, as well as "deeper, richer ties with their extended families" (Lareau, 2003, p. 749).

What Lareau discovered in her study is that in the middle-class parents' approach of concerted cultivation, the children developed an emerging sense of entitlement. This conclusion was reached through a method called triangulation. That is, the researchers used multiple sources of data *and* multiple researchers analyzing the data to interpret the results. Teams of three researchers (including Lareau) observed every family, and they also gathered data in different ways, including both interviews and participant observation. Without the observation piece, the researchers might not have come to the conclusion that the parenting approaches were leading to entitlement. Researchers observed the children's entitled behaviors in doctors' offices and classrooms, and were able to infer from the other data points, including parental interviews, that the concerted cultivation approach leads to child entitlement.

On the flip side, Lareau also concluded that the natural growth model resulted in a growing sense of constraint among working-class and poor children. This is characterized by being cautious, only speaking when being spoken to, and distrusting authority figures like school officials. Again, while one of the children indicated that he knew his mother mistrusted school officials in an interview, the researchers were also able to validate this while observing the mother interact with teachers during the parent–teacher conferences. Here we can see conflict theory in action on many levels; working-class and poor parents are structurally disadvantaged in society, and the constraints of social class are recreated within the family on the individual level for children. Within this one study, we can see conflict theory on both the micro- and macro-levels, and we can also see how researchers invoke theory using research methods designed to capture the theoretical complexities with multiple data sources and techniques.

Conflict theory in practice

There are several ways in which educators, practitioners, and family policy makers can apply conflict theory in their work with individuals and families. One of the most important places where family scholars can utilize conflict theory is in the development of policy. As we outlined in Chapter 1, the demographic landscape of American families is changing. Right now, the Family and Medical Leave Act (FMLA) of 1993 (2006) mandates that businesses with over 50 employees offer 12 weeks of unpaid leave for employees to care for loved ones (e.g., a newborn, a family member with dementia). From a conflict perspective, we need to ask several questions about this policy, such as who it benefits, who it includes, and who it leaves out.

First, the policy does not include employees working for businesses with fewer than 50 employees. This means that small businesses are exempt from offering family leave to their employees. Also, when considering a life event like the birth of a baby, FMLA allows for 12 weeks of *unpaid* leave. In an economy where most families are dependent on two incomes to sustain a basic standard of living, could they truly sustain three months without a second pay check? If they can, the next thing to consider is who will leave work to take care of the newborn. Traditional notions of gender would suggest that the mother should stay home with the baby, but this is also supported by the economic realities of employment as well. Women still only make about 80 percent of what men make (Bureau of Labor Statistics, 2010), and therefore it would make the most economic sense to lose the income from the parent who brings home the lower salary (usually the woman). That way, the family keeps the man's salary for the duration of the maternity leave.

Applying conflict theory to practice – or in this case, policy development – allows us to see clearly how macro-level structures affect families on the micro-level. Policies that are supposed to support families when they need it the most could actually be creating intrafamily conflict. Not only does FMLA particularly disadvantage single-parent families that simply cannot afford to go three months without pay, but it also has the potential to create conflict within the family if and when the couple disagrees over who should stay home with the newborn. Over time, women are assumed to be the caregivers not only for children, but also for parents who need help or caregiving as they age. This pattern of gendered expectations not only has the potential to create strain within couples and families, but it also re-creates disadvantage on the macro-level. Women are more likely to leave the workforce to care for family members, which limits their earning potential, including access to promotions, but also social security and retirement. Over time, women who leave the workforce for caregiving accumulate disadvantage because they lose out on earnings, pension, and other wealth that accumulates for those who are able to persist in the workforce (Gibb et al., 2014).

Conclusion

Conflict theory has provided important ideas that allow researchers and practitioners to put the theory to use beyond the conceptual level. Once critiqued as a grand theory, limited in application, family scientists have developed ways in which conflict theory can be applied to multiple levels of family conflict.

Additionally, it is important to highlight how conflict theory is applicable to the study of families across the globe. Access to legal protections is an important consideration for conflict theorists and family scholars, so Box 3.3 highlights how same-sex marriage is protected in some nations, but not others. Why do you think this is? How would conflict theorists explain the differences between the countries we highlight? We challenge you to consider these global applications of the theory as you move on to the discussion and reflection questions, and areas for further study, in the concluding pages of this chapter.

Box 3.3 Global Comparisons of Same-Sex Marriage

There are variations from country to country when it comes to legalizing same-sex marriage. Consider these examples:

Argentina, Canada, Netherlands, Spain Universal same-sex marriage is allowed.
Mexico, United Kingdom Same-sex marriage is allowed in some jurisdictions.
Armenia, Italy, Nepal Same-sex marriage is pending or under consideration.
Cuba, Gambia, Saudi Arabia, South Korea Same-sex marriage is illegal.

Source: www.pewforum.org/2015/06/26/gay-marriage-around-the-world.

Multimedia Suggestions

www.zachwahls.com

This is the homepage of Zach Wahls, who testified before the Iowa House Judiciary Committee in 2011. This webpage contains links to see what Zach is up to, read his latest blogs, his interviews, and information on his book, *My Two Moms* (2012).

Activate your theory app: Can you find examples of Bourdieu's different types of capital in Wahls's materials (his speaking engagements, his blog posts, or in his bio)?

http://www.epi.org/resources/budget/

This is the website for the Economic Policy Institute's "Family Budget Calculator." This budget calculator is updated annually, and allows users to enter their family type (i.e., one parent, one child), and the city and state where they live. Based on those demographics, the budget provides estimated monthly expenses for housing, food, child care, transportation, health care, taxes, and other necessities. This website is useful for students to understand the costs associated with raising children, which are often underestimated. Students can also compare their budget results to the federal poverty line, and average salaries and wages in their areas.

Activate your theory app: Calculate your budget, based on your current family status. Add up all of your current expenses (including education) *on top* of what is listed for you, and compare the two figures (what you live on now, and what is needed to maintain a basic standard of living calculated by the website). How do the two compare? Run other numbers, for single parents or two-parent families with two children. Are you surprised by the results?

Arrested Development (2003–2006 and 2013)

In this comedic television series, a dysfunctional wealthy family is in desperate need of the show's main character, Michael Bluth, to pull them out of impending financial ruin. This show illustrates micro-level conflict, as the family members compete for resources within the family. The show also provides examples of cultural and symbolic capital, via the patriarch George Bluth's past abilities to talk his way out of illegal business practices. The family's capital contrasts with the career aspirations of their son-in-law Tobias, which include being an actor. Throughout the series, Michael is forced to bring the family together, illustrating conflict management, and sometimes, conflict resolution and consensus.

A scene from *Arrested Development*, 2003, cr. Mitchell Hurwitz, 20th Century Fox Television

Activate your theory app: See if you can find examples of Bourdieu's concepts of economic, cultural, and social capital in this series as well. How does the family protect its members due to their different types of capital? How does that compare to your own family?

Weeds (2005–2012)

This comedy-drama is also featured in family systems theory (Chapter 6), and involves a widowed mother (Nancy) of two who begins selling marijuana to support her family after her husband dies suddenly. She has trouble managing this new financial endeavor and the day-to-day duties of being a mother, which illustrates conflict management on a micro-scale. This show also provides examples of cultural and social capital, because Nancy often has to rely on her new network of acquaintances (drug dealers) to solve her problems. Her cultural capital changes *because* of her new job, and so too does her economic capital.

A scene from *Weeds*, 2005, cr. Jenji Kohan, Lionsgate Television/Showtime Networks

Activate your theory app: Are there examples in this series of conflict theory on a macro-scale? Think about the families whose hard work and (sometimes) illegal operations make Nancy's family's standard of living possible. How does conflict theory on a macro-level apply to the entire community?

Further Reading

Ehrenreich, B., *Nickel and dimed: On (not) getting by in America* (New York: Macmillan, 2010). Barbara Ehrenreich writes about her experience as an undercover journalist working in low wage jobs across the country in order to investigate the repercussions of the 1996 Welfare Reform Act. She posed as a waitress, hotel maid, house cleaner, nursing home aide, and Walmart salesperson and found that the lived realities of low-wage workers include needing two low-wage jobs just to afford basic necessities of food, shelter, and transportation to and from work. Readers should be able to identify conflict theory on both macro- and micro-levels, because the author delves into the realities of her own as well as her coworkers' lives, as they face employment, child care, chronic illness, and domestic violence.

Hochschild, A. R., *The time bind: When home becomes work and work becomes home* (New York: Holt, 1997). Arlie Russell Hochschild exposes a source of conflict that working families face: parents are putting in more hours at work to support their families. This, in turn, creates more stress at home and pushes parents into seeking more work time to escape the tension at home. Hochschild notes that this attempt to escape work–family conflict creates even more difficulties because parents inevitably must spend time repairing the damage left in the wake of their compulsion to work.

Jaramillo-Sierra, A. L., and Allen, K. R., "Who pays after the first date? Young men's discourses of the male provider role," *Psychology of Men and Masculinity, 14* (2013), 389–399 (doi:10.1037/a0030603). This qualitative study asked male college students to describe their perceptions of payment arrangements in dating relationships with women. While all participants believed that men should pay for the first date, four discourses of the types of provider roles were found for after the first date: (a) the self-centered provider, who has a negative and unequal perception of women, and an exchange payment discourse; (b) the chivalrous provider, who has an idealized perception of women, and a responsible provider payment discourse; (c) the chivalrous-equal sharing provider, who has an idealized perception of women, and an equal sharing payment discourse; and (d) the mutual provider, who perceives women as equal, and holds an equal sharing payment discourse.

Kozol, J., *Rachel and her children: Homeless families in America* (New York: Random House, 2006; originally published 1988). Jonathan Kozol tells "Rachel's" story of homelessness in an attempt to critique New York's welfare policy during the 1980s. While this book is not a scientific study of families, it is a nonfiction piece that helps readers understand how families are affected by public policies, bureaucracy, and homelessness; Kozol tells the story of real people, like Rachel and her family, who are not lazy, crazy, or misfits. Rather, they suffer from inefficient, inappropriate policies that are supposed to help them.

Mills, C. W., *The power elite* (New York: Oxford University Press, 1956). This book, one of the most important sociological texts, explains how the interests of the military, corporations, and political realms of society determine social reality. C. Wright Mills also examines how wealthy families contribute to the power elite's domination of most of the free world. This text is useful for scholars in family studies, sociology, and other disciplines because it debunks taken for granted ideas when thinking about families, including just how powerful affluent families truly are when they transmit wealth from generation to generation, thereby reproducing the class structure on a global scale.

Questions for Students

Discussion Questions

1. Why is it important to understand both the external and internal causes of conflict over resources? How do both interplay to create advantage or disadvantage within and outside of families?
2. Do families on the inside track experience conflict, given their access to almost unlimited resources? On the flip side, is it possible to experience very little within-family conflict in lane 4 (structurally the most disadvantaged lane)? Explain and provide support for your answer.
3. Using conflict theory, explain how each of the lanes on the inequality track are dependent on one another. Could the inside lane function without the other lanes? What about the outside lane – are families in the working poor dependent on the three inside lanes? Why/why not?
4. Which other theories from this textbook are most similar to and different from conflict theory?
5. Describe the types of capital. How do they change over time; that is, in what ways do different social institutions besides the family give individuals access to different types of capital?
6. Describe what would happen if we were to apply Marx's original conflict theory to modern society. Does the theory work for today's society?

Your Turn!

Imagine that you were charged with determining the strengths and weaknesses of the Family and Medical Leave Act of 1993 using conflict theory. Your employers want a solid theoretical analysis of the Act, as well as suggestions for change based on the strengths and weaknesses. Using terms from this chapter, describe the policy and make suggestions based on both external and internal sources of conflict.

Personal Reflection Questions

1 Consider where you might be situated on the inequality track presented in this chapter. Who is in the other lanes? Can you think of examples from your own life of either access to privilege, or barriers that caused disadvantage for you and your family? How did those external forces influence the struggle over resources within your family?
2 Consider how much different your life might be if you moved up or down a lane. What influence would that have on your possible pathways? Is it possible for large numbers of people to move up a lane? What about down? How are all of the lanes dependent on one another?
3 Give an example of how your family has experienced internal conflict and how you managed or resolved the conflict.
4 Thinking about your own family, describe what types of economic, social, cultural, and symbolic capital you have. How does your capital help or harm your chances of moving up a lane?
5 Consider Lareau's conceptualization of parenting approaches: concerted cultivation and natural growth. Which one most closely resembles how you were raised? If you plan to have children, which approach will you most likely use? Why?
6 Conflict theory can be used to study families on very different levels, ranging from analyzing structural-level inequalities to conflict between siblings over resources. What aspect of conflict do you find most interesting? Micro or macro? In what ways?

References

AARP (American Association of Retired Persons) (2001). *In the middle: A report on multicultural boomers coping with family and aging issues*. Washington, DC: Belden Russonello and Stewart.

Adams, B. N., and Sydie, R. A. (2002). *Classical sociological theory*. Thousand Oaks, CA: Sage.

Allen, K. R., Blieszner, R., and Roberto, K. A. (2011). Perspectives on extended family and fictive kin in the later years: Strategies and meanings of kin reinterpretation. *Journal of Family Issues, 32*, 1156–1177. doi:10.1177/0192513X11404335.

Appelrouth, S., and Edles, L. D. (2011). *Classical and contemporary sociological theory: Text and readings*. Los Angeles: Pine Forge Press.

Bernard, J. (1982). *The future of marriage*. New Haven: Yale University Press.

Blank, O., Knowles, L. L., and Prewitt, K. (1970). *Institutional racism in America*. Englewood Cliffs, NJ: Prentice Hall.

Bourdieu, P. (1990). *In other words: Essays towards a reflexive sociology*. Palo Alto, CA: Stanford University Press.

Bureau of Labor Statistics (2010). *Women in the labor force: A databook*. U.S. Department of Labor. At http://www.bls.gov/cps/wlftable17-2010.htm.

Cherlin, A. J. (2010). Demographic trends in the United States: A review of research in the 2000s. *Journal of Marriage and Family, 72*, 403–419. doi:10.1111/j.1741-3737.2010.00710.

Dilworth-Anderson, P., Williams, I. C., and Gibson, B. E. (2002). Issues of race, ethnicity, and culture in caregiving research: A 20-year review (1980–2000). *Gerontologist, 42*, 237–272. doi:10.1093/geront/42.2.237.

Family and Medical Leave Act of 1993, 29 U.S.C. § 2601–2654 (2006).

Farrington, K., and Chertok, E. (1993). Social conflict theories of the family. In P. G. Boss, W. J. Doherty, R. LaRossa, W. R. Schumm, and S. K. Steinmetz (eds), *Sourcebook of family theories and methods: A contextual approach* (pp. 357–384). New York: Plenum.

Gibb, S. J., Fergusson, D. M., Horwood, L. J., and Boden, J. M. (2014). The effects of parenthood on workforce participation and income for men and women. *Journal of Family and Economic Issues, 35*, 14–26. doi:10.1007/s10834-013-9353-4.

Gilman, C. P. (1998). *Women and economics: A study of the economic relation between men and women as a factor in social evolution*. Mineola, NY: Dover. (Originally published 1898.)

Heath, S. B. (1983). *Ways with words: Language, life and work in communities and classrooms*. Cambridge, UK: Cambridge University Press.

Henderson, A. C. (2013). Defining caregiving relationships: Using intergenerational ambivalence theory to explain burden among racial and ethnic groups. In S. Marrow and D. Leoutsakas (eds), *More than blood: Today's reality and tomorrow's vision of family* (pp. 289–303). Dubuque, IA: Kendall Hunt.

Hochschild, A., and Machung, A. (1989). *The second shift: Working parents and the revolution at home*. New York: Viking.

Jackson, J. B., Miller, R. B., Oka, M., and Henry, R. G. (2014). Gender differences in marital satisfaction: A meta-analysis. *Journal of Marriage and Family, 76*, 105–129. doi:10.1111/jomf.12077.

Kahlenberg, R. D. (ed.) (2010). *Affirmative action for the rich: Legacy preferences in college admissions*. New York: Century Foundation Press.

Lareau, A. (2003). *Unequal childhoods: Class, race, and family life*. Berkeley: University of California Press.

Luescher, K., and Pillemer, K. (1998). Intergenerational ambivalence: A new approach to the study of parent–child relations in later life. *Journal of Marriage and the Family, 60*, 413–425. doi:10.2307/353858.

Marx, K. (1977). *The economic and philosophic manuscripts of 1844*, in a single vol. with K. Marx and F. Engels, *The communist manifesto*, ed. Dirk J. Struik, trans. Martin Milligan. New York: International. (Originally published 1844 and 1848.)

Piven, F. F., and Cloward, R. A. (1971). *Regulating the poor: The functions of public welfare*. New York: Random House.

Quinney, R. (1970). *The social reality of crime*. Boston: Little, Brown.

Ritzer, G. (2010). *Sociological theory* (8th edn). New York: McGraw-Hill.

Sassler, S. (2010). Partnering across the life course: Sex, relationships, and mate selection. *Journal of Marriage and Family, 72*, 557–575. doi:10.1111/j.1741-3737.2010.00718.x.

Silverstein, M., and Giarrusso, R. (2010). Aging and family life: A decade review. *Journal of Marriage and Family, 72*, 1039–1058. doi:10.1111/j.1741-3737.2010.00749.

Solomon, S. E., Rothblum, E. D., and Balsam, K. F. (2005). Money, housework, sex, and conflict: Same-sex couples in civil unions, those not in civil unions, and heterosexual married siblings. *Sex Roles, 52*, 561–575. doi:10.1007/s11199-005-3725-7.

Sprey, J. (1969). The family as a system in conflict. *Journal of Marriage and the Family, 31*, 699–706. doi:10.2307/349311.

Sprey, J. (1979). Conflict theory and the study of marriage and the family. In W. R. Burr, R. Hill, F. I. Nye, and I. L. Reiss (eds), *Contemporary theories about the family: General theories/theoretical orientations* (vol. 2, pp. 130–159). New York: Free Press.

Sprey, J. (1999). Family dynamics: An essay on conflict and power. In M. Sussman, S. K. Steinmetz, and G. W. Peterson (eds), *Handbook of marriage and the family* (pp. 667–685). New York: Plenum Press.

Stack, C. B. (1974). *All our kin: Strategies for survival in a Black community*. New York: Harper & Row.

Taylor, R. J., Chatters, L. M., Woodward, A. T., and Brown, E. (2013). Racial and ethnic differences in extended family, friendship, fictive kin, and congregational informal support networks. *Family Relations, 62*, 609–624. doi:10.1111/fare.12030.

Wahls, Z. (2011). *What makes a family*. Testimony to the House Judiciary Committee, Iowa State Legislature. At http://lybio.net/tag/zach-wahls-transcript/.

Wahls, Z. (2012). *My two moms: Lessons of love, strength, and what makes a family*. New York: Penguin.

Ward, M. C. (1971). *Them children: A study in language and learning*. New York: Holt, Rinehart, & Winston.

Wilson, M. N. (1989). Child development in the context of the Black extended family. *American Psychologist, 44*, 380–385. doi:10.1037/0003-066X.44.2.380.

4

Symbolic Interactionist Theory

Think about a celebrity you like – maybe it's your favorite actor or actress, professional athlete, comedian, or musician. You may follow his or her career as it develops over time, and you may also notice news articles about his or her personal life. Oftentimes, celebrities get married and/or divorced for very different reasons when compared to the general population. Why is that? What does marriage mean to a celebrity couple that differentiates it from what it means to the rest of us? Finally, even while we know that celebrity marriages typically do not last long, why do we sometimes truly feel surprised when we learn that our favorite celebrity couple is splitting up?

Symbolic interactionist theory is considered to be one of the most influential theories in family science, as it provides scholars with a useful framework to understand how symbols, interactions, and social context explain marriage and family dynamics. In this chapter, we discuss the history of symbolic interactionist theory and how the principles and key concepts can be used to understand individuals, families, and the meanings associated with both. Symbolic interactionism, as it is also called, helps us answer questions about how we create meaning in our everyday lives, and how those social constructions contribute to our views of families. In order to gain a fuller understanding of how symbolic interactionism works, we start with a case study that illustrates how individual definitions of family can carry very different meanings, depending on one's particular perspective and experience.

Case Study

Jeremy, the subject of our case study, is a 32-year-old man who has just started graduate school after taking some time in his twenties to explore what he truly wanted to do. He has had several romantic relationships, one in particular that was serious and ended after a year-long engagement. He has dated on and off, but hasn't found anyone he really clicks with.

Jeremy was raised by his father after his mother split from the family and moved hundreds of miles away. He and his brother grew very close with his father, but Jeremy still has not found a way to truly trust women. He always thought he would love to get married and have children, but at this stage in his life, he is not sure if it will happen. He has several wonderful friendships, one in particular with a woman who is in a similar situation. Ana, a 34-year-old single woman with a very successful career, has dated off and on but has decided to forego marriage and instead have a child on her own. After spending thousands of dollars at a sperm bank, Ana began to feel frustrated and hopeless. Ana and Jeremy did try dating once, but it wasn't in the cards.

Ana finally built up enough courage to ask Jeremy if he would consider being her sperm donor. This would save her thousands of dollars because his donation would come at no financial risk to her. Jeremy immediately agreed to do it – he told Ana he was flattered that she would ask him to be a donor, and that

Family Theories: Foundations and Applications, First Edition. Katherine R. Allen and Angela C. Henderson.

he would be honored knowing that even if he did not end up starting his own family someday, he had helped contribute to the creation of a life so that Ana could have a family. He also felt secure knowing that this child would be raised by a responsible, intelligent, caring, and loving mother. Ana had a legal contract drawn up that released Jeremy from any financial or parental obligation. The two agreed to the legal terms – bound by the fact that they do not and will probably never have a sexual relationship – and embarked on the journey of intrauterine insemination.

Contrast the realities of this scenario with how we view love, family, and marriage. What can we glean from this case study about Jeremy's view of love and family? How have his experiences both as a child and now as an adult contributed to his feeling of honor at having been asked to contribute to creating Ana's family? What will Ana's child symbolize to the two of them? Symbolic interactionism helps us understand how we construct meanings that are always changing based on our interactions with one another. Symbolic interactionists argue that objects do not have meaning outside of themselves; instead, they arise out of social interactions and are highly dependent on context. Think about how "pregnancy" can mean very different things to different people, depending on the situation. We could hypothesize that pregnancy to a 13-year-old girl in Sudan, Africa means something vastly different than it does to a married couple who have been trying to conceive for 10 years. Symbolic interactionists examine these differences, and which processes we go through to create meanings and labels, why they differ from culture to culture, and how they change over time. Given how diverse families are, and how adaptable this theory is, it should be no surprise that this theory is one of the most popular theories used for studying families across the globe.

What Is Symbolic Interactionist Theory?

Symbolic interactionist theory is used by researchers in sociology, family science, social psychology, and other areas, to explain how processes of interaction produce meanings. This theory examines how humans define objects, but not in the typical sense you would think about "objects." For social scientists and theorists, an **object** can refer to ideas, roles, social norms, behaviors, or actions (Blumer, 1969). This means that whatever we do, we are constantly in the process of creating and re-creating meaning through interactions. Therefore, nothing has meaning without human interaction, not even human beings! George Herbert Mead (1934), one of the founding theorists, argued that infants are blank slates when they are born, and without socialization, they would not become "human." The **self** develops through social interaction:

> The self is something which has a development; it is not initially there, at birth, but arises in the process of social experience and activity, that is, develops in the given individual as a result of his relations to that process as a whole and to other individuals within that process. (Mead, 1934, p. 135)

Therefore, we define reality based on the personal meanings things have for us. These meanings can be based on something we already deem to be true about an object, because it is what we were told or what we learned through interactions with others. Let's contrast how each theory you have read about so far, functionalist theory (Chapter 2) and conflict theory (Chapter 3), would view the social issue of divorce. For functionalists, reality is defined by preexisting systems that are interdependent. Divorce, then, signifies that one part of a system became dysfunctional, which led to the divorce. Conflict theorists argue that reality is best understood by examining who has access to power, and who does not. Therefore, conflict theorists would analyze divorce in relation to the power dynamic between spouses, between those with greater financial security (i.e., men) and those who have no financial support should they choose to end a marriage (i.e., women). According to these two macro-level theories, our realities are predetermined; we cannot escape the boundaries of social class and overarching social systems that structure our lives.

Symbolic interactionists, on the other hand, argue that *we* – individuals – define reality. **Symbolic interactionism** is a micro-level theory, which, as outlined in Chapter 1, considers processes at the individual level. Symbolic interactionists start from the assumption that *we* create boundaries that exist in society, not some external system, or social institution that is separate from us. Instead, cultural realities, including symbols, language, meaning, identities, and expectations, are all created from the "bottom up." In this way, using symbolic interactionism as a theoretical framework gives individuals substantial influence, or agency, over how reality is constructed. Here, we outline the history of symbolic interactionist theory, including the many theorists who have contributed to its development over the past century.

History and origins

Symbolic interactionism is a unique theory in that it consists of the perspectives of many different theorists, and has been in use since the nineteenth century. The underpinnings of this theory are drawn from **pragmatism**, which argues that the meaning of objects lies in their practical use (Appelrouth and Edles, 2011). Noted pragmatists such as Charles S. Peirce (1839–1914), William James (1842–1910), and John Dewey (1859–1952) were interested not in fixed ideals, but instead in how objects, ideas, and behaviors depend on how the *individual* defines them (Appelrouth and Edles, 2011; LaRossa and Reitzes, 1993). While this may seem like a minor switch in orientation from studying macro- to micro-level processes of social phenomena, it represented a major shift in the social sciences. Symbolic interactionist theory is interested in local definitions, or the ones that we immediately assign to things, instead of prescribed definitions of reality. This shift in focus meant that objects, interactions, events, and situations are essentially devoid of meaning without someone perceiving them.

For example, imagine showing your grandfather how to set up a Facebook account for the first time. It may be difficult for you to remember your very first time using the website or application, so you have a hard time explaining to him what it "is" without inadvertently telling him what it means to *you*. How do you explain what Facebook "is" to someone unfamiliar with it? You might say that it is a website where you can post pictures of yourself to share with friends, and see pictures of them as well. You might cautiously explain what a "selfie" is, and how to "tag" people in your photos. Your grandfather might wonder why on earth he would be interested in posting pictures of himself on a website. Sensing his resistance, you switch your description to something he might find useful. You suggest that maybe he would like to at least have a Facebook account so that he can keep up on current events, see pictures of all of his grandchildren (your siblings and cousins), and keep abreast of what they are doing on a daily basis, even though they live hundreds of miles away. You, on the other hand, have little interest in seeing the loads (too many, in your opinion) of pictures your uncle and his wife post of their children losing their first teeth, winning a trophy in soccer, or singing in a school concert. Instead, you are much more interested in your friends' posts, pictures of people you find attractive and are interested in dating, and funny videos and pop culture updates. Facebook, then, does not have objective meaning as an "object" out in cyberspace. Instead, it depends on *how people use it*. And, just like you and your grandfather, different people use it for very different reasons. This suggests that it is not objective truths that symbolic interactionists are after; instead, they are much more interested in the **subjective** experiences we have with objects and how we make meaning of those experiences through social interaction.

Once pragmatists laid the groundwork for a new orientation to explaining the social world, symbolic interactionism flourished, and is still in use today. Below, we outline both the theorists whose work falls under the umbrella of symbolic interactionism, as well as the key concepts that are foundational for understanding how this theory can be used to study individuals and families.

Key concepts

Looking-glass self As one of the earliest symbolic interactionists whose work built directly on James's idea of the self, Charles Horton Cooley is best known for his theory of the **looking-glass self**. This concept describes how an individual's sense of self develops based on beliefs about how he or she is perceived by significant others (Cooley, 1902). The looking-glass self involves three steps. First, we imagine how we appear to others. This involves an internal thought process whereby we think first about what others

Box 4.1 At a Glance: Symbolic Interactionist Theory

Symbolic interaction People act toward things based on the meaning those things have for them, and these meanings are derived from social interaction and modified through interpretation.

Self Our "social" self is created by going through the sequential stages of (a) imitation, (b) play, and (c) the game.

Significant others Humans give greater weight to the perspectives of certain others.

Generalized other An organized set of attitudes that are common in the group to which an individual belongs.

Looking-glass self A person's beliefs about how he or she is perceived by significant others.

Dramaturgy Social life is like a drama or stage play.

Impression management The process by which we attempt to manage others' perceptions of our social performances.

Emotion work Unpaid emotional work that one undertakes in relationships with loved ones.

Emotional labor Managing emotions in a paid work environment.

might think about us, before the interaction occurs. Essentially, this is the first step in getting ready for the day. We try on clothing, style our hair, and look in the mirror while doing so. We choose clothing to wear based on where we are going and who we will see. We imagine how our clothing will be perceived; we might change clothes several times before stepping out for the day because we know certain clothes give off a certain "look." The second step occurs when the interaction actually takes place, when we interpret others' reactions. When we interact, we take in facial expressions, gestures, and communication about our appearance and overall presentation. The third and final step in this process occurs when we use those interpretations to develop a self-concept. Perhaps someone looked surprised at your appearance, or at something you did or said in a social interaction. This third step can occur both during and after the interaction, where we process what others' reactions were and use them to adjust or modify our self-concept. Based on signals we received during interaction, we internalize the view of others, and it shapes our future behavior.

This process undoubtedly occurs within families. As the primary socializing unit, the family responds to our presentation of self before any other group. Both negative and positive self-concepts are built starting as early as infancy, where parents and family members express both approval and disapproval of our actions, behaviors, and words, and babies begin to internalize the reactions of those around them. As we develop, our sense of self is highly dependent on this social mirror. Consider Jeremy from our case study. He told Ana that he felt honored that she asked him to be a donor. His perception of merely being asked to help her start a family was meaningful for him, because it meant he would have a chance at contributing to the creation of a life with someone he respected and admired. For Jeremy, the interaction and meaning associated with it was very influential in developing his sense of self. His interactions with Ana as well as others led him to feel flattered to be asked; his "social mirror" reflected back to him that Ana thought he was a great person and that she would be thrilled to carry his child. These interactions invariably tell us a lot about meanings and symbols that operate at the societal level. By analyzing the process of the looking-glass self, Cooley argued that we can glean quite a bit about how society works on a broader level.

Stages of developing self-consciousness Considered to be one of the founders of social psychology, George Herbert Mead contributed significantly to the development of symbolic interactionism during the twentieth century (Morris, 1962 [1934]). His contributions were arguably more complex than that of Cooley (1902), conceptualizing a more detailed examination of how the individual mind and self both arise out of the social process. According to Mead, the mind, or individual psychology (how the mind works), is intelligible only in terms of social processes (Appelrouth and Edles, 2011). The mind develops by using symbols and language, deriving meaning from interactions, which includes an internal conversation of gestures, or considering alternative lines of conduct based on past interactions. Inherent in this process, then, is the ability to be self-conscious, or reflexive, and consider how one's actions are affected by others, and how those actions may be altered in the future.

Contrary to Cooley, Mead outlined the specific stages humans go through to arrive at the pinnacle of self-development, referred to by Mead as taking the role of the "other." There are three stages of intersubjective activity that we go through to get to this phase: (a) we learn language as early as infancy, based on interactions with our caretakers, (b) we imitate others in the play stage, and (c) we truly become self-aware as a member of an organized community in the game stage. Going through each of these stages is crucial to developing a "self," and becoming self-conscious. Humans enter the play stage typically during childhood, when children are able to take on a role they observe in those around them. An example would be a little boy pretending to be a superhero; as a result of playing this role, children are able to learn that they are both subject and object. This means that the child understands the difference between his true "self" and the role he is acting out. He has specific gestures, language, and maybe even a costume that he uses to "act out" the role of superhero. In the play stage, the child can only take on and understand one role at a time; it is merely "play."

The game stage, on the other hand, is referred to as such because it is best understood in the context of a game. This phase of development occurs when children are able to more fully understand their sense of self *in the context of others*. That is, Mead explained the roles of others as part of a larger set of interactions. Mead gave the example of a baseball game to illustrate this stage:

> But in a game where a number of individuals are involved, then the child taking one role must be ready to take the role of everyone else … He must know what everyone else is going to do in order to carry out his own play. He has to take all of these roles … In the game, then, there is a set of responses of such others so organized that the attitude of one calls out the appropriate attitudes of the other. (Morris, 1962 [1934], p. 151)

Therefore, the game stage is a much more sophisticated and mature understanding of group roles and dynamics than the play stage. During early socialization, children enrolled in organized sport learn not only their own place in the game, but they also learn the roles of all others who are involved with them in the game. They also need to comprehend the rules of the game, which condition the various roles. Granted, this analysis does not apply to very young children who, for example, play soccer and chase the ball around like a swarm of bees, each of them trying to kick the ball at once. Instead, the game stage involves a more mature understanding of positioning and each individual player's role and expectations. Once humans are able to truly understand their role, the role of their teammates, and the purpose of the game, then they become much closer to understanding the generalized other.

The **generalized other** refers to an organized set of attitudes that are common in the group to which an individual belongs. According to Mead, when the individual can view herself from the standpoint of the generalized other, "self-consciousness in the full sense of the term" is attained (Morris, 1962 [1934], p. 195). Of course, it is important to note here that just because children are enrolled in a sports team, it doesn't mean that they are truly "done" developing. We are constantly exposed to the attitudes of the generalized other throughout our entire lives. There are multiple generalized others that are specific to different contexts; think of it as a set of expectations associated with different groups. For example, we have a general idea of what the expectations of parents are in any given society. At the most basic level, parents are supposed to care for their children, provide basic necessities, and help socialize them to become full members of society. However, those expectations will vary from culture to culture, and have definitely changed over time. For example, Ana, from our case study, has experienced some pushback from her grandparents for choosing to start a family on her own. The generalized other that her parents experienced growing up in a traditional, conservative era suggests that getting pregnant out of wedlock is frowned upon. Ana's grandmother has told her more than once that she disapproves of her decisions "because a child needs a father." However, this view is becoming outdated as society evolves and we redefine what it means to be a family. The generalized other changes over time as social norms change. Think about how access to birth control, adoption, artificial insemination, and sperm banks have changed the way we view families over time. Before these resources were available, individuals were limited in how they were able to start (or prevent) having a family. But now, access to different technologies and second-parent adoption opens up possibilities for individuals to define and redefine "family." Symbolic interactionism is unique compared to the other theories presented in this book, because it allows family researchers, practitioners, and policymakers to focus on how our interactions with these "objects" – laws, policies, technologies – change over time, making room for new realities and meanings for individuals and families.

As you are probably starting to see by reading through the different theorists' approaches and contributions to symbolic interactionism, this framework represents a variety of theoretical ideas about families (see Figure 4.1). While it would be impossible to cover every theorist and concept in this chapter, we do present six key theorists important to the application of symbolic interactionism to the family. While Cooley and Mead are considered classical symbolic interactionists, Blumer, Goffman, Hochschild, and Stryker, covered below, are more contemporary theorists who drew on the work of earlier scholars.

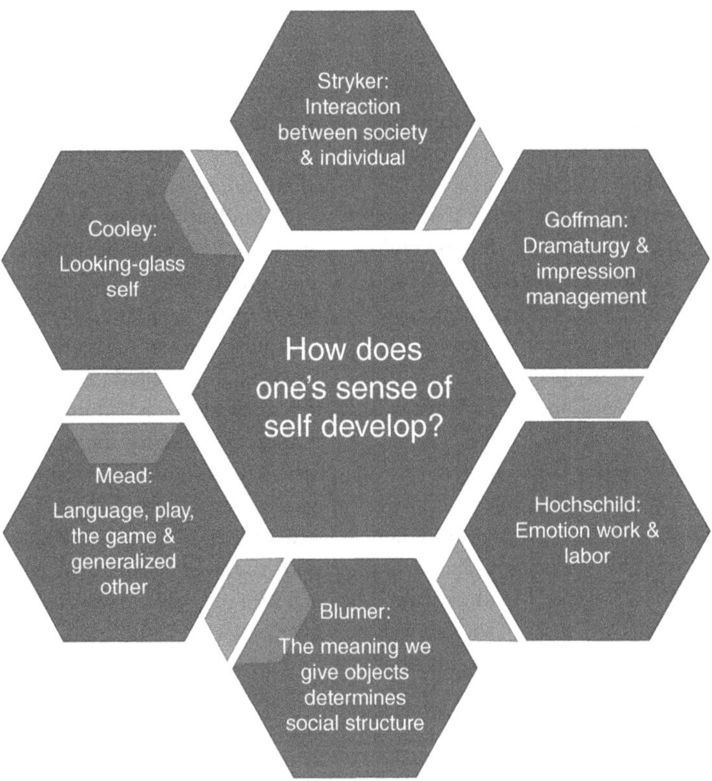

Figure 4.1 Comparison of symbolic interactionists' view of self

Naming symbolic interactionism Though Mead and Cooley contributed to the broad framework we now know as symbolic interactionist theory, it was not until the latter half of the twentieth century that Herbert Blumer (1969) officially coined the phrase "symbolic interactionism." As a student of Mead, Blumer based most of his theoretical insights on Mead's work. Like Mead, Blumer argued that social structure does not determine individual action; instead, humans engage in interaction in order to make sense of the world around them, thereby creating a **conversation of gestures**. The social structures that are external to humans are significant "only as they enter into the process of interpretation and definition out of which joint actions are formed" (Blumer, 1969, p. 75). What this means is that rules, laws, regulations, and social institutions are only effective in guiding our behavior if they are relevant to us. Consider laws that exist "on the books" but do not affect how we go about our daily lives. In Connecticut, it is illegal to walk across the street on your hands, and it is also illegal for anyone to try to stop a child from playfully jumping over puddles of water (Brandeslaw.com, 2016). In Nebraska, a parent may be arrested if his or her child cannot hold back a burp during a church service. There are dozens more examples of these types of laws that are still in existence, but likely not enforced or prosecuted. This reinforces Blumer's assertion that "it is the social process in group life that creates and upholds the rules, not the rules that create and uphold group life" (1969, p. 19). While parents may be embarrassed if their children burp in church, it is likely not because they fear arrest, but instead they fear social judgment from their peers.

Impression management and dramaturgy Erving Goffman contributed much to the study of this theory, even though he did not see himself as a symbolic interactionist (Appelrouth and Edles, 2011). He drew heavily from many social theorists, but derived his most famous concepts from Mead's assertion that we "divide ourselves up in all sorts of different selves with a reference to our acquaintances ... There are all sorts of different selves answering to all sorts of different social creations" (Morris, 1962 [1934], p. 142). In this excerpt, Mead hinted at the possibility that we actively present a different "self" to significant others, depending on the situation. Goffman (1959) elaborated on this in one of his most famous works, *The Presentation of Self in Everyday Life*, which describes how face-to-face interactions can be likened to theatrical performances.

Inherent in Goffman's conceptualization of symbolic interactionism is the presence of motivation. By suggesting that "all the world is a stage," Goffman (1959) argues that social actors try to control or guide the impression others form of them, which is referred to as **impression management**. We manipulate performances based on who is in the "audience" and what kind of impression we are trying to achieve. Goffman also identified a **front stage**, where we tailor a performance for an audience, and a **back stage**, where we retreat from the performance. Socialization, then, consists of learning to perform on the stages of life.

As you read this and consider Goffman's conceptualization of **dramaturgy**, or the idea that life is acted out like a stage drama or play, you can probably identify times in your own life where you attempted to control others' impressions. Let's revisit the example of Facebook from earlier in this chapter. Have you ever *not* posted a photo to Facebook because it would give off an impression to your Facebook audience you are not comfortable with? Maybe your grandfather (who is now on Facebook, thanks to you!) would not approve of the photos of you partying with your friends, so you maybe share them only with a specific audience. Indeed, researchers from several different disciplines have delved into the world of social media analysis to investigate how impression management occurs in an online setting (Chou and Edge, 2012; Rosenberg and Egbert, 2011). This line of research indicates that Facebook users tend to present themselves in a favorable way, which gives the impression that they are happy. As a result, individuals who utilize Facebook frequently come to have the impression that others have better lives than they do. Though Goffman did not analyze social media as a "stage" where people manage impressions, it fits well for the purposes of studying his concepts.

When it comes to every day interaction among family members and loved ones, Goffman's concepts offer valuable insight as well. For instance, consider the "stage" you perform on as part of your interactions with your immediate family. It is likely that you find yourself in the back stage, where you can retreat from acting out a concerted performance, more often than the front stage, because at home we are able to truly be ourselves. Indeed, Goffman argues that in the back stage, "the performer can relax; he can drop his front, forego speaking his lines, and step out of character" (Goffman, 1959, p. 112). You may have seen your family members stepping out of character at home as well; perhaps your parents show anger, resentment, and disappointment at home when only the nuclear family is present, but put on a "face" when there are guests in the home. Viewing these exchanges within the context of a performance adds a level of complexity to understanding what meaning we derive from interaction. Goffman's theory helps us imagine not only how we and others *should* appear in social situations, but also how self-interest and preservation motivates our presentation of self. If you want to borrow the car to take your friends to a party, you have most likely learned over time which "self" to present to your parents when you ask for the car. This skill is learned and honed over time, and is undoubtedly salient for families, couples, and children as they interact over the life course.

Emotions Arlie Russell Hochschild (1979; 1983) has published extensively on issues of the family, and you will read about her work in other chapters, such as conflict theory (Chapter 3) and feminist theory (Chapter 8). In this chapter, we present her earlier work, which focused on the management of emotions and nicely complements Goffman's interactional model. To Hochschild, emotions are "biologically driven" (1983, p. 219), and directly tied to behavior as we engage in interaction. We perform **emotion work** when we attempt to change a feeling so that it is appropriate for the situation. Social guidelines dictate what emotions are appropriate and when, which means we have to actively produce and manage them. Hochschild notes the gendered difference in emotion work, pointing out that men and women "do" emotions much differently, and for different reasons. Women, who in general have far less access to power, wealth, and authority, turn their emotions into a resource and offer it to men as a gift in return for the resources they lack (Hochschild, 1983). Particularly among middle-class families, women tend to engage in "emotion work that affirms, enhances, and celebrates the well-being and status of others" (Hochschild, 1983, p. 165). Men, on the other hand, have the "socially assigned task of aggressing against those that break rules of various sorts, which creates the private task of mastering fear and vulnerability" (Hochschild, 1983, p. 163). Have you ever heard the infamous words, "Wait until your father gets home!" uttered in frustration by someone's mother? Emotion work can manifest itself in various ways, so when you really think about it, chances are you can identify it in many different types of family communication.

Hochschild (1983) extends the idea of emotion work into the paid labor force, suggesting that **emotional labor** also exists to "sell" emotions to customers. Emotional labor is increasingly common in the service industry and is regularly used by restaurant servers, flight attendants, and retail salespeople, among others. Individuals working in such roles have to sell emotion as part of their service in order to increase tips or have satisfactory performance evaluations. This includes smiling, being courteous and pleasant, and other methods of what Hochschild refers to as *surface acting*, which is when individuals alter their displayed emotions, but not their private emotions (e.g., having a terrible day but not letting it show to your customers). *Deep acting* occurs when both the inner and outer feelings are altered because of the pressure to perform emotional labor. Finally, *genuine acting* refers to when our felt emotions are already congruent with expressed emotions. In her description of genuine acting, Hochschild references the global trend of transnational carework that we discussed in Chapter 1. Referring to this type of global emotional labor as a heart transplant, Hochschild and Ehrenreich (2003) describe how women from less developed countries leave their own young families and elderly family members to work as nannies or caregivers in affluent countries such as the United States. By transplanting their own love and care from their own family to a new family they now work for, women have to manage their own grief and anguish from leaving their families behind in their home countries.

Roles and identity Sheldon Stryker (1959; 1964) is best known for his work on identity theory, which

Box 4.2 Symbolic Interactionist Theory in Pop Culture: *About a Boy*

A scene from *About a Boy*, 2002, dir. Chris Weitz and Paul Weitz, Universal Pictures

About a Boy was released in 2002 as a film and was recently adapted into a television series that premiered in 2014. One of the main characters in the film, Will, is a self-centered bachelor whose primary goal in life is avoiding responsibility. He meets Marcus, a bright, "geeky" 12-year-old boy, and after a while, the two become friends as Marcus seeks Will out for help and advice. Marcus's mother, Fiona, struggles with depression as a single mother. She and Marcus have a hard time connecting.

Throughout this film, we can see examples of Cooley's looking-glass self. Marcus blames himself for his mother's instability, and he also gets teased at school and has very few friends. Marcus's interactions with his mom are shaped by his perception of himself in the relationship as her "savior." His perception of himself as the one who makes his mom happy transcends into his "self" at school, as one of the most famous scenes from the film depicts him singing at the school concert because his mom likes to hear him sing. Unfortunately, his peers make fun of him for this, which leads to Marcus's negative self-concept. The positive side is that it makes his mom happy and he receives praise *from her* for it. Each interaction – at home and at school – has spillover effects and creates a unique perspective for Marcus to seek out other options – other "father figures" – like Will. Marcus also tries to set up his mother and Will on a blind date in order to have another person around to help him care for his mother. Clearly, he perceives himself as his mother's caretaker and one of the only people who can make her happy. He has internalized this responsibility based on his interactions with his mother, and he is imagining a life with "three" – a father figure, a mother, and himself. This symbolism is very powerful for Marcus and drives his behavior most of the film.

draws on Mead and actually counters the work of Blumer. Stryker introduced a social-structural view of symbolic interactionism, centered on the reciprocal relationship between self and society. That is, Stryker argued that a theoretical framework must be able to move from the level of the person to that of large-scale social structure and back again (Stryker, 1964). This is in opposition to earlier symbolic interactionist work that suggested that interactions determined social structure, not the other way around. Stryker, on the other hand, believed that society and the individual are integral to one another; understanding one is impossible without taking the other into account.

Stryker's most famous concepts, then, make up the middle ground that earlier symbolic interactionist work was arguably missing: roles and identities. Individuals fulfill roles, or behavioral expectations and meanings that are attached to positions located in the social structure (Appelrouth and Edles, 2011). Roles are structural in nature, but are filled by individuals, who in turn internalize those roles and build the concept of the "self." Thinking back to Ana from our case study, we can see that she wants to someday soon fulfill the role of mother. To her, this role in society carries weight and importance. In addition, Ana specifically wants to be able to carry her own biological child. She could have chosen to adopt, or to become a foster parent, but those roles carry different meanings and are situated differently in the social structure. Taking these factors into account, we are analyzing Stryker's (1980) structural side of identity. At the same time, we must analyze the micro-level processes that are impossible to untangle from Ana's decisions. Ana's sense of identity as a biological mother to her child is part of the sense of "self" she wants to achieve. Of the roles she could choose to fulfill on her journey to becoming a mother, being a biological mother carries more meaning for her. Using this example, we can see how **identity** (internalized expectations and meaning) and roles (structure) are inevitably both responsible for contributing to the complexity of the "self." The number of identities a person possesses corresponds to the number of structured role relationships in which he or she participates (Appelrouth and Edles, 2011).

Stryker's (1980) theoretical contributions to symbolic interactionist theory also include the concept of **identity salience**, which suggests that our identities are arranged in a hierarchy. This means that your identities, as a student, child, sibling, parent, worker, or best friend, are all arranged in order of importance in the construction of your identity. Identity salience is evident in the concept of a **significant other** (Stryker, 1964), in that greater priority is given to the perspectives of certain individuals over others. Depending on the situation you find yourself in, you are most likely to invoke an identity that is more important to you. As an example, let's imagine that you and your significant other are having a heated fight that may end the relationship. The problem is, you also have an important exam the next day, so you are thinking about how to best handle this situation. According to Stryker, you will make a choice based on which identity is most salient to you at that time. Which would you choose?

Evaluating Symbolic Interactionist Theory

Strengths of symbolic interactionist theory

As you are noticing throughout this book, all theories have strengths and weaknesses. Symbolic interactionist theory is a very popular family theory because its tenets can be easily applied from one research setting to another. Unlike functionalist theory (see Chapter 2), symbolic interactionist theory is not a "grand theory" that purports to explain "the facts." Rather, this theory is applicable to multiple ways in which human beings and their circumstances change over time.

One of the most influential of all the family theories Symbolic interactionist theory has a long history in the field, and it is considered one of the "classical" theories in sociology. Yet, at the same time, the theory remains relevant to contemporary applications and has stood the test of time in family science. Although functionalism has had many critics, symbolic interactionism has never gone out of style. In fact, LaRossa and Reitzes (1993) claim that this theory has had the greatest impact on the study of families since its original application. Symbolic interactionist concepts such as "significant other" have made their way into popular culture and everyday speech. The theory provides an excellent way to utilize concepts about how family members develop a shared sense, or symbolic reality, of the world.

Easy to integrate with other theories Symbolic interactionist theory is often combined with other perspectives because no other theory does a better job of understanding how human beings are socialized and interact with one another on a micro level of analysis. For example, early family theorists combined symbolic interactionism, as a micro perspective, and structural functionalism (Chapter 2), as a macroperspective, that led to the creation of family developmental theory, which we discuss in Chapter 5. In a recent example, which we describe below, Glass and Few-Demo (2013) combined symbolic interactionist theory with Black feminist theory. These innovative theoretical pairings deepen our understanding of family process because the theory so richly describes the complex and diverse ways humans learn how to be members of families through social interaction.

Highly compatible with qualitative research methods Many family theories are rich with ideas and explanations, but do not translate well into the practice of guiding a research study. For example, in Chapter 5, we will find that family developmental theory is considered conceptually rich, but methodologically poor. That is, many theories in the field are very useful in organizing concepts and providing an explanation of family process and structure, but when scholars try to put the theory into research practice, it is difficult to create hypotheses that are easily answered through research methods. Unlike other theories that are very difficult to operationalize, however, symbolic interactionism goes hand in hand with qualitative research methods (Bogdan and Biklen, 2007). Symbolic interactionist theory provides the foundation for research studies that explore how human beings interact and make meaning in the world.

Symbolic interactionist theory undergirds the qualitative research practice of grounded theory methodology (Daly, 2007; Gilgun, 2013; LaRossa, 2005). This method provides a set of rules, or guidance, in helping researchers generate theory from the "ground up." That is, this theory presumes that more relevant and accurate depictions of the lives of real people can only be generated from the actual observation and interviewing of people in their own social context. In their classic study of staff/parent communication on neonatal units, Bogdan, Brown, and Foster (1982) presented a grounded theory they called "Be honest but not cruel" to explain how doctors and nurses in an intensive neonatal care unit temper the information they share about an infant's chances of survival with the infant's parents. It would be difficult to obtain such a complex understanding of family trauma unless we saw it firsthand and generated theory from those observations. Thus, researchers ground their practices of data collection and analysis in everyday life experience and allow a theoretical explanation to emerge inductively (see Chapter 1, Figure 1.2, "The scientific process and theory building").

Weaknesses of symbolic interactionist theory

Despite its popularity and usefulness, symbolic interactionist theory is not without its critics. Primarily, critics have charged that in promoting Burgess's (1926) idea of the "family as a unity of interacting personalities," the individuality, interpersonal conflicts, and social structural inequalities that challenge unity are obscured (Cheal, 1991). Next, we examine three critiques that have been directed at symbolic interactionist theory. We also note that many of the limitations of this theory have been addressed by recent scholars, and it is, in the long run, maintaining its reputation as a central family theory.

Overestimates the role of human agency One of the main critiques of symbolic interactionist theory is the emphasis on human agency. The controlling nature of macrosystems are downplayed in this theory, which gives individual actors more power in determining their reality (also called the subjective fallacy) than external forces allow (LaRossa and Reitzes, 1993). In this sense, symbolic interactionist theory does not give as much weight to the conflict and inequality created by the economy, social institutions, and embedded stereotypes and systematic discrimination. As an example, symbolic interactionists would be interested in Ana and Jeremy's story and how they come to define their own situations and definitions of family. A macro-level theorist would criticize this perspective for not taking into account the forces outside of Ana and Jeremy that directly affect their choices. For instance, Ana is undoubtedly affected by our pronatalist society, which highly values having children. This is not the case around the world. Indeed, in some countries like India, governments have enacted policies aimed at reducing the number of births. At one point, the Indian government offered new cars for both men and women who volunteered for sterilization (BBC News, 2011). In addition, macro-level theorists would ask what other forces led to Ana's choice not to adopt: Was adoption too expensive? As you can see, critics of symbolic interactionism argue that by focusing on the dyad as the primary unit of analysis, the issue of power as an objective reality is obscured. Families differ by their ability to define what is real in their lives. In another example, minority group families and immigrants still must contend with the objective reality of prejudice and discrimination against their families that are imposed by external laws and structures outside of their control. Ana and her child will undoubtedly face questions about where the child's father is, and why Ana and Jeremy did not get married, because they do not fit the "ideal" that is defined at the structural level of society. In addition, imagine Ana as a Black woman; would she be perceived differently for being a single mother, based on her race? Or, what if Ana is White and Jeremy is Black, and the child they create is biracial? Thus, symbolic interactionism is critiqued for not focusing on such larger, macro-level factors as racism, classism, and heterosexism.

Not a unified theory Another major critique of symbolic interactionist theory is that it is more of a loose collection of concepts than a formal, or grand, theory that attempts to explain human actors in families and society (Hill and Hansen, 1960). Although the very notion that it is even possible or necessary to have a grand theory such as Sigmund Freud's theory of psychosexual development (Gay, 1995) or Talcott Parsons's (1951) theory of structural functionalism to explain individual and family development has been widely criticized, most theorists from the symbolic interactionist tradition have not been willing or successful in developing the concepts into a formal and systematic theory. Consider the long history of symbolic interactionism, and the many versions that contributing theorists have added to the framework. Because the theory has been so adaptable, it is criticized for being *too* flexible and offering only a "mixed bag" of concepts (LaRossa and Reitzes, 1993, p. 154).

Downplays the role of emotion As a theory of social interaction, symbolic interactionism has been criticized for not being sensitive to the irrational, unconscious, and biological mechanisms that also control human behavior (Smith and Hamon, 2012). In some ways, this criticism is unfounded because earlier theorists, such as Cooley, in his notion of the looking-glass self, did suggest that emotions provide the motivation for individuals to engage in social relationships. As is often the case with theories that have stood the test of time, new theorists have built upon the criticisms by addressing the neglected aspects of the original theory. As noted above, Hochschild (1979) developed a theory of emotion work that explains how men and women learn to consciously manage their emotions in dealing with culturally appropriate gender identities (e.g., women as responsible for family work, men as responsible for breadwinning) when both spouses work outside the home (Erickson, 2005).

An alternative theory app: family systems theory

In this chapter, we have presented the key concepts, historical origins, modern applications, and strengths and weaknesses of symbolic interactionist theory. It is both useful and interesting to compare theories to more easily pinpoint the differences between them, so in this chapter, we will compare symbolic interactionist theory to family systems theory, which we cover in more detail in Chapter 6.

As it has been observed in this chapter, symbolic interactionist theory takes into account micro-level social relations to help us understand how individuals within families are socialized and develop identities, as well as how they communicate and go about their daily lives. Family systems theory, on the other hand, gives us a "panoramic" view of all the subsystems that both influence and are influenced by families. A subsystem within a family can consist of dyads or triads – the dyad could be the two parents, and a triad could be three children. For each subsystem within the family unit, the pathways of communication are endless: the parents may argue over a child's behavior, which affects the child as well as his or her siblings. Family systems theory also takes into account hierarchies that exist within families, allowing researchers to analyze who in a family has the most and least amount of power, and how that influences family communication. This theoretical perspective allows for an analysis of interaction and symbols, but approaches the study of families from a more holistic perspective while doing so.

Working with Symbolic Interactionist Theory: Integrating Research and Practice

Now that we have described the historical origins, key concepts, and strengths and weaknesses of symbolic interactionist theory, we turn our attention to how the theory can be used in practice. We then analyze an empirical study that was rooted in this theory in order to see how scholars put the theory to work in a research project. Finally, we present ideas about how the theory informs policies associated with race, adoption, and families.

Symbolic interactionist theory today

Kerry Daly (2003) utilizes and expands ideas associated with symbolic interactionist theory to distinguish between the ways that families actually live their lives and the ways that scholars theorize about how families live their lives. Using the concept of **negative spaces**, he says that there are many aspects of everyday family activities that we have not seen or given a name to as we attempt to explain how family members interact with one another. He theorizes that culture is an important way to understand the inner workings of families because cultural categories reveal what we value, as evidenced through how we dress and speak, what we believe, and how we make meaning of family experience. Thus, culture provides us with a "tool kit" that guides us toward meaning and action (Swidler, 2001).

In contrast to looking at the spaces of family life that are elusive, or hidden from view, family scholars mostly theorize about families as if cultural context does not matter. Daly (2003) proposes that we need to make visible the varied and unique ways that families construct meaning as they interpret cultural codes and beliefs. He suggests three negative spaces that are important for understanding the meaning-making process in families.

The first of these three negative spaces concerns the realm of belief, feeling, and intuition. Here, Daly (2003) gives attention to the less rational and logical aspects of our lives. Although scholars typically study attitudes and activities, much of family life, in contrast, is characterized by very charged feelings such as love, care, envy, anger, hurt, and disappointment. As Hochschild (1979) has found, the family's emotional climate is highly charged, and families operate by unspoken feeling rules. For example, in some families, crying and feelings of sadness are frowned upon. Yet, these negative spaces are important to explore for how feelings are allowed to be expressed. Feelings are often ambivalent, or comprised of both positive and negative emotions. For example, positive emotions such as love and care can be trumped by the feeling of burden and resentment. Other aspects of the feeling side of families are expressed through spirituality, religion, and how a family interprets the "realm of the sacred." We can gain deeper insight into family interactions by examining their rituals. Further, the stories, or myths, that families tell about themselves are one of the chief ways they reveal what they believe is important. By understanding how emotions, spirituality, and the "inherited myths" are passed down through the generations, we can gain a deeper insight into their inner workings. Returning to our case study, how do you think the family culture in which Ana grew up differed from Jeremy's family culture? Ana was raised in a two-parent nuclear family, and has a sister who is married with a son. Jeremy, on the other hand, grew up in a one-parent household after being abandoned by his mother. What stories and myths about the way families are supposed to be and look like were probably passed down to these two individuals? How have they affected their desires for having a biological child that one raises on a daily basis (Ana) or contributing to the creation of a life, but not being involved in the child's daily life (Jeremy)?

The second of these negative spaces concerns consumption and the meaning that things reveal about family life. Families are constantly exposed to messages that promote the motivation to accumulate things. The objects we buy are an expression to others about what we value and what we can afford; these expressions of consumption are often invisible but very present within families. As an example, think about your own family's consumption patterns. Did your parent(s) buy generic brands of food at the grocery store, or was everything organic and/or name brand? Have you ever noticed how other families "do" food consumption? Some families eat out five times a week, and yet other families eat home-cooked meals every night. What we eat and what we are exposed to within our families says a lot about how we value brands, types of consumption (restaurant prepared or prepared at home by a parent or the entire family), and the "image" we are trying to give off.

The things that we buy also divide a family. An example Daly (2003) gives is of an adolescent who gets a nose ring, and the potential conflict this brings with his or her parents. Furthermore, consumption is a negative space in which individuals in families communicate facts about their social class, gender, age, occupation, educational level, and the like. Think about the cars that people buy and the number of cars per family. What does it communicate about an individual and a family to drive a sedan, a jeep, a luxury car, a smart car, a used car, or a minivan? Each of these vehicles conveys a message about its owner and occupants. Some families swear they will never succumb to the convenience of a minivan; culturally, the minivan sends the message of a "soccer mom" that not all families are comfortable with. In fact, makers of a popular family minivan, Toyota, have produced a comical parody video that highlights a White married couple with two kids. The couple raps about "lookin' slick" in their swagger wagon (Toyota, 2010). This indicates efforts by car manufacturers to continually reach families' negative spaces of consumption, always trying to bring in new buyers and keep their products "hip."

Finally, the third negative space concerns the location of family members in time and space. Daly (2003) describes how the relation between home and work or home and community create "territories of self" and boundaries within and between families. For example, what happens to family time when a parent has a long commute to work? How does a couple's ability to be emotionally close differ when they live in the same home, or when they live apart and have a "commuter" marriage? How much time in housework is spent when one owns a large house, or rents a small apartment? Technology, as well, is a major influence on time and space in family life. Today, many family members communicate through texting, rather than picking up the phone and calling one another. Even the concept of "picking up the phone" is outdated, as stationary telephones are being replaced by cell phones that can be kept on one's person at all times. Time and space are thus examples of negative spaces that new theoretical perspectives on symbolic interactionist theory suggest we should consider when studying the complex meaning-making process in families.

Symbolic interactionist theory in research

In their qualitative study of 11 Black lesbian couples, Valerie Glass and April Few-Demo (2013) ground their analysis in symbolic interactionist theory, but also integrate how Black feminist theory (Few, 2007) is useful to address the issue of power. This study is an example of how well symbolic interactionism blends with other theories. By combining these theories, the authors were able to show that Black lesbian couples had unique sources of support and constraint from their various communities. For example, extended family members were more likely to accept their daughter's lesbian partner as a "friend," rather than seeing the two women as a couple. Although they downplayed the lesbian relationship by desexualizing it, they did not reject their daughter or her "friend." Given the great importance of family and kinship ties in the Black community, families were able to deal with the contradiction of keeping a lesbian daughter close without having to approve of the lesbian relationship. Further, given the significance of religion in the Black community, many of the couples still participated in religious services, but did so as individuals, not as a couple.

Symbolic interactionist theory allowed Glass and Few-Demo (2013) to interpret the cultural contradictions of being a lesbian and being a Black woman whose family traditions value kinship and church communities. At the same time, the lesbian couples had to deal with subtle racism in the lesbian, gay, bisexual, transgender or queer (LGBTQ) community, and a bias against parenthood (10 of the 11 couples had children living in their home). It was hard to find family-friendly spaces for lesbian parents in their communities, as most of the women lived in rural locations outside of the urban areas that have large and diverse LGBTQ members. Still, the constraints of race, gender, sexual orientation, geography, and maternal status did not stand in the way of creating a "homeplace" that honored their lesbian and family identities. As Glass and Few-Demo (2013) explain, Black feminist theory defines **homeplace** as a self-supporting safe space where minority individuals can experience the safety, affection, and full acceptance not available in the wider society (hooks, 1997). Thus, the integration of symbolic interactionism and Black feminist theory allowed the authors to uncover how women with racial and sexual minority status interpreted and enacted contradictory cultural values, symbols, and roles in self-supporting ways.

Table 4.1 Racially stratified adoption fees

Race/Ethnicity	Gender	Due	Cost
African American	Unknown	Any day	$17,000 + legal fees
African American	Girl	October 15th	$17,000 + $4,500 legal fees
African American	Girl	September 26th	$17,000 + $6000–8000 medical expenses
African American	Unknown	November 18th	$17,000 + $6,000-8,000 medical expenses (Mom smokes cigarettes)
African American	Boy	October 22nd	$17,000 + $6,000–8,000 medical expenses (Mom smokes cigarettes)
Biracial (African American/ Native American)	Girl	August 18th	$22,500 + $2,500 legal fees + medical expenses
Biracial (Caucasian/African American)	Girl	October 12th	$25,000 + $8,000–10,000 medical expenses
Biracial (Caucasian/Hispanic)	Unknown	September 15th	$30,500 + $4,500 legal fees
Biracial	Boy	Late October	$30,000 + $7,000 legal fees
Caucasian	Unknown	Late October	$28,000 + $8,000 legal fees
Caucasian	Unknown	February	$29,000 + $7,000 legal fees (Mom would like an open adoption with a few visits per year)

Source: Examples shown at NPR, 2013.

Symbolic interactionist theory in practice

There are several ways in which educators, practitioners, and family policy makers can apply symbolic interactionism in their work with individuals and families. Though symbolic interactionism has been critiqued for not being applicable to studying macro-level phenomena, one of the areas where this theory is relevant is in the study of racially stratified adoption fees.

As a family studies practitioner or researcher, you will likely confront the issues of adoption and/or racial discrimination, either separately or perhaps together. The two issues are important to consider together because transracial adoptions are increasing annually in the US (Lee, 2003) *and* how much a family will pay to adopt is directly related to the race of the child. Table 4.1 presents the race-based cost differential for one adoption consulting group that links potential parents with adoption agencies.

Why is such a macro-level system important to the application of symbolic interactionism? It is important because the ways in which we make meaning of race varies from person to person and culture to culture. The demand for healthy White infants is higher than the supply (Sokoloff, 1993). While this may seem on the surface to be a macro-level issue, it is important to note that from a symbolic interactionist perspective, there is much to be said about perceptions of race, and individual and family identity. Indeed, sociological researchers have found that prospective adoptive parents prefer a child who shares similar traits with them, such as race/ethnicity, so they may better resemble a biologically formed family (Ishizawa and Kubo, 2014). In addition, families with biological children have pursued international adoptions so that the adopted child would not look different from the siblings (Kubo, 2010). The family in these cases prefers to have a racially matched family, hesitating to adopt transracially because of the fear that they would be criticized, for instance, by the Black community for not being culturally equipped to raise Black children (Brooks, James, and Barth 2002). Therefore, from a symbolic interactionist standpoint, we can see evidence of the looking-glass self, the importance of the family identity, and how the meaning we assign to individuals based on race are key to understanding racially stratified adoption fees.

Conclusion

Symbolic interactionism has provided important ideas that allow researchers and practitioners to put the

Box 4.3 Global Comparisons of Wedding Rituals

Weddings are a major cultural event in which community values and meanings are revealed. Many western countries tend to place more focus on the two partners. But in traditional cultures, families and entire communities are more central. At the same time, wedding ceremonies and celebrations combine elements of old and new customs. The following examples reveal that each society demonstrates what is important to them through the rituals associated with major life events. Although particular practices may vary, the elaborate nature of weddings, in terms of adornment, food, celebration, and the like, are evidence that these events are festive occasions that are meant to include the couple, their families, and their community (Droesch, 2013). Here, we examine wedding traditions from around the world.

China One of the new customs to emerge in contemporary China is the wedding album. The bride and groom hire a professional photographer to pose them in different locations and outfits prior to their wedding. The highly stylized album does not contain pictures of the wedding ceremony itself.

India Although there are many celebrations and rituals before, during, and after the traditional Hindu wedding ceremony, one of the most elaborate rituals is the Mehndi ceremony. Mehndi is an art form using henna dye, in which the bride's palms, wrists, arms, legs, and feet are decorated in elaborate and colorful designs.

Jamaica Weddings in Jamaica involve the entire community. Receptions have traditionally been held in the groom's home. They are lavish celebrations with flowers, food, games, dancing, and music, and often last for days.

Sami Lapland weddings of the Sami people include the entire community (from 600 to 2,000 guests). The bride and groom wear elaborate decorations in the form of traditional footwear made of reindeer skin, and silver jewelry historic to their community.

United States A long-standing tradition in the US is for the father to "give away" the bride to her new husband. More recently, both parents have walked their daughter down the aisle. Receptions often vary by how much money the couple, or their parents, can afford to spend.

Source: *World wedding traditions*, at www.worldweddingtraditions.net.

theory to use beyond the conceptual level. From its earliest days as a theory of self and mind, to its current uses as a theory that helps us understand emotions and social contexts, symbolic interactionist theory covers a wide range of territory regarding the micro-processes in families.

Additionally, it is important to highlight how this theory is applicable to the study of families across the globe. Marriage patterns and wedding rituals differ vastly, depending on the country's culture and history. Why do you think this is? How would symbolic interactionists explain the differences between the countries we highlight in Box 4.3? We challenge you to consider these global applications of the theory as you move on to the discussion and reflection questions, and areas for further study, in the concluding pages of this chapter.

Multimedia Suggestions

https://sites.google.com/site/sssinteraction/

The Society for the Study of Symbolic Interaction (SSSI) is an international professional organization of scholars and researchers who study issues such as identity, language, and everyday life. SSSI publishes the journal *Symbolic Interaction*, hosts an annual conference where scholars present their latest work, and offers a number of honors and awards, including the George Herbert Mead Award for Lifetime Achievement, the Charles Horton Cooley Award for Recent Book or Article, and the Herbert Blumer Graduate Student Paper Award.

Activate your theory app: Browse through the website and see if you can find other examples of current theorizing and/or contemporary research studies using this theory in the conference program and recent journal issues.

https://www.youtube.com/watch?v=ybDa0gSuAcg

This video was created by US high school student Kiri Davis in 2006 as a follow-up to Kenneth and Mamie Clark's famous doll study from the 1930s and 1940s. In the video, Kiri shows 21 young Black American children either a White or Black doll with the exact same features except for skin color. Kiri asked the children similar questions to the ones the Clarks asked: which doll they would prefer to play with, which one was nice, and which one was bad. The final question asked the children which doll was most similar to them. Fifteen of the children chose the White dolls over the Black dolls, giving reasons similar to the ones the Clarks heard. These results indicate that even among very young children, individuals' self-concept and identities are very important to understanding structural issues of racism.

Activate your theory app: How can we explain the interactions in the video using symbolic interactionist concepts? Consider how individuals' self-concepts and identities develop when it comes to experiencing structural (albeit invisible) issues of racism.

House of Cards (2013–present)

Symbolic interactionist theory is evident in nearly every film and television show because the theory is so adaptable and applicable, which makes it hard to narrow down the focus to just one example. The Netflix original series *House of Cards,* which is based on a British TV drama by the same name, illustrates many of the concepts we have discussed in this chapter. Impression management is a common tactic used by the main characters, Frank Underwood and his wife, Claire, who are masters at manipulation throughout this series. Oftentimes, they socially construct and manipulate situations after they have internalized others' opinions of them. An example of this is when Frank uses reporter Zoe Barnes to leak stories about his rivals in Washington. He and Claire utilize the looking-glass self as well; they carefully imagine others' impressions of them, and then respond to those impressions by manipulating information. Frank's ascension to the seat of the President of the United States is a clear example of him being fully aware of all the other important "actors" in politics, and thus engineering several situations that led ultimately to his becoming the most powerful man in the free world.

A scene from *House of Cards*, 2013, cr. Beau Willimon, Netflix/Sony Pictures Television

Activate your theory app: Has Frank developed through to the "game" stage, according to Mead? How does self-centeredness play a role in identity development?

Seinfeld (1989–1998)

Seinfeld is a television sitcom set in New York City, featuring the main character (Jerry Seinfeld) and his friends and acquaintances. This show has multiple examples of symbolic interactionism, as characters navigate dating, engagement, relationships with their families, and friendships. In one episode, the family of his friend George celebrates a holiday they invented themselves called "Festivus," which serves as an alternative to the commercialization of Christmas. Interestingly, this idea was so popular when it was depicted on the show that it has made its way into popular American culture and is celebrated by *Seinfeld* fans every year. This is a great example of how individuals attach meaning to cultural symbols and they can emerge out of individual-level interactions.

A scene from *Seinfeld*, 1989, cr. Jerry Seinfeld and Larry David, Sony Pictures Television

Activate your theory app: What aspects of Cooley's looking-glass self are evident in this show? What about the "generalized other"?

Further Reading

Blakely, K., "Busy brides and the business of family life: The wedding-planning industry and the commodity frontier," *Journal of Family Issues, 29* (2008), 639–662 (doi:10.1177/0192513X07309453). Kristin Blakely built upon Hochschild and Ehrenreich's (2003) ideas about the commercialization of intimate life to examine how families now "outsource" work that has traditionally been done within the home. Such work includes takeout meals as a substitute for home cooking, the use of nannies to care for children as a substitute for maternal care, dry-cleaning as a substitute for doing the family's laundry, maid service, dog walking, birthday party planning, and a host of other activities that were once the primary responsibility of women. To this list, Blakely added the role of wedding planning as a new "commodity frontier" in which domestic work has expanded into the paid labor market. She suggested that this increasing outsourcing of family work may allow for women to work outside the home, but it is not without its costs. As we become more and more detached from the actual work of caring for self and family, we may experience greater disenchantment and isolation from the very emotions and activities that keep us tied to one another.

Burr, W. R., Leigh, G. K., Day, R. A., and Constantine, J., "Symbolic interaction and the family," in W. R. Burr, R. Hill, F. I. Nye, and I. L. Reiss (eds), *Contemporary theories about the family: General theories/Theoretical orientations* (New York: Free Press, 1979), vol. 2, pp. 42–111. In this classic article, Wesley Burr and colleagues describe the history of the application of symbolic interactionism to the study of families. They attempt to integrate the concepts associated with symbolic interactionist theory into a formal theoretical framework from which propositions can be used to guide research. This article provides a comprehensive review and comparison of the various schools of thought associated with the theory, such as the Chicago School that emphasized the subjective development of self through interaction, and the school of thought that emphasized the objective roles and structures that are more deterministic in guiding human behavior in families.

Hochschild, A. R., *So how's the family? And other essays* (Berkeley: University of California Press, 2013). This book is a collection of some of Arlie Russell Hochschild's prolific work on contemporary family life. She addresses her current work on issues such as the use of surrogate mothers (e.g., wombs) to provide wealthy families with children they could not otherwise have. She also elaborates upon her ongoing work on how emotional labor is managed in families and other institutional settings such as the workforce. The essay on "the two-way global traffic in care" applies an analysis of Goffman's (1959) concept of "backstage behavior" to how migrant care workers come to work for wealthy families in developed countries. Their work is both necessary to support their own families back home but also poorly paid and devalued in their host countries.

Killoren, S. E., Updegraff, K. A., Christopher, F. S., and Umana-Taylor, A. J., "Mothers, fathers, peers, and Mexican-origin adolescents' sexual intentions," *Journal of Marriage and Family, 73* (2011), 209–220 (doi:10.1111/j.1741-3737.2010,00799.x). In this study of 246 families, the authors used a symbolic interaction perspective to address the serious sexual risks of Latino adolescents, who have the highest teen birthrates compared to any other ethnic background, and higher rates of sexually transmitted infections than non-Latino Whites. They examined the interrelated roles of mothers, fathers, and deviant peer affiliations (with deviance being measured as the likelihood to use drugs, lying about one's age to buy or do things, etc.) in the choices Mexican immigrant youth and US-born Latino youth make about their sexual activity. Contrary to expectations, they found that levels of parental acceptance and disclosure to parents did not differ across the two groups. A major factor, however, was that being born in the US increased the likelihood that Latino youth would be influenced by the negative behaviors of their peers.

Marsiglio, W., and Hinojosa, R., "Managing the multifather family: Stepfathers as father allies," *Journal of Marriage and Family, 69* (2007), 845–862 (doi:10.1111/j.1741-3737.2007.00409.x). This is one of the first studies to examine stepfathers' interaction and relationships with their stepchildren's biological fathers, thus extending our knowledge of how men co-construct their identities and relationships in families. The authors conducted in-depth interviews with 46 stepfathers and found that 18 of these men had some degree of regular and ongoing contact with the biological father. Contrary to masculine gender rules of competition, many of the men developed friendly and cooperative relationships with one another. The findings indicate that these men were able to successfully challenge conventional masculinity norms and create new definitions of stepfather relationships. Their ability to construct their identities in a "fatherly way" rather than an authoritarian or competitive way allowed them to develop relationships with biological fathers as allies who are committed to the needs of the children they share.

Questions for Students

Discussion Questions

1. Generate a list of all of the types of family labor you can think of. Which family members tend to perform each task?
2. How does gender affect the way that emotions are managed in families and at work?
3. Considering that symbolic interactionism is easy to pair with other family theories, can you think of one that has very different assumptions and is not easily paired with this theory?
4. How would you use symbolic interactionist theory to guide a quantitative research study?
5. How is backstage behavior expressed on the internet, or in other electronic communication?
6. In what ways do you think families are "a unity of interacting personalities"? In what ways does the concept of family conflict (Chapter 3) challenge this view?

Your Turn!

You are a school counselor and happen to overhear some middle schoolers' conversation as you are walking down the hall one day. They are joking and laughing about a new way of greeting each other called "grazing." For male students, this involves grazing another male's groin area to say hello. Female students graze each others' breasts. As a school administrator, you immediately become concerned about sexual harassment, so you stop the children and intervene. Once you get back to your office, you come up with a game plan on how to address the entire student body about this new trend before it gets out of hand. What do you decide is the best approach? How can the theories you have read about in this chapter inform your conversation with other school administrators about how to handle this? Come up with a communication plan and base it on at least one of the theorists' concepts and theoretical framework.

Personal Reflection Questions

1 Give an example of how you may have experienced the looking-glass self as you grew up. How did family members or loved ones contribute to your self-perception?
2 How would you define your "self"? How has your sense of self been shaped by your family's interaction?
3 Describe a situation in your family in which it was very important to manage your emotions. Now, find examples in other societies around the globe where the cultural context dictates a different way of emotion management. What do you notice in this cultural comparison of emotions?
4 Who are the significant others in your own life? How long have these relationships lasted? How have they changed over time?
5 What are your reference groups as a college student?
6 What are the metaphors and negative spaces that describe the kind of family in which you grew up?

References

Appelrouth, S., and Edles, L. D. (2011). *Classical and contemporary sociological theory: Text and readings*. Los Angeles: Pine Forge Press.

BBC News (2011, July 1). *India: Rajasthan in 'cars for sterilisation' drive.* At http://www.bbc.co.uk/news/world-south-asia-13982031.

Blumer, H. (1969). *Symbolic interactionism: Perspective and method*. Englewood Cliffs, NJ: Prentice Hall.

Bogdan, R. C., and Biklen, S. K. (2007). *Qualitative research for education: An introduction to theories and methods* (5th edn). Boston: Pearson.

Bogdan, R., Brown, M. A., and Foster, S. (1982). Be honest but not cruel: Staff/parent communication on neonatal units. *Human Organization, 41*, 6–16. doi:10.17730/humo.41.1.03x7x4214201v7p2.

Brandeslaw.com (2016). *Strange laws still on the books.* At http://www.brandeslaw.com/Lighter/lawsob.htm.

Brooks, D., James, S., and Barth, R. P. (2002). Preferred characteristics of children in need of adoption: Is there a demand for available foster children? *Social Service Review, 76*, 575–602. doi:10.1086/342996.

Burgess, E. (1926). The family as a unity of interacting personalities. *The Family*, 7, 3–9.

Cheal, D. (1991). *Family and the state of theory.* Toronto: University of Toronto Press.

Chou, H. T. G., and Edge, N. (2012). "They are happier and having better lives than I am": The impact of using Facebook on perceptions of others' lives. *Cyberpsychology, Behavior, and Social Networking, 15*, 117–121. doi:10.1089/cyber.2011.0324.

Cooley, C. H. (1902). *Human nature and the social order.* New York: Schocken.

Daly, K. J. (2003). Family theories versus the theories families live by. *Journal of Marriage and Family, 65*, 771–784. doi.10.1111/j.1741-3737.2003.00771.x.

Daly, K. J. (2007). *Qualitative methods for family studies and human development.* Los Angeles: Sage.

Droesch, K. (2013, September 29). Wedding traditions from around the world. *Huffington Post.* At www.huffingtonpost.com/2013/09/29/wedding-traditions_n_3964844.html.

Erickson, R. (2005). Why emotion work matters: Sex, gender, and the division of household labor. *Journal of Marriage and Family, 67*, 337–351. doi:10.1111/j.0022-2445.2005.00120.x.

Few, A. L. (2007). Integrating Black consciousness and critical race feminism into family studies research. *Journal of Family Issues, 28*, 452–473. doi:10.1177/0192513X06297330.

Gay, P. (ed.) (1995). *The Freud Reader.* New York: Norton.

Gilgun, J. F. (2013). Qualitative family research: Enduring themes and contemporary variations. In G. W. Peterson and K. R. Bush (eds), *Handbook of marriage and the family* (pp. 91–119). New York: Springer.

Glass, V. Q., and Few-Demo, A. L. (2013). Complexities of informal social support arrangements for Black lesbian couples. *Family Relations, 62,* 714–726. doi:10.1111/fare.12036.

Goffman, E. (1959). *The presentation of self in everyday life.* New York: Doubleday.

Hill, R., and Hansen, D. A. (1960). The identification of conceptual frameworks utilized in family study. *Marriage and Family Living, 22,* 299–311. doi:10.2307/347242.

Hochschild, A. R. (1979). Emotion work, feeling rules, and social structure. *American Journal of Sociology, 85,* 551–575. doi:10.1086/227049.

Hochschild, A. R. (1983). *The managed heart: Commercialization of human feeling.* Berkeley: University of California Press.

Hochschild, A. R., and Ehrenreich, B. (eds) (2003). *Global woman: Nannies, maids, and sex workers in the new economy.* New York: Metropolitan.

hooks, b. (1997). Homeplace (a site of resistance). In D. S. Madison (ed.), *The woman that I am: The literature and culture of contemporary women of color* (pp. 448–454). New York: St. Martin's Press.

Ishizawa, H., and Kubo, K. (2014). Factors affecting adoption decisions: Child and parental characteristics. *Journal of Family Issues, 35,* 627–653. doi:10.1177/0192513X13514408.

Kubo, K. (2010). Desirable difference: The shadow of racial stereotypes in creating transracial families through transnational adoption. *Sociology Compass, 4,* 263–282. doi:10.1111/j.1751-9020.2010.00274.x.

LaRossa, R. (2005). Grounded theory methods and qualitative family research. *Journal of Marriage and Family, 67,* 837–857. doi:10.1111/j.1741-3737.2005.00179.x.

LaRossa, R., and Reitzes, D. C. (1993). Symbolic interactionism and family studies. In P. G. Boss, W. J. Doherty, R. LaRossa, W. R. Schumm, and S. K. Steinmetz (eds), *Sourcebook of family theories and methods: A contextual approach* (pp. 135–163). New York: Plenum.

Lee, R. M. (2003). The transracial adoption paradox: History, research, and counseling implications of cultural socialization. *Counseling Psychologist, 31,* 711–744. doi:10.1177/0011000003258087.

Mead, G. H. (1934). *Mind, self, and society.* Chicago: University of Chicago Press.

Morris, C. W. (ed.) (1962). *Mind, self, and society. Vol. 1 of Works of George Herbert Mead.* Chicago: University of Chicago Press. (Originally published 1934.)

NPR (2013, June 27). *Six words: "Black babies cost less to adopt."* Race Card Project: Six-Word Essays. At http://www.npr.org/2013/06/27/195967886/six-words-black-babies-cost-less-to-adopt.

Parsons, T. (1951). *The social system.* New York: Free Press.

Rosenberg, J., and Egbert, N. (2011). Online impression management: Personality traits and concerns for secondary goals as predictors of self-presentation tactics on Facebook. *Journal of Computer-Mediated Communication, 17,* 1–18. doi:10.1111/j.1083-6101.2011.01560.x.

Smith, S. R., and Hamon, R. R. (2012). *Exploring family theories* (3rd edn). New York: Oxford University Press.

Sokoloff, B. Z. (1993). Antecedents of American adoption. *The Future of Children, 3,* 17–25. doi:10.2307/1602399.

Stryker, S. (1959). Symbolic interaction as an approach to family research. *Marriage and Family Living, 21,* 111–119. doi:10.2307/348099.

Stryker, S. (1964). The interactional and situational approaches. In H. T. Christensen (ed.), *Handbook of marriage and the family* (pp. 125–170). Chicago: Rand McNally.

Stryker, S. (1980). *Symbolic interactionism: A social structural version.* Menlo Park, CA: Benjamin/Cummings.

Swidler, A. (2001). *Talk of love: How culture matters.* Chicago: University of Chicago Press.

Toyota (2010, May 2). *Swagger wagon.* At http://www.youtube.com/watch?v=ql-N3F1FhW4.

5

Family Developmental Theory

Have your family members ever given you a hard time about when you are going to get married? Or, if you're already married, maybe they ask when you are going to have kids. Or, if you already have one child, why don't you have another? Family members, usually older than you, are notorious for trying to push young adults through the family life cycle stages, giving out cautionary advice that always starts with "Wait until you … [fill in the blank]!" Maybe they are trying to tell you what it's like to move from being a couple to being married for three, seven, or even forty years. Young parents are often forewarned of what the transition is like going from two to three children, or from having babies to having teenaged children. Or, maybe even farther down the road, you hear your retired grandparents talking about how wonderful retirement is, and how you need to keep working hard now, so you can enjoy it later! It might be difficult to imagine that far into the future, but given how central the family life cycle is to how we see the world, it should be no surprise that family members who have "been there, done that" are trying to give us advice (wanted or unwanted!) about what to expect.

Family developmental theory considers each of these "stages" as part of the family life cycle, which is the central concept in this theory. Unlike other theories that you may have read about in a psychology or child development class, such as Sigmund Freud's model of psychosexual development (Gay, 1995), Erik Erikson's (1968) eight-stage model of human development, or Jean Piaget's (1952) four-stage model of cognitive development, family developmental theory does not begin with the individual. It begins with the creation of a family – the family of procreation. Because it was first developed in the 1950s, family developmental theory reflected the type of family that scholars envisioned back then: First, a man and a woman marry, then their first child is born and they transition from being a couple to being parents, and then they go through the stages of expanding and contracting their family. The family life cycle begins with a marriage and ends with the death of both spouses. For each stage in the life cycle, there are expectations and developmental tasks assigned to individuals in those stages. Think about the rituals we enact in modern society associated with "entering" these stages of the family life cycle. For example, we give baby showers for mothers-to-be, filled with advice from women who have been through the stage the pregnant woman is about to enter. We usually have an idea of what to expect in each stage (based on the generalized other concept that you read about in Chapter 4 on symbolic interactionism), but for the most part, we learn and develop as we go through the family life cycle.

Given how we've described family developmental theory so far, you may already be noticing that this theory has roots in both functionalist theory (Chapter 2) and symbolic interactionist theory (Chapter 4). This is because family developmental theory is the result of merging the macro-analyses of structural functionalism, the micro-analyses of interactionism, and the element of time. Thus, family developmental theory deals with the structural level (major social institutions), the interactional level (family dynamics and processes), and the individual level (personality

Family Theories: Foundations and Applications, First Edition. Katherine R. Allen and Angela C. Henderson.

variables), as they progress through sequential stages over time (Hill and Rodgers, 1964).

When first proposed, family developmental theory was hailed as the first major conceptual framework with a focus on the family. Specifically, it was created to place marriage and family in the center of how we study and understand the ever evolving nature of family interaction across the life of a family (Hill and Hansen, 1960). At the time when it was first conceptualized, this theory positioned the social group of the nuclear family as the key starting point for theorizing about and studying individual personality, family dynamics, and social institutions as they intersect over time (Mattessich and Hill, 1987). One of the major areas of study that this theory helps scholars understand is how families accomplish the tasks and milestones that are necessary for families to fulfill their normative roles in society at each stage of family life cycle (Aldous, 1978). Further, as the first family theory to factor in a temporal dimension, family developmental theory came before both life course theory (Chapter 9) and family ecological theory (Chapter 10). In order to gain a fuller understanding of how this theory works, we start with a case study that illustrates how members of the same family experience different stages of the family life cycle, and how their interactions with each other contribute to varying developmental outcomes.

Case Study

The subject of our case study, Margo, was very sheltered by her parents, and learned very early to rely on her mother, Karen, for emotional support. Margo was handled with "kid gloves" her entire life; when she married an underemployed drifter, her parents pretended he was a good guy and spent thousands of dollars on a lavish wedding. Their marriage was rocky, to say the least. Margo had to work two jobs to support her husband because he could not hold down a steady job. Because of this, she struggled to find a way to manage her stress and strain. Her mother secretly intervened in Margo's life every step of the way, saving her from declaring bankruptcy, and buying her a home to live in when she and her husband were forced out of their own home. Karen also paid for Margo's moving expenses when she finally filed for divorce from her husband after three years, and moved back home with her parents.

After a few years, Margo moved out of her parents' home, remarried, and she and her new husband gave birth to a son. On the surface, their family appeared happy, healthy, and normal. However, Margo never learned how to cope with anger, frustration, or sadness. She sank into a deep depression after giving birth, and asked Karen to move in with her so that she could help her take care of her newborn son. Having just retired herself, Karen was having a difficult time adjusting to being home with her husband all the time. He was verbally abusive and controlling, making him very unpleasant to be around. Karen loved being needed, and welcomed the distraction of her daughter and grandson as a way to help her avoid her own relationship strain and the uncertainties associated with retirement.

Contrast this family scenario with how we envision love, marriage, and raising children before we enter these family life cycle stages. How is it that what we envision sometimes does not turn out to be true, when we eventually go through certain stages of the life cycle? Further, did Margo go through the appropriate developmental stages at the normative time, or was she protected too much, never learning coping skills or strategies? And how was Karen transmitting values to Margo by avoiding conflict in her own marriage? Family developmental theory helps us understand how families move through developmental stages as they age, beginning with marriage, raising and launching children, having grandchildren, retirement, and death. This theory was developed to specifically analyze families, so it gives great insight into the stages both Margo and her mother have gone through thus far, including the developmental issues encountered along the way. This theory also helps us see how families deal with change, transitions, and timing of events across their lives, and how they affect other family members along the way. Here, we present the concepts of family developmental theory, as well as important theorists who contributed to this perspective, including modern adaptations that make it applicable to today's changing families.

What Is Family Developmental Theory?

Family developmental theory is used to explain the unique functions, processes, and mechanisms for change associated with the family unit. The family unit is unique in that it is the social institution charged with the responsibility of regulating human reproduction, socialization, and survival. As we mentioned earlier, this theory was introduced to study families specifically, which makes it unique when compared to other theories, which were borrowed from other social or psychological sciences and applied to families.

One of the biggest draws of using family developmental theory is that it helps scholars understand how families change over time. Think about your own family and how it has changed since you were a toddler. Think about how you have changed, how your parent(s), siblings, grandparents, and even your extended family have changed! Therefore, one of the most important concepts to consider when using this theory is the concept of **family development**. Family development is a longitudinal process of going through a hierarchical system of age and stage related changes. All families experience a normative process of expansion and contraction throughout the family's history due to a multitude of changes; birth, death, marriage, divorce, graduation, retirement, or any other developmental milestone. Family development can also involve a family crisis, like the one Margo from our case study experienced when she divorced her first husband and needed to move back home to reestablish financial and emotional security. Family crises will be discussed in more detail in Chapter 11 when we introduce family stress and resilience theory, but for now it is important to know that crises can and do often propel the family unit into the next phase of development. Traditionally, however, families have been defined as progressing through approximately eight stages that are marked by different family configurations, roles, relationships, and tasks. Because the family unit is a unique structure in society, all families are obligated to perform common functions. Thus, there is a normative structure to families that is generally comparative across all families.

Given that this theory was developed to specifically analyze families, it assumes that "the typical family" is defined as a nuclear or conjugal unit that begins with the wedding of two young adults and continues until the death of the last spouse. This theory also suggests that each family begins the **family life cycle** with marriage, which signals the start of a new **family of procreation**, when partners start a new family of their own. Moving into the stage of procreation propels the family forward to new roles associated with parenthood. Then, once children leave the family nest, the family contracts back to the married couple. The family created by the original married partners ends when both of them die.

Family developmental theory argues that moving through these **family stages** is predictable across all families. Yet, because society has changed significantly since this theory was developed, the nature of families as the unit for carrying out the reproductive function has changed as well. Scholars have altered the original concepts to include variations linked to additional aspects of marriage and parenthood. For example, not all family life cycles begin with the first stage of marriage. Some families form when one person has a child and is not married to the child's other parent. In another example, not all marriages end with the death of the spouses. Some families experience divorce, become a single-parent family, and thus end with the death of the remaining parent (Hill, 1986). And, not all families are limited to the nuclear unit. Families may be headed by intergenerational adults, as in families headed by a grandmother and a mother (Burton, 1996; Nelson, 2006). Some families also incorporate the sibling relationship as part of the family cycle (Aldous, 1978). Still other families are headed by one or more lesbian or gay parent (Goldberg, 2010). Thus, what began as the family life cycle concept of normative stages of marriage and parenthood, has evolved to accommodate variations in family roles and processes (Glick, 1947; 1988).

History and origins

As we have pointed out throughout this book, it is important to examine the historical context in which a theory was developed in order to fully understand how the theory was originally meant to be applied.

Family developmental theory was developed in the mid-twentieth century specifically for studying families' unique structural and dynamic qualities as a social group. As noted above, family developmental theory borrowed from functionalist theory (Chapter 2) and symbolic interactionist theory (Chapter 4) and added the concept of multiple dimensions of time, which are individual time, social process time, and historical time (Rodgers, 1973). By borrowing from functionalist theory, the family developmental approach incorporated structural concepts such as **position** (i.e., the location of a family member in the family system), role (i.e., the dynamic aspect of a position), and **norms** (i.e., societal expectations). By borrowing from symbolic interactionist theory, the developmental approach incorporated Burgess's (1926) concept of the family as a unity of interacting personalities.

In addition, family developmental theory borrowed the concept of **ontogenic change** from individual theories of human development (e.g., Erikson and Piaget) in order to explain how growth occurs through hierarchical stages (Bengtson and Allen, 1993). Ontogenic change refers to how an organism – in this case, a family and/or individual family members – changes and matures over time. Since the day you were born, you have gone through several stages of development that are necessary for maturation; your caregivers taught you how to walk and talk, and you were potty trained. You went through puberty and adolescence, and now are likely to be in the stage of young adulthood or older. Families, by definition, are supposed to contain necessary elements that assist in moving their members through these changes, with one stage building upon the previous stage. One of the things that makes this theory unique is its emphasis on how the *family* is the guiding force behind moving members through these changes; no other social institution can perform these same tasks. Think about your own life; you likely did not go to preschool to learn what it means to love your family. You learned what family means and what roles certain family members play by watching, and modeling, your own family members.

Because of families' unique characteristics, as a social institution, families are supposed to be pre-programmed to develop through stages that typically correspond to the age structure of parents and children over time. At each stage of the family life cycle, families are destined to perform unique developmental tasks associated with sexuality, reproduction, caregiving, and intimacy that no other system in the social structure can do.

Given that family developmental theory was conceptualized using the twentieth-century nuclear, heteronormative, and pronatalist family unit as the model for its stages, a strong debate has emerged on the relevance of this theory to explain family growth and change in the face of major demographic and historical shifts. As a result, the life course perspective (see Chapter 9) emerged as a new paradigm to liberate the family life cycle from the gridlock of rigid stages and roles and to take into account the dynamic interplay among individual, family, and sociohistorical time (Bengtson and Allen, 1993; Rodgers and White, 1993). Further, James White and David Klein (2008) have updated the work of earlier family developmental theorists and combined their ideas with the life course approach. White and Klein's family life course development framework is a modern adaption and update of the three original perspectives that went into making family developmental theory: the individual life span, family process and structure, and social-historical context. Most recently, the White and Klein model has been again revised, as we note later in this chapter.

Assumptions of family developmental theory

You may already be picking up on some of the assumptions of this theory, but let's take a closer look at how the earliest framers of family developmental theory (e.g., Duvall, 1957; Hill and Hansen, 1960; Hill and Rodgers, 1964; Rowe, 1966) have identified the taken-for-granted assumptions of this theory. Aldous (1978) succinctly consolidated these ideas into five underlying assumptions. The first assumption is that "family behavior is the sum of past experience of family members as incorporated in the present as well as in their goals and expectations for the future" (Aldous, 1978, p. 15). This means that understanding a family's history is important to be able to understand current and future behavior. Think about Margo from our case study – based on how she was raised, it should be no surprise that her mother would do whatever it takes

Box 5.1 At a Glance: Family Developmental Theory

Family development The family is a social group in which growth occurs through the unfolding of predictable stages.

Family life cycle Families progress through a series of normative stages that begin with marriage, expand with adding children, contract with launching children, and end with the death of both spouses.

Family stage Families can best be studied by dividing up the structural changes in marriage and parenthood into model segments that all families experience.

Family time Families are long-lived groups with a history that incorporates three elements: individual time, social process time, and historical time.

Family developmental tasks Society assigns certain activities, or tasks, which families are expected to perform in order to ensure the survival of the family unit and the socialization of its members.

Societal-institutional dimension The family is charged with the responsibility of regulating reproductive roles of marriage and parenthood. As one of the key social institutions, families are influenced by broader cultural values and goals that dictate what is normal and valued.

Group-interactional dimension Families are a semi-closed system of interaction, where each individual family unit varies in the ways in which it enacts the societal-institutional expectations for family life.

Individual-psychological dimension The individual is the basic unit of the family, and each individual has a unique genetic makeup and unique family roles.

to step in and rescue her from experiencing both the ups *and* downs of adult life. Her mother sheltered her during childhood, and continues to do so even as an adult.

The second assumption builds off of this idea, and posits that "families develop and change over time in similar and consistent ways" (Aldous, 1978, p. 15). This assumption presumes that family behavior and change are fairly predictable by stage and age structure. Therefore, all new parents, regardless of their circumstances, can expect to go through a major transition period when the family composition changes from two to three members. Becoming parents is a predictable pattern in the life of a family, and will be experienced in similar ways across all families. That's why expectant parents are warned about "never getting a full night's sleep again!" after a baby is born. Indeed, this is one of the reasons that pregnancy preparation books and parenting advice are so popular: people want to know how others got through similar life cycle stages without pulling their hair out!

The third assumption is that "humans not only initiate actions as they mature and interact with others but also they react to environmental pressures" (Aldous, 1978, p. 15). This means that human beings both shape and are shaped by the behavior of other family members as well as by the broader social system. Families are interdependent units – they must accommodate the individual needs of members as well as the norms and expectations of society. An example of the third assumption is what happens when a child "fails to launch." In contemporary society, young adults' transition from the family home to their own independent lives can be compromised by the lack of guaranteed and plentiful employment opportunities (Arnett, 2000). Although many young adults now go to college, they may have to move back home for a time until they can find secure employment. The family must readjust to economic realities, and make room once again for their adult children in the home. Another example of this can be seen in the recent extension of US health insurance laws, where parents may now carry their adult children on their policies until the child is 26.

The fourth assumption is that "the family and its members must perform certain time-specific tasks set by themselves and by persons in the broader society" (Aldous, 1978, p. 15). This assumption refers to the concept of individual and **family developmental tasks** that are associated with each time of life. An individual and a family unit have normative goals that they must accomplish in order to move forward to the next level of development. According to Aldous (1978), a developmental task requires coming to terms with reality, or taking responsibility for work life, family life, community life, and the like. Have you ever heard someone joke about "you know you're an adult when …!"? Examples could range from "you get excited about getting a vacuum as a gift" or "you spend your Saturdays at Home Depot." These examples illustrate how with each new stage in the life cycle, we fulfill roles and engage in behavior that can be vastly different from the preceding life cycle stage. Your "ideal Saturday night" in your twenties probably looks pretty different when compared to your thirties or forties. Therefore, as we age and move through life cycle stages, our developmental tasks change, and we adapt accordingly. This is necessary for individual fulfillment, family functioning, and societal well-being.

Finally, Aldous's fifth assumption is that "in a social setting, the individual is the basic autonomous unit" (1978, p. 15). This assumption means that the family system as a whole is dependent on the actions and reactions of its *individual* members. An example of the fifth assumption is when a stay-at-home parent decides to get a job outside the home; all of the individuals in the whole family system must make adjustments in response to the actions of one member. Teenage children will no doubt have new chores to do, the other parent may have to take on more housework or spend less time on the job, and caring for aging parents may become more difficult and stressful. Families are systems in which the individual members are interdependent. What happens to one person has implications for the others.

Key concepts

Family developmental theory offers a wealth of concepts that are appealing to multiple audiences and easy to apply in education and practice. Many of the concepts derived from family developmental theory have become part of our everyday language, so we often just assume we know their meaning. This is also the case with concepts from other theories we describe in this book. For example, in Chapter 4, we pointed out that the concept of "significant other," taken from symbolic interactionist theory, has become a common phrase that you hear everyday. And in Chapter 2 regarding functionalist theory, we described the concepts of "instrumental and expressive roles" that are gender related. These concepts, too, have entered the popular vernacular. Similarly, as you read on in this chapter, you will discover that concepts derived from family developmental theory are also part of our common vocabulary.

The family life cycle This concept is the most enduring contribution of family developmental theory, because it offers a way to logically segment the shared experiences in families as they progress over time. Embedded in this concept are the normative stages associated with the initiation, expansion, contraction, and dissolution of a marriage. Marriages are expanded with the addition of children, and as the children leave home, families contract. Marriage ends with the death of the first spouse, and the family life cycle dissolves upon the death of the second spouse. This concept provides an index of how roles are allocated in families over time. According to Mattessich and Hill (1987), there are three key components – persons, roles, and role patterns – of family structural organization that appear and disappear over the life cycle of a family of procreation. "Persons" refer to individuals who enter or leave the family life cycle through transitions such as birth, marriage, launching, and death. "Roles" refer to the family activities associated with each family position that must be enacted. "Patterns of roles" are interactive or transactive behavior which are "adjusted to meet the changing demands of family members and society, in accordance with the resources available to the family at any point in its career" (Mattessich and Hill, 1987, p. 443).

The family life cycle, as originally proposed by Evelyn Duvall (1957), consists of eight stages. Family stages are determined by the number of roles/positions in the family (e.g., Stage 1 and Stage 7 consist only of the married couple), and by the age and role of the oldest child (e.g., Stages 2 to 5). Figure 5.1 depicts the original normative model of the eight stages.

Here, we describe each of the stages, role positions, and family goals (i.e., developmental tasks) that are

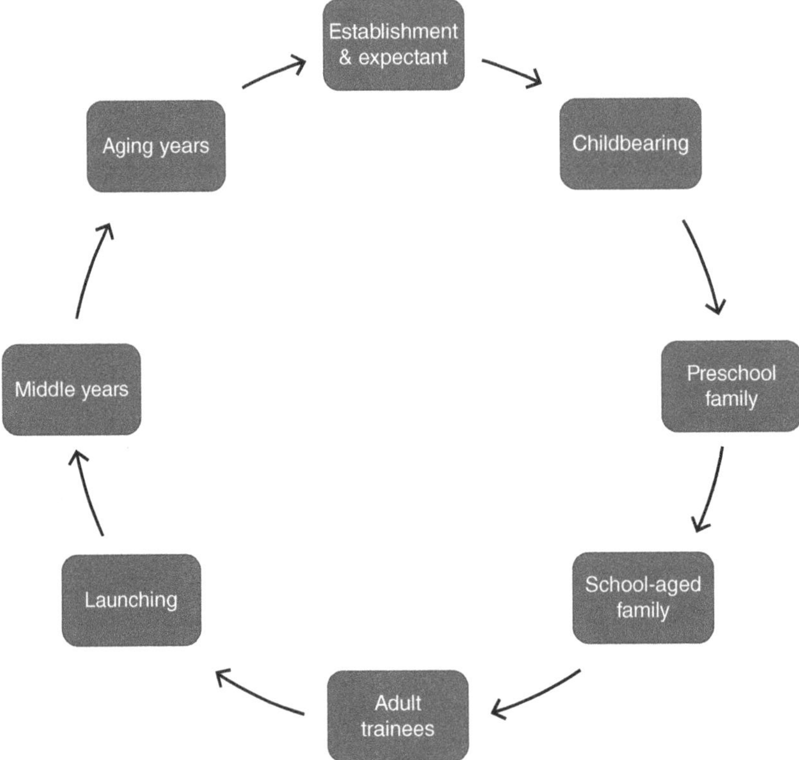

Figure 5.1 The normative family life cycle

associated with each phase of the family life cycle as originally conceptualized (Hill and Rodgers, 1964).

Stage 1, Establishment and expectant, starts the family life cycle with the marriage of a man and a woman, both of whom are conceptualized as young adults. In this stage, there are only two members in the family, and they fulfill the traditional roles of husband and wife. This stage lasts about one year. The primary task of this stage is for the young couple to adjust to living as a married pair. As they adjust to marriage, the wife becomes pregnant and the couple must adjust to pregnancy and planning for the transition to parenthood when they will add a child to their family constellation.

Stage 2, Childbearing, changes the family structure from that of a husband and a wife to the parental roles of mother and father, and adds the third role of child. This stage lasts about two years. The developmental task of Stage 2 is to reorganize the family unit around the needs of infants and begin to add additional children to the family.

Stage 3, Preschool family, includes the husband/father, wife/mother, son/brother, and daughter/sister, in various combinations, depending on the number and gender of the children born. Stage 3 lasts about four years. The developmental tasks of Stage 3 continue with the family reorganizing around the needs of infants and now preschool children.

Stage 4, School-aged family, is identified as a stage that lasts about seven years. It consists of the parents, and approximately three children. Note that three children was the average number of children per family in the 1950s and 1960s (Glick, 1988). These children probably range in age from very young to preadolescent. The developmental task of this stage is the reorganization of the family to fit into the expanding world of school-aged children.

Stage 5, Adult trainees, now includes the parents and up to four of their children, where the oldest child is a teenager, and the youngest child is a preadolescent. This stage lasts about seven years, and the developmental tasks include allowing the children to have greater freedom in terms of taking on responsibility for their own lives.

Stage 6, Young adult launching, now adds a third generation: grandparents. By this stage, young adult children marry and start their own nuclear families, and their parents become grandparents. The developmental tasks of Stage 6 include parents returning to a more egalitarian relationship now that their children are launched (note that the assumption of traditional gender roles was very evident in the original statement of this theory). This stage lasts about eight years.

Stage 7, Middle years, returns the family life cycle to just two members, the postparental older adults. Here, the family consists of a husband/grandfather and a wife/grandmother. This stage lasts about 14 years. The family has now reorganized around the marital pair. As parents disengage from their roles as caregivers for dependent children, and enter into the last half of life, they may experience loneliness and even a crisis of meaning. This has been referred to as "the empty nest syndrome" though currently, it is associated with an adjustment phase instead of a problem. The major developmental task of Stage 7, then, is for the married couple to reengage in new social roles that bring meaning and fulfillment, in the absence of caring for and supporting children.

Stage 8, Aging years, takes the married couple up to the loss of one, then both, spouses. This stage lasts anywhere from 7 to 13 years. It is important to note that when Hill and Rodgers (1964) first conceptualized this stage of the family life cycle, the average life expectancies for men (age 74) and for women (age 77) were much younger than they are today in most developed countries. Indeed, the average life expectancy at birth in Japan in 2013 was 80 for men and 87 for women; in the United States in 2012, it was 76 for men and 81 for women (WHO, 2016). The major developmental tasks of this stage are for adjusting to a narrower type of life, and then adjusting to widowhood. Younger generations must also cope with the death of the oldest generation, once their family life cycle ends.

It should be obvious by now that the original model of the family life cycle needed to be revised and updated as scholars recognized that it was idealizing only one type of family: the marriage of two heterosexual parents and their own children. In fact, one of the originators of the theory, Reuben Hill (1986), recognized that many families only include one parent, and he provided an updated model of the family headed by a single parent.

Another major revision of the family life cycle concept addressed the increasingly common stepfamily form. As Stewart explained (2007, p. 48), Papernow's (1993) adaptation of the family life cycle to "the stepfamily cycle" provides a very concrete model for educators, therapists, and other professionals in their work guiding stepfamilies through the reconstitution phase of family life. Papernow proposed three stages of the life cycle and seven components. In the early stage, stepparents must address the developmental tasks of "fantasy," "immersion," and "awareness." In the middle stage, the developmental tasks are "mobilization and "action." Finally, in the later stage, stepparents and stepchildren experience the developmental tasks of "contact" and "resolution." Papernow's stepfamily life cycle model builds upon the normative model of the family life cycle by taking a longitudinal perspective and segmenting critical transitions into stages. On the other hand, Papernow's model recognizes far more conflict and difficulty among family members than the more rosy view of family development characterized in the original model. This more realistic view of the inevitability of conflict and the need for its resolution in the family (as discussed in Chapter 3) suggests a departure from the original structural-functional roots (Chapter 2) of family development theory that make it less relevant to contemporary families.

Family developmental tasks For each stage of the life cycle, there are major goals that family members must accomplish. Rodgers defined a developmental task as:

> A set of norms (role expectations) arising at a particular point in the career of a position in a social system [e.g., father], which, if incorporated by the occupant of the position as a role or part of a role cluster, brings about integration and temporary equilibrium in the system. (1973, p. 51)

As an example, there are several tasks that accompany the life cycle stage of adolescence:

> (a) The alteration of the parent–adolescent relationship in order to allow the adolescent to move more freely out of and back into the family environs; (b) a renewed focus on marital issues and parental career interests; and (c) taking on a greater role in caregiving for older family members. (Gavazzi, 2013, p. 306)

Developmental tasks must be accomplished in an orderly fashion in order for the family to successfully reorganize to the next level of family structure and interaction. Failure to accomplish these normative goals at each stage in the life cycle can lead to individual unhappiness, family stress, disapproval by society, and difficulty in accomplishing the goals of future stages (Havighurst, 1972 [1948]).

Family developmental tasks have many features. First, there are developmental tasks associated with each one of the family life cycle stages, and family members are simultaneously at different stages of development when they are required to meet them. In Gavazzi's (2013) example of families with adolescents, the adolescent's developmental tasks include becoming independent from his or her parents, but the parents' developmental tasks include an increasing focus on caring for aging parents. Accomplishing developmental tasks can be very complex, especially when there are multiple family members. Imagine the developmental tasks associated with adjusting to marriage that involve only two people, compared to adjusting to having adolescents in a family.

Second, there are more general developmental tasks that are ever changing and span the entire family life cycle (Rowe, 1966). Duvall (1957) described these as the need to establish and maintain: (a) an independent home; (b) satisfactory ways of getting and spending money; (c) mutually acceptable patterns in the division of labor; (d) continuity of mutually satisfying sex relationships; (e) open system of intellectual and emotional communication; (f) workable relationships with relatives; (g) ways of interacting with associates and community organizations; (h) competency in bearing and rearing children; and (i) a workable philosophy of life. Chances are you have not spent a lot of time thinking about each of these tasks unless you have had to address them firsthand in the midst of a relationship. It would be interesting to see how your list of developmental tasks would change from age 20, to age 30, 40, 50, and beyond. What kind of sex life do you expect to maintain, as a 20-year-old thinking forward to marriage? What types of household tasks did you have to do growing up, compared to what your spouse/partner will expect of you if and when you marry or cohabitate? You might be surprised if you wrote down your developmental tasks for the stage you are in, and the stages you will enter, and observe how they might stay the same or change over time.

It is important to note that the accomplishment of developmental tasks is more of an ideal than a reality (Rowe, 1966). Family members have rarely "caught up" with themselves and with the normative expectations. Some developmental tasks inevitably carry over to the next stage, as we have seen in the example of young adults' "failure" to launch and become completely independent of their parents' financial support. Although developmental tasks are essential features of how families change and grow, they are not an "all or nothing" proposition. For example, do you ever completely transition to adulthood or adjust to the loss of a loved one? Perhaps it is better to think of developmental tasks as guideposts, rather than endpoints. Still, as normative expectations, we can all identify what we are "supposed" to do. We are supposed to get a high school diploma, a job, a spouse, children, our own home, and so on. The order in which we do these things and the people we do them with, however, are much more variable than the developmental task concept implies.

Family career Several scholars have expanded the concept of the family life cycle to include the **family career**. Rodgers defined the family career as "the most general statement of the dynamics of the family over time" (1973, p. 19). This concept allows us to concurrently examine the life of the family as a social group that includes individual members, the family as a whole system, and the family in transaction with the broader society. Aldous (1978), however, suggested that the concepts of family career and family life cycle are synonymous.

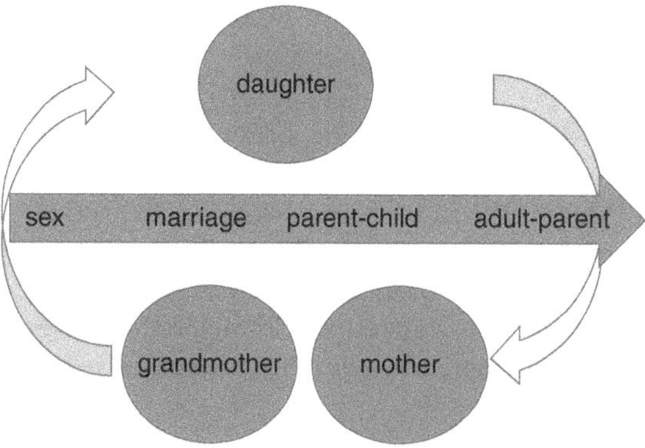

Figure 5.2 The lifetime family and the lineage family

In one of the most important revisions of the family life cycle concept, Harold and Margaret Feldman, a husband and wife team of family scholars, addressed some of the critiques of family developmental theory. They proposed a new schema for "recycling" it. Feldman and Feldman (1975) proposed that there are actually two types of family "histories" (see Figure 5.2). The first is the lifetime family, or the family of ego, which consists of four subcareers: the sex experience career, the marital career, the parent–child career, and the adult–parent career. Although "ego" (i.e., a person) can be in several of these careers simultaneously, the person's family career is linear and spans his or her lifetime. The other concept offered for "recycling" the family life cycle idea is the lineage family, which lasts through time over generations.

The lineage family is actually cyclical, in that at any given time, there is a different role occupant in each position of the family, but the same positions always exist, no matter who fills them. Thus, in our case study, Margo has been in the position of child and mother. Karen has occupied the same positions, with the addition of grandmother, though at different points in time. The two dimensions of lifetime family and lineage family allow us to understand families from the perspective of those who do marry and have children, and those who do not. For example, a woman will be a daughter throughout her life but may not be a wife, mother, and grandmother (Allen and Pickett, 1987).

Evaluating Family Developmental Theory

Strengths of family developmental theory

Like all of the theories we describe in this book, family developmental theory has both strengths and weaknesses. Family developmental theory is the first of its kind to be created by scholars with a unique focus on families, and it is the first to integrate multiple conceptions of time. This theory also integrates both micro- and macro-perspectives. Further, family developmental theory captures the popular imagination, given the fact that it is the human condition to be born, develop, and eventually die. Many of its concepts, including family life cycle and family developmental tasks, are common in our everyday language and shared understanding of families.

Incorporation of time A very important contribution of family developmental theory has been the conceptualization of families through the perspective of time. This is the first theory to analyze family process and structure through the dimension of time. This allows researchers to measure family dynamics and structural shifts in roles, positions, and norms at both short-term (e.g., cross-sectional) and long-term (e.g., longitudinal and historical) levels. By taking time into account, family change can be measured within each stage and across the stages that comprise the entire life cycle of the family. The perspective of time helps researchers understand the immediate impact of having a baby on a marriage, as well as the long-term consequences of raising children to adulthood and launching them out into the world.

Universal framework for understanding the family life cycle The family life cycle concept is an idea that we see in all aspects of popular society. Shakespeare wrote about "the wheel has come full circle" in the play *King Lear*. The biblical passage in *Ecclesiastes* 3:1–2 reminds us: "To every thing there is a season, and a time to every purpose under the heaven: A time to be born, and a time to die" (King James Bible). In the late 1950s, folk singer Pete Seeger put the Ecclesiastes passage to music in the song "Turn! Turn! Turn! (To everything there is a season)," and this song has been covered by

Box 5.2 Family Developmental Theory in Pop Culture: *The Lion King*

A scene from *The Lion King*, 1994, dir. Roger Allers and Rob Minkoff, Walt Disney Pictures

The Lion King, released in 1994, is an animated Disney movie centered on the lion family of King Mufasa, Queen Sarabi, and their newborn male cub, Simba. This film has several examples of family developmental theory throughout the story. As male heir, Simba is now destined to inherit the throne from his father, which makes Mufasa's brother, Scar, incredibly jealous. Scar goes on a mission to destroy both Simba and Mufasa because of this, which demonstrates his difficulty in dealing with the expectations of "middle age." Having never started a family of his own, we cannot analyze Scar's movement through the family life cycle as a father, but we can see how he covets power because of the norms associated with the development of a family. He most likely resents the norms associated with inheritance, because if Mufasa (assumed to be the eldest male) had not started a family of his own, Scar would have inherited the throne when Mufasa died. However, because of the norms associated with royalty and inheritance, it is assumed that Mufasa had to select a mate and procreate in order to keep the throne in his family line.

One of the most famous songs from this film, *Circle of Life*, illustrates family developmental theory as well. The song, with lyrics written by Tim Rice and music composed by Elton John, describes moving through the circle of life, as depicted in this stanza:

> In the circle of life, it's the wheel of fortune
> It's the leap of faith, it's the band of hope
> Till we find our place on the path unwinding
> In the circle, the circle of life.

These lyrics allude to the various phases of the life cycle, including both happy and sad times. It accompanies the part of the film when Mufasa is giving Simba a tour of the Pride Lands, teaching him the responsibilities that come with inheriting the animal kingdom and becoming a leader. While human families do not typically train children to inherit wealth, property, or prestige until much later in life, the analogy of moving through family life cycle stages is still relevant.

Related to that, we can see examples of the various generations in this film, as Simba and Nala are the replacement generation for Mufasa and Sarabi. After Mufasa dies in a stampede orchestrated by Scar, Simba and Nala become the king and queen, and have a lion cub themselves. The film ends with the pride's elder, Rafiki, holding up the baby cub to all the lions in the pride below and everyone sings the *Circle of Life*.

many bands ever since, from the Byrds to U2. The cycle concept was also popularized in the television program *The Wonder Years*, and spoofed in an episode of *The Simpsons*.

Thus, the family life cycle concept has broad appeal because it is intuitively helpful in characterizing the fact that we are born, we couple, we reproduce, we change, and we die. We do this not simply as individuals, but as individuals who associate with others and help one another fulfill the mandates of society. The family life cycle concept is so engrained in the very fabric of society, including religion, myth, literature, economics, politics, and education, that it provides a useful model for communication. Try to think of a context in which the family is not the major institution to accomplish the developmental task of raising children to a healthy adulthood. There are only rare exceptions to this idea, and even then, the thought of them is discordant to how we are taught, throughout the world, to partner and raise our children.

Applicable to family life education Family developmental theory is one of the most effective conceptual frameworks for applying concepts to family life education. This theory is the basis for community programs designed to help families accomplish the developmental tasks associated with the family life cycle. Programs include marriage preparation classes, marriage enrichment classes for mid-life married couples, support groups for new mothers and their babies, transitioning to retirement for older family members, and dealing with loss and bereavement. Rather than taking an individualistic approach that is common in psychotherapy, family life education focuses on the family as the target of support and change (Mattessich and Hill, 1987). For example, a family life educator assigned to Margo's case would identify stages in the life cycle where Margo or her mother need to still work on accomplishing the appropriate developmental tasks. Instead of leaning so heavily on her mother for rescue, should Margo instead try to push her own boundaries of development and work together with her new husband to grow stronger as a couple and parents? A family life educator could suggest several routes for Margo and her mother to take in order to get their families back on track developmentally.

Weaknesses of family developmental theory

Despite its strengths, family developmental theory also has several weaknesses. Although many scholars have updated the theory, it is still critiqued for oversimplifying the conceptualization of family stages, ages, and cycles. On balance, however, family developmental theory has been incorporated into other theories and in that sense, it still remains relevant today. Next we consider the primary weaknesses of this perspective.

Too static Family developmental theory was very useful in the early years of merging individual psychosocial theories with family roles and careers. However, it soon became apparent that the equating of family roles with static positions did not allow scholars to consider family diversity and variation. By static, we mean that the theory put too much emphasis on the actual "faces" of the occupants of normative roles by characterizing unchanging definitions of the positions of husband/wife; father/mother; child/sibling. As we have noted throughout this book, however, families come in a wide variety of forms, and family members do not necessarily have to be related by blood or marriage. Because of the many ways that families are organized and change over time, both within and across societies, the original static proposal of common stages, roles, and positions gave way to the individual variations that can be captured by a life course perspective. Although family developmental theory has continued to evolve in order to accommodate the criticisms, the main result is that family developmental theory has been overshadowed by life course theory (Chapter 9) or by a combination of the individual life course and the family cycle models, as shown in White, Klein, and Martin's recent revision of the approach entitled "The life course developmental framework" (2015, ch. 5).

More conceptually useful than empirically useful In a critique of the family life cycle concept, Nock (1979) assessed the usefulness of family developmental theory as stronger in terms of identifying concepts, than in actually operationalizing those concepts in research. The family life cycle concept has wide popular appeal as a metaphor for the stages of birth, life, and death that all humans, indeed all living things, experience. Yet, it is very hard to measure a stage, let alone measure it in terms of the age span of its occupants. How do we compare families in the "preschool age" stage when there is so much variation across family types and sizes? Further, the cross-cultural comparisons are very difficult, depending on demographic factors such as the average life span, the birthrate, the interactions across the generations, among others, that occur within and between different societies. With an endless supply of variation, you can see that although the concept is intuitively appealing, utilizing it in scientific research is quite a challenge.

Ignores family problems Another major critique of family developmental theory is that it ignores some of the most problematic aspects of family life. The theory assumes that families will adjust positively to the major events and transitions of the family life cycle (Cheal, 1991). After all, these events and transitions are normative and expected. But what about the all too common problems that occur in families due to violence, substance abuse, job loss, and the like? The theory cannot adequately address these issues because, like functionalist theory (Chapter 2), it defines them as deviant and abnormal. A related issue is that this theory assumes that families proceed through the life cycle in an orderly manner, and that they adhere to a socially structured time frame. But, family events and transitions do not occur at the same time and in the same order for everyone. Parents are not always in their early twenties when they have their first child. Many families may never experience an "empty nest" because it is increasingly common for adult children to not leave home. In the case of childlessness, some family roles and transitions are never experienced. However, the theory promotes the idea that families develop on the same schedule, that they complete each stage of the family life cycle, and that they accomplish their developmental tasks in a mostly positive manner.

An alternative theory app: feminist theory

In this chapter, we have presented the key concepts, origins and background, and modern applications as well as the strengths and weaknesses of family developmental theory. In earlier chapters, we have mostly compared theories that have had both similarities as well as differences. In this chapter, however, we take a different approach. Family developmental theory and feminist theory (Chapter 8) definitely have more differences than similarities, as we outline next.

To start, consider your own desires and dreams about family. Do you want to get married, or have children? Do you think every one of your classmates has the same dreams and desires? Feminist theory contrasts sharply with family developmental theory in that it does not assume that all individuals want the same things in life. Some women and men do not want to marry, or have children, or perhaps they want to cohabit or even have children as single parents. These models do not "fit" into the framework of family developmental theory, because they do not fit into the linear stages of the family life cycle. The heart of feminist theory is the emphasis on differences, whether they emerge out of socially constructed ideas about gender or intersections of race, class, gender, and other systems of privilege and oppression. Not all individuals *want* the same things in life, and even more important is the fact that not everyone has *equal access* to the same goals and dreams. Feminist theory emphasizes each of these factors in turn in Chapter 8.

Working with Family Developmental Theory: Integrating Research and Practice

Now that we have defined family developmental theory, described the historical origins and key concepts, and pointed out its strengths and weaknesses, we turn to how the theory can be used in practice. We provide an example of current theorizing, analyze an empirical study that was guided by family developmental theory, and describe how the theory informs the practice of family policy.

Family developmental theory today

Many contemporary family scholars have provided alternative models to the family life cycle concept. One area in which such alternative theorizing has occurred is in the family therapy field. Notably, Monica McGoldrick and her colleagues (McGoldrick, Carter, and Garcia-Preto, 2011; McGoldrick and Hardy, 2008) have provided a corrective to the ways that the original version of the family life cycle reflects the standard nuclear family arrangement, and thus minimizes and ignores differences in family experience by race, class, gender, sexual orientation, ethnicity, and religion. Their recent work in expanding the family life cycle is much more inclusive of the diverse ways individuals experience families, including family households, communities, and cultural groups.

Also a family therapist, Suzanne Slater (1999) revised the family life cycle concept and applied it to the lesbian couple's family experience. She proposed that there are five stages in the lesbian family life cycle that couples go through, and that these stages are predictable and normative for lesbian couples. Like the traditional family life cycle concept, Slater's model takes a positive view of her subjects' experiences. She suggests that the lesbian family life cycle model is a way to help lesbian partners positively reframe their efforts to live and thrive in a homophobic society. The lesbian family life cycle model is aimed at helping women understand that the transitions they are experiencing as they age are not deviant or unique, but rather common to other lesbian families. This positive reframe has the goal of helping lesbians sustain a successful lesbian family life.

In Slater's (1999) scheme, the first stage of the lesbian family life cycle is "the formation of the couple." In this stage, the women must adjust to the disruption in their lives caused by the emotional and sexual excitement of a new partnership. The second stage is "ongoing couplehood." At this point, the couple is creating their own rituals and patterns as they become comfortable with one another. The third stage is "the middle years." This is the time when the women make a commitment to one another and start to make plans for their future. The fourth stage is "generativity," in which partners become aware of their own mortality. Typically, by mid-life, women who have lived with the social prejudices of homophobia and heterosexism have come to the generativity stage earlier than others. The final stage is "lesbian couples over sixty-five." Although many lesbian couples have weathered the storm of multiple layers of prejudice, old age is a time of dealing with the accumulation of stresses associated with being an older lesbian.

Criticisms of Slater's model include that it presents only a positive perspective on lesbian couple family life, and it focuses on White, middle-class lesbians in committed relationships, thus mirroring the heterosexist notions of families (Lev and Sennott, 2013). In spite of these drawbacks, Slater's model has also been hailed as an important step in updating the family life cycle concept to more realistically reflect diverse family structures.

Family developmental theory in research

John Davies and Douglas Gentile (2012) utilized a family developmental perspective to examine media use and effects in their study of families consisting of one child, as compared to families consisting of several children. They address the impact on families of living in a media-saturated environment. They cite research on family media habits, and note that children use, on average, 7.5 hours of media a day, with media use measured by screen time (e.g., television, movies, video games, and computers). It is interesting to note that these figures do not include the amount of media use per day in school, or in using a cell phone. Thus, children spend more than half of their waking hours in "screen time." Parental monitoring of children's media time use also varies by child age. Young children (approximately three to five years old) watch more educational programming than school-aged children (approximately 6 to 12 years old). By the time children are in elementary school, they are spending more time with their peers than their parents, typically on video-gaming devices in their bedrooms.

Building upon Duvall's (1957) eight-stage model of family developmental theory, Davies and Gentile (2012) selected the three stages in the family life cycle that include children: (a) families with preschool children, ages 2 to 6 years, (b) families with school-age children, ages 6 to 13 years, and (c) families with adolescent children, ages 13 to 20 years. Importantly, the authors updated the social context in which families develop to include the technological revolution that has taken over in families. The major research question they asked was how the media habits of families differ according to the three family developmental stages with children. They were especially interested in the influence that siblings have on children's media use. They wanted to know in what ways it might matter if children viewed television with a sibling or a parent. To test their hypotheses, they used two independent samples: (a) a nationally representative sample consisting of 527 parents with children living at home and between the ages of 2 and 17; and (b) a convenience sample consisting of 1,257 families who attended a MediaWise parent education program created by the National Institute on Media and the Family.

As expected, the authors found that families with adolescent children had less healthy media viewing habits than families with younger children. Parents of teenagers provided significantly less monitoring of their children's media use, reported that their teens were participating in fewer alternatives to screen time than younger children, and that they themselves were less consistent about enforcing family rules that restricted media use. The authors interpreted these findings in light of family developmental theory: They suggested that what counts as normative media use has escalated in our media-saturated society today. Media use now peaks in the adolescent years. Because parents have come to expect that their adolescents will engage in less healthy media habits, they have relaxed their standards for controlling their children's access. The importance of siblings for media use was more equivocal. On the one hand, families with siblings showed more healthy media habits than families with only children. On the other hand, having only one child tends to make parents more anxious about that child, and thus motivates them to develop positive interactions that will foster healthier media habits. What is interesting to consider here is how this issue would differ depending on the cultural context; how do children in developing countries experience the media? Are parents socialized to be aware of and care about media consumption in all countries and cultures around the world? As a family theorist, it's important to take these global considerations into account.

Family developmental theory in practice

There are several ways in which educators, practitioners, and family policy makers can apply family developmental theory in their work with individuals and families. One of the most important places where this theory can be applied is in working with young adults who are making decisions about reproduction and family.

You may be familiar with the phrase "childless by choice" – it represents a fairly recent movement among men and women who reject the pronatalist ideology that values childbearing. In fact, the media has featured young women's stories of frustration with being counseled out of and even denied sterilization procedures by their medical providers, because they are too young (Pearson, 2014). Given that family developmental theory outlines childbearing as a natural and essential stage of the family life cycle, it is important to consider the potential challenges this might create for individuals who do not want to have children. This issue is particularly salient for women who prefer to be childless, because their options for permanent sterilization are limited until they reach a certain age. The official stance of the American College of Obstetricians and Gynecologists (ACOG) is that "women who have completed their childbearing are candidates for sterilization" (Pearson, 2014). Each provider may interpret this statement differently: Does it mean that women have to have had a child to be eligible? Or does it mean women have to be over age 35 to be considered eligible? As a practitioner, you may very well confront this issue as perhaps a nurse, family life educator, therapist, policymaker, or health care worker. How would you help your clients with this issue and navigate available options?

While the official statement of the ACOG may seem arbitrary, it is important to understand that researchers in obstetrics and gynecology have reason to be concerned with women choosing permanent sterilization in their twenties. Research has shown that up to 26 percent of women regret their decision to undergo sterilization (Bartz and Greenburg, 2008; Curtis, Mohllajee, and Peterson, 2006). In addition, this research also indicates that the factor most strongly associated with regret is age; women under the age of 30 are much more likely to regret the decision when compared to older women (Bartz and Greenburg, 2008). Given what we know about family developmental theory, including its strengths and weaknesses, how can we evaluate this issue? Should the ACOG's stance on permanent sterilization change, according to this theoretical perspective? How does the theory's history and origins help us understand its applicability to issues of reproductive rights and family planning in an ever changing world?

Conclusion

Family developmental theory has provided important ideas that allow researchers and practitioners to understand the predictable stages that guide families through the events and transitions associated with marriage and reproduction. Once championed as the first theory to place the family unit in the center of analysis, family

Box 5.3 Global Comparisons of Age of Majority (Legal Adult Status)

Societies differ in the age at which a child is recognized or declared as an adult in law. According to World Law Direct (2010), age of majority is the "chronological moment when a child legally ceases to be considered a minor and assumes control over their persons, actions and decisions, thereby terminating the legal control and legal responsibilities of their parents or guardian over and for them." Depending on the society, adult status can confer certain rights: to marry, to vote, to drive a car, to move out of the parental home, to have sexual intercourse, to drink alcohol, to get a bank account or credit card, to serve in the armed forces, and the like. Consider how various jurisdictions and countries confer the age of majority:

United States The age of majority is 18, and is consistent across all states except for three. The exceptions are age 19 in Alabama and Nebraska, and age 21 in Mississippi.

Indonesia The age of majority varies by gender: age 18 for men and age 15 for women.

Scotland The age of majority is 16.

Brazil The age of majority is 18, with the exception of the right to vote (age 16).

Canada The age of majority varies (either ages 18 or 19) by provincial and territorial jurisdiction.

Senegal The age of majority is 18 for both men and women, but the minimum age for marriage is 18 for men and 16 for women.

developmental theory has been challenged by the vast diversity that characterizes families nationally and internationally. However, the theory has proven to be remarkably useful in terms of a general understanding of how humans conduct their intimate lives and care for the young. The life cycle concept is a powerful metaphor for family growth and change, and no other theory has done better in highlighting what is unique and enduring about families everywhere.

One area of interest to family scholars across the globe is when adolescents are considered legal adults. In Box 5.3, we highlight the age of majority in several cultures. How would family developmental theorists explain the differences between the countries we highlight? We challenge you to consider these global applications of the theory as you move on to the areas for further study and the discussion and reflection questions in the concluding pages of this chapter.

Multimedia Suggestions

www.ted.com/talks

Search for Jennifer Senior for a Ted Talk that touches on the stages of the life cycle that involve parenting. She refers to a "parenthood crisis" that characterizes modern parenting. Senior's talk is based on her 2014 book *All joy and no fun*, which explores how children reshape their parents' lives. She describes in her talk how "we got here," pointing out that the word "parent" was not widely used as a verb until the 1970s. Senior uses this illustration to show that modern parenthood is riddled with anxiety, and suggests that we rethink how we raise our children.

Activate your theory app: After watching this clip, can you think of examples you have witnessed or heard about in your own life of this parenting challenge? Consider the type of parents affected by this challenge – does it include every demographic, or just a specific group?

www.advocatesforyouth.org

This website serves as a resource for anyone working with young adults as they navigate the life cycle and make decisions about their reproductive and sexual health. It includes resources, links to partner organizations, and information for activists who seek to influence public policy in this area.

Activate your theory app: Consider the issues facing today's youth on this website: how could family developmental theory be used to help practitioners address these concerns?

This Is 40 (2012)

This comedy film depicts what it is like for parents to turn 40. Pete and Debbie struggle with the issues of moving through various life cycle stages, including raising a "school-aged family" while moving toward "middle age." They also have to address Pete's financial support of his father, while trying to also maintain a romantic sexual relationship with each other. To add fuel to the fire, they find out that at 40, Debbie is pregnant. This film illustrates several concepts from family developmental theory as the family members each deal with change, unexpected timing, and norms associated with moving through each stage in the life cycle.

A scene from *This Is 40*, 2012, dir. Judd Aptow, Universal Pictures

Activate your theory app: Have norms associated with specific "decades" of life changed over time? If this film was made a quarter-century ago, what decade do you think it would have targeted as an important stage for adult parents?

The Notebook (2004)

This popular romantic-drama tells the story of a couple, very much in love, at two stages in the family life cycle. The film begins at the present time in a nursing home where an older gentleman, Duke, reads from his "notebook" to an older lady. Duke tells the story of Noah and Allie, a young couple who first meet as adolescents and they have the perfect summer together on a southern island. The young lovers, Noah and Allie, are torn apart, however, because Allie's wealthy parents do not approve of the "local" boy, Noah. Allie's mother even calls him "trash." Noah eventually goes off to fight in World War II, and Allie meets a sophisticated and wealthy lawyer, to whom she becomes engaged. However, Allie realizes that she has loved Noah all along, and breaks her engagement to her fiancé. The interesting twist in the story is that it becomes apparent that Noah and Allie are actually Duke and the woman he is reading to, and that Noah/Duke has been telling Allie (who suffers from memory loss) the story of how they met. The story ends with the two of them confirming their love and dying peacefully together. Thus, true to the normative family life cycle, their own family began with their marriage and ended in their deaths.

A scene from *The Notebook*, 2004, dir. Nick Cassavetes, New Line Cinema

Activate your theory app: As we pointed out earlier in this chapter, one of the weaknesses of family developmental theory is that it ignores family problems. How were the problems facing this couple solved in this film?

Further Reading

Cicirelli, V. G., "Attachment relationships in old age," *Journal of Social and Personal Relationships, 27* (2010), 191–199 (doi:10.1177/0265407509360984). This research emphasizes attachment patterns in old age, a stage in the life cycle that does not receive quite as much attention when it comes to attachment and relationships. Victor Cicirelli sheds light on this process, taking into account how deceased family members, the onset of disability, or experiencing widowhood may affect older adults' attachment patterns. Based on Bowlby's (1988) assertion that individuals are dependent on others throughout the life span, this work highlights one stage of the life cycle in helping us understand how attachment and relationships inevitably change over time.

Furstenberg, F. F., Jr, "On a new schedule: Transitions to adulthood and family change," *The Future of Children, 20* (2010), 67–87 (doi:10.1353/foc.0.0038). Frank Furstenberg discusses the major changes that have occurred in marriage and family patterns within the context of global and economic changes. These changes have affected the way that young people experience the transition to adulthood. Unlike other western nations, the United States does not invest heavily in education, health care, and job benefits for young adults. As a result, dependency on parents continues into the third decade of life, delaying the start of the family life cycle for current youth. Moreover, youth who come from economically disadvantaged families have a more difficult time attaining independence from their family of origin than youth from families with more ample support. Now, youth operate on a newly extended timetable in terms of being launched from the parental home and transitioning to adulthood. They can no longer expect the type of predictable schedule posited by family developmental theory.

Murkoff, H., *What to expect when you're expecting*, 4th edn (New York: Workman, 2008). Hailed as America's "pregnancy bible," this is often the first book read by women and their partners when they discover they are expecting a baby. Updated for current family life, this popular "how to" manual addresses everything from getting pregnant, to keeping healthy during pregnancy, to adjusting to having a newborn baby, and to getting back in shape. Dads are also addressed. Although mostly written from the perspective of the positive side of pregnancy and childbirth, this book also addresses pregnancy loss. It provides an accessible and authoritative voice to help women and their partners anticipate this key part of the family life cycle.

Murray, C. I., Toth, K., Larsen, B. L., and Moulton, S., "Death, dying, and grief in families," in S. J. Price, C. A. Price, and P. C. McKenry (eds), *Families and change: Coping with stressful events and transitions*, 4th edn (Thousand Oaks, CA: Sage, 2010), pp. 73–95. Death is a crisis experienced by all families. This article suggests the most helpful way to understand death, dying, and grief includes a developmental model that takes into account individual, familial, and cultural dimensions simultaneously. This broader perspective is needed because the way that most industrialized societies deal with death tends to sensationalize the public nature of death (e.g., death by murder, death by war, death by natural disaster). These kinds of death are splashed across the news on a daily basis. There is a major difference between the public events and the private nature of death in families. Death is often an invisible process with little anticipatory socialization in how to deal with it. Family developmental theory proposes that the end of the family life cycle includes the experience of coping with the loss of a spouse and the ultimate death of both married partners, but very little support is given for the grief process. Colleen Murray and colleagues show that it is important to take into account how death affects the individual family members, the family unit as a whole, and the social context in which it occurs.

Ward, M., and Bélanger, M., *The family dynamic: A Canadian perspective* (Toronto: Cengage Learning, 2011). This book highlights family dynamics in Canada, including how families move through the life cycle. This text provides insight into how a nation's laws and policies affect families' access to marriage, child care, and assisted reproduction. In addition, some interesting comparisons included in this book emerge when considering Canadians' experiences of immigration, transnational marriages, adoption, and grandparents raising grandchildren. As an example, the Canadian census includes grandparents raising grandchildren (with no parents present) as a legal definition of family.

Questions for Students

Discussion Questions

1 In what ways is the concept of the family life cycle still relevant for families in the twenty-first century? In what ways is it not?
2 Considering the cultural differences of families around the world, how might family developmental theory be applied in different economies or settings?
3 How do family developmental tasks cause conflict in families, depending upon the person's position in the hierarchical structure?
4 Like some other theories you have read about in this book, family developmental theory was proposed in the United States during a time of economic prosperity. Does this model fit for racial and ethnic minorities, living in varying conditions throughout the world?
5 Consider the developmental tasks associated with the different stages of the family life cycle. Are there some that can be accomplished in alternative ways (i.e., outside the family unit)?
6 Compare and contrast family developmental theory with conflict theory (Chapter 3). What do they have in common? How do they differ?

Your Turn!

Most individuals do not necessarily "map out" how they expect to move through stages of the life cycle; instead, we typically daydream or imagine ourselves in the future. For this activity, we ask you to put pen to paper and draw/write out what you envision is your next stage in the life cycle. Write your career goals, where you will live, and how much you expect to earn. Then, envision the next stage of your life cycle, drawing where you are currently according to Figure 5.1 in this chapter, and where you are headed next. Answer the basic questions of "who/what/where/when/how/why" regarding the next stage in your life cycle. Be specific, detailing even the small things, like if or how the household labor will be divided, who will do carework (if applicable), and how you will maintain any individual interests, hobbies, or activities in the face of new changes.

Personal Reflection Questions

1 What family developmental tasks did you and your parents struggle with the most, and at what ages?
2 Meet with one or more of your older relatives and talk about their experience of the family life cycle. How does their experience differ from your own?
3 If you plan to marry, do you intend to go through a marriage preparation class? If so, what do you hope to learn as you prepare for this major change?
4 Are there films other than the ones discussed in which the circle of family life is evident? Name one of your favorites and explain why it fits with family developmental theory.
5 Thinking about your own progression in the family life cycle thus far, are there any developmental tasks that you have accomplished outside of your family? Or, are there any developmental tasks not listed as part of family developmental theory that your family *did* help you achieve?
6 Meet with a classmate, either virtually or in person, and discuss differences and similarities you've each experienced thus far in the family life cycle. Are there cultural or religious differences you can identify? What similarities exist, and why?

References

Aldous, J. (1978). *Family careers: Developmental change in families*. New York: Wiley.

Allen, K. R., and Pickett, R. S. (1987). Forgotten streams in the family life course: Utilization of qualitative retrospective interviews in the analysis of lifelong single women's family careers. *Journal of Marriage and the Family, 49*, 517–526. doi:10.2307/352197.

Arnett, J. J. (2000). Emerging adulthood: A theory of development from the late teens through the twenties. *American Psychologist, 55*, 469–480. doi:10:1037/0003-066X.55.5.469.

Bartz, D., and Greenberg, J. A. (2008). Sterilization in the United States. *Reviews in Obstetrics and Gynecology, 1*, 23–32.

Bengtson, V. L., and Allen, K. R. (1993). The life course perspective applied to families over time. In P. Boss, W. Doherty, R. LaRossa, W. Schumm, and S. Steinmetz (eds), *Sourcebook of family theories and methods: A contextual approach* (pp. 469–499). New York: Plenum.

Bowlby, J. (1988). *A secure base: Parent–child attachment and healthy human development*. New York: Basic Books

Burgess, E. (1926). The family as a unity of interacting personalities. *The Family, 7*, 3–9.

Burton, L. M. (1996). Age norms, the timing of family role transitions, and intergenerational caregiving among aging African American women. *Gerontologist, 36*, 199–208. doi:10.1093/geront/36.2.199.

Cheal, D. (1991). *Family and the state of theory*. Toronto: University of Toronto Press.

Curtis, K. M., Mohllajee, A. P., and Peterson, H. B. (2006). Regret following female sterilization at a young age: A systematic review. *Contraception, 73*, 205–210. doi:10.1016/j.contraception.2005.08.006.

Davies, J. J., and Gentile, D. A. (2012). Responses to children's media use in families with and without siblings: A family development perspective. *Family Relations, 61*, 410–425. doi:10.1111/j.1741-3729.2012.00703.x.

Duvall, E. M. (1957). *Family development*. Philadelphia: Lippincott.

Erikson, E. H. (1968). *Childhood and society* (2nd edn). New York: Norton.

Feldman, H., and Feldman, M. (1975). The family life cycle: Some suggestions for recycling. *Journal of Marriage and the Family, 37*, 277–284. doi:10.2307/350961.

Gavazzi, S. (2013). Theory and research pertaining to families with adolescents. In G. W. Peterson and K. R. Bush (eds), *Handbook of marriage and the family* (3rd edn, pp. 303–327). New York: Springer.

Gay, P. (ed.) (1995). *The Freud Reader*. New York: Norton.

Glick, P. C. (1947). The family cycle. *American Sociological Review, 12*, 164–174. doi:10.2307/346771

Glick, P. C. (1988). Fifty years of family demography: A record of social change. *Journal of Marriage and the Family, 50*, 861–873. doi:10.2307/352100.

Goldberg, A. E. (2010). *Lesbian and gay parents and their children: Research on the family life cycle*. Washington, DC: American Psychological Association.

Havighurst, R. J. (1972). *Developmental tasks and education* (3rd edn). New York: David McKay. (Originally published 1948.)

Hill, R. (1986). Life cycle stages for types of single parent families: Of family development theory. *Family Relations, 35*, 19–29. doi:10.2307/584278.

Hill, R. L., and Hansen, D. A. (1960). The identification of conceptual frameworks utilized in family study. *Marriage and Family Living, 22*, 299–311. doi:10.2307/347242

Hill, R., and Rodgers, R. H. (1964). The developmental approach. In H. Christensen (ed.), *Handbook of marriage and the family* (pp. 171–211). Chicago: Rand McNally.

Lev, A. I., and Sennott, S. L. (2013). Clinical work with LGBTQ parents and prospective parents. In Goldberg, A. E., and Allen, K. R. (eds), *LGBT-parent families: Innovations in research and implications for practice* (pp. 214–260). New York: Springer.

Mattessich, P., and Hill, R. (1987). Life cycle and family development. In M. B. Sussman and S. K. Steinmetz (eds), *Handbook of marriage and the family* (pp. 437–469). New York: Plenum.

McGoldrick, M., and Hardy, K. V. (eds) (2008). *Re-visioning family therapy: Race, culture, and gender in clinical practice*. New York: Guilford Press.

McGoldrick, M. B., Carter, B., and Garcia-Preto, N. (2011). *The expanded family life cycle: Individual, family, and social perspectives* (4th edn). New York: Pearson.

Nelson, M. K. (2006). Single mothers "do" family. *Journal of Marriage and Family, 66*, 781–795. doi:10.1111/j.1741-3737.2006.00292.x.

Nock, S. L. (1979). The family life cycle: Empirical or conceptual tool? *Journal of Marriage and the Family, 41*, 15–26. doi:10.2307/351727.

Papernow, P. (1993). *Becoming a stepfamily*. San Francisco: Jossey-Bass.

Pearson, C. (2014, October 28). *Meet the 20-somethings who want to be sterilized*. HuffPost Women. At http://www.huffingtonpost.com/2014/10/24/female-sterilization-young-women_n_5882000.html.

Piaget, J. (1952). *The origins of intelligence in children*, trans. M. Cook. New York: Norton.

Rodgers, R. H. (1973). *Family interaction and transaction: The developmental approach*. Englewood Cliffs, NJ: Prentice Hall.

Rodgers, R. H., and White, J. M. (1993). Family developmental theory. In P. G. Boss, W. J. Doherty, R. LaRossa, W. R. Schumm, and S. K. Steinmetz (eds), *Sourcebook of family theories and methods: A contextual approach* (pp. 225–254). New York: Plenum.

Rowe, G. P. (1966). The developmental conceptual framework to the study of the family. In F. I. Nye and F. M. Berardo (eds), *Emerging conceptual frameworks in family analysis* (pp. 198–222). New York: Macmillan.

Senior, J. (2014). *All joy and no fun: The paradox of modern parenthood*. New York: HarperCollins.

Slater, S. (1999). *The lesbian family life cycle*. Chicago: University of Illinois Press.

Stewart, S. D. (2007). *Brave new stepfamilies: Diverse paths toward stepfamily living*. Thousand Oaks, CA: Sage.

White, J. M., and Klein, D. M. (2008). *Family theories* (3rd edn). Thousand Oaks, CA: Sage.

White, J. M., Klein, D. M., and Martin, T. F. (2015). *Family theories: An introduction* (4th edn). Thousand Oaks, CA: Sage.

WHO (World Health Organization) (2016). Global Health Observatory data repository: Life expectancy; data by country. At http://apps.who.int/gho/data/node.main.688?lang=en.

World Law Direct (2010). *Age of majority*. At www.worldlawdirect.com/forum/law-wiki/27181-age-majority.html.

6

Family Systems Theory

Have you ever had a roommate whose housekeeping quirks really made you wonder? Did she leave piles and piles of dirty dishes in the sink? Over time, some people might come to the conclusion that the roommate was just unclean, or perhaps lazy, or one might even go so far as to say she was simply disgusting. However, as a family theorist, it is important to take a look at the bigger picture to understand behavior. It is easy to use a simple individualist viewpoint, where we focus on the individual and assume that the problem is unique to that person. Most likely there are other contributing factors we need to consider before seeing the behavior as innate and unchangeable. Perhaps the roommate is rebelling from having a very strict upbringing where she was harshly punished for not doing her chores. Or maybe her parents did all the chores, so she does not know where to start, or she just assumes someone else will do them, which is what she has expected and experienced for nearly 20 years of her life. In any case, systems theorists look at the *whole* – not just the parts – of the system before interpreting behavior. Family systems theorists wonder what else is going on in the family to help understand issues and conflicts. Family systems theorists ask: How is the problem related to other processes, such as parenting styles, expectations for siblings, and how well members of a family communicate? With family systems theory, every contributing factor is taken into account, because we cannot understand any part of the system without looking at the whole picture.

One way to envision how family systems theory works is to think about a family portrait you have seen. With that image in your mind, look at the subjects in the photo, the landscape behind and next to the subjects, and take in each aspect of the picture. Family systems theory gives us this type of panoramic, 3-D view of family; no aspect can be taken for granted, ignored, or left unexamined. Consider, when imagining the portrait, what the weather is like that day, what the family members are wearing, whether a family member is in a wheelchair, how close it is to meal time, if there is a barking dog nearby, whether or not anyone either in the photo or even behind the lens was having a bad day or had a misunderstanding with someone else before or while the photo was taken. When you think about it, the possibilities are endless! Family systems theorists take into account all of the interrelated parts when examining family dynamics and issues. Our case study gives us a closer look at family dynamics and how each part of the system contributes to the overall stability (or instability) of a family.

Case Study

When Jackson's mother married her second husband, Jackson not only gained a new father, but he also became a sibling for the first time. His stepfather's son, Dustin, just a year younger, came to live with them. The new brothers couldn't be more different. Jackson was an introvert who liked anything to do with science fiction. He was especially into the Harry Potter books and films. In addition, Jackson and his mother were very close during his childhood. Jackson's biological father died when he was only four, so for the past 10 years, it was just the two of them. At bedtime, he and his mother would take turns reading chapters from the

Family Theories: Foundations and Applications, First Edition. Katherine R. Allen and Angela C. Henderson.

Harry Potter books out loud to one another. Jackson was a good student in school and an avid reader. For a 14-year-old boy, he was uniquely emotionally tuned in to those around him. He was also quiet and shy.

Dustin, on the other hand, was much more outgoing than Jackson. The main reason he came to live with his dad was because his mother said she could not control him. Going to live with his father, stepmother, and stepbrother also meant that he was moving up in the world. His father lived in an exclusive suburb with excellent schools and safe neighborhoods. This was very different for Dustin, who had grown up in an apartment in inner city Boston.

Since Dustin was so outgoing, he immediately made friends with the cool kids at Jackson's school. Dustin also was taller and tougher than Jackson, a difference that only exaggerated Jackson's difficulties fitting in with his peers. Jackson became increasingly withdrawn and now spent most of his time alone in his room. Formerly an A student, his grades began to drop. He became more and more belligerent toward his mother and would barely speak to his stepfather. His stepfather tried to use the same discipline techniques on both boys, but Jackson resented the fact that he was no longer treated as special. Jackson's mother worried about his adjustment to his new family situation and felt torn in her loyalties to her old family, consisting of her first husband and Jackson, and to her new family that included her second husband and his son.

When she got a call from Jackson's teacher that he was no longer turning in his assignments, she knew he needed help. Her new husband was furious and suggested disciplining Jackson at home, but she was able to convince him that Jackson needed to see a therapist first. She contacted a therapist so that Jackson could get the individual attention and help he needed. When she explained Jackson's problems to the therapist, the therapist said that the whole family needed to come to the session. Jackson's mother was stunned: why did they all have to go when it was Jackson who was acting out?

Why was Jackson's mom so shocked that the therapist wanted to see the whole family? Why would there be a difference between addressing Jackson's behavior from an individual perspective, compared to a family perspective? What could be learned from focusing on family dynamics, loyalties, and the introduction of new "parts" into the family system? Family systems theorists would argue that individuals do not function in isolation: family members are interdependent. Their behaviors are best understood in terms of the interrelatedness of all of the parts of a system, including the history of all members, the back story of the family unit, and the interplay of family dynamics as a result. Therefore, when we use family systems theory, we are equipped to look beyond the problem – we take a panoramic, 3-D view – to help frame the underlying issues contributing to the system as a whole.

What Is Family Systems Theory?

Family systems theory is concerned with the ways that parents and children, spouses, and extended family members mutually influence and communicate with one another. This theory focuses on the relationships that make up a system, rather than just the system as a whole. This theoretical lens allows for a closer examination of the "inner workings" of systems, such as rules that govern the behaviors of individuals in the family, as well as within the subsystems that comprise the family unit. A **family system** is defined as a unit of interdependent individuals. Subsystems are units within the family that can be examined on their own in relation to the larger unit. Examples are a parental subsystem, sibling subsystem, aunt–nephew subsystem, and grandparent–grandchild subsystem. Families, as systems, seek to maintain their existing boundaries and patterns. Understanding each of these dynamics as part of the larger whole – including patterns of interaction, communication, and resistance to change – is the key to applying family systems theory (Anderson, Sabatelli, and Kosutic, 2013; Broderick and Smith, 1979; Holmes and Huston, 2010).

Family systems theory emerged from general systems theory (GST), a perspective that explains the wholeness and the interconnection among all parts in the system. Systems theory was developed in order to identify how all types of systems – especially those that are mechanical or inanimate – function in universal ways (von Bertalanffy, 1973). Many scholars argue that general systems theory contains universal principles that can be applied to any context, whether inanimate or living. For example, an information system, a weaponry system, a governmental system, and a family system, all share the same characteristics according to systems theory. They are composed of interconnected parts that affect and are affected by their environments. In order to understand how any of these systems operate, you have to understand the system as a whole (White, Klein, and Martin, 2015).

Other scholars, however, argue that applying general systems concepts to families requires some adjustment. As living systems, families must be understood differently than inanimate systems. Human beings are unpredictable. We are motivated by different things, and our choices and preferences even change over time, as do the social forces surrounding us. Because of a family's ever changing dynamics, family systems theory as we know it today was developed by scholars and therapists in psychology, sociology, and family science who studied and worked with families, particularly in addressing their emotional and behavioral problems (e.g., Ackerman, 1984; Beavers and Hampson, 2000; Cowan et al., 1996; Minuchin, 1985; Olson, 2000). This perspective is concerned with the ways that interrelated individuals in families are affected whenever a change is introduced into any one part of the family system; that change will affect all other members in the system (e.g., a parent gets a new job and the family must relocate; a new baby is born and the older children have to adjust to another family member). Family systems theorists are concerned with the interactions and emotional issues that arise in everyday life, whether they are in the **family of origin**, which is the family one is born into, or the family of procreation, which as we learned in Chapter 5 regarding family developmental theory, is the family one establishes by marriage. These interactional patterns and processes occur among spouses, between parents and children, and they echo across the generations in the extended family. As we explained in the case study involving Jackson and his family, a family systems perspective helps us to uncover patterns that are often unseen and unspoken, as in the case of how a child's "acting out" behaviors are a clue to broader issues in the family system (O'Gorman, 2012).

History and origins

There are many variations to systems theory. In this section, we examine the emergence of the theory as it was first developed in the mid-twentieth century, and then address how it was applied to the study of families. Thus, although we emphasize systems theory as applied to families, we also point out that like other theories, family systems theory is interdisciplinary in its roots and current applications.

General systems theory Compared to conflict theory (Chapter 3) and symbolic interactionist theory (Chapter 4), general systems theory is a relatively new perspective. It is a perspective that crosses scientific disciplines, with roots in physics, biology, engineering, statistics, and other physical and mathematical sciences. Whitchurch and Constantine explain that GST was developed during World War II out of desperation because more sophisticated weaponry was needed in combat with enemy forces:

> extensive use of airplanes in warfare during World War II necessitated intensive research on antiaircraft gunnery to improve accuracy of aiming at moving targets from ships rolling on ocean waves. Therefore, mathematical theory of prediction was developed to calculate the positions of enemy aircraft ahead of their current positions to enable ammunition to meet airplane targets in mid-air. Of course, accurate tracking of the target required constant comparison of the aim of the antiaircraft gun with the movements of the target and tracking the gun's own position. This was a self-monitoring process by the antiaircraft gun that became known as *cybernetic feedback*. (1993, pp. 326–327)

A key feature of GST is the ability to look inside of a system to examine what processes keep it functioning. This notion is based on the science of **cybernetics**, developed by mathematician Norbert Wiener (1967). Cybernetics provides a model for understanding the forms and patterns that steer a system and allow that system to self-regulate. While this process seems macro-level in nature, by examining overall functioning of a system, what is unique about cybernetics is the ability to explore the patterns of communication and control that a system develops to maintain stability.

Systemic patterns change when confronted with the new information and constraints that are constantly bombarding the system. This process of change is similar to how families operate on a daily basis and over time. Cybernetics deals with the internal rules that govern a system in order to keep it functioning. For example, cybernetics explains how a thermostat adjusts itself in order to maintain the desired temperature, or how the circuits in the brain control behavior in animal systems (Broderick, 1993). Therefore, GST takes into account both the functioning of the overall unit, as well as how the unit reacts to and adapts to changes, new information, constraints, and roadblocks over time. This allows researchers to really understand how units function on a much deeper level than, for example, a more macro theory like functionalism (see Chapter 2).

The emergence of family systems theory Following World War II, psychiatrists and sociologists who studied families started to think about families as systems. This development led to the growth of family therapy (a departure from the biologically and individually oriented field of Freudian psychoanalysis that dominated psychiatry). Family systems theory was used to explain how a young person might develop schizophrenia by positing that the mother's influence was the most important in creating the conditions under which this psychiatric disorder developed (Bateson et al., 1956). The argument was based on the idea that mothers created a **double bind** situation that occurs when a person is given two commands that contradict each other. For example, a double bind is created when the parent repeatedly asks for more affection from the child, and at the same time, shows through their body language (e.g., stiffens when they touch) that they are rejecting that affection. The double bind is said to create a paradoxical straightjacket, maintained with unspoken rules that family members must uphold this "crazy-making situation" (Broderick, 1993, p. 34). Although eventually critiqued by feminist family therapists as mother blaming, sexist, and male-centered (Luepnitz, 2002 [1988]), the application of GST to family social science had begun.

Family systems theory, then, is built on the idea of **holism**: the whole family should be studied. The subsystems within families need to be understood as part of a larger hierarchy, defined by internal boundaries. This suggests that one or more subsystems can have more power than others. For instance, a father–son subsystem may have access to more resources within the family because they are considered important in decision-making processes. A father may place more trust in his son to manage his estate instead of his wife or daughter after he dies. These subsystem dynamics and boundaries that are created within families need to be understood in terms of a hierarchy that carries theoretical significance when studying families. In Box 6.3 later in this chapter, we provide examples of how the gendered hierarchy persists and is reflected in different forms around the globe.

Family scholars have also examined how broader social systems and external boundaries affect families (Grych, Oxtoby, and Lynn, 2013). In one of the classic studies that examined societal level influences, Bowen (1985) studied societal functioning around the issues associated with juvenile delinquency. Many societal subsystems are engaged when youth are involved in criminal acts. Bowen's study showed the interconnectedness of law enforcement agencies, the legal and judicial systems, public schools, and social service agencies in addressing this social problem (Comella, 2011). Further, family systems theory is helpful in understanding the links between how families operate in the home, and how families operate in contexts related to but outside the home, such as family businesses (Norton, 2011) and religious institutions (Crimone and Hester, 2011; Pinkus, 2006).

Like many other theories we cover in this book, family systems theory has evolved and changed over time. One of the major applications of family systems theory is in the area of family therapy, and there are many variations that characterize this clinical field. Some family systems models emphasize intergenerational relationships (e.g., Bowen, 1985). Other models emphasize experiential communication patterns (e.g., Satir, 1988). The circumplex model (Olson, Sprenkle, and Russell, 1979) provides a way to study and assess the insider's view of a family, where each member provides a perspective of the family's flexibility (i.e., balance) and cohesion (i.e., closeness). Still other family systems models are emotionally focused and emphasize attachment relationships in adulthood (Johnson, 2004). A structural version of family systems theory

Box 6.1 At a Glance: Family Systems Theory

- A family consists of interdependent individuals.
- The family system consists of interdependent subsystems.
- The family system, subsystems, and individual members seek to maintain equilibrium.
- The whole (family) is greater than the sum of its parts (individuals and subsystems).
- The whole family has to be examined in order to understand family dynamics.
- Families differ in the degree to which they are cohesive or disengaged.
- Families are organized by open and closed boundaries.

uses techniques such as reframing in order to restructure family rules and boundaries. Reframing involves relabeling an event or problem and putting it in an entirely different context so that it alters the way family members view it (Goldenberg and Goldenberg, 2013). Social constructionist models of family systems theory rework the metaphor of systems and focus on the way we weave the stories of our lives into a coherent narrative; therapists try to intervene in self-defeating narratives and help people to rewrite their past, present, and future story lines in order to actively change their lives (White and Epston, 1990). Taken together, family systems theory can be applied to the study of family in various ways, taking into account multiple points of conflict, difference, communication patterns, and many other contributing factors. Again, this perspective allows for a panoramic view, where we are able to focus in on any one variable or facet of a family in order to paint a more accurate picture of family dynamics.

Key concepts

There are several main concepts that characterize family systems theory, all of which are useful as a "map for understanding everyday and erratic family behavior" (Galvin, Dickson, and Marrow, 2006, p. 320). Family scholars and practitioners have taken general systems theory concepts and adapted them to the particular context of the family.

Family system A family system refers to the overarching entity that contains individuals who are related to one another by birth, marriage, adoption, and choice. Family systems also include nuclear arrangements of two generations where much of family drama unfolds, multigenerational relationships where the carryover of family of origin dynamics across the generations are visible, and connections with the wider society, which push and pull family members together and apart. Within this family unit, members' emotional functioning is established, perfected, and challenged (Broderick, 1993; Rosenblatt, 1994; Rothblaum et al., 2002; Whitchurch and Constantine, 1993). In one of the classic statements of family systems theory, Virginia Satir (1988), who has been called "the mother of family systems theory," described families as "people-making" organizations where our sense of self-worth and our ability to communicate with one another are first formed and developed. Rather than emphasize their problems, Satir focused on the good intentions of families to create authentic and sensitive relationships with one another, while still valuing the individual self. In addition, Satir furthered family systems theory by emphasizing the developing self in the context of the family. One of the goals of healthy development is to have an individual sense of oneself, and to be able to share oneself with others.

Like a theatrical performance, each family member knows the part they have to play in order to keep the system running smoothly. As interactional patterns are rehearsed over and over again, the players repeat their parts, sometimes not even aware of what they are doing. Family roles are often assumed; each system is governed by a set of invisible rules that everyone seems to understand, but are often subconscious in nature. As an example, in many families, it is assumed that when a child is ill, the mother will stay at home and care for the child. This typically is not stated in a family "handbook" or part of a larger set of family rules that are formally discussed. Instead, most families run on assumptions about the roles each family member fulfills. It is important to examine these assumptions because some families may operate with traditional family roles, and others may decidedly try to share household duties and caretaking more equally. Part of what makes family systems theory so useful to family therapists is that it attempts to take into account the "bigger picture" – starting from square one, how does the couple (a subsystem, which we discuss in more detail below) feel about enacting specific roles in the family? How do the children interpret parents' fulfillment of these roles?

Going back to our case study, Jackson's family consists of both biological and stepfamily relationships. There seems to be an unstated assumption that Jackson's new stepfather will be the disciplinarian of the children in the home; after all, one of the primary functions of fathers has been to fulfill that role. Jackson resents the authority his stepfather is trying to impose on him. Instead of addressing the parenting issues that arise when a new family system is formed, as in the case of remarriage, the tendency is to blame, or scapegoat, one person as the problem, while ignoring ways in which the whole family contributes to the problem. Families have unwritten rules that can become problematic under stress. In Jackson's family, he has become the scapegoat.

Related to the idea of performance and roles is the idea of subsystems within families. Subsystems exist as part of the larger family unit, and usually consist of one of three primary relationships in families: marital (or adult partnership), parental (parent–child relationships), and sibling subsystems (brothers, sisters, stepsiblings, etc.). Each of these dyads or triads has specific patterns of communication and could be hierarchically situated above or below any of the other dyads or triads. For example, in a one-parent household, the eldest male child may be seen as a partial breadwinner/adult partner because both his financial help and his leadership are needed to run the household. Younger siblings may both defer to him and also resent him for exerting power over them. We elaborate on this process in the sections below.

Satir (1988) suggests that there is a typology of basic family communication styles that are particularly evident when families are under stress. This typology is based on her many years of therapeutic practice with families all over the globe, where she came to view and intervene in problematic behaviors based upon the roles that family members play. The first type is the placater. This person tries to please, probably based on feelings of worthlessness. The placater might say, "Whatever you want is okay, I'm just here to make you happy." The second type of family member is the blamer. This person wields the power in families, and communicates to others through finger pointing and saying "You never do anything right," or by redirecting attention away from himself or herself by shirking responsibility. A third type is the super-reasonable person, who tries to be logical and distanced from any emotionality at all costs. This person masks his or her vulnerability by maintaining a cool and calm demeanor, and thus keeping others at bay. A fourth type is the irrelevant person, who tries to distract others in the family from any intense interaction. Let's say that the family members are having an argument. Rather than addressing the conflict directly, the irrelevant person might try to make a joke about something related to the discussion, but ultimately distracts attention away from the conflict. Finally, a fifth type is the congruent communicator, who is the only person willing to be authentic and honest in family interactions. Satir and other systems theorists have emphasized that these types can be found in any family, or in any combination. As Goldenberg and Goldenberg observed, if a "blamer" is married to a "super-reasonable" person, communication is hampered when the wife complains bitterly "We hardly ever make love anymore; don't you have any feelings for me?" and the husband responds coldly: "Of course I do, or I wouldn't be married to you. Perhaps we define the word love differently" (2013, p. 261). By being super-reasonable, the husband is not addressing the wife's feelings of hurt that he might not love her anymore. Similarly, an irrelevant spouse would probably hear the complaint, either brush it off with a joke or offhand remark, and then maybe change his or her behavior slightly in the future. The possibilities for communication according to family systems theory are endless; no one is functioning independently of one another. We turn next to the concept of influence and interdependence.

Mutual influence As is true in any system, individuals, relationships, and subsystems that comprise the family system are interdependent, or mutually influential. This means that what happens in any one part of the family system affects every other component (Grych, Oxtoby, and Lynn, 2013). That is, if we were to dissect the communication patterns of each member of a family of five, several pathways would emerge. First, there is the dyad of the partner/spouse relationship. The couple that originally fell in love and decided they wanted to have children has their own relationship that needs time, energy, and emotion *separate from* that of the rest of the family. However, when that relationship is not tended to, it can deteriorate over time. If the quality of the partner/spouse relationship declines, it will undoubtedly affect the emotional well-being of others living in the house. The parents may take out frustrations with their spouse on the child(ren), creating a negative communication pathway that emanates from outside of the child/parent relationship. This misplaced emotional expression could create strain among siblings, echoing all across each and every member of the household. What is important to understand is that for every shift between a subsystem in a family, other family members will inevitably be affected by it, negatively or positively.

The same systemic process is found with external causes of strain; if a child or parent has a bad day at school or work, the ripples of that external interaction will be felt inside the rest of the family in one way or another. This ripple effect also applies to family members who do not communicate or show strain or stress to the rest of the family. Even if a family member is either incapable of communicating or withholds emotions and attitudes from other members of the family, this action will still affect the other family members in the overall system. Indeed, the components of the family system are organized into a whole that transcends the sum of its individual parts (Goldenberg and Goldenberg, 2013). That is, even if we only have five people in a family, the pathways of communication and influence are infinite. See Figure 6.1 for an illustration of mutual influence in family relationships.

In this illustration, we can see that the entire family is greater than the sum of its parts. This means that though there are only five people in the family, there are multiple pathways for communication and influence. The eldest child may feel the brunt of the argument between the parents; this in turn leads to jealousy of the youngest child, who is too young to process the weight of the emotions. The middle child tries to keep peace and resolve the conflict, leading to more communication between child and parent. Each of these parties to the functioning of the overall system can play a vital role in reaching or preventing equilibrium in the family as a whole.

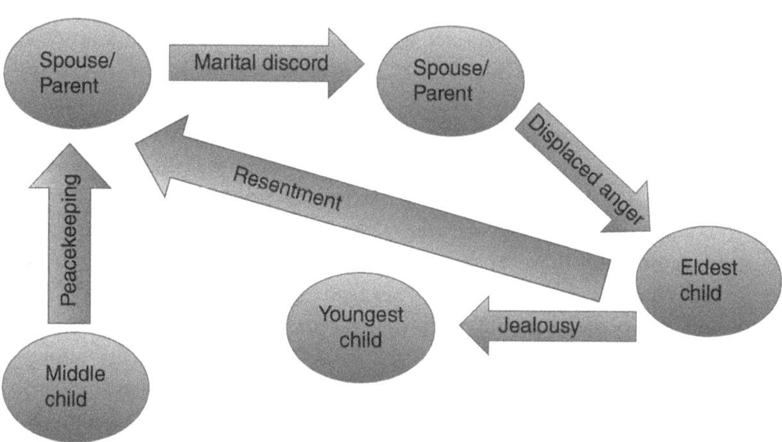

Figure 6.1 Pathways of communication using family systems theory

Hierarchy Family subsystems are arranged hierarchically. This layering is related to the power structures in families (Whitchurch and Constantine, 1993). Traditionally, husbands have had more power than wives. Parents are above young children in the family hierarchy, and thus have more power than their offspring. Older siblings can function as pseudo parents, expected to take on the caregiving for younger siblings. Hierarchies are not necessarily problematic, unless unhappiness or dissatisfaction develops within the family (Benson et al., 1995). For example, if an older sibling has to quit school to care for younger siblings while the parents work, that sacrifice can have serious consequences for the child who is unable to finish school. The eldest child both carries more power than the younger two but can also take on more unnecessary burden when there is conflict, because of his place in the family hierarchy. The unspoken rules about hierarchy can also work in the opposite direction. In our case study, Jackson had been his mother's closest confidant for 10 years, following the death of his biological father and before his mother married his stepfather. Now, his place in the family hierarchy is threatened by his mother gaining a new partner. Further, Jackson is no longer the only child in the family. All of a sudden, he has to share his home with an unwelcomed stepbrother.

Boundaries In order to conceptualize families as a "system," it is important to be able to draw boundaries so that we can separate out and filter what is included and what is not. Thus, family systems theory requires us to visualize the various parts of a system in discrete units; in short, to draw a **boundary** (Whitchurch and Constantine, 1993). In family systems theory, boundaries can be permeable or impermeable. A permeable boundary is open to interchange from outside the system. An impermeable boundary, by contrast, is closed to the outside. By their very nature, families are open systems because there is always some interaction with the environment, but families differ in the degree to which they are bounded. Families with flexible boundaries are more likely to be engaged with the outside world, whereas families with inflexible boundaries are more likely to be tightly knit and withdrawn from external social contact. A family system that places a premium on privacy, for example, would be less likely to seek family therapy when experiencing a major shift (e.g., transitioning to parenthood; a child acting out in school; forming a stepfamily; coping with a chronic illness) than a family system that valued the expertise and assistance of outside professionals. As we can see in our case study example, although Jackson's mother was open to finding help for Jackson's so-called behavioral problems, her initial instinct was to locate an individual therapist to deal with Jackson one-on-one. A family with more flexible boundaries, on the other hand, would be more open to seeking professional help for the entire family.

Feedback Given its roots in cybernetics and technology, feedback is probably a concept unique to family systems theory. **Feedback** is a way of capturing the interdependence function of systems – that individuals in family systems influence one another. Feedback can be either negative or positive. Negative feedback puts a stop to communication or behavior in order to bring the system back to equilibrium. Positive feedback, on the other hand, responds to the stimulus by allowing change in the overall functioning of the system. An example of positive feedback would be if one of the spouses suggested the couple attend therapy, in order to address the mix-up in communication that occurred to cause the discord in the first place. Negative feedback, on the other hand, would prevent such change from happening. The spouses would continue in their pattern of communication, and the negative emotions would trickle down to the children and back up to the parents like they always do when that situation occurs. In sum, positive feedback helps the system to innovate and change, while negative feedback dampens efforts to change by helping the system achieve and maintain stability. A healthy family system needs a balance of both positive and negative feedback loops. That is, families need enough flexibility to allow change but enough restraint to keep change from getting out of control (Whitchurch and Constantine, 1993). You can see the challenge of balancing flexibility and restraint in families, particularly when they undergo many major changes at once. Jackson's family, for example, was dealing with remarriage, stepparent/stepchild relationships, introduction of a new sibling into the family system, ongoing grief from the death of a parent, and the normal developmental challenges associated with adolescence.

Equilibrium Seeking a balance between change (positive feedback loops) and stability (negative feedback loops) is referred to as **equilibrium**. In the face of change, all systems seek to return to the "status quo," or homeostasis. Families are no exception in their efforts to stabilize themselves. Equilibrium does not mean, however, that there is some universal harmonious state that all systems seek. Rather, each family operates according to rules that they have developed in order to protect their own survival. Because families are diverse in structure, the balance that families seek does not look the same across families. The key to equilibrium is that families seek to stabilize according to their own internal rules. Each family has its own blueprint for reaching equilibrium, and equilibrium can look different in open or closed family systems. What works to create balance for some families may not work for all.

Intergenerational family patterns One of the hallmarks of family systems theory is that family problems and recommendations for change can be uncovered by studying family patterns from an intergenerational perspective. One of the primary techniques for uncovering intergenerational family patterns is the genogram. Based in Bowen's (1985) family systems theory, the genogram protocol was further developed by McGoldrick, Gerson, and Petry (2008) as a clinical technique to use in helping individuals understand the intergenerational context of family dynamics and problems.

The genogram consists of structural and emotional systems used to represent one's family. Structural symbols include boxes for males, circles for females, diamonds for pets, with a double square for the **index person** (e.g., the person whose life is featured in the genogram). In our example in Figure 6.2, the index person is Jason. Emotional symbols include a double line indicating a strong or special relationship between two people, a wavy line indicating a conflictual

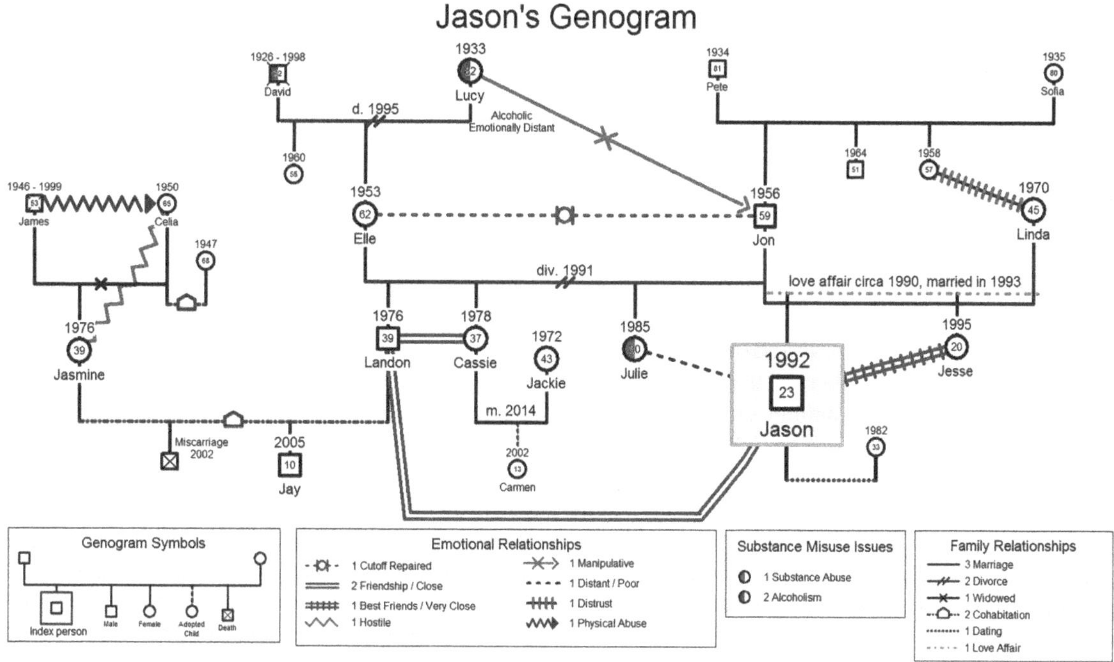

Figure 6.2 Genogram illustration
Source: www.genopro.com.

relationship, a double slash for a divorce, and a shaded symbol indicating substance abuse problems. It is most helpful to go back at least three generations in order to get more factual information, and then to interview older family members about their emotional journeys. Figure 6.2 depicts a rendering of how a genogram can be used to understand family dynamics.

Family cohesion: enmeshment versus disengagement Family systems theory is concerned with the degree to which family members feel close to one another. This idea reflects the concept of family cohesion, which refers to a continuum between the extremes of high cohesion to low cohesion. High cohesion is characterized by **enmeshment**, where family members are highly dependent upon one another, and closed off to others external to the family system. Enmeshed families have a high sense of "we-ness" and a low sense of "I-ness." On the other hand, low cohesion is characterized by **disengagement**, where family members tend to operate independently of one another. Extreme forms of disengagement can challenge the loyalty that family members feel toward one another. At the same time, families may also contain elements of both enmeshment and engagement. The classic example of enmeshment and disengagement in a family can be found in the middle-class, two-parent home that has been idealized in western society as superior to all others. In such a family, fathers are highly disengaged because they are expected to work long hours and support the family financially, and mothers are highly enmeshed, because their primary role is to take care of children and tend to the nurturance of the family (Goldenberg and Goldenberg, 2013).

Because flexibility is seen as a goal, according to family systems theory, neither of these extremes is considered to be healthy. Families can also vacillate between these poles. In our case study, Jackson's experience in a single-mother family, where it was just Jackson and his mom, reveals enmeshment. They did everything together and were bonded by the death of Jackson's dad. When his mother remarried, the old pattern of enmeshment was challenged. Change can be very unsettling to individuals and thus destabilize the family system as a whole. Box 6.2 includes an example of these family processes in the film *The Blind Side.*

Evaluating Family Systems Theory

Strengths of family systems theory

Family systems theory has many strengths. It is rooted in the application of theory to examine how families interact, allowing theorists a look at very complex processes that affect family members, both individually and as a whole, and it is applicable beyond studying the family as a stand-alone unit. Here we elaborate on these strengths.

Practical application Family systems theory is a very practical theory that is easy to apply to everyday life. Systems concepts can be easily translated into commonsense language that is accessible to a wide variety of individuals and families. One of the most helpful tenets of family systems theory can be captured in the idea that "if something isn't working, more of the same won't work." For example, if your car does not start, continuing to try to start it by turning the ignition is not going to make it start. Perhaps you should check the battery! In family systems terms, if Mom continually tells you to clean your room, and you do not clean your room, then Mom's repeated reminders to clean your room are not likely to be successful. Some other intervention is needed. In another example, as a practical theory, family systems concepts resonate with real people's lives. The work of social worker and therapist Brené Brown (2012) on the power of vulnerability has reached millions via her internet videos and Ted Talks. Brown's ideas about positive energy and the courage to change one's life are grounded in family systems theory.

Intervention Because of its emphasis on understanding family communication patterns and relationship processes, family systems theory is also useful for developing intervention programs to help families when they are experiencing troubles. Military family research is a key area for family systems theory (Drummet, Colman, and Cable, 2003; Faber et al., 2008; Paley, Lester, and Mogil, 2013). For example, research has shown that children whose parents are in the military experience greater loneliness and depression when their parents are deployed and thus away from home for months at a time. An effective

Box 6.2 Family Systems Theory in Pop Culture: *The Blind Side*

A scene from *The Blind Side*, 2009, dir. John Lee Hancock, Warner Bros. Pictures

Family systems theory is illustrated throughout the movie *The Blind Side*, which is based on a true story and novel written by Michael Lewis (2006). The main character, Michael, is an African American youth who had been in foster care with different families throughout his childhood because of his mother's drug addiction. In the beginning of the movie, an upper middle-class White woman, Leigh Anne Tuohy, sees him walking alongside the road in cold weather, and takes him in for the night. Over time, Michael becomes part of the family. The family as a unit has to adjust to the new member in order to maintain equilibrium. The father and daughter are skeptical at first, but over time make adjustments and the positive feedback loops allow the family to change and grow as a result.

In order to secure Michael a football scholarship to a Division I school, the family hires tutors to help increase his grade point average. When recruiters from both Tennessee and Ole Miss visit with Michael to encourage him to sign with their schools, Leigh Anne and her family become part of an investigation by the National Collegiate Athletic Association (NCAA) into whether or not the Tuohy family taking Michael in was a violation of NCAA booster regulations. This illustrates the concepts of boundaries, where external forces permeate the open boundaries of the family and disrupt the system. Because of the investigation, Michael becomes angry with the Tuohy family and flees to his mother's apartment in the projects. Over time, Michael does return to the family and chooses to attend Ole Miss. The processes of reconnecting and establishing healthy communication patterns between all members of the family unit is well illustrated throughout this film.

intervention has been to use technology, such as emails, Skype, and webcams, to keep parents and children in touch and communicating with each other (Blaisure et al., 2012).

Applicable to other aspects of family research In addition to its cybernetic and clinical roots, family systems theory is used in a variety of other contexts to study families. To extend individual and family development beyond the parent–child relationship, Cox (2010) applied systems theory to sibling relationships, and showed that the sibling subsystem is often more influential than the parental subsystem. Further, the sibling subsystem is the longest lasting tie. An application of this finding is that sibling relationships are very important for members of the baby boom generation, described in Chapter 9 on life course theory. As life expectancy is increasing and members of the baby boom are becoming senior citizens, they are more likely to have a sibling than a spouse in old age. Systems theory has also been used to examine the inclusion of pets as members of families, and thus address the therapeutic value of pets (Walsh, 2009). Another key research topic is how role reversals between parent and child can be handed down through the generations (Macfie et al., 2007). Role reversals often occur in families where parents have alcohol or drug addictions, or are unable to function as responsible parents due to incarceration or severe illness. In such cases, children are subject to "adultification" where they are required to function as a substitute parent or partner, thereby crossing hierarchical family boundaries (Burton, 2007).

Weaknesses of family systems theory

As we discussed in Chapter 1, no theory holds all the keys. Despite the numerous strengths of systems theory, there are some challenges in applying this perspective to families. These challenges are detailed here.

Possibility of stereotyping Just as family systems theory is very applicable to many different contexts, it is also very easy to apply it in superficial and stereotyped ways. Considered from a gender perspective, for example, the systemic concepts of "overfunctioning" and "underfunctioning" can be seen as disrespectful to families, particularly if a family member is gravely ill and requires a great deal of care. Such concepts are typically based on gender stereotypes, in which women are said to overfunction, and men are said to underfunction, without recognizing that the reverse is often true as well.

Simplifies complex relationships Another area in which systems theory is uncritically applied concerns sibling order and relationships. Assumptions about the sibling subsystem can be alluring but inaccurate. It is tempting to reduce sibling personalities to birth order characteristics (e.g., only children are selfish; eldest children are high achievers; middle children are scapegoats or the family clown; youngest children are pampered), because there can be a grain of truth in any stereotype (Bradshaw, 1988; Conley, 2004). However, sibling relationships are highly complex, multifaceted, and vary by cultural context. For example, in China, parents favor oldest sons over daughters and younger sons. Yet, in the US, older women tend to favor their youngest daughters when relying upon adult children for care and support (Suitor, Gilligan, and Pillemer, 2013).

Minimizes power dynamics in families One of the strongest critiques of family systems theory is that it minimizes, and even ignores, the power differences between men and women, and adults and children, in families. By proposing that a family's problems arise only from dysfunctional interpersonal relationships, family systems theory ignores how gender and generation ascribe different and unequal power to family members. A critique of family systems theory is thus a critique about how power is distributed unevenly in families. As feminists (Chapter 8) have observed, power differences in families reflect the broader social and political context (Luepnitz, 2002; Silverstein and Goodrich, 2003). By assuming that each member of the family has an equal responsibility and vested interest in family dynamics, family systems theory hides that some members of families are more "equal" than others (Leslie and Southard, 2009).

An alternative theory app: family ecological theory

In this chapter, we have laid out the key concepts, origins and background, and modern applications as well as the strengths and weaknesses of family systems theory. In Chapter 5, we compared two very different theories to activate your theory app; in this chapter, we compare two theories that are fairly similar to emphasize how over time, theories build on one another to adapt to new considerations in family theory.

Family systems theory is considered a foundational theory in family studies because it allows practitioners and researchers to take the "whole family" into account. Family ecological theory (Chapter 10) takes this perspective as well, but broadens the lens of analysis to include the environment and institutions that exist surrounding families. According to family ecological theory, humans directly modify their environments and are influenced by external forces as well. Consider Jackson from this chapter's case study. If we were using family ecological theory to study him, we would take a much closer look at the external environment in which his family interacted. Jackson had access to excellent schools and lived in a safe neighborhood, so we could determine that his family has tangible privileges compared to other families. Because of this, his mother was able to afford to go to therapy with him and other family members. At the same time, we need to note that family ecological theory would consider the historical reality that psychological services might not even exist to benefit Jackson and his family. Fifty years ago, sending a child (particularly a male child!) to counseling would have been unheard of. In this way, we can see how family ecological theory broadened the lens through which family theorists could analyze behavior by taking into account even larger macro-level forces than family systems. In comparison, family systems theory seems like a fairly micro-level theory, even though it is not!

Working with Family Systems Theory: Integrating Research and Practice

Now that we have described the historical origins, key concepts, and strengths and weaknesses of family systems theory, we turn our attention to how the theory can be used in practice. We then analyze an empirical study that was rooted in family systems theory, in order to see how scholars put the theory to work in a research project. Finally, we present ideas about how the theory informs the practice of family policy.

Family systems theory today

Paul Rosenblatt (1994), a family therapist, contends that family systems theory offers rich metaphors that are useful in understanding both family functioning and family change. Key metaphors of family systems theory include the family as a machine, prison, container, river, house, etc. A metaphor is a figure of speech, or analogy, in which "words or actions that literally denote one kind of object or idea are used in place of another" (Rosenblatt, 1994, p. 1). Metaphors are evocative and can help trigger emotions and ideas that need to be dislodged in order facilitate growth or resolution. In today's multicultural society where we recognize that no one single metaphor can capture so many types and dimensions of family, we need diverse metaphors to characterize the multiple realities of families.

Family systems metaphors are particularly useful in understanding how families deal with loss, trauma, death, and grief. Consider Rosenblatt's (2013) example of the death of a child. First, even though family members are connected to one another, grief over the death of a child can make individuals less available or less tuned in to one another. In the face of such tragedy, the family system can cease communicating and "shut down" altogether. Second, because families seek to maintain the system as it was, after a child dies, family members may still act and think in ways that keep the child "alive" in the system. It is not uncommon for parents to "talk to" their deceased child. Or, they may begin to focus all of their attention on how the surviving child is faring. Third, because a family is a system of rules that are typically unspoken, if a family member tries to grieve in ways that violate the family rules, it could make others uncomfortable and push the griever to "change back" to the ways that are expected. Some families allow intense emotion to be expressed, but other families may try to shut it down. These metaphors of connection, maintenance, and rules help us understand how processes of change, such as grief and loss, operate in families. Because families are systems that are more than the sum of their parts, how families cope with loss, and change of all kinds, is a family affair, not just an individual one.

Family systems theory in research

In a rare longitudinal study that incorporated *both* mothers' and fathers' perspectives, Holmes, Sasaki, and Hazen (2013) examined changes in the family system when young married couples experience the transition to parenthood. In most studies, only mothers have been asked to report on family transitions, a practice that family systems theorists criticize. Instead, a family systems perspective says that all of the individuals in the family have a unique, though interdependent, experience. The authors used quantitative research methods to study 125 married couples, by giving them a series of measurements at three points in time: prenatal, eight months after birth, and when the child was two years old.

Many subsystems are disrupted or created during the transition to parenthood due to the introduction of a new family member. In addition to the individual level issues (e.g., whether a parent experiences depression during the adjustment to having a child), there are relationship level components to consider, such as the parental marriage, particularly in terms of how contradictory emotions are experienced (e.g., how love *and* conflict are both present in a marriage). The transition to parenthood, then, is a hotbed of new challenges because several individuals and subsystems are being disrupted as the family system attempts to reestablish equilibrium after the addition of a new member. As a rule, family systems seek balance and resist change, making them vulnerable to stress when change does occur. The husband–wife relationship, the mother–child relationship, the father–child relationship, and the eventual sibling–sibling relationship are just a few of the subsystems that are put on high alert upon the birth of a child. Further, given the interrelatedness of all members in the system, how each member is affected and responds impacts everyone else. According to family systems theory, there is pressure to restabilize. Some parental subsystems have a smoother transition than others.

When a major milestone such as the birth of a new baby occurs, family systems theory predicts that family relationships and patterns become unstable. The resulting disequilibrium can intensify existing family problems (e.g., conflict between spouses) and also allow positive adjustments as the family seeks homeostasis in order to rebalance in light of the new disruptions to the system. Holmes, Sasaki, and Hazen (2013) sought to understand why some couples are able to navigate the transition to parenthood more easily than other couples. They hypothesized that parental gender (being a mother or father), infant gender (whether the first child is a boy or a girl), infant temperament (whether the infant is fussy and reactive, or calm and easily soothed), the emotional climate in the family (whether individuals are depressed), how realistic the parents' expectations are about having a new baby, and the presence of both love and conflict between husbands and wives, will affect the transition to parenthood for men and women. Ultimately the authors asked, what is it about variations among mothers, fathers, infants, marriages, and families that facilitates a smooth or rocky adjustment to parenthood?

One of the main findings had to do with fathers, which is important because so little research actually incorporates the perspectives and voices of fathers. In this study, the baby's reactivity and the baby's gender were factors in fathers' adjustment. The authors found that fathers' marital conflict increased if they had a fussy baby, or if they had a daughter, a finding that corresponds to the worldwide preference for boys, or at least for the firstborn to be a boy. The study also had many implications for family intervention, so as to educate and prepare new parents with realistic expectations about how their lives would be affected when introducing an infant into the family system.

Family systems theory in practice

Over the course of 40 years, Murray Bowen (1985) developed a version of general systems theory that he applied to the study and treatment of emotional processes in families. Like Bateson et al. (1956), Bowen originally used family systems theory in relation to families who had a member diagnosed with schizophrenia. Over time, Bowen and his collaborators developed their version of family systems theory to include society's role in contributing to dysfunctional or toxic family interactions and to helping us understand that problems with emotional functioning occur in all families, including so-called "normal families" (Broderick, 1993; Kerr and Bowen, 1988). Bowen's family systems theory is a very appealing one for family scholars and practitioners because it recognizes that in order to understand emotional functioning in family relationships, one must become an expert in one's own emotional functioning in relationships. This theory teaches that we are all susceptible to observational blindness, and that becoming adept at recognizing the "triggers" that cause you to react in certain ways is a helpful skill in human services and other helping professions (Comella, 2011).

Bowen (1985) proposed several interrelated ideas that are very influential in how scholars and clinicians think about internal family dynamics, particularly in the therapeutic setting. For example, **differentiation of self** refers to one's sense of being an individual compared to being related to others. This concept captures a person's ability to distinguish what they think from what they feel, and to respond appropriately to anxiety and stress (Baucom and Atkins, 2013; Kerr and Bowen, 1988). Another very helpful idea is that of **triangulation**, when a three-person relationship occurs and two of the members of the relationship exclude the third. A triangle is formed in order to stabilize the family unit (Titelman, 2008). The classic example is when the parental interaction becomes overly stressful, a child is pulled in ("triangulated") to smooth things over between the parents (McGoldrick, Gerson, and Petry, 2008; Taylor, Robila, and Fisackerly, 2013). Emotional units, in Bowenian theory, refer to the system of interlocking triangles that help to maintain the family system in the face of chronic anxiety, conflict, and other intense emotions (Comella, 2011). **Emotional cut-off** refers to the extreme distancing that family members can experience as a way of coping with heightened anxiety. When such intensity is activated, an "emotional divorce" may be a way of coping with the swell of emotions that occur. Family transitions (e.g., the birth of a new child; when a young adult moves out of the parental home; the death of an aging parent) are crucial times when emotional cut-off often occurs. In this way, a major jolt to family equilibrium that triggers stress and emotional withdrawal may also be seen as an adaptive reaction.

Conclusion

Family systems theory has provided important ideas that allow family researchers and practitioners to put the theory to use beyond the conceptual level. Stemming from general systems theory and cybernetics, scholars have developed ways in which systems theory can be applied to the study of families as a unit using multiple levels of analysis, and analyzing both internal and external shifts in systems. Family systems theory helps us to understand the interacting dynamics of the entire family, providing a more comprehensive view that moves beyond the perspective of individual family members. One of the most important parts of family systems theory is helping us understand that we are all responsible for our own part in any interaction, and what we do impacts the whole system. Understanding how a system operates helps each one of us to initiate changes that are needed for healthy family interaction.

Finally, it is important to understand how family systems theory is applicable to the study of families across the globe. Earlier in this chapter, you read about hierarchies within families. How families are structured as a system will affect the type of communication, established boundaries, and feedback loops. In Box 6.3, we consider how concepts associated with family hierarchies are represented in different countries and regions of the world. We challenge you to consider these global applications of the theory as you move on to the areas for further study and the discussion and reflection questions in the concluding pages of this chapter.

Box 6.3 Global Comparisons of Family Hierarchies and Gendered Power

Though of course there are exceptions everywhere, most countries still value men's lives over women's. The United Nations report *The world's women 2010: Trends and statistics* (2012) provides demographics from various countries regarding gender traditions practiced in countries around the world. From the UN's analysis, it is clear that women have less power than men in terms of all major indicators of well-being, including that they are more likely to live in poverty; they are more likely to be subjected to violence both in and outside their home; they have less access to education and employment; and they are overwhelmingly responsible for child care. Consider the various practices around the globe in which male dominance in families (e.g., family hierarchy) is reproduced and put into action.

Preference for sons In many Asian countries, there is a shortage of women, most likely due to practices that reflect the preference for sons over daughters. For example, there is a high prevalence of prenatal testing for the sex of the child and the abortion of female fetuses. The sex ratio at birth is about 109 to 117 males to every 100 females in Asia. And, in countries such as Korea, families are hierarchically organized around the eldest male, who is consulted in important decision-making and management of the family. This hierarchy is arranged both by age (oldest men are the most important) and gender (women are least important).

Rapid aging of the population The world population is rapidly aging, but the increases are more significant in some parts of the globe than others. One of the most rapid changes in the aging of society has occurred throughout southern, northern, and western Europe, in countries such as England, France, Italy, and Norway. In southern Europe, for example, 25 percent of the population is 60 years of age or older. In the gender hierarchy, women provide the primary care for older and younger family members. Yet, as women live longer than men, most of the aging population is female. These demographics have implications for the well-being of aging women in particular: who will provide care for them as they become old?

International migration of the workforce Women are now just as likely as men to seek employment away from their home countries. Most immigrant workers come from developing countries, and migrate to one of the 30 developed nations. Migrant women are typically employed as housekeepers and nannies, in countries such as Canada, Japan, and Israel. They often migrate from countries in which they have few opportunities to make a living and support their children, countries that include those in southern and northern Africa and Central America. Although they join wealthy households, as workers who are paid to care for others, their place in the family hierarchy is at a very low level.

Multimedia Suggestions

www.gottman.com

John Gottman's (1994) research has become well known for predicting whether or not a married couple is likely to get divorced. Over his career, Dr Gottman and his wife Dr Julie Gottman have been able to successfully predict and explain factors leading to divorce with an over 85 percent accuracy rate. The Gottman Institute's website provides links to research articles, relationship help, educator training, parenting advice, and clinical training for family practitioners and individuals.

Activate your theory app: There is a strong emphasis on research throughout this website. Where can you see evidence of theory? Can you see evidence of other theories, besides family systems theory, on this website?

www.thebowencenter.org

This website, of the Bowen Center for the Study of the Family, provides information on family systems theory as well as recent research using the theory. The website also provides links to information on clinical services for families, upcoming meetings, training materials, and other publications that are helpful for family therapists, teachers, and other practitioners.

Activate your theory app: How could this website resource be used for practitioners, researchers, and teachers who are not going into the field of family and marriage therapy?

Weeds (2005–2012)

This television series was featured in Chapter 3 (conflict theory), but we are featuring it again in this chapter because it is useful to illustrate how family theorists can use the same content to see very different theories and concepts. The main character, Nancy, is a widowed mother of two boys who begins selling marijuana to support her family after her husband dies suddenly. She has very different relationships with each of her sons, which create important subsystems within the family that add to the overall functioning of the family system. In addition, this show illustrates the concept of feedback, both negative and positive, as it guides Nancy's behavior and decision-making when it comes to her family.

A scene from *Weeds*, 2005, cr. Jenji Kohan, Lionsgate Television/Showtime Networks

Activate your theory app: Are there similarities between how conflict theory (Chapter 3) and family systems theory can be applied to this television show? What about the other theories covered so far in this book?

Nurse Jackie (2009–2015)

This dark comedy-drama portrays Jackie, a married mother of two daughters who is addicted to narcotics. Her addiction eventually leads to divorce, which only complicates the parental relationship as they seek to deal with the acting-out behavior of their older daughter, Grace. In the language of Bowenian family systems theory, Grace becomes the "symptom bearer" or "identified patient." Although family dynamics include the secrecy around drug addiction, it is Grace's behavior that brings the family into therapy.

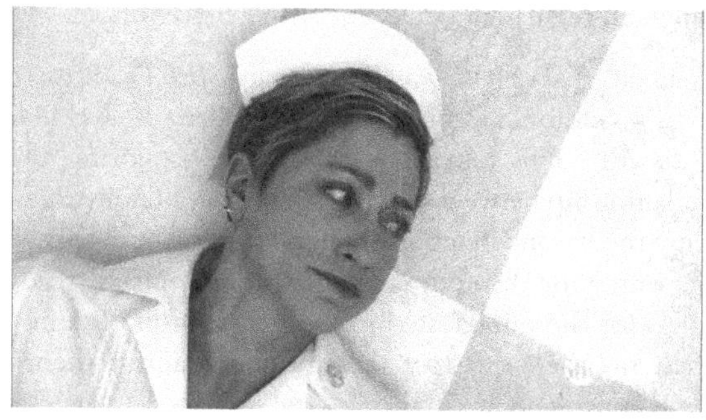

A scene from *Nurse Jackie*, 2009, cr. Liz Brixius, Evan Dunsky and Linda Wallem, Lionsgate Television

Activate your theory app: Describe the subsystems found in this television show. How does each subsystem interact with other aspects of Jackie's family? Consider how feedback affects each system as well.

Further Reading

Boss, P., *Loss, trauma, and resilience: Therapeutic work with ambiguous loss* (New York: Norton, 2006). Pauline Boss expands on and applies her theory of ambiguous loss to understanding how stress and trauma can be treated in clinical practice in order to enhance coping, resiliency, and health for individuals and their families. The theory of ambiguous loss deals with both absence and presence in families. A family member could be psychologically absent but physically present, as in the case of a parent with dementia. A family member could also be physically absent but psychologically present, as in the case of a son missing in action during a war. These experiences of ambiguous loss can keep family members frozen in grief. Treatment and understanding should focus on resiliency, which is "the ability to regain one's energy after adversity drains it" (p. 27).

Lerner, H. G., *Marriage rules: A manual for the married and the coupled up* (New York: Penguin, 2013). Harriet Lerner writes widely popular and readable books about women's emotional lives and their interpersonal relationships. She applies Bowen's family systems theory to marriage, family, and friendship ties. In her recent book, Lerner provides suggestions that hit the "hot spots" in marriage and other long-term relationships, including how to fight fair, listen well, avoid overtalking and defensiveness, establish boundaries, deal with difficult family members, and handle your partner's relationship with technology.

Kantor, D., and Lehr, W., *Inside the family: Toward a theory of family process* (San Francisco: Jossey-Bass, 1975). In this highly influential text, David Kantor and William Lehr provide one of the classic revisions of general systems theory by applying systems concepts to the micro-level of family interaction. They propose that the family system is composed of three subsystems: the family-unit subsystem, the interpersonal subsystem, and the personal subsystem. This book was one of the first to show that seemingly simple family processes are actually very complex rules for governing and regulating family members' behaviors.

Journal of Feminist Family Therapy (*JFFT*) (http://www.tandfonline.com/toc/wfft20/current#.UrH8yOIswt0). This journal is devoted to exploring the relationship between feminist theory and family therapy theory and practice. *JFFT* offers a comprehensive resource for theoretical, applied, and empirical readings for those interested in the intersection of family systems theory, family therapy, and feminist theory and practice. Check the journal website for articles regarding the treatment of mental health issues, trauma, intimate partner violence, and relational problems.

Regalia, C., Manzi, C., and Scabini, E., "Individuation and differentiation in families across cultures," in M. A. Fine and F. D. Fincham (eds), *Handbook of family theories: A content-based approach* (New York: Routledge, 2013), pp. 437–455. The authors examine the dual concepts of individuation (i.e., how individuals develop their identity) and differentiation (i.e., how parents and families either support or hinder the individuation process) in cultural context. They give examples of how the development of the self is reflective of different cultural norms and practices. For example, collectivist cultures, often found in Asian countries, differ from western societies, such as those in North America and the United Kingdom, by emphasizing the greater influence of the extended family and wider community in how a person becomes "a social being" (p. 442). In India, for example, individual identity is best seen as a "familial self" because of the emphasis on respect for the authority of older generations.

Questions for Students

Discussion Questions

1 Do you think the general systems metaphor can be applied in a universal way? That is, do family systems resemble inanimate systems, or are there aspects of living systems (e.g., families) that are unique and not reducible to the metaphor of a machine?
2 Which metaphor of family systems theory most appeals to you?
3 Systems theory in family science has been very effective in terms of family therapy and marital communication research. What are other areas where you might apply "systemic thinking"?
4 How is family systems theory different from functionalist theory (Chapter 2)? How is it similar?
5 Describe how family systems theory would apply to the study of a Mexican American family newly immigrated to the US. Does family systems theory take into account issues such as culture shock, generational change, and assimilation?
6 In what ways do the new technologies (Skype, Facetime, etc.) facilitate family interaction and cohesion when family members are living in separate cities, nations, or continents? How can technology be used to strengthen families and intervene in problems of loneliness, isolation, and other associated stressors? Are there particular strategies that are useful for children who are separated from their parents?

Your Turn!

Construct a family genogram by going back to as many generations as you know, using the concepts and symbols in the McGoldrick, Gerson, and Petry (2008) book and Figure 6.2 as a resource. Locate an older relative (e.g., a grandparent, a great aunt, a third cousin) to help you fill in the gaps of key genogram components such as birth, death, marriage, divorce dates, and other key patterns that have happened in the past several generations. What are the patterns that you notice across the generations? How have they affected your life?

Personal Reflection Questions

1 Use a family systems perspective to analyze and describe a family whose origin is very different from your own. Select a family who you consider to be very different. Are there meaningful ways to understand such differences, using family systems theory?
2 Consider your parents' and grandparents' generations, and what was considered to be normal communication for them growing up. Has "normal" shifted over time? How are hierarchies and subsystems related to communication styles, across these generations?
3 How do you understand sibling relationships? Where are you in the birth order: an only child, a youngest, an oldest, or somewhere in the middle? How do your gender, sexual orientation, race, and other characteristics affect your sibling relationships?
4 Think about an experience in your family where there is an emotional cut-off. How did this family process begin? Who is helping to maintain it? What need does it serve? What are ways you could intervene to help your family become "unstuck"?
5 Are there other systems to which we can apply concepts of family systems theory? What about your "fictive kin" – or non-blood related friends you consider family?
6 What is an example in your own life of the systems notion that "if something isn't working, more of the same won't work"? Have you ever found yourself caught in such a cycle of resistance to change? What helped you break the pattern and try a new strategy?

References

Ackerman, N. J. (1984). *A theory of family systems.* New York: Gardner.

Anderson, S. A., Sabatelli, R. M., and Kosutic, I. (2013). Systemic and ecological qualities of families. In G. W. Peterson and K. R. Bush (eds), *Handbook of marriage and the family* (3rd edn, pp. 121–138). New York: Springer.

Bateson, G., Jackson, D. D., Haley, J., and Weakland, J. (1956). Toward a theory of schizophrenia. *Behavioral Science, 1,* 251–263. doi:10.1002/bs.3830010402.

Baucom, B. R., and Atkins, D. C. (2013). Understanding marital distress: Polarization processes. In M. A. Fine and F. D. Fincham (eds), *Handbook of family theories: A content-based approach* (pp. 145–166). New York: Norton.

Beavers, W. R., and Hampson, R. B. (2000). The Beavers systems model of family functioning. *Journal of Family Therapy, 22,* 128–143. doi:10.1111/1467-6427.00143.

Benson, M. J., Curtner-Smith, M. E., Collins, W. A., and Keith, T. Z. (1995). The structure of family perceptions among adolescents and their parents: Individual satisfaction factors and family system factors. *Family Process, 34,* 323–336. doi:10.1111/j.1545-5300.1995.00323.x.

Blaisure, K. R., Saathoff-Wells, T., Pereira, A., Wadsworth, S. M., and Dombro, A. L. (2012). *Serving military families in the 21st century.* New York: Routledge.

Bowen, M. (1985). *Family therapy in clinical practice.* New York: Jason Aronson.

Bradshaw, J. (1988). *Healing the shame that binds you.* Deerfield Beach, FL: Health Communications.

Broderick, C. B. (1993). *Understanding family process: Basics of family systems theory.* Newbury Park, CA: Sage.

Broderick, C., and Smith, J. (1979). The general systems approach to the family. In W. R. Burr, R. Hill, F. I. Nye, and I. L. Reiss (eds), *Contemporary theories about the family* (vol. 2, pp. 112–129). New York: Free Press.

Brown, B. (2012). *Daring greatly: How the courage to be vulnerable transforms the way we live, love, parent, and lead.* New York: Gotham.

Burton, L. (2007). Childhood adultification in economically disadvantaged families: A conceptual model. *Family Relations, 56,* 329–345. doi:10.1111/j.1741-3729.2007.00463.x.

Comella, P. A. (2011). Observing emotional functioning in human relationship systems: Lessons from Murray Bowen's writings. In O. C. Bregman and C. M. White (eds), *Bringing systems thinking to life: Expanding the horizons for Bowen family systems theory* (pp. 3–30). New York: Routledge.

Conley, D. (2004). *The pecking order: Which siblings succeed and why.* New York: Pantheon.

Cowan, P. A., Cohn, D. A., Cowan, C. P., and Pearson, J. L. (1996). Parents' attachment histories and children's externalizing and internalizing behaviors: Exploring family systems models of linkage. *Journal of Consulting and Clinical Psychology*, *64*, 53–63, special section on attachment and psychopathology. doi:10.1037/0022-006X.64.1.53.

Cox, M. J. (2010). Family systems and sibling relationships. *Child Development Perspectives*, *4*, 95–96. doi:10.1111/j.1750-8606.2010.00124.x.

Crimone, M. W., and Hester, D. (2011). Across the generations: The training of clergy and congregations. In O. C. Bregman and C. M. White (eds), *Bringing systems thinking to life: Expanding the horizons for Bowen family systems theory* (pp. 197–207). New York: Routledge.

Drummet, A. R., Coleman, M., and Cable, S. (2003). Military families under stress: Implications for family life education. *Family Relations*, *52*, 279–287. doi:10.1111/j.1741-3729.2003.00279.x.

Faber, A. J., Willerton, E., Clymer, S. R., MacDermid, S. M., and Weiss, H. M. (2008). Ambiguous absence, ambiguous presence: A qualitative study of military reserve families in wartime. *Journal of Family Psychology*, *22*, 222–230. doi:10.1037/0893-3200.22.2.222.

Galvin, K. M., Dickson, F. C., and Marrow, S. R. (2006). *Systems theory: Patterns and (w)holes in family communication*. Thousand Oaks, CA: Sage.

Goldenberg, H., and Goldenberg, I. (2013). *Family therapy: An overview* (8th edn). Belmont, CA: Brooks/Cole.

Gottman, J. M. (1994). *What predicts divorce: The relationship between marital processes and marital outcomes*. Hillsdale, NJ: Lawrence Erlbaum.

Grych, J., Oxtoby, C., and Lynn, M. (2013). The effects of interparental conflict on children. In M. A. Fine and F. D. Fincham (eds), *Handbook of family theories: A content-based approach* (pp. 228–245). New York: Norton.

Holmes, E. K., and Huston, A. C. (2010). Understanding positive father–child interaction: Children's, fathers', and mothers' contributions. *Fathering: A Journal of Research, Theory, and Practice about Men as Fathers*, *8*, 203–225. doi:10.3149/fth.1802.203.

Holmes, E. K., Sasaki, T., and Hazen, N. L. (2013). Smooth versus rocky transitions to parenthood: Family systems in developmental context. *Family Relations*, *62*, 824–837. doi:10.1111/fare.12041.

Johnson, S. M. (2004). *The practice of emotionally focused marital therapy: Creating connections* (2nd edn). New York: Brunner/Mazel.

Kerr, M. E., and Bowen, M. (1988). *Family evaluation: An approach based on Bowen theory*. New York: Norton.

Leslie, L. A., and Southard, A. L. (2009). Thirty years of feminist family therapy: Moving into the mainstream. In S. A. Lloyd, A. L. Few, and K. R. Allen (eds), *Handbook of feminist family studies* (pp. 328–339). Thousand Oaks, CA: Sage.

Lewis, M. (2006). *The blind side: Evolution of a game*. New York: Norton.

Luepnitz, D. (2002). *The family interpreted: Psychoanalysis, feminism, and family therapy*. New York: Basic. (Originally published 1988.)

Macfie, J., Mcelwain, N. L., Houts, R. M., and Cox, M. J. (2007). Intergenerational transmission of role reversal between parent and child: Dyadic and family systems internal working models. *Attachment and Human Development*, 7, 51–65. doi:10.1080/14616730500039663.

McGoldrick, M., Gerson, R., and Petry, S. (2008). *Genograms: Assessment and intervention* (3rd edn). New York: Norton.

Minuchin, P. (1985). Families and individual development: Provocations from the field of family therapy. *Child Development*, *56*, 289–302. doi:10.1111/j.1467-8624.1985.tb00106.x.

Norton, J. (2011). Bringing Bowen theory to family business. In O. C. Bregman and C. M. White (eds), *Bringing systems thinking to life: Expanding the horizons for Bowen family systems theory* (pp. 219–227). New York: Routledge.

O'Gorman, S. (2012). Attachment theory, family system theory, and the child presenting with significant behavioral concerns. *Journal of Systemic Therapies*, *31*, 1–16. doi:10.1521/jsyt.2012.31.3.1.

Olson, D. H. (2000). Circumplex model of marital and family systems. *Journal of Family Therapy*, *22*, 144–167. doi:10.1111/1467-6427.00144.

Olson, D. H., Sprenkle, D. H., and Russell, C. S. (1979). Circumplex model of marital and family systems: I. Cohesion and adaptability dimensions, family types, and clinical applications. *Family Process*, *18*, 3–28. doi:10.1111/j.1545-5300.1979.00003.x.

Paley, B., Lester, P., and Mogil, C. (2013). Family systems and ecological perspectives on the impact of deployment on military families. *Clinical Child and Family Psychology Review*, *16*, 245–265. doi:10.1007/s10567-013-0138-y.

Pinkus, S. (2006). Family systems: Applying a family systems perspective for understanding parent–professional relationships: A study of families located in the Anglo-Jewish community. *Support for Learning*, *21*, 156–161. doi:10.1111/j.1467-9604.2006.00422.x.

Rosenblatt, P. C. (1994). *Metaphors of family systems theory: Toward new constructions*. New York: Guilford Press.

Rosenblatt, P.C. (2013). Family systems theory as a tool for anyone dealing with personal or family loss. *The Forum: Quarterly Publication of the Association for Death Education and Counseling*, *39*(1), 12–13.

Rothblaum, F., Rosen, K., Ujiie, T., and Uchida, N. (2002). Family systems theory, attachment theory, and culture. *Family Process*, *41*, 328–350. doi:10.1111/j.1545-5300.2002.41305.x.

Satir, V. (1988). *The new peoplemaking*. Palo Alto, CA: Science and Behavior Books.

Silverstein, L. B., and Goodrich, T.J. (eds) (2003). *Feminist family therapy: Empowerment in social context*. Washington, DC: American Psychological Association.

Suitor, J. J., Gilligan, M., and Pillemer, K. (2013). Continuity and change in mothers' favoritism toward offspring in adulthood. *Journal of Marriage and Family*, *75*, 1229–1247. doi:10.1111/jomf.12067.

Taylor, A. C., Robila, M., and Fisackerly, B. (2013). Theory use in stepfamily research. In M. A. Fine and F. D. Fincham (eds), *Handbook of family theories: A content-based approach* (pp. 280–297). New York: Norton.

Titelman, P. (ed.) (2008). *Triangles: Bowen family systems theory perspectives*. New York: Haworth.

United Nations (2012). *The world's women 2010: Trends and statistics*. At http://unstats.un.org/unsd/demographic/products/Worldswomen/WW2010pub.htm.

von Bertalanffy, L. (1973). *General system theory: Foundations, development, applications* (rev. edn). New York: George Braziller.

Walsh, F. (2009). Human–animal bonds II: The role of pets in family systems and family therapy. *Family Process*, *48*, 481–499. doi:10.1111/j.1545-5300.2009.01297.x.

Whitchurch, G. G., and Constantine, L. L. (1993). Systems theory. In P. Boss, W. Doherty, R. LaRossa, W. Schumm, and S. Steinmetz (eds), *Sourcebook of family theories and methods: A contextual approach* (pp. 325–352). New York: Plenum.

White, J. M., Klein, D. M., and Martin, T. F. (2015). *Family theories: An introduction* (4th edn). Thousand Oaks, CA: Sage.

White, M., and Epston, D. (1990). *Narrative means to therapeutic ends*. New York: Norton.

Wiener, N. (1967). *The human use of human beings: Cybernetics and society*. New York: Avon.

7

Social Exchange Theory

In a world where sitcoms have increasingly been replaced by reality television, it is interesting to consider just how *real* reality shows truly are. Is it possible that producers are puppeteering the reality characters from behind the scenes? Further, is it possible that when romantic relationships occur on reality television, they are predetermined and maybe not based on what many of us consider to be "true" love? As much as we would like to believe the contrary, the truth is that most of these shows are actually scripted, and the "romance" we see, even when it is supposed to be real, is created and sold to us for other reasons. The same goes for shows that depict families and their daily lives as reality television.

Imagine being privy to conversations that occur around the proverbial "board room" table between television producers and actors' and actresses' agents. Producers are fishing for a romance to sell, and agents know that even staged on-air romances boost the familiarity of and likability of their clients. Perhaps what occurs behind these closed doors is similar to a draft for sports teams. The typecast heartthrob character is sought after for the romance, as is the shy, girl-next-door character. In exchange for their agreeing to be a part of an on-screen romance, they are promised more air time, appearances on talk shows to promote the show, and other endorsement deals. The romance we see on television, then, is hardly what it is in reality. Each of these deals is struck behind the scenes, perhaps before filming even begins, and is based on a pragmatic cost/benefit analysis. Further, think about the power relations that are present during the discussion of the "plot" of the show. Who holds the power, and who wants it? Is the exchange that occurs between the actors, actresses, agents, and producers balanced, or imbalanced? Are there intrinsic (e.g., internal) or extrinsic (e.g., external) rewards to anyone involved, by striking a deal to create a romance for the show? What happens if one of the actors develops feelings for someone else on the set, or even more complicated, if they already have a partner off-screen? When it comes to love and relationship negotiation, the costs, benefits, and intrinsic and extrinsic rewards for behavior have real consequences for individuals and families.

Social exchange theory provides family researchers and practitioners with a useful way to understand how dating, marriage, and family relationships can often be based on the use of exchange in decision-making. In this chapter, we discuss the history of social exchange theory, and how the principles and key concepts apply to the study of families and individual relationships. Social exchange theory helps us answer questions about how individuals within families and other relationships negotiate the "best deal" for themselves, based on the availability of power, rewards, and costs. In order to gain a fuller understanding of how this theory works, we start with a case study that illustrates how romantic relationships and families can be understood using the concepts of social exchange.

Case Study

Stefan and Christina have been married for over 10 years, and have three children. Both parents work outside the home, and have negotiated the roles inside the household to be fairly equitable. For example, Christina loves to cook, so Stefan does the dishes.

Family Theories: Foundations and Applications, First Edition. Katherine R. Allen and Angela C. Henderson.

They take turns driving the children to and from school and soccer, helping the seven and nine year olds with homework, volunteering in the children's classrooms, and other activities. Their youngest is only 18 months old, so they even take turns changing dirty diapers and preparing her for bedtime. They each get time to themselves as well: Christina exercises four days a week, and Stefan plays in a recreational softball league. Their family life is busy, with most weekdays and weekends scheduled down to the hour because of all they have going on. The five of them are satisfied with the arrangements, and are a very close-knit family that works together well as a unit. Their roles have each been negotiated so that Stefan and Christina feel like they spend quality time alone, with each other, as well as with each of the children, thanks to their distribution of household labor.

One aspect of the couple's lives that is still relatively unbalanced is Stefan and Christina's work lives. Christina has a prestigious job that offers her flexibility, travel, and contract work that supplements the family's income so that they can take family vacations together, renovate their home, and still have money left over for savings. Stefan, on the other hand, is at a standstill in his career. He has hit the earning ceiling in his occupation – making 40 percent less than Christina – and has recently started looking for other jobs in his field. The problem is, his area of expertise is so specific that a promotion would mean the family would need to relocate. He spent years working on his specialized graduate degree and his only jobs have been in a specific area within higher education. Stefan has really struggled with feelings of depression and despair, constantly comparing himself to his wife in terms of salary and flexibility and overall happiness because Christina is arguably at the peak of her career.

Ten years into their marriage, Stefan has a meltdown and admits to Christina that he cannot do it anymore. Though it goes against the way he has approached his career his entire adult life, he decides to leave his position and seek out a job in a different field. He loves his family and his children, and does not want the family to relocate because financially, it would not make sense to move everyone for his lower-paying job. Instead, Stefan tells Christina that he has "come to terms" with his career being secondary to hers. It took 10 years and extensive thought, but he tells her he is okay with not being the main breadwinner. He starts stepping aside for Christina to excel in her career by fulfilling the traditionally "feminine" roles of taking time off of work to care for sick children and doing more at home so that Christina has less to worry about and can focus more time and energy on her career. This decision did not come without costs; Stefan struggled with feeling emasculated, disappointed professionally, and resentful towards his wife. However, in the end, Stefan told Christina he does not want to be on his deathbed and be known for being a great employee; he wants to be known for being a good father and husband. He truly embraces his new perspective of his identity, and the family is stronger because of it.

Think about the complexities associated with both Stefan and Christina's relationship as well as their family life as a whole. Throughout the time they have been together, they have had to negotiate the costs and benefits of each step of their relationship. The first two times they relocated, it was for Stefan's career. It was not until the last eight years that Christina's career really took off, which both contributed to the financial security of the family as well as the overall family functioning because her schedule was much more flexible than Stefan's. In fact, her security and flexibility contributed to the couple's decision to have a third child. For each step in their lives, Stefan and Christina had to consider the available resources, rewards, costs, and commitment as they moved forward. Some marriages dissolve when the couple faces a crossroads like this; why did that not happen for Stefan and Christina? In addition, what might have happened if Stefan and Christina had not had children? Would the relationship be more fickle, and subject to dissolution? Social exchange theory helps researchers and practitioners frame family issues in terms of the balance between individuals' self-interest, norms of reciprocity, and available alternatives.

This theoretical framework focuses on how dependence in a relationship can lead to commitment and persistence. Social exchange theorists might suggest that Christina's level of financial dependence on Stefan is relatively low, but at the same time, she relies heavily on him to perform the *unpaid* tasks of child-rearing and household management. His devotion to their family is vital to her success. In addition, until

Stefan came to terms with his place in the family as the secondary breadwinner, he struggled with his self-interested desire to continue moving up in his career at the cost of his family's stability and security. Although these issues appear on the surface to be at the level of the individual, social exchange theory suggests that these decisions are not made in a vacuum. At the core of these seemingly individualistic decisions, there is – at a minimum – the presence of at least one other person; thus, the name social *exchange* theory! This perspective gives researchers and practitioners unique insight into how relationships are formed, maintained, and dissolved, and how they are affected by family growth and change.

What Is Social Exchange Theory?

Social exchange theory posits that all human relationships can be understood in terms of a cost-benefit analysis and the exchange of resources available to participants. When it comes to families, this theory is useful for examining relationships at their inception, sometimes before they are even formed! Why did you enter into your current relationship? Or, why are you *not* currently in a relationship? This theory's applicability does not stop at the onset of a relationship; it also can be used to understand how relationships shift, grow, and change over time, as well as why they end. One of the major assumptions of this theory is the idea that people act out of **self-interest** and are interdependent on one another (Lawler and Thye, 1999). This means that individuals have something of value to bring to a relationship, and during interaction they decide whether or not to exchange those "goods" and in what amounts (Lawler, 2001). It is important to remember that self-interest does not need to always be conceptualized as a negative, greed-driven act. In fact, it could be argued that most people are involved in relationships because of a sense of fulfillment, which is a guiding force of human interaction (Roloff, 1981). Therefore, whether willing or even able to admit it, people often form relationships based on the consideration of "what's in it for me?" while also considering possible alternatives.

While this might seem harsh when applied to loved ones, think about your own selection of a significant other. In response to the questions raised earlier about your past and current relationship status, make a list of three to five reasons why you answered the way that you did. Are you single by choice? If so, what is the driving force behind that preference? Chances are, your reasons for whatever your relationship status is have roots in social exchange theory. Maybe you *prefer* to not be controlled by a significant other. Maybe you no longer felt attracted to the other person you were last in a relationship with. On the contrary, if you are in a relationship, examine *why* that is the case. Does the other person build up your self-confidence? Does she or he support you when you need it? Really consider the heart (no pun intended) of the relationship and whether or not self-interest plays a role. Also consider what you depend on the other person for, and vice versa. Maybe what we define as "love" is in reality just an exchange of feelings that we experience when we are around the other person. Maybe we feel inseparable or so compatible that we cannot imagine a day without that person. Is interdependence at the heart of that feeling? Is it in our best interest to build a life with the person we most enjoy spending our time with, because it is fulfilling? At the core of these considerations is social exchange; emotional support, connections, trust, and obligations are all elements in a relationship that can be exchanged between two people.

Considering relationships in that way, hopefully it can become easier to see beyond the quantitative, economics-based cost-benefit analysis and apply this theory to love and relationships, as well as to your own individual preferences. In fact, most of the other theories you have read about in this book have focused on the family as the unit of analysis. By contrast, social exchange theory begins with the individual as the unit of analysis. As originally proposed by George Homans (1958), any social entity (e.g., a person, a family, a social structure such as work) can be understood at the level of the individual. The "self-interested" individual is in the center of an exchange analysis. As such, "the needs, wants, and desires of an individual account for his or her actions" (Perry-Jenkins and MacDermid, 2013, p. 386). Therefore, it may be useful to consider your own preferences, needs, and experiences in *any* relationship, and how they have influenced the outcome. If you have heard (or given) the excuse "it's not you, it's me" when a relationship is ending, you probably already understand the basis of this theoretical framework. When we hear that phrase, we often consider it to be a clichéd excuse for ending a relationship, a "cop-out" of sorts. In reality, the person using that phrase may actually be telling the truth because his or her own self-interest is at risk. In most relationships, we *do* try to do what is best for ourselves, and we *do* often put ourselves first, knowingly or not. Below, we go into more detail about the historical underpinnings of this theory that contribute to where this framework is today, including its usefulness and applicability to individuals, relationships, and families.

History and origins

As with all theories, it is important to examine the historical context in which the theory was developed. Social exchange theory has a rich history across a range of academic fields, such as cultural anthropology, economics, behavioral psychology, and sociology. Over time, the theory has been adapted to a number of other contexts, and is especially relevant in the study of interpersonal relationships and families today. The origins of the theory are rooted in two basic philosophical principles: utilitarianism and behaviorism. Utilitarianism refers to a view held by early economists, such as Jeremy Bentham and John Stuart Mill, that humans are rational and self-interested, and they try to maximize the "benefits or utility from transactions or exchanges with others in a free and competitive marketplace" (Sabatelli and Shehan, 1993, p. 387). Essentially, when people make "utilitarian" decisions, they are doing what is best for themselves.

Another key influence on the origins of exchange theory can be found in the work of cultural anthropologists, particularly Claude Lévi-Strauss, who went beyond the individual level of rational exchange, and conceptualized exchange as collectivist, whereby social norms and institutions regulate interpersonal exchanges (Sabatelli and Shehan, 1993). This means that cultural expectations dictate what types of exchanges we participate in, and are decided at the societal level as opposed to the individual level. Later in this chapter, we discuss arranged marriages as an example of the collectivist type of social exchange theory.

Behaviorism, on the other hand, focuses on how individuals participate in behavior based on operant learning theory and reinforcement. This concept was developed by B. F. Skinner and attempted to explain the persistence of exchange relations. Behaviorists examine why people engage in behaviors time and time again. This aspect of social exchange theory helps us understand why some men or women, for example, are attracted to a certain *type* of significant other, even if that relationship does not on the surface appear to be in the person's best interest. For instance, consistently dating the "rebel" type fulfills a need, and after dating several rebels over a period of time, the behavior becomes a pattern. Something about that type of significant other elicits a profit and payoff. Indeed, Cook and Rice explain that "behavior is a function of payoffs" (2003, p. 54) that can be found in the exchange of activity between at least two individuals.

One of the early theorists who developed the **behavioral psychological approach** to exchange was George Homans (1958). Not only was he interested in exchange as an interaction of activity, but he was also influential in proposing that reinforcement principles keep an exchange going over time. Homans's early work on exchange theory focused mostly on the psychological aspects of exchange as it occurred between a dyad, or two individuals. Homans believed that social exchange was based on three reinforcement principles: (a) success proposition, (b) stimulus proposition; and (c) deprivation-satiation proposition. **Success proposition** provides the basis for social exchange in that it supposes that when individuals are rewarded for their actions, they repeat them. Then, a **stimulus proposition** leads the individual to respond to a stimulus that provided a reward in the past. Finally, **deprivation-satiation** refers to when the reward itself loses value after it has been given too often in the recent past to hold high value.

Essentially, this early model specifically investigated why individuals would engage in exchange, and also why the exchange might cease to exist. In Homans's (1958) view, humans continue to participate in an exchange (or relationship) until participation ceases to be rewarding. An example of this would be the beginning stages of romantic relationships. Early on, partners often engage in romantic gestures like showering their love interest with flowers, compliments, and gifts. Initially, these acts might elicit excitement and appreciation of the newness of the relationship. However, over time, if the gifts and attention continue, their power to reward wears off. At this point, deprivation-saturation is reached and therefore the reward loses value. The receiver may even start to get sick of all the attention. Feeling so saturated with such attention, according to Homans's early conceptualization of social exchange, could end the relationship.

Peter Blau (1964) was another early social exchange theorist who contributed to this theoretical perspective with his sociological background. Blau moved beyond analyzing the reinforcement principles of the dyad and of instrumental (i.e., learned) behavior. Building upon an **economic-utilitarian framework**, Blau extended exchange theory to a model that included an understanding of the institutions and organizations that emerge out of social exchange. In doing so, Blau abandoned Homans's behavioral psychological analysis and instead focused on sociological issues such as power, inequality, and norms of legitimation (Appelrouth and Edles, 2011).

Blau focused on **power**, which he defined in a similar way to sociologist Max Weber as "the probability that one actor within a social relationship will be in a position to carry out his own will despite resistance" (Blau, 1964, p. 115). By stepping back to analyze not only the exchange, but also the power dynamics involved in the exchange, Blau added a level of complexity to the theoretical framework. Essentially, Blau conceptualized social life as a "'marketplace' in which participants negotiate with each other in an effort to make a profit" (Sabatelli and Shehan, 1993, p. 391). Conceptualizing the exchange process in this way insinuates that there are alternative courses of action that individuals can pursue, and the decision process itself involves considering one alternative over the other as part of the exchange. Individuals competing for power in the marketplace seek rewards that can fall into four general classes: social approval, money, esteem or respect, or compliance (Sabatelli and Shehan, 1993). Of course, the dominant social norms will dictate what is valued more (or less) in an exchange. In this way, we can see how Blau's model of social exchange extends beyond just the individual-level decision; it also takes into account how dominant ideals and norms play a part in the exchange. Indeed, Blau defined **norms of reciprocity** and norms of fairness to account for the social history of the exchange. The more individuals engage in exchange, the more trust is built and feelings of reciprocity are strengthened. At the same time, both parties need to perceive the exchange as fair and equitable for it to continue, and these perceptions are often defined at the cultural or social level.

Think back to the case study: had Stefan and Christina built their lives together in a different era, gendered cultural expectations might have made their particular exchange impossible. It has not always been socially acceptable for women to work outside the home, much less earn more than their husbands. Similarly, Stefan may also experience derogatory jokes from his male peers for taking on much of the housework and childcare responsibilities in order to make it possible for his wife to become more successful in her career. The interplay of cultural norms and the availability of power both affect the exchange in Stefan and Christina's relationship.

Blau (1964) also introduced the influence of viable alternatives to the analysis of exchange: if individuals in the exchange have alternatives to receive benefits *outside* of the relationship, they have more power than someone who does not have viable alternatives. This leads to **imbalanced exchange**, where one individual becomes dependent on the person with more power because they have few rewards to offer and no alternatives to turn to besides the more powerful individual in the exchange already. What are the rewards Stefan could access if he ended the relationship? If he felt emasculated by Christina, he might have chosen to file for divorce and find a partner who made less money than he did so he could regain some relative power. On the flip side, the financial obligation he would have by paying child support to Christina may be too costly, and essentially outweigh the benefit of finding a new partner. Therefore, given the alternatives, the relationship remains stable.

While Homans and Blau laid the groundwork for exchange theory, John Thibaut and Harold Kelley (1959) elaborated on the theory to include relationship stability *and* satisfaction. That is, while Stefan and Christina's relationship may persist, how can we explain their relationship satisfaction in terms of the exchange? Thibaut and Kelley suggest that it is important to consider the partners' perceptions of the comparison level (CL) and the comparison level for alternatives (CLalt). According to Thibaut and Kelley, the **comparison level** (CL) is a standard by which people evaluate the rewards and costs of a given relationship in terms of what they feel is deserved and/or realistically obtainable (Sabatelli and Shehan, 1993). In other words, individuals compare their own situations to the societal norms for people in similar situations. If they perceive that aspects of their relationship fail to meet their expectations, their global assessments of the relationship will be low. On the flip side, if someone feels they "have it made" in their relationship, their relationship satisfaction would be high. Christina, from our case study, may feel especially satisfied in the relationship depending on what she values out of the exchange. If she values freedom and independence from the "apron strings" of home and children, and prefers to spend energy on work, then the sacrifices Stefan is making for their family likely lead to her relationship satisfaction. She may see her colleagues at work struggle with work–family balance, which gives her a comparison standard by which to judge her own situation, making her feel lucky to have the balance she has.

At the same time, Thibaut and Kelley suggest it is important to consider the available alternatives, if there are any. The **comparison level for alternatives** (CLalt) refers to "the lowest level of relational rewards a person is willing to accept given available rewards from alternative relationships or being alone" (Sabatelli and Shehan, 1993, p. 398). In other words, individuals may consider whether or not alternatives would bring more rewards and fewer costs than their current situation. In this way, CLalt provides a measure of stability rather than satisfaction. Figure 7.1 provides an illustration of CLalt using Stefan from our case study.

As you can see, the right side of the scale is tipped in favor of Stefan staying in the relationship because

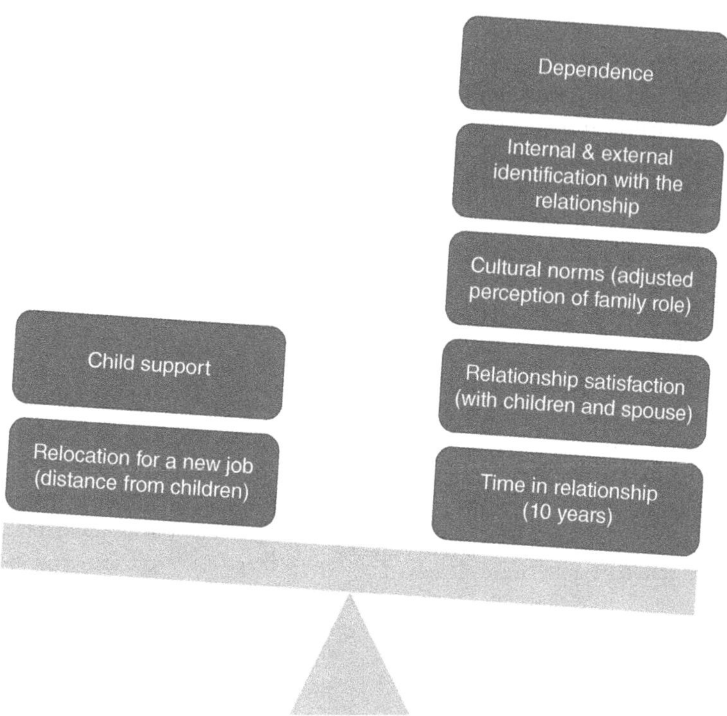

Figure 7.1 Comparison level for alternatives (CLalt): Stefan

Box 7.1 At a Glance: Social Exchange Theory

Rational choice The assumption that individuals make decisions about their relationships by trying to maximize benefits and minimize costs.

Power The ability of one person in a social relationship to get his or her own way despite resistance from the other.

Rewards Any satisfaction, gratification, status, or relationship that one enjoys, and therefore, would like to experience with greater frequency.

Costs Any factor that would deter an activity, such as a punishment, that results from engaging in one behavior over another. There are three types: *investment costs* (time and effort), *direct costs* (resources given to another in an exchange), and *opportunity costs* (rewards available in other exchanges that were foregone as a result of participating in a particular relationship).

Norm of reciprocity Social expectations or rules that dictate that people should help those who have helped them, and that they should not harm those who have helped them.

Comparison level The evaluation of the profitability of a relationship against what we feel we deserve.

Comparison level for alternatives The lowest level or relationship rewards a person is willing to accept in light of rewards that are available from alternative relationships or being alone.

Profit What is left after reward minus cost is calculated.

the alternatives (on the left) are too costly, and serve as barriers to relationship dissolution. At the same time, the right side of the scale represents several aspects of CLalt: (a) Stefan's dependence on the relationship; (b) his internal identification with the relationship (beliefs about divorce) and external factors (economic considerations); (c) cultural norms (acceptable for men to take on a more expressive role in the family); (d) relationship satisfaction (love, fulfillment, and meaning); and (e) time in the relationship. It is important to note here that CLalt is a subjective assessment, and is dependent on an individual's perception that better alternatives exist, regardless of whether or not they *are* actually better. In addition, this model is more complex than it may appear as applied to Stefan; it predicts stability, while taking satisfaction into account. That means that unstable relationships may persist for lack of a better alternative. At the same time, relationships may become unstable in spite of high levels of satisfaction and may remain stable in spite of low levels of satisfaction.

Key concepts

Now that we have examined the history of social exchange theory, we will define some of the key concepts that are used in this theory. From its origins in the broader fields of economics, psychology, and sociology, among others, it is clear that social exchange theory has a rich history in the family related disciplines. For example, because social exchange theory is concerned with the costs and rewards of work and family life for individual actors and intimate partners, exchange principles enter into couples' and families' decision-making "about where to work, how much to work, whether and when to marry, when to have children, and even when to divorce" (Perry-Jenkins and MacDermid, 2013, p. 386).

Rational choice The concept of **rational choice** represents a theory in and of itself; it is important to social exchange theory because it provides the basis from which we conceptualize human interaction. Social exchange theory assumes that humans will make decisions based on a rational cost-benefit analysis of any situation. Note that the word "rational" has colloquial meanings that we should not confuse with the meaning we intend to explain here. Typically, we associate the word "rational" with "sane" or "sensible"; someone is making a decision with a clear head. Instead, from a theoretical standpoint, rational choice means that no matter what the mental state of the actor, she or he will act based on the aim to maximize their own personal advantage (Friedman, 1953). As we have pointed out thus far in the chapter, this type of orientation to decision-making can also be applied to issues of love, romantic relationships, and families.

Resources In addition, according to rational choice theorist James Coleman, humans have several types of **resources**, or capital, to exchange (Adams and Sydie, 2002). The first kind is physical capital, which is tangible and observable. An example would be a farmer's tractors and equipment, land, and other assets that help run the farm. A second kind of capital is human capital, which is less tangible than physical capital, and refers to the knowledge and skills a person acquires. Individuals acquire human capital through furthering their education, acquiring wealth, and "moving up" in society. A third kind of capital is social, and this is the least tangible form because it is embodied in social relationships. A good example of this type of capital is the old adage "I'll scratch your back if you scratch mine." When it comes to social relationships, these mutual expectations operate on two conditions: (a) a level of trustworthiness to be able to believe that the obligation will be met; and (b) the individuals interacting in the exchange need to understand the extent of the obligations (Coleman, 1994). It is important to point out that social capital is not easily exchanged, however. First, individuals need to have access to investing in social capital, which often occurs within "'closed' social networks in which most individuals either directly or indirectly (as in a friend of a friend) are known one another" (Appelrouth and Edles, 2011, p. 457). This prerequisite of network access is not easily overcome. In order to access a network to which we do not belong, sometimes we have to take a chance in investing in a social structure we are not yet a part of. An example would be volunteering or interning at a company before becoming employed there. The investment of time and resources into the social structure is high, and the risk that it might not pay off is also high. However, once an individual has access to social capital, the more likely she or he is to benefit from social exchange and reciprocity. At its core, Coleman's conceptualization of social capital champions the ideas of fairness and commitment, both essential for establishing and maintaining healthy family relationships. Note that we present a somewhat different view of capital in Chapter 3, when we describe conflict theory; another form of capital is symbolic, as developed by Bourdieu (1990).

Norms of reciprocity Reciprocity occurs when individuals return one exchange for another of equal value. These exchanges can be positive (e.g., sharing carpooling duties with other parents) or negative (e.g., saying no to a request for help to "pay back" an individual for refusing to do the same thing for you previously). In his examination of social exchange and power in families, Scanzoni (1979) has studied norms of reciprocity in marriage, focusing specifically on how it influences marital role consensus, marital conflict, and marital stability. For the most part, norms of reciprocity serve to stabilize marital relationships because over time, reciprocity becomes patterned behavior. This tends to be stabilizing because at the beginning of relationships, individuals can feel indebted or obligated to participate in reciprocal exchange. In a marriage, however, these exchanges become part of the established partnership and are expected.

Cost-benefit analysis A **cost-benefit analysis** is usually carried out at the beginning of a relationship to help us decide whether or not a relationship is worth investing in. It involves a process for calculating the value of a relationship in terms of potential rewards and costs. The potential **costs** of a relationship are those things that we see as negative: giving up freedom or settling for a partner who does not have the most desirable qualities. The **rewards** or benefits of a relationship are those things that we see as positive: desirable personality traits, physical attractiveness, positive emotions, and so on. This type of cost-benefit analysis follows an economic model that can predict the overall value of the relationship as well as net profits to those involved.

Intrinsic and extrinsic rewards Blau differentiated between two different types of rewards because "linking intimate relations to exchange processes runs counter to our conventional understanding of such relations" (Appelrouth and Edles, 2011, p. 142). Thus,

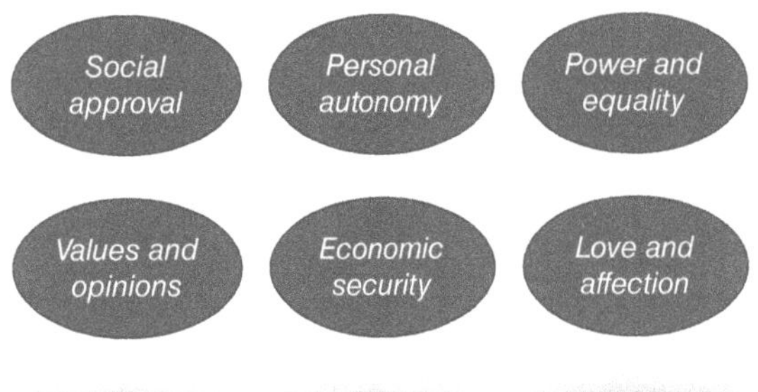

Figure 7.2 General sources of rewards and costs

Blau added these two concepts to aid in our understanding of how rewards could be perceived by the receiver. **Intrinsic rewards** are both "tangible and intangible things we find pleasurable in and of themselves, not because they provide the means for obtaining other benefits" (Appelrouth and Edles, 2011, p. 461). An example would be going on a walk with loved ones on a beautiful hiking trail. **Extrinsic rewards**, on the other hand, are things that are detached from the actual relationship one is involved in. That is, the relationship may be a means to an end; the "end" is the extrinsic reward. As an example, someone who just wishes to get married and have children as soon as possible may settle for a partner who is not their "ideal" type. The end goal – getting married and having kids before age 40 – is more important than the actual emotional value placed on the relationship.

Figure 7.2 depicts some of the considerations that individuals use in evaluating the best ways to maximize their rewards, reduce their costs, and secure the most profits (or least losses). Nye (1979) explains that the process of weighing alternatives in order to make the best choices is a critical part of social exchange. He states that there are several generalized sources of rewards and costs that are at the heart of social exchanges. For example, social approval is a major source of exchange. To gain social approval is to maximize one's ability to receive respect, admiration, and prestige, and to minimize social disapproval and rejection. Security, as well, is a generalized source of rewards and costs, in that security can entail having a home, health insurance, and an income, but without those commodities, life can be very insecure.

Bargaining The concept of bargaining, which refers to the ways that couples distribute resources, derives from Gary Becker's (1981) classic exchange/economic model of marriage, which is based on rational choice theory. Using micro-exchange principles, Becker hypothesized that men and women seek to maximize the utility of their marriage by comparing benefits and costs, and that they may choose divorce if they expect it to increase their own welfare (Braver and Lamb, 2013). Bargaining is based on the proposition that men and women compete as they seek mates, which creates a marriage market. According to Becker, this explains not only why most adults are married, but also why potential mates are hierarchically arranged, compared, and evaluated according to their wealth, education, and other valuable characteristics (Becker, 1981). In essence, the courting process involves bargaining for the best deal on a partner, within the restrictions "imposed" by market availability.

Power Social exchange theory posits that marriage and family relationships are microstructures in which power – and compliance – are exercised and experienced (Scanzoni, 1979). As we discuss in Chapter 8 on feminist theory, gender is a primary way through which power operates in families, and partners must constantly negotiate their own perceptions of fairness in terms of contributions to childcare, housework, and paid labor (Thompson, 1991). From a utilitarian perspective, marriage is basically an economic arrangement where "money talks." And, money often talks in different ways for men and women. In a study comparing how couples from the US and Australia bargain about time spent in housework, for example, Bittman et al., (2003) used exchange theory to explain gender differences in marriage. They found that women were able to decrease their time spent in housework, but only if their earnings did not exceed their husbands' income. Conversely, for men, they found that gender is more important than money; men did not increase their share of housework even if they earned less. For men, their gender allows them the privilege of doing less housework than their wives, but for women, their options are to either allow some housework to stay undone, or to purchase household services (e.g., housecleaning). These findings are a useful example of social exchange theory when it comes to

Box 7.2 Social Exchange Theory in Pop Culture: *The Tudors*

A scene from *The Tudors*, 2007, cr. Michael Hirst, Sony Pictures Television

The Tudors is a historical fiction television series set primarily in sixteenth-century England and aired in the United States, Canada, and Britain from 2007 to 2010. Given the norms and expectations of that era, it should be no surprise that social exchange theory would apply well to this series. The traditional expectation for royalty required that the king and queen would give birth to a son who could inherit the throne. In the beginning of the series, King Henry VIII is married to Catherine of Aragon, who had only given birth to a daughter (Mary). The patriarch of the Boleyn family saw this as an opportunity to put their daughter Anne forward to become one of Henry's lovers, hoping that this would earn them greater favor (in terms of wealth, property, and titles). King Henry fell in love with Anne, but she refused to sleep with him unless he married her. Thus, the king requested an annulment of his marriage from the Pope, which was eventually granted, but in the process the king and his cardinals all but destroyed their relationship with the Catholic Church.

Anne gives birth to a daughter, Elizabeth, followed by two miscarriages. Because Anne does not produce a son and heir to the throne, she loses the king's favor, and he begins another affair. In order to get pregnant again, Anne sleeps with her brother. When this is discovered by the king, both she and her brother are executed.

The king goes on to marry Jane Seymour, who gives birth to their son and only heir to the throne, Edward, right before she dies from complications of childbirth. Throughout the series, we can see that families in court are constantly trying to win the king's favor. The king has to consider the costs and benefits to every move he makes. His decisions are presumably based on rational calculation and maintaining the power balance. He is dependent on his lovers only to provide him sexual gratification, and his wives to provide him a male heir. The same goes for his appointed advisors and counselors; if they cross the king, they are likely banished from court or murdered, so that the king maintains his power.

understanding how power (and gendered expectations) influence marital exchange.

Equity theory Equity theory is a type of social exchange theory that emphasizes the principle of **distributive justice**. Homans (1961) explained distributive justice as the expectation that each person in an exchange relation will expect that their rewards will be proportional to their costs. That is, the greater the rewards, the greater the costs, and the greater the investments, the greater the profit (Ekeh, 1974). In equity theory, a relationship can be considered equitable if the ratio of benefits to contributions is the same for both partners. An inequitable relationship is one in which one partner is overbenefiting from the relationship, and the other partner is underbenefiting. To be underbenefited in a relationship means that you are giving more to the relationship than you are receiving. Although the partner who is overbenefiting from the relationship can also feel negative emotions like stress and guilt, the inequity of the relationship bears a greater cost to the underbenefited, who may experience even more intense feelings of anger, depression, and the like because their contributions may be unacknowledged or devalued (Dainton and Zelley, 2006, p. 247). As an example, think about who provides most of the care for older relatives in families. Typically, caregiving for older men is provided by daughters, wives, and daughters-in-law. Sons may provide instrumental support, in the form of financial assistance, but the lion's share of the work is provided by close female kin. Thus, men tend to overbenefit in family relationships, and women tend to underbenefit. Nowhere is this more apparent than in the relationships of adult brothers and sisters. Sisters tend to provide much more care for their parents than do brothers, and yet brothers get more credit for the (more limited) work they perform (Connidis, 2010).

Evaluating Social Exchange Theory

Strengths of social exchange theory

Like all theories, social exchange theory has both strengths and weaknesses. The strengths include its widespread popularity and usefulness as a comprehensive theory of humans, couples, and families in their social and economic contexts.

The economic metaphor is highly adaptable to multiple contexts One reason social exchange theory is very versatile and applicable to many areas of study is the succinct nature of the economic metaphor. When reduced to the calculus of reciprocally trading resources in the marketplace in order to maximize profits, it is easy to see how this metaphor is as applicable to the international stock market as to the interpersonal exchanges of love, social approval, and power. The elegance of the simple mathematical equation of rewards minus costs equal outcome (e.g., Rewards – Costs = Outcome) offers a shorthand way to understand rational human action and transaction (Dilworth-Anderson, Burton, and Klein, 2005). And, when examining family relationships, the economic metaphor helps to explain the investments parents and children make to one another over time as a primary way to efficiently meet members' needs by minimizing risks and maximizing benefits (Silverstein, 2005).

Social exchange concepts bridge the gap between research and practice Social exchange theory is easy to put into practice (Roloff, 1981). How many times, when facing a difficult decision, have you pulled out a pen and paper, and drawn two columns, with pros on the one side, and cons on the other? This very effective problem-solving strategy shows just how intuitive and useful social exchange principles are for everyday life. For example, theoretical concepts such as rewards, costs, bargaining, and comparison level have often been applied in clinical practice (Bagarozzi, 1993). Therapists try to help individuals and couples bring to light the underlying rules and values they use to negotiate with one another and make mutually beneficial decisions. Therapists also know that human behavior that seems illogical on the outside does have some underlying rationality that reflects a person's way of assessing information and investments in order to lead to the most satisfactory outcome.

Social exchange theory is highly testable in research One of the major hallmarks of social exchange theory is that it is easily translatable into testable hypotheses. The simple elegance of its theoretical propositions are parsimonious and fit the requirements of experimental quantitative research (Nye, 1978). (Also, see Chapter 1, Figure 1.2 for an explanation of the scientific process as it relates to theory building.) Because the theory translates so well into research, a systematic, incremental approach, rather than a haphazard approach, has been used to refine and expand the theory (Collett, 2010). Further, many of the complicated relationships that comprise the family can be put to a test. Nye (1979) describes an array of family contexts that can be proposed and then tested in research. In Nye's description of social exchange theories, a few of the more than 120 testable propositions (e.g., hypotheses) are: (a) middle-class employed mothers are more likely to have more "disposable time" than lower-class employed mothers; (b) the more highly educated the woman, the more nonmonetary rewards are obtained from employment; (c) the more highly educated the woman, the less physically tiring the work (Nye, 1979, p. 14). In addition to these hypotheses about social class and education in families with employed mothers, Nye also proposes hypotheses about topics such as ages and number of children, race and employment of mothers, timing of marriage and parenthood, sexual behavior, social networks, divorce, family violence, and communication.

Weaknesses of social exchange theory

Despite its strengths, social exchange theory is not without its weaknesses. As we have found in most of the family theories described in this book, some of its strengths are also some of its weaknesses.

Assumes individuals rationally calculate costs and benefits One of the limitations of exchange theory is that it presumes that individuals are rational and act out of self-interest. However, what about behavior that is motivated by emotionality or altruism? This theory even presumes that altruism is rational, because "the person will predictably be rewarded by approval both by the person helped and by others who are aware of the act" (Nye, 1979, p. 8). Viewing even altruism as strictly rational and self-interested seems to trivialize the importance of moral principles that dictate values such as kindness, forgiveness, and self-sacrifice. For example, would you say that Mother Teresa's work on behalf of the poor is motivated by self-interest? Fortunately, recent research on the role of emotions in personal relationships is beginning to address the purely rationalistic, instrumental understanding of social exchange to include more of its intangible qualities (Lawler and Thye, 1999).

Studies of family relationships have not kept pace with new exchange concepts In spite of the simple elegance and appeal of the language of costs, rewards, and outcomes, more recent research shows that family scholarship has not moved beyond these seminal ideas and taken advantage of new developments in the sociological study of exchange theory. Collett (2010) charges that the new research now allows us go past the earlier ideas about how individuals participate in exchange relationships, by examining the role of the social relationship itself – and not the individual – as the mechanism of exchange. Further, by studying the relationship, there are new possibilities for examining the importance of trust, commitment, perceptions of fairness, and positive emotions in how marital and family relationships are developed and maintained.

Oversimplifies the influence of power at the macrostructural level Feminist scholars (see Chapter 8) argue that the individual level is not sufficient to understand how bargaining occurs in marriage, basically because it minimizes the complex role of gender and power in intimate relationships (Komter, 1989). Bargaining, at the micro-structural level, is influenced by how power is distributed at the macrostructural level, in the ways that law, politics, and social structures inequitably shape opportunities and access to resources. For example, gender norms that provide men with greater earning power enter into their private relationships with their wives by the expectation that men do not have to share equally in housework. Only interpreting behavior as a function of personal preferences and resources, and not acknowledging that gender privilege derives from social institutions, is thus a major limitation of exchange theory.

An alternative theory app: life course theory

In this chapter, we have laid out the key concepts, origins, and modern applications as well as the strengths and weaknesses of social exchange theory. Although social exchange theory primarily uses a micro-level of analysis, it is useful to think about how it compares to life course theory, which you will learn about in Chapter 9.

Life course theory is a theoretical framework researchers use when they want to understand the ways in which time, culture, context, and the interdependence of family relationships influence people's lives. This theory contrasts with social exchange theory, which examines the exchange that takes place within families. However, one of the strengths of life course theory is that it can be used to analyze issues such as relationship or familial exchange as it relates to time. For instance, if a social exchange theorist is interested in studying a newly married couple's division of household labor, we would examine how a couple negotiates who does the cooking, cleaning, and laundry, among other tasks. However, isn't it true that "who does what" changes over time, during the course of a marriage, or even raising children? Life course theory allows for this type of analysis – examining how roles shift over time, taking into account cultural shifts like the social acceptance of men being more involved in children's lives, and so on. In a way, life course theory can enhance almost any theoretical perspective because it allows researchers to take these external variables into account.

Working with Social Exchange Theory: Integrating Research and Practice

Now that we have defined social exchange theory, described the historical origins and key concepts, and pointed out its strengths and weaknesses, we turn to how the theory can be used in theory, research, and practice. We provide an example of current theorizing, analyze an empirical study that was guided by social exchange theory, and describe how the theory has been applied to understanding the very important issue of family financial management.

Social exchange theory today

Social exchange theory has come a long way since its founders – Homans (1958), Blau (1964), Thibaut and Kelly (1959), and Emerson (1976) – first conceptualized the role of rewards, costs, resources, alternatives, and opportunities as a set of principles and propositions, rooted in behaviorism and utilitarian economics, that explain the "importance of the informal actions of small groups" (Collett, 2010, p. 281). And, when J. N. Edwards (1969) and Nye (1978) first applied social exchange principles to family relationships, the cognitive and behavioral actions of individuals were still the focus of how exchanges are negotiated. Today, however, new research on the importance of emotion in social exchange has allowed scholars to move beyond the rational, cognitive elements of exchange and examine the affective component. The affect theory of social exchange, developed primarily by Lawler (2001), is just as important in explaining how relationships develop, continue, or come to an end (Collett, 2010).

Previously, social network research, originally developed by Emerson (1976), focused on "negatively connected" exchanges, which propose that exchange and commitment to one relationship come at the expense of exchange and commitment to another relationship. Collett (2010) gives the example of a stay-at-home mother who pours her energy and resources into taking care of her children and home, and no longer has the resources to share her time or energy in her relationship with her best friend. But, by shifting the focus to a "positively connected" network, you can see how it is possible for this woman to duplicate and transfer her resources to other relationships besides those with her husband and children. One of the key concepts in this new conceptualization is that if exchanges, such as time and energy, are nonduplicative and nontransferable, they get used up. But if shifted to a positive connection, duplicative exchanges (such as moral support or financial assistance) can be transferred. Even though this woman is not earning outside income, her husband's financial support can be used to pay someone else to care for her children or home so that she has free time to spend with her friend. In this way, she is positively connected, and her relationships with others are not compromised or dissolved.

Social exchange theory in research

As we have shown, social exchange theory is very useful across many fields of study and also provides a common language for discussing how different cultures around the world engage in marital bargaining. In a rare study of the collectivist-oriented society, Nepal, in rural South Asia, Jennings (2014) sought to understand marital conflict and divorce by using a cost-benefit approach. Investigations of this type are very uncommon, and this study revealed the importance of conducting research on what is considered a western topic in a society very unlike the US. The author conducted a quantitative study using a sample of 674 couples from the Chitwan Valley Family Study in Nepal. This is a very unique and important data set, because data from South Asian countries are rare.

Although divorce is still uncommon and stigmatized in this traditional society, the author found that individualist factors, such as marital discord, were more important predictors of divorce than cultural dictates to remain married. They found that even though women have little household power and few opportunities to support themselves, they still would prefer to get out of marriages for their own emotional well-being and physical safety. Thus, marital quality was still highly valued by these wives, so much so that they were willing to risk financial insecurity in order to leave a marriage characterized by conflict and unhappiness. Further, the women found alternatives to living in a harsh marriage. Some planned to move back in with their parents, others chose separation and living in separate households; still others found a new partner and remarried soon after they divorced their previous husband. Of interest, then, is that "both spouses' perceptions of discord are important for marital outcomes, even in settings where the costs of marital dissolution are relatively high" (Jennings, 2014, p. 476)

Social exchange theory in practice

There are several areas where social exchange theory can be applied in practice. Next, we elaborate on how the social exchange perspective has been applied to understanding ways that families manage their finances. Family financial management, which is the allocation of income and material resources, is one of the crucial functions of family life (Bennett, 2015). In the typical model of how family financial management operates, the family is seen as a singular unit. Husbands are seen as the primary breadwinner, wives work only for extras (if at all), and children are dependent upon parental support. More recent insights into family financial management, however, reveal that the accumulation and distribution of finances are subjected to gendered and economic power structures and roles. The economic history of the family is anything but equal; it is very important to consider not only who earns money, but also who controls how it is spent. As we have learned in other chapters, one of the major concerns of family life is who has control over money and wealth. Just like in conflict theory (Chapter 3), conflict over where resources go can be managed and overcome by the ability of family members to cooperate with one another, regardless of who holds more power.

Another consideration in understanding how families negotiate the utilization of financial and material resources is that families are very diverse. Rather than assuming that the economic processes in families are alike despite differences in family structure, age, gender, and income, among others, it is important to consider the unique ways that social class, age, gender, race, and other important circumstances impinge on family relationships and individual members' ability to participate in family financial decision-making, pooling resources, engaging in paid work, and living under the same roof. Thus, in trying to work with families regarding their finances, practitioners must consider an array of different situations, including working families; couples in retirement; remarried families in which biological or stepchildren may or may not live in the couple's household; and unemployment.

Consider all the scenarios where understanding family finances in light of social exchange theory is important. As noted in the case study, a marriage and family therapist would benefit from knowing that Stefan and Christina have struggled with meaning associated with financial power in the past. Though it seems like the couple has worked out many of the issues associated with their exchange, it may inevitably arise in both small and big ways in their future. How does "flex" or "fun" money get allotted in their household? Does Christina get more, because she brings in more? What about family wealth and inheritance? Depending on the financial status of each of their parents, Christina and Stefan may subconsciously consider who may inherit more money, or which parent will require caregiving and/or long-term care as they near the end of life. Since Stefan is taking on more traditionally "feminine" roles in his family so Christina can work more, does that mean he would also assume caregiving responsibilities for their parents? Clearly, the breakdown of gendered earning norms, along with familial wealth, inheritance, and financial planning, have real consequences. Each of these issues can contribute to relationship quality, which undoubtedly affects not only the couple's relationship, but the relationship with their children and extended family as well.

Box 7.3 Global Comparisons of Caregiving for Older Adults

Countries around the world have different ways of addressing the needs of the older adult population, depending on their customs and norms of intergenerational exchange. Below, we highlight four countries' approaches to caring for older adults.

Netherlands In the Netherlands, all citizens receive a monthly pension at age 65 of about $1,000 for individuals and $1,400 for couples (M. Edwards, 2004). Unlike in the US, individuals do not have to have a work history to qualify for this government pension, but they do have to have been residents of the Netherlands for a minimum of 50 years. Netherlands residents over the age of 65 also receive an annual "holiday allowance" of $700 to offset the costs of vacation travel. Considering that all Dutch citizens have government insurance for medical conditions and nursing-home care, and prescription drugs are available with few or little co-payments, some Netherlands residents over the age of 65 can live quite well relatively speaking.

Israel Citizens of Israel receive universal health coverage for medical services and hospitalization, but long-term care insurance is only available to citizens with low incomes. This leaves a large number of family caregivers in Israel without respite. One reason for this situation is because Israeli families are caught between the Jewish code of law, which defines caring for elders as a moral obligation, and modern pressures of employment and a longer lifespan (National Alliance for Caregiving, 2002). The Israeli government is considering providing a subsidy to caregivers in the form of a modest tax credit and wage compensation for employment leave. The argument against paying caregivers is that "such a government policy would demean, and in effect, decrease, any feelings of family responsibility for elders" (National Alliance for Caregiving, 2002, p. 8).

China The Confucian ideal of filial piety toward family elders has traditionally meant that elderly parents and grandparents are cared for by family in the home. However, recent demographic shifts have made it difficult for families to fulfill this traditionally held value. Chinese young adults are migrating from rural to urban areas, a demographic shift that increases the geographical distance between children and parents. In addition, until abolished in 2015, the one-child policy had created the "4:2:1" problem, which refers to the typical four grandparents and two parents for every one working Chinese person. Interestingly, analysts suggest that perceptions of "value" by both those involved in the exchange – those paying for the care (potentially the Chinese government) as well as those receiving the care – are of utmost importance. That is, the system that is adopted must address the cultural expectations that Chinese elders are to be honored and cared for in their later years (Shobert, 2012).

Italy Italians have previously favored norms of reciprocity and caring for older adult family members at home, but that was before a major demographic shift occurred that has put Italians in a tight spot. Historically, large Italian families meant built-in caregivers, but family sizes have been steadily shrinking over the past several decades. In 1950, Italy had five adult children for every elderly parent; today, that number has shrunk to only 1.5 (D'Emilio, 2007). Italians generally still prefer to be cared for at home, so they have begun to rely on foreign caregivers to take the place of family. Older adults do have access to a program that provides help to subsidize the costs of hiring a caregiver, but currently there is a waiting list.

As we can see, the choices available to families are dependent on the cultural expectations and the institutional support (or not) given to caregivers and their families. Caregivers must weigh the costs and benefits by examining the options available to them, especially when it comes to norms of reciprocity, and the comparison level for alternatives of care.

Conclusion

Since its origination in economics and its elaboration in the field of developmental psychology and sociology, social exchange theory continues to be applicable to the study of relationships and families today. This theory has also been used extensively to study issues of aging and family, particularly when it comes to norms of reciprocity and caregiving. Social norms of exchange differ significantly around the world, depending on the economic, cultural, and religious expectations that surround intergenerational exchange. Box 7.3 considers how social exchange theory is applicable to the study of families across the globe. It presents information from four different countries to highlight the cultural differences that exist when it comes to caring for older adults.

Multimedia Suggestions

www.gerontology.vt.edu/docs/MetLife%20Elder%20Abuse_Older%20Adults%20Tips_051711.pdf

Many older adults, regardless of age, race, social class, gender, or health status, can be exploited financially by a loved one or caregiver. A comprehensive report on this topic, *The Metlife study of elder financial abuse: Crimes of occasion, desperation, and predation against America's elders* (2011), was commissioned by the Metlife Mature Market Institute and completed by Karen Roberto and Pamela Teaster from the Center for Gerontology at Virginia Polytechnic Institute and State University (www.gerontology.vt.edu) and the National Committee for the Prevention of Elder Abuse (www.preventelderabuse.org). The report offers many helpful suggestions to both seniors and their caregivers for preventing elder financial abuse. Advice for seniors includes (a) stay active and avoid isolation; (b) monitor your own financial affairs; (c) keep legal documents in a safe, secure location; (d) protect your passwords; (e) beware of telephone solicitations; and (f) know what to do if you believe you are a victim of financial abuse.

Activate your theory app: Consider how social exchange theory could help explain issues like elder financial abuse. How do power relations change over the life course, and provide opportunities for exploitation between family members?

www.fresnostate.edu/craig/ifb/index.html

Given the rising popularity of the merger of work and family life, many universities and corporations now offer research and services to foster and support family businesses. For example, the Institute for Family Business is housed in the Craig School of Business at California's Fresno State University. Their mission is to essentially preserve the family business heritage by "wedding" economic development and the family firm in service to the community. In addition to disseminating research findings, they offer a variety of monthly events on ways to improve and market family firms. Some of the topics on their website have been "The six things you're doing wrong on Facebook," "Surviving Thanksgiving"; and "Legislative updates: Employment, taxes, and regulations for 2015."

Activate your theory app: Although we learned about social exchange theory on a more micro-level (e.g., within families), how does the information on this website pertain to social exchange on a more macro-level (between families)?

Arranged (2007)

This film follows the story of two young schoolteachers, one an Orthodox Jewish woman and the other a devout Muslim woman. It is based loosely on a true story told to the filmmaker, and has won multiple independent film awards. Both of these young women are going through the process of having their marriages arranged. In addition to examining their relationship, the film also contains latent messages about cultural ignorance, religion, and friendship, and how these issues reflect micro- and macro-level social exchanges. The film explores the benefits of a deep friendship, but in the context of its costs.

A scene from *Arranged*, 2007, dir. Diane Crespo and Stefan Schaefer, Cicala Filmworks

Activate your theory app: How do the two main characters in this film weigh the benefits against the costs associated with traditional cultural norms that discourage their friendship? What do they each have to "give up" to maintain their friendship?

The Bachelor (2002–present)

This American reality television show is set up to help an eligible man choose from a pool of 25 women to find a woman he wants to propose to on the show's finale. The show features the bachelor getting to know the women, going on dates, and ultimately presenting roses each week to only the women he wishes to see remain on the show as a possible mate. Inevitably, contestants are criticized for being on the show to only increase publicity for their own careers, as opposed to being truly interested in finding a spouse. The same could be said for the bachelor, as only one of the couples actually got married after the on-air proposal. After 19 seasons of the show, it is clear that the show does not actually lead to love and marriage; instead, several of the contestants and bachelors have been offered roles in other television shows and have increased their celebrity status as a result of appearing in *The Bachelor.*

A scene from *The Bachelor*, 2002, cr. Mike Fleiss, Warner Bros. Television

Activate your theory app: Are there other popular reality television shows that we could apply social exchange theory to? How often do you think the reality behind the production of these shows is really producers, agents, and writers making the "best deal" instead of what we see on television?

Further Reading

Becker, G. S., *Gary S. Becker – biographical* (1992), at www.nobelprize.org/nobel_prizes/economic-sciences/laureates/1992/becker-bio.html. Gary Becker, a political conservative, was an economist who ventured into the study of marital relationships and family economics. He was awarded the Nobel Prize in 1992 for extending the domain of micro-economic analysis to a wide range of human behavior and interaction, including nonmarket human behavior. In the family social sciences field, Becker's work has been applied to an array of topics including marriage, divorce, fertility, and the work–family interface. In this account, he tells the story of his own life in relation to his family, his political and intellectual beliefs, and his achievements in the realm of family economics.

Hirshman, L. R., and Larson, J. E., *Hard bargains: The politics of sex* (New York: Oxford University Press, 1998). The authors, both legal scholars, posit that heterosexual relationships are ones in which couples must bargain about their sexuality. This bargaining is not just a matter of private negotiations between a man and a woman. Rather, sex is political, and private negotiations about what, where, when, and how to be sexual take place under increasingly public scrutiny.

The sexual landscape is always in flux. What was considered scandalous in previous eras (e.g., showing skin in the Victorian era) may be taken for granted today. And what is considered illegal in some cultures (e.g., wives' adultery is punishable by death) is considered with more neutrality in others. Further, regardless of advances women have made in their economic lives, sexual politics still require hard bargains in navigating sexual access, sexual cooperation, and sexual practices. Hard bargains mean that we must negotiate the costs and benefits of sexual interaction, and consider the empowerment and disempowerment of partners in sexual relationships. Ultimately, sexuality is of the body, mind, heart, and spirit, but all of these are grounded in broader issues of cultural beliefs and practices associated with law, politics, and religion.

Horan, S. M., "Further understanding sexual communication: Honesty, deception, safety, and risk," *Journal of Social and Personal Relationships, 33* (2016), 449–468, doi:10.1177/0265407515578821). In this study of 183 young adults with an average age of 22 years, Sean Horan used affection exchange theory, a variation of social exchange theory, to examine the role of honesty and dishonesty in disclosing one's sexual history to new partners. Although benefits of disclosing one's sexual history include having accurate information that can affect whether one wants to take health risks with a new partner, there are also costs, such as possible rejection or judgment. Horan found that individuals who tended to omit the number of their previous partners (e.g., practiced dishonesty) were also uncomfortable with other aspects of safer sex communication (such as decisions about condom use). Further, the more informal the relationship (e.g., friends with benefits, compared to committed partners), the less likely the individuals were to communicate about sexual topics at all. Interestingly, about 60 percent of the participants reported that in the past, they had been deceptive in disclosing the number of previous sex partners, with 20 percent of those saying they never disclosed this information. Implications of this study suggest that young people should be provided with health education that moves beyond simply stressing condom use, and focuses on the role of communication and sexual safety during any type of sexual activity.

Schwartz, P., *Peer marriage: How love between equals really works* (New York: Free Press, 1994). Pepper Schwartz is a professor of sociology at the University of Washington, a popular relationship and sex columnist for the *New York Times* and *Glamour Magazine* (among other publications), a radio personality, and a consultant for organizations such as AARP, Perfectmatch.com, and WebMD. In *Peer marriage*, she analyzes interviews with egalitarian couples who are consciously trying to undo traditional gender norms in their families. Schwartz found four general characteristics of peer marriages: First, couples had no more than a 60/40 split in terms of doing housework and childcare. That is, couples did not achieve an equal share of 50 percent each. Second, partners believed that each person in the relationship had equal influence and decision-making power. Third, both partners felt that they had equal control over the family economy. Finally, each partner's work had equal weight in the marriage. As in our case study of Stefan and Christina, regardless of earning ability, peer couples shared money, decision-making, childcare, and housework. There was no hidden hierarchy. Schwartz concluded that a relationship based on "deep friendship" is much more realistic than a marriage rooted in the romantic ideals of gender differences. Yet peer marriage also has its costs, because the process of negotiating and reshuffling power and equity in a relationship can be physically and emotionally draining. On balance, Schwartz shows how relationships that are based on equality, intimacy, and friendship can lead to a deeply rewarding and long-lasting partnership.

Sprecher, S., Wenzel, A., and Harvey, J., *Handbook of relationship initiation* (New York: Psychology Press, 2008). In this comprehensive volume, Susan Sprecher and her colleagues address many topics regarding how relationships are formed, maintained, experienced, and dissolved. Although multiple theories are used by the various authors in the book, exchange and equity theories are present in many of the chapters. In addition to the topics we would expect to find in a scholarly resource on attraction, self-disclosure, relationship processes and structures, and when relationships dissolve, there are chapters on more recent ways of starting and pursuing relationships, such as speed dating, hookups, MySpace, and internet matchmaking services.

Questions for Students

Discussion Questions

1 Compare and contrast social exchange theory with family stress and resilience theory (Chapter 11). Are these two theories similar in any ways? How are they different?
2 Although social exchange theory has primarily been applied at the micro-level of analysis (e.g., the individual), describe ways that it is also useful at the macro-level (e.g., how social institutions and unequal power structures impact individual choices).
3 Critique the popular belief that men offer their wealth and women offer their beauty when entering a relationship. Do you think this idea is still prevalent today? If not, how do you think ideas about this gender stereotype are changing?
4 What other family relationships, other than romantic or parent–child, can be studied using social exchange theory?
5 How might social exchange theory be used to study LGBTQ relationships? If you were to update the theory to provide a broader applicability to *all* families and relationships, what would need to be added or reconsidered?
6 Provide examples of the different types of capital that individuals have, and how each type can be used in an exchange relationship.

Your Turn!

When you plan to enter an intimate partnership – either in terms of a cohabiting or a married relationship – how do you think you will distribute (or, pool) your money? Do you plan to set up separate bank accounts? A joint account? Or, do you plan to have a "yours, mine, and ours" system, where you both pool resources and also maintain your own control over a separate account? What are the rewards and costs of the particular financial arrangement you set up?

Personal Reflection Questions

1 Have you ever known someone who repeats the same pattern again and again in relationships? Consider how those choices may be a result of reinforcement, deprivation-satiation, and the comparison level for alternatives.
2 Make a list of "ideal" qualities you find desirable in a partner, and another list of what you feel you bring to relationships. Consider your lists in light of social exchange theory and reward, costs, profits, and comparison level.
3 Do you think it is possible for individuals to act in altruistic ways, without expecting something in return? If so, describe the altruistic actions of someone you admire and assess these qualities in relation to the concept of rational choice.
4 Think about power dynamics in the relationships either you have been involved in, or for someone close to you. Is it truly possible to have an equal share of power in a dyadic relationship? Why, or why not?
5 How do you "rationalize" your choices to put your own needs ahead of the needs of someone you love? Under what conditions do you think it is okay to act solely in self-interest?
6 What is the most "irrational" thing you ever did? As you reflect on it, do you think there are some rational aspects to this as well?

References

Adams, B. N., and Sydie, R. A. (2002). *Contemporary sociological theory*. Thousand Oaks, CA: Pine Forge Press.

Appelrouth, S., and Edles, L. D. (2011). *Classical and contemporary sociological theory: Text and readings*. Los Angeles: Pine Forge Press.

Bagarozzi, D. A. (1993). Clinical uses of social exchange principles. In P. Boss, W. Doherty, R. LaRossa, W. Schumm, and S. Steinmetz (eds), *Sourcebook of family theories and methods: A contextual approach* (pp. 412–417). New York: Plenum.

Becker, G. S. (1981). *A treatise on the family.* Cambridge, MA: Harvard University Press.

Bennett, F. (2015). Opening up the black box: Researching the distribution of resources within the household. *NCFR Report: Family Resource Management, FF63*, F1–F3.

Bittman, M., England, P., Sayer, L., Folbre, N., and Matheson, G. (2003). When does gender trump money? Bargaining and time in household work. *American Journal of Sociology, 109*, 186–214. doi:10.1086/378341.

Blau, P. M. (1964). *Exchange and power in social life.* New York: Wiley.

Bourdieu, P. (1990). *In other words: Essays towards a reflexive sociology*. Palo Alto, CA: Stanford University Press.

Braver, S. L., and Lamb, M. E. (2013). Marital dissolution. In G. W. Peterson and K. R. Bush (eds), *Handbook of marriage and the family* (3rd edn, pp. 487–516). New York: Springer.

Coleman, J. S. (1994). *Foundations of social theory.* Cambridge, MA: Harvard University Press.

Collett, J. L. (2010). Integrating theory, enhancing understanding: The potential contributions of recent experimental research in social exchange for studying intimate relationships. *Journal of Family Theory and Review, 2*, 280–298. doi:10.1111/j.1756-2589.2010.00062.x.

Connidis, I. A. (2010). *Family ties and aging* (2nd edn). Thousand Oaks, CA: Pine Forge Press.

Cook, K. S., and Rice, E. (2003). Social exchange theory. In J. Delamater (ed.), *Handbook of social psychology* (pp. 53–76). New York: Springer.

Dainton, M., and Zelley, E. D. (2006). Social exchange theories: Interdependence and equity. In D. O. Braithwaite and L. A. Baxter (eds), *Engaging theories in family communication: Multiple perspectives* (pp. 243–259). Thousand Oaks, CA: Sage.

D'Emilio, F. (2007, July 6). New twist on old world: Aging Italians rely on nuns, immigrants. *USA Today*.

Dilworth-Anderson, P., Burton, L. M., and Klein, D. M. (2005). Contemporary and emerging theories in studying families. In V. L. Bengtson, A. C. Acock, K. R. Allen, P. Dilworth-Anderson, and D. M. Klein (eds), *Sourcebook of family theory and research* (pp. 35–57). Thousand Oaks, CA: Sage.

Edwards, J. N. (1969). Familial behavior as social exchange. *Journal of Marriage and the Family, 31*, 518–526. doi:10.2307/349775.

Edwards, M. (2004, November/December). As good as it gets: What country takes the best care of its older citizens? The Netherlands rates tops in our exclusive survey of 16 nations. But no place is perfect. *AARP The Magazine*, 47–53.

Ekeh, P. P. (1974). *Social exchange theory: The two traditions.* Cambridge, MA: Harvard University Press.

Emerson, R. M. (1976). Social exchange theory. *Annual Review of Sociology, 2*, 335–362. doi:10.1146/annurev.so.02.080176.002003.

Friedman, M. (1953). *Essays in positive economics.* Chicago: University of Chicago Press.

Homans, G. C. (1958). Social behavior as exchange. *American Journal of Sociology, 63*, 597–606. doi:10.1086/222355.

Homans, G. C. (1961). *Social behavior: Its elementary forms.* New York: Harcourt, Brace & World.

Jennings, E. (2014). Marital discord and subsequent dissolution: Perceptions of Nepalese wives and husbands. *Journal of Marriage and Family, 76*, 476–488. doi:10.1111/jomf.12104.

Komter, A. (1989). Hidden power in marriage. *Gender and Society, 3*, 187–216. doi:10.1177/089124389003002003.

Lawler, E. J. (2001). An affect theory of social exchange. *American Journal of Sociology, 107*, 321–352. doi:10.1086/324071.

Lawler, E. J., and Thye, S. R. (1999). Bringing emotions into social exchange theory. *Annual Review of Sociology, 25*, 217–244. doi:10.1146/annurev.soc.25.1.217.

National Alliance for Caregiving (2002). Third international conference on family care: Conference report. At http://www.caregiving.org/data/conferencereport.pdf.

Nye, F. I. (1978). Is choice and exchange theory the key? *Journal of Marriage and the Family, 40*, 219–233. doi:10.2307/350754.

Nye, F. I. (1979). Choice, exchange, and the family. In W. R. Burr, R. Hill, F. I. Nye, and I. L. Reiss (eds), *Contemporary theories about the family: General theories/theoretical orientations* (vol. 2, pp. 1–41). New York: Free Press.

Perry-Jenkins, M., and MacDermid, S. M. (2013). The state of theory in work and family research at the turn of the twenty-first century. In M. A. Fine and F. D. Fincham (eds), *Handbook of family theories: A content-based approach* (pp. 381–397). New York: Routledge.

Roloff, M. E. (1981). *Interpersonal communication: The social exchange approach.* Beverly Hills, CA: Sage.

Sabatelli, R. M., and Shehan, C. L. (1993). Exchange and resource theories. In P. Boss, W. Doherty, R. LaRossa, W. Schumm, and S. Steinmetz (eds), *Sourcebook of family theories and methods: A contextual approach* (pp. 385–411). New York: Plenum.

Scanzoni, J. (1979). Social processes and power in families. In W. R. Burr, R. Hill, F. I. Nye, and I. L. Reiss (eds), *Contemporary theories about the family: Research-based theories* (vol. 1, pp. 295–316). New York: Free Press.

Shobert, B. (2012, April 1). Senior care in China: Challenges and opportunities. *China Business Review.* At http://www.chinabusinessreview.com/senior-care-in-china-challenges-and-opportunities/.

Silverstein, M. (2005). Testing theories about intergenerational exchanges. In V. L. Bengtson, A. C. Acock, K. R. Allen, P. Dilworth-Anderson, and D. M. Klein (eds), *Sourcebook of family theory and research* (pp. 407–410). Thousand Oaks, CA: Sage.

Thibaut, J. W., and Kelley, H. H. (1959). *The social psychology of groups*. New York: Wiley.

Thompson, L. (1991). Family work: Women's sense of fairness in marriage. *Journal of Family Issues, 12*, 181–196. doi:10.1177/019251391012002003.

8

Feminist Theory

Why is it that when parents are expecting a child, they typically have reasons for wanting a boy or a girl? Why do men sometimes feel it is important to have a son, to "pass down" the family name? Is it a safe assumption that their son would even want to get married someday, and that he would want his partner to take his name? What if he is unable to marry legally in the country where he lives, if he is gay? In dual career families, which parent feels more pressure to stay at home after a child is born? What about families where one parent is a maid/nanny for an upper-class White family? Who does she rely on to raise her own children?

Questions about gender, power, social change, and intersectionality are addressed in a feminist perspective. Like family science overall, feminist theory has a broad, interdisciplinary background. In this chapter, we focus on the ways in which family scholars typically use and integrate feminist theories to study individual experience and family relationships within a social context. Feminist theory was originally grounded in a concern about gender equality, calling into question the inherent right and necessity of men to serve as the head of families, nations, and society. Over time, feminist theory has evolved to consider how issues of race, class, sexual orientation, age, nationality, and disability, among others intersect to create different experiences of privilege, opportunity, and oppression. Ultimately, feminist theory critiques the status quo and generates suggestions for social change. Now, we turn to a story about feminism, intersectionality, and social change to set the stage for how this theory is used to explain family issues.

Case Study

As a freshman in college, Luke felt excited on the day that his history professor began her lecture on the history of feminism. Many of the events the professor covered hit home for him; he had heard stories about how his mother had been active in the feminist movement since her first days in college, in the early 1970s. She had marched in many parades for women's rights – for reproductive freedom, for the Equal Rights Amendment, and for equal rights for lesbians and gay men. He had been on some of these marches as a kid, especially the Take Back the Night march in his hometown.

Yet, he noticed his classmates begin to roll their eyes and whisper about the "angry feminist" professor who was lecturing. Luke didn't view the professor as angry at all, and felt conflicted about what his peers were saying because his entire life, he'd known firsthand what feminism looked like. He distinctly remembers being proud of his mother. She had been a single parent most of his life and had been the sole support of their family. They were very close and yet she gave him his space. His home was more relaxed than most of his friends', and that was one of the reasons his high school friends felt comfortable about coming over to hang out. He respected his mother for working full-time, and taking care of their family, and also being an activist in their community. To him, feminism was a positive word, and he had benefited from his mother's actions and work on behalf of equality.

As a young boy, Luke's eyes were opened to seeing exactly what his mother was fighting for. He remembers one time when he was very young – and too

Family Theories: Foundations and Applications, First Edition. Katherine R. Allen and Angela C. Henderson.

young to understand gender inequality – when he asked his mother what the "wage gap" was because he had overheard her talking about it with her friends at dinner. His mother told him that girls do not get paid the same amount as boys when they are grown-ups. In response, Luke asked his mother, "Is that because the girls don't work as hard as the boys?" and of course his mother responded by saying that no, in fact, sometimes girls have to work even harder to get treated the same as boys. Luke remembers this conversation as a defining moment during his childhood; he didn't fully believe his mother because it did not make sense. After that conversation, he began to pay more attention to his female classmates. After a few weeks of observation, he told his mother one day after school, "You're right, mom! I watched the girls in my class and they get their work done faster than the boys! Maybe girls should get *more* money!"

Because of his exposure to activism and observing inequalities starting at a very young age, Luke knew about feminism through his mother's life – she lived it, believed it, and fought for it. He knew firsthand what a feminist was. How do you think he handled hearing his classmates bash feminism and the professor for simply telling its history? How did feminism get such a bad rap? Feminists grapple with this very question, as they try to untangle the difficulties of disrupting a long-standing system of ideas about what is "normal," what masculinity and femininity are supposed to look like, and why we struggle so much accepting the idea that men and women should be treated equally.

What Is Feminist Theory?

Feminist theory is grounded in the struggle for gender equality. This struggle is caused by the belief that women's lives are perceived as less important than men's lives, and that men are the standard against which women are compared. When compared to men, women inevitably come up short; they are seen as less than men. Feminist theory guides the practical or activist part of feminism, which is called **praxis**. Thus, feminist theory and feminist activism are both important in uncovering gender prejudice, demystifying power dynamics, and working toward social change (Acker, Barry, and Esseveld, 1983).

There are many variations of feminism, and feminists believe that the inability to capture feminism in one single perspective is its very strength (Elam and Wiegman, 1995). Yet, there are several common themes regarding women and their experiences in society that motivate the integration of feminist theory and feminist activism (Baber and Allen, 1992). First, feminism embodies the belief that women are exploited and oppressed as subordinates in a hierarchical social system that affords privilege to elite White males. Second, feminism is committed to the empowerment of women and to improving the conditions of their lives. Finally, feminism emphasizes that women's experiences, values, and activities are meaningful and valued.

In family studies, feminist scholars have used feminist theory to name unequal power arrangements in families that persist by generation and gender (Allen, Walker, and McCann, 2013; Ferree, 1990; Walker, 1999). Feminist theory brings to the forefront issues in the family that are grounded in gender inequality, such as perceptions that men cannot be stay-at-home parents, or that all women have an instinct to be mothers. Feminist theory in family studies analyzes the ways in which gender intersects with other forms of oppression and privilege to structure individual and family life (Allen, Lloyd, and Few, 2009). Currently, feminist theory is used to explain how individuals "do gender" in families (West and Zimmerman, 1987). Important, too, are the ways in which systems of oppression, such as patriarchal power (Collins, 1990) and intersectionality (McCall, 2005; Shields, 2008) operate to structure opportunities in individual and family life. We will return to each of these concepts later in the chapter.

History and origins

Because feminist theory is linked to feminist activism, the theory is always under scrutiny, particularly in terms of how well feminist thought has led to real changes and improvements in society. As we describe throughout the chapter, feminist theory is one of the theories most open to critique and revision as feminist priorities are refined and changed. Thus there are many variations of feminist theory as it has evolved over time. Feminists have characterized the history of

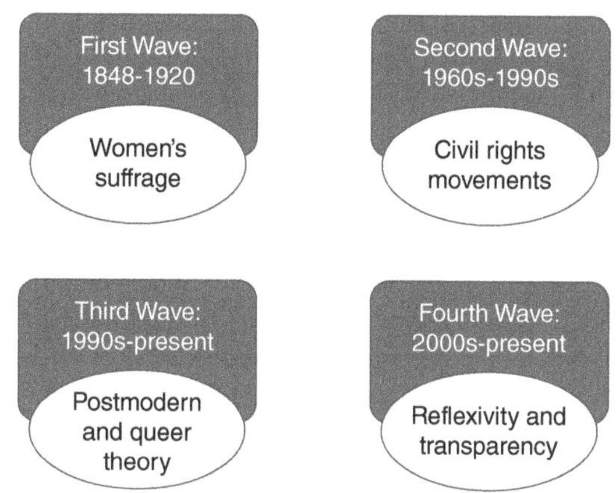

Figure 8.1 Four waves of feminism

feminist theory and activism over the past two centuries in terms of **waves of feminism**. Although thinking about feminist theory and activism in terms of waves is useful (see Figure 8.1), it is important to remember that these waves overlap, and the time frames we identify are only estimates. Yet, by examining this history over time, we can see the effectiveness of feminist thinking on changing and improving women's lives and the lives of their family members.

First wave feminism The dawn of current feminist theory is rooted in the nineteenth and early twentieth centuries and was spurred by women's efforts to gain the right to vote as well as their involvement in the Abolitionist movement to end slavery in America. This first wave was roughly a 70-year period, dating from 1848 with the Women's Rights Convention in Seneca Falls, New York, calling for women's suffrage and culminating in the passage of the 19th Amendment to the US Constitution in 1920, guaranteeing women the right to vote. During this time, feminist leaders such as Susan B. Anthony, Charlotte Perkins Gilman, Elizabeth Cady Stanton, Sojourner Truth, and many others organized around issues that young people simply take for granted today, including women's voting rights, married women's rights to inheritance and divorce, the end of slavery for African Americans, and contraceptive availability (Freedman, 2002).

Charlotte Perkins Gilman, for example, was a first wave feminist who focused on issues that were arguably ahead of her time; Gilman advocated for mothers' access to public day care and cooperative kitchens so they could free themselves of domestic duties and focus on careers. However, given that women were not afforded federal protections against job discrimination based on sex until much later, Gilman was not accepted as an established author until after her death (Lemert, 2008). In fact, during this time, women were not considered first-class citizens; they were not allowed to vote, and married women did not own their own property. Their legal rights were dependent upon the will of their fathers or husbands. The rights that women take for granted today came many years later, after much struggle and many setbacks. After women secured the right to vote in the US in 1920, feminism went underground, at least as a topic of national attention. The Great Depression, World War II, and the postwar period of the 1950s consumed national attention.

Second wave feminism Second wave feminism took root in the midst of the social upheaval of the Civil Rights Movement for African Americans and the antiwar movement against the Vietnam War in the 1960s. Yet, several influential books that addressed the status of women had already set the stage. One of the most important texts was written by French philosopher Simone de Beauvoir. In *The Second Sex*, de Beauvoir (2011 [1949]) explained how women are socially constructed as "other"; they are objectified and stereotyped as less than men. Her ideas about women's treatment in a male-constructed patriarchy were highly controversial, because they critiqued the status quo as oppressive to women and led the way to challenging other forms of oppression.

Another defining event was the publication of Betty Friedan's book *The Feminine Mystique* in 1963 Friedan reignited a national women's movement by analyzing how empty women's lives were, especially for married, middle class White mothers, who did not work outside the home and were expected to find fulfillment in caring for others. Friedan called this "the problem that has no name," and wrote about it in a way that spoke to millions of women. Through Friedan's book, women came to understand that their second-class status was due to political injustice affecting all women, not personal failings inherent to them as individuals (Coontz, 2011).

During the 1960s, as social and political unrest was intensifying, women began to mobilize for their own civil rights. They met in consciousness-raising groups to speak out against repression of their bodies, lack of educational and occupational opportunities, confinement to the home, and abuse, with the goal of working toward legal and political reform. Luke's mother, from our case study above, came of age during second wave feminism. Her sense of being limited as a female in a man's world, combined with the emerging understanding of social injustice in the broader society, sparked her feminist consciousness. This merger of the personal and the political inspired her to become a lifelong feminist activist and to teach these values and practices to her son.

Second wave feminism was a time in which feminist theory proliferated. **Liberal feminism**, probably the most common type, pushed for women's equality with men (Okin, 1989). In this case, women were going after their "equal share of the pie." Liberal feminism spoke primarily to middle-class women who sought careers and financial parity with men.

Socialist feminism, rooted in Marxist class theory (see conflict theory, Chapter 3), posited that capitalism and its relation to **patriarchy** (a system of male dominance) were responsible for women's second-class citizenship (Mitchell, 1971). Another group of women previously overlooked were working-class women who did not have the financial security that middle-class women experienced. They often worked in jobs that were physically exhausting, where they had little control over their time (Stacey, 1990).

Radical feminism offered a major challenge to the pervasiveness of patriarchy by seeking to uncover the root cause of the mechanisms of women's oppression and men's privilege with the goal of creating massive social change (Morgan, 1970). Radical feminist theory critiqued the ways that all social institutions (e.g., law, education, family, military) conspired to oppress women and elevate men. One of the first analyses of the devaluation of women's labor with a call for radical change was Ann Oakley's (1974) analysis of housework among middle- and working-class women in Britain. Oakley applied concepts of gender, power, social stratification, and deviance to understand why women's work in the home was unpaid, invisible, devalued, and monotonous, yet essential to the maintenance of families. Oakley made the hidden intersections of gender, class, and power more visible.

The variations on feminist theorizing continued to ripple. Major challenges to liberal feminist thought in the second wave came from women whose experiences were not represented by the singular concept of gender. Gender, they argued, was not the only cause of women's oppression, and the experiences of White, middle-class, heterosexual feminists did not reflect all women's experiences. **Womanist feminism** was developed by women of color. They were among the first to challenge the liberal paradigm, arguing that race, gender, and class cannot be separated (Combahee River Collective, 1982). Black women, for example, have had very different experiences of work, given the frequent necessity to be both providers and caregivers for their own children, and historically, other women's children (Collins, 1990). Another major challenge to second wave feminist thought came from lesbian standpoint theory. **Lesbian feminism** combined sexual orientation with gender theory, by critiquing the concept of "compulsory heterosexuality" (Rich, 1980), where all women were presumed to be heterosexual, and those who were not were considered deviant.

These feminist critiques about the variations in women's experiences went hand-in-hand with changes in family life as well. As more middle-class women were returning to the paid labor force, issues such as the lack of childcare, women's double burden of work at home and in the labor market, and the invisibility of housework, were exposed by feminist activism and scholarship. Feminist activism took on issues that no one else had conceptualized: abortion, rape, sexual harassment, wife abuse, child abuse, and pornography (Freedman, 2002). In family studies, feminist theory began to explain how power impacted family members in hierarchical ways, based on gender (male, female) and generation (fathers/mothers; sons/daughters) (Osmond and Thorne, 1993; Walker and Thompson, 1984).

Barrie Thorne (1982) summarized how the feminist critique of mainstream family theory opened the way to reclaiming "the family" for more critical analysis, rather than thinking about family roles and relationships as natural. First, feminists challenged traditional family theory as presuming that "The Family" always referred to one type: a monolithic structure of an unchanging entity associated with nuclear relationships, the home, and bonds of love (see Chapter 1). All other forms were labeled as deviant. Second, Thorne described how, although the family appears to be embedded in the most natural and biological of relationships (e.g., birth, sickness, death), feminists have argued that the family should be analyzed by "emphasizing the social organization of sexuality, reproduction, motherhood, the sexual division of labor, and the division of gender itself" (1982, p. 6). Third, feminists critiqued family theory as functionalist (Chapter 2), where the gendered division of labor became translated into a language of roles that thereby "glosses over the complexity of behavior in actual families and falsely assumes that expressive and instrumental activities are mutually exclusive" (1982, p. 8). These early insights laid the groundwork for future analysis of the social construction of gender and the concepts that are now accepted as "doing gender" (West and Zimmerman, 1987) and "doing family" in diverse kinds of families (see Nelson, 2006; Perlesz et al., 2006, for examples). "Doing" refers to the fact that gender is a social construction, not a natural or biological difference.

Thus, feminist theorists, activists, and critics in the second wave demonstrated the necessity of full economic, reproductive, and sexual justice for women through social activism. Emerging challenges that led to a new movement included the necessity of looking beyond western borders to the understanding of feminisms on a global scale (transnationalist feminism), the ways in which young women did and did not resonate with feminist ideas and practice, the experiences of men (men's studies), critical race theory (Burton et al., 2010; Few-Demo, 2014), and the questioning of the very utility of feminist theory itself (Elam and Wiegman, 1995).

Third wave feminism The second wave faded through the challenges of women whose lives did not fit the dominant culture's mandate of being heterosexual, White, first world, young, able-bodied, and thus as close to men's privilege as possible. Third wave feminism acknowledged that no singular version of feminism can reflect all women's experiences or needs for legal justice and social change in terms of economic disadvantage, race, sexual orientation, ability, age, nationality, and other major forms of social difference. In an essay entitled "Age, race, class, and sex: Women redefining difference," Audre Lorde wrote eloquently about her experiences as "a forty-nine-year-old Black lesbian feminist socialist mother of two, including one boy, and a member of an interracial couple" (1985, p. 114), and how all of these identities were inseparable. Therefore, one of the main lessons learned from the second wave that was carried forth into the third wave was about the politics of difference: feminist theory is not a unified body of knowledge, but is particular to the situation at hand (De Reus, Few, and Blume, 2005). That is, a single woman in an executive position raising a child on her own is likely to have paid help; a single woman without financial resources is likely to rely on family networks, if they are available, or to face difficult choices between work and childcare.

Two of the major theoretical modifications that emerged during the third wave are postmodern feminism and queer theory. First, **postmodern feminism** deconstructs gender systems and the practices that uphold them, primarily through challenging and exposing what has come to be seen and accepted as normal and natural (Baber, 2009). This theory suggests ways to "undo gender" (Butler, 2004). For example, a postmodern approach to women's reproductive lives challenges the motherhood mandate, which assumes that all women want to reproduce. This approach also challenges the belief that motherhood is the most satisfying of any role a woman could have. Postmodern feminism questions these taken-for-granted assumptions because they are not true for everyone.

Second, **queer theory** calls attention to the social construction of sexual orientation, rather than it being regarded as a mental illness, a medical issue, or an essential identity category. Instead of focusing on how lesbian, gay, bisexual, transgender, or queer (LGBTQ) individuals deviate from society's norms, queer theory questions the very foundation of heterosexuality as being normal, and thus, "queers" the concepts of identity, sexual orientation, and family (Oswald, Blume, and Marks, 2005). Queer theory challenges the taken-for-granted assumption that everyone is and should be heterosexual, and it exposes how social institutions maintain heteronormativity through pressures to conform. For example, rituals associated with major family events are designed to reinforce heteronormative expectations. Think about the greeting card section of any major store. What kinds of cards are there? Who is depicted in the cards – straight couples or gay couples? There are sections for "husband," "wife," and each card is filled with humor embedded in the assumption that all people identify as heterosexual. Queer theory helps us see the injustice in the heterosexist realities of our everyday lives, and offers creative new ways for doing research about LGBTQ individuals and their allies, as van Eeden-Moorefield and Proulx's (2009) study on using cyber-feminist methods to study gay men's perceptions of couple identity demonstrates.

Another contribution of third wave feminism has been the insistence on including international perspectives, that of global feminisms. Now, feminist theorizing is stretching beyond representations of women as a universal group, and recognizing that women's experiences are socially created, and vastly different depending upon geographic and national circumstances. Consider Lubbe's (2013) description of LGBT-parent families in nonwestern societies. In many African countries, for example, same-sex relationships are illegal, allied with strong sanctions, such as imprisonment. This enforces silence and hiding among gay and lesbian individuals, rendering their families invisible. Yet, the way that individuals combine gender, sexual orientation, and economic circumstances in families does not typically resemble western ways. Woman-to-woman marriage exists in southern African countries, but it is not labeled as lesbian (Lubbe, 2013). Thus, whereas women's friendships might be a topic of study in the US, female infanticide or illiteracy may be more salient in a developing country. This trend toward international feminisms that attempts to fully integrate the voices and experiences of transnational authors challenges the very notion of "what is feminism?"

Fourth wave feminism Fourth wave feminism grew out of the recognition by contemporary young women that women's quest for full personhood, though improved, still has a long way to go. Women realized that the societal belief that they could "have it all" was not working. There were still many barriers to key issues such as equity in marriage and parenthood, lesbian rights, and economic advancement. These recognitions were born of young women's reflection on their own experience of the persistence of the **glass ceiling**, despite the many battles that had already been won. The glass ceiling refers to the invisible barrier that keeps women and other minority group members in lower-level positions by denying them the same opportunities for career advancement as White, privileged men. The metaphor of "glass ceiling" calls attention to how the barrier is not overtly acknowledged, thus making it very hard to challenge and change.

Additionally, fourth wave feminism has emerged in recent years to address a renewed interest among young people in feminist research and activism (Baumgardner, 2011). Young feminists are revealing bolder integrations of what was once called (in second wave feminism) the "personal is political." For example, the online magazine *Everyday Feminism* provides definitions of basic feminist theory and terms, such as patriarchal intersectionality, and also provides interesting articles on self-worth, sex, love, body image, violence, work, and the like. In our case study, Luke is identifying as a fourth-wave feminist. He respects and appreciates the work for equality in which his mother engaged, and does not take his own privilege for granted, as if it was a birthright simply by being male.

One aspect of the new feminist theorizing among young scholars and activists includes a more explicit use of self-reflection in research and writing (see Christensen, 2015; Magalhães and Cerqueira, 2015), which is referred to as **reflexivity**. In family science, feminist theory is perhaps the only framework that values the use of personal experience in understanding the research process. Reflexivity refers to the conscious, reflexive practice of applying feminist knowledge to one's own life and scholarship (Allen, 2000). Feminist reflexive practice helps to keep the researcher honest by constantly recognizing the tension between sameness and difference in studying gender and its intersections. Feminists have broken new ground in many areas by recognizing the connection between the oppression they were experiencing in their own lives and how it connected to macro experiences as well.

Box 8.1 At a Glance: Feminist Theory

Gender equality Feminists are concerned with ensuring gender equality for all individuals.

Intersectionality How multiple systems of oppression, such as race, class, gender, sexuality, religion, age, and nationality intersect to create advantage or disadvantage.

Praxis Putting theory into practice by working for social change, both locally and globally.

Patriarchy A system of male dominance in which men have more privilege, power, and worth than women.

Reflexivity The conscious, reflexive practice of applying feminist knowledge to one's own life and scholarship.

Doing gender Gender is a social construction and performance, not a biological given.

Privilege and oppression Power differences in society create social institutions and interactions that value the elite group and create disadvantages for minority groups.

As an example, Slater (2013) incorporates her own experiences with growing up, graduating, and moving into adult roles as a college teacher into her research on disabled youth. Rather than distancing themselves as researchers, young feminist thinkers are critically engaging their own process of how feminism affects them. They are changing the ways in which we can utilize feminist principles of repression and revolt. In family studies, theorizing by including personal reflections on the research process, though supported by some feminist scholars (Allen, Lloyd, and Few, 2009; Lather, 2007), is still rare. Yet this transparency can be helpful in understanding why the researcher has a vested interest in the topic.

Key concepts

As we have discussed, the major areas of feminist theorizing include equality, power, privilege, oppression, and intersectionality. Now we address how these concepts are defined and utilized in both feminist theory and family studies. The feminist historian Estelle Freedman has identified four key principles of the nature of feminism, as both a theory and praxis: "Feminism is a belief that women and men are inherently of equal worth. Because most societies privilege men as a group, social movements are necessary to achieve equality between women and men, with the understanding that gender always intersects with other social hierarchies" (2002, p. 7).

Equal worth Women's experiences in the home and the workplace are as valuable as men's. The idea of equal worth challenges the view that men's ways of knowing, living, and being in the world are superior, and thus women are expected to aspire to be the same as and equal to men. Instead, the assumption of equal worth is that whatever work women have been engaged in, whether traditional female activities such as childbearing, child-rearing, parent care, or teaching, is just as valuable as the work that has historically been done by men (Freedman, 2002). Valuing women's experience means that men's lives are not the gold standard for measuring worth; women's experiences have a significant impact on social and political life.

Privilege Some individuals and groups have more advantages than others. **Privilege** refers to the taken-for-granted rights, both legal and informal, that certain people have in society, by virtue of their gender, race, class, sexual orientation, age, and other ways in which society structures and regulates human relations. Peggy McIntosh (1995) has pointed out that male privilege, just like White privilege, is an invisible knapsack of benefits that one takes along the road of life. In the family realm, male privilege includes the greater value placed on male children, as expressed in the parental preference for boys in many cultures, which can be traced back to rules of inheritance that may no longer be relevant in contemporary society. These invisible privileges also include men's formal rights, such as the right to vote or hold political office, which did not become a reality for women in the US until 1920. While it may seem that women can run for elected office just as easily as men, think about the scrutiny we place on women who run for offices such as president and vice president of the US. Do we ask the same questions of men and women running for the same office? Do men have to tell us how they will juggle taking care of children with their job in the Senate? Conversely, do we place more scrutiny on women for wanting to take on such a prestigious job?

Another way of thinking about the invisible knapsack is to consider everyday realities for men and women – activities that are conducted in a more private way than running for public office. Think about how the physical labor is traditionally divided in the household. Who does the "inside" chores, and who usually performs the "outside" chores? Women traditionally do cooking, cleaning, laundry, and primary childcare. Each of these duties has to be completed every day; families usually eat three meals a day, and everyone wears clothing that needs laundering at least once a week. Cleaning – or at the very least, picking up – needs to be done every day (e.g., making beds and doing dishes are both daily activities). Men, on the other hand, are usually responsible for "outdoor" duties – mowing the lawn and shoveling the snow, and perhaps taking out the trash. These tasks are *not* completed every day; mowing is not only a weekly task, but it is only necessary during certain seasons. Trash usually does not need to be taken out every day, but perhaps twice or three times a week. Without analyzing these major differences in the division of labor between men and women, we are reproducing privilege. Privilege is invisible because it occurs without anyone even thinking about it. We go about our daily lives thinking that we are just "doing what's always been done," when in reality, we are recreating advantage and disadvantage without thinking twice. This taken-for-granted quality is what makes privilege so powerful – we have to stop and think to really see it.

Social movements When individuals start to become aware of the differential treatment and unearned privileges operating at the personal, familial, and societal levels, they are developing a **consciousness** about unequal privilege. Consciousness-raising at the individual level helps to spark a broader social movement. The Women's Liberation Movement that began to take shape in the 1960s explicitly addressed justice for women as a primary concern (Freedman, 2002). A social movement involves the collective activism toward social change that is essential to feminism. Activist involvement includes individual participation, such as taking a women's studies class during college, or providing your child with gender-neutral toys. It can also involve participating in nationalist or global movements that work toward women's human rights and full citizenship in developing countries or those that still bar women from full participation in society, including the right to education (Naples, 2002). Yet, while women may participate in a variety of social movements, including civil rights, ecology, socialism, and religious fundamentalism, these movements are not feminist if they overlook or affirm patriarchal authority. A social movement is feminist when it is rooted in the critique of "male rule" (i.e., patriarchy) and places the improvement of women's lives in the center of vision (Freedman, 2002).

Social hierarchy So far, we have primarily addressed feminism as a critique of gender differences (men versus women). However, the most important lesson of the past several decades of feminist theory and feminist activism is the recognition that gender is integrally related to other social locations, especially those based on class, race, sexuality, and culture. The deconstruction of the universal concept of "woman," in which gender is essentialized, has occurred because of the critiques by women of color, lesbians, bisexual women and transgender individuals, poor and working-class women, transnational women, and multiracial and multicultural men and women, as we noted above. Freedman states,

> Despite the prevalence of hierarchies that privilege men, in every culture some women (such as elites or citizens) enjoy greater opportunities than many other women (such as workers or immigrants). Some women always have higher status than many men. If we ignore these intersecting hierarchies and create a feminism that serves only the interests of women who have more privilege, we reinforce other social inequalities that disadvantage both women and men in the name of improving women's opportunities. (2002, p. 8)

Freedman is referring to the ways in which multiple statuses can intersect to create advantage or disadvantage, opening up feminist theory to a broader understanding of these multiple statuses, including class, race and ethnicity, sexual orientation, disability, and age, among others. For example, how gender operates in families is contextual. That is, gender is expressed very differently depending upon the gender of the other person with whom one parents (sexual orientation and marital status) or the gender of the child (age and generation) (Goldberg, 2010; Tasker, 2013). Gender is further complicated by differences across the social and economic resources men and women bring to families. Gender matters in many different ways within families and across families.

Intersectionality and systems of oppression Feminist theory has expanded to go beyond gender hierarchy and incorporate multiple systems of oppression. Systems of oppression are the interlocking hierarchies that stratify and objectify individuals in society. As a result of this stratification, certain groups are defined by the dominant society as subordinate. As we described in Chapter 3 on conflict theory, members of the elite have greater access to opportunities and rewards. They have the power to define experience, create meaning, establish the rules, and dole out sanctions (Collins, 1990; Few-Demo, 2014).

Social locations such as race, class, gender, sexuality, religion, and nationality have the ability to mutually construct one another (Collins, 1990; Mahler, Chaudhuri, and Patil, 2015). **Intersectionality** is the politics of location, where each of us simultaneously experiences privilege and disadvantage (Few-Demo, 2014; McCall, 2005). As depicted in the inequality track (Chapter 3), privilege means that to the degree that a person occupies more highly valued social positions (e.g., a wealthy White man), they have more doors opening, with less effort. A person with privilege is less likely to be stopped by the police, more likely to get into a prestigious school, and more likely to find a suitable mate. However, every person does not live up to the "ideal" of "having it all." So this means that some social positions are less valued than others. Being gay, compared to being heterosexual, is more devalued. Thus, a wealthy White man who is gay deals with those intersections: he is privileged because of his gender, race, and class status, but disadvantaged and marginalized because of his sexual orientation. And this has consequences for becoming a father. It has been difficult for gay men to have children, given the stereotypes and stigma against them. However, gay men with financial resources are able to pay for surrogacy arrangements, again a function of how class intersects with gender and sexual orientation in impacting family life (Berkowitz, 2009; Goldberg, 2012).

Hegemonic masculinity Patriarchy – defined earlier in the chapter as a system of male dominance – is enforced through hegemonic masculinity. **Hegemonic masculinity** is the "practice that defines men's roles, expectations, and identities as superior to women" (Connell and Messerschmidt, 2005, p. 832). Hegemonic masculinity is fairly easy to achieve for some, but definitely not all men. The ideal of hegemonic masculinity includes being successful, heterosexual, married/in a relationship with a woman, aggressive, dominant, strong, wealthy, and powerful. See Figure 8.2 for an illustration of contemporary American ideas of masculinity.

The words inside the "man box" in Figure 8.2 are prescriptions for how men *should* behave. The words outside of the box are the terms used to describe men when they fail to fit into the "man box." Even though not all men can achieve these "ideals" of masculinity, it is still the standard by which men are judged. In addition, for hegemonic masculinity to work as the rule for men, it also requires women to emphasize femininity. That is, these ideals of masculinity are *not* to be performed by women. Women are supposed to fulfill ideals that directly oppose hegemonic masculinity; women are supposed to be meek, subordinate, delicate, pretty, dependent on men, and sexual (but not too sexual).

Think about this dichotomy of prescribed gender performance in relation to the man box – what do you notice about the words used to describe men who do not fit in the box? Most of the words are feminine in nature, which means that as a society, we value masculinity and not femininity. If we are putting a man down, we use feminine words to describe him, or worse, we use negative or slanderous words that are associated with women (e.g., bitch; wussy) to describe him. This lends weight to the idea that in

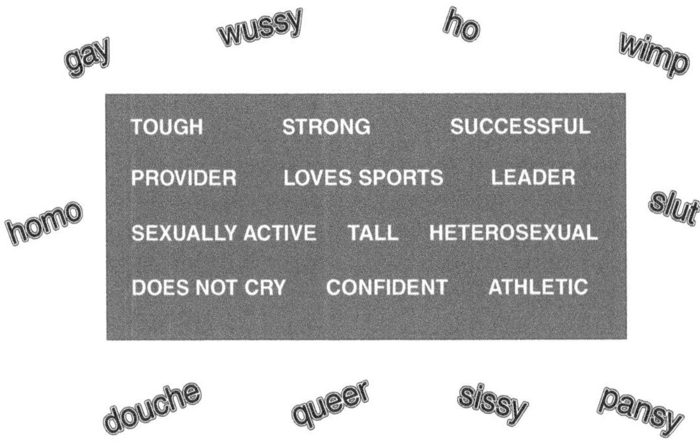

Figure 8.2 The "man box"

order for hegemonic masculinity to be powerful and functional, we need women to emphasize feminine traits. In turn, when men deviate from the masculinity norm, we label them with derogatory feminine words. This helps maintain the dichotomized notions of how to "do" gender in our society. Together, hegemonic masculinity and emphasized femininity set the standard by which all members of society – regardless of their race, class, gender, or sexual orientation – are evaluated.

Box 8.2 Feminist Theory in Pop Culture: *Tough Guise*

A scene from *Tough Guise*, 1999, dir. Sut Jhally, Media Education Foundation

Jackson Katz, a leading gender violence prevention trainer, has produced two documentaries to critique contemporary notions of masculinity in America. *Tough Guise* and *Tough Guise 2* examine rates of domestic violence, and the stunning statistic that men commit over 90 percent of violent crimes in society. Yet, until recently we have not examined the social construction of masculinity (the "tough guise") with a critical eye. Katz illustrates how hegemonic masculinity has developed over the past 60 years, and gives a particularly poignant example of the size of boys' action figures. Since the toy G.I. Joe was first created in 1963, his biceps have been steadily enlarged.

One of the most intriguing aspects of these documentaries is the practical application of the ideas. Katz breaks down not only media messages about masculinity, but also how we communicate with and about boys, and the toys we let our children play with. For these reasons, these documentaries are also good examples of both micro- and macro-levels of gender analysis.

Evaluating Feminist Theory

Strengths of feminist theory

Feminist theory in family studies has many strengths. It is one of the most dynamic, exciting, adaptable, and controversial of all the theories. And because of its variability – that there are so many versions of feminist theory – it can also be a challenge in trying to use it. As we have discussed throughout this chapter, feminist theory is full of complexity and contradiction.

Critique of power dynamics in families Feminist theory is the only perspective in family studies that directly challenges inequality and power dynamics in marriages and families and seeks to enact private and public social change. Feminist theory began with challenging the normative family structure of the separation of gendered family roles. Feminists challenged this taken-for-granted family structure by uncovering issues such as invisible labor, family violence, unequal distribution of power in families, and many other concepts (Walker and Thompson, 1984). Feminist theory allowed us to "rethink the family" and ask new questions about how gender is reproduced in families, and how it can be deconstructed in order to disrupt power inequities (Thorne, 1982). Feminist theory also offers possibilities for reconstructing families from women's experiences, thereby decentering the prevalence of patriarchy (Baber and Allen, 1992).

Valuing and hearing women's voices Another major strength of feminist theory is that it takes the voices of the people it studies seriously. A good deal of the family research guided by a feminist perceptive has used qualitative methods to go straight to the source and document the experiences of those who have been oppressed – in their own words. We first learned about the gendered nature of housework – invisible, unappreciated, unpaid, and delegated to women – by interviewing women about their responsibilities in the home (Lopata, 1971; Oakley, 1974). New insights are gleaned by investigating unexamined topics, listening to women and their family members, and by paying attention to their experiences. In another example, MacTavish (2007) examined family and community life for low-income parents and children living in a rural mobile home park. By taking the perspective of the people she studied, MacTavish was able to uncover not only their feelings of exclusion but also to support it with evidence of class-segregated schooling, exclusionary recreation programs, and social stigma. Listening to the voices of women and their families, and taking them seriously is a hallmark and strength of feminist theory.

Adaptable to change A third strength is that feminist theory is constantly being revised in light of new knowledge, social changes, and the reflexive quality of feminist scholars to critique themselves and each other. Feminism is a dynamic and fluid theory that is not satisfied with the status quo; it is a contentious theory that challenges scholars and activists to not settle for outdated concepts and easy solutions. Thus, feminists have studied gender in families, first from the perspective of biological sex roles and gender roles, and after critiquing their own ideas, feminist theory has contributed new ideas that shed light on the limitations of sex and role as theoretical concepts. Instead, gender as a set of relations, about how men and women "do gender," replaced earlier and more static ideas about sex or gender roles (Risman, 2004; West and Zimmerman, 1987). And, feminists have introduced the concept of intersectionality to the study of gender, so that we now understand that how we do gender intersects with how we do class, race, family, and the like (Collins, 1990). No doubt, as we write these words, there are newer ideas about feminist theory that will replace them.

Weaknesses of feminist theory

Just as there are many strengths to feminist theory, there are also many criticisms. As we have noted, sometimes the strengths of a theory can also be its weaknesses. Feminist theory attempts to deal with very complex social and personal issues and ground them in a political context, hence leading to debates about its usefulness as a way to look at the world from an intellectual standpoint.

Is it a theory or an ideology? A common criticism of feminist theory is that it is not a theory, but an ideology. What this means is that concerns over gender inequality are part of a perspective, or way of looking at the world, but without "testable" propositions like other theories. As an example, structural-functionalism theory (Chapter 2) would suggest that the reason that nearly 50 percent of marriages end in divorce is because the family has outsourced needs that were previously met *inside* the family. Therefore, if you were to examine this phenomenon using functionalist theory, you would measure family members' use of external social institutions, such as going to a therapist for emotional support, compared to when family members used to stay inside the private realm of the family to get those needs met. Prior to the Industrial Revolution that began in western countries several centuries ago, family members worked at home, educated children at home, received religious teachings from the patriarch (father) of the household, and grew and prepared all of their food at home. Each member of the family had a specific "job," which is very different from how a contemporary family functions. Therefore, the testable proposition using structural-functionalist theory would be: "Divorce rates have increased since the Industrial Revolution because of modern society's reliance on external social institutions." Using feminist theory, on the other hand, you would examine the ways in which gendered ideologies have shifted over time and how women's and men's roles have changed as a result. Critics who argue that feminism is not a theory suggest that while examining gender roles in the family is important, it is not specific enough to be testable. Instead, they suggest that feminism is more of a political ideology. It is important to point out, however, that the same argument could be made for conflict theory (Chapter 3), which presupposes that all social order is determined by access to wealth and power. These are underlying processes that affect and predict how families operate, and are undoubtedly important to examine.

Does it have to be explicitly feminist to be a feminist theory? One of the challenges in finding feminist theory in family studies is that authors often do not name their work explicitly as being feminist (Ferree, 2010; Thompson and Walker, 1995; Walker, 2009; Wills and Risman, 2006). Several commentaries and studies over the past three decades have challenged the impact that feminist theory and research have made in family studies. Part of this issue has to do with the fact that scholars often use concepts of gender, power, and multiple social locations which are derived from feminist theory, but do not name them as such. This example of not giving credit where credit is due is akin to saying, "I'm not a feminist, but …" The very fact that some people do not want to identify their work as feminist, and yet have benefited by the changes created by feminist scholars and activists, is some indication of its controversial nature. It also indicates the relevance of feminist theory for challenging the status quo belief that all individuals are equal in society.

Difficulty of measuring intersectionality Intersectionality is an exciting and useful theoretical concept, as it acknowledges that gender alone is not complex enough to measure privilege, opportunity, and oppression in people's lives. Rather, our lives are shaped by how gender intersects with other forms of social stratification. Intersectionality, as an academic concept, is relatively easy to understand. Methodologically, however, it is very difficult to measure, particularly in quantitative research (Bowleg, 2008; McCall, 2005). Ferree (2010), as we will discuss in the section entitled "Feminist theory today," suggests ways of conceptualizing intersectionality as either locational or relational, and these definitions offer suggestions for how to measure intersectionality in ways that retain the benefits of its theoretical complexity.

An alternative theory app: functionalist theory

In this chapter, we have laid out the key concepts, origins and modern applications, as well as the strengths and weaknesses of feminist theory. For most students, at first glance, feminist theory stands in stark contrast to functionalist theory. However, it is still useful to consider how we would "switch" apps to explain the same phenomenon from perspectives that are seemingly polar opposites.

Think back to Chapter 2, when you learned about functionalists Talcott Parsons and Robert Merton. Parsons's theory of social change argued that change occurs slowly, over time, and that perfect equilibrium among all systems is a goal, but is rarely achieved.

Merton extended this line of thought and argued that not all individuals in a society can "fit" into the preexisting social institutions, which naturally produces deviance. Think about this in relation to how feminist thought has evolved over time. The first wave focused on giving women legal rights, the second wave on questioning stay-at-home motherhood mandates and giving voice to women of color. The third and fourth waves expanded to include LGBTQ voices and pushing the boundaries of traditional notions of feminism in academia. Each of these changes would not have been possible without considering the functionality of "deviant" voices, and how over time, the cultural system adapts to include new perspectives. There is a place in society for the "other" voices – to disrupt and evoke change in a preexisting system. Therefore, the functionalist model of social deviance and social change helps us understand how feminism has come to be what it is today.

Working with Feminist Theory: Integrating Research and Practice

Feminist theory today

Given the complexity of intersectionality as a theoretical and methodological concept, Myra Marx Ferree (2010) provided two ways to conceptualize it. The first type, **locational intersectionality**, is concerned with the identities and social positions of disadvantaged groups, such as those who are poor, members of a minority group, LGBTQ, old, or disabled. This perspective gives voice to individuals with multiple oppressed social locations, and helps others to understand how people with those multiple intersections actually experience such disadvantages. For example, in Nelson's (2006) qualitative study of single mothers, the women created their own families in a way that conformed to the idealized traditional family model, even though they had not been able to achieve this ideal family in their own lives. They created this by having their mothers serve as placeholders for the husbands they did not currently have, but they hoped to secure in the future. They relied on their own mothers to provide housing, financial security, and child-rearing support, so that they could complete the dream of becoming a traditional family. According to Ferree, Nelson's study is an exemplar of a locational intersectional analysis by revealing how a woman's social locations of being a divorced, single mother reflect societal-level institutional constraints, such as the risk of poverty.

The second type, **relational intersectionality**, theorizes that intersectionality affects every individual, not just the most oppressed and marginalized. It moves beyond locational intersectionality to examine the institutional practices and social processes that interact to produce patterns of inequality for all individuals (Ferree, 2010). Identity, then, is not static, but shifts with changing cultural discourses and social institutions. In their study of how poor women of color dealt with the welfare system, Dodson and Schmalzbauer (2005) used the relational approach to interpret their strategies and "habits of hiding" to exercise caution when interacting with social work professionals who had the power to exert control over them by denying them needed resources.

Feminist theory in research

Kathleen Gerson's research, *Children of the Gender Revolution*, was an in-depth interview study of 120 young men and women between the ages of 18 and 32 from diverse social classes and racial/ethnic groups. She found that their family relationships, not family type (e.g., single parent, two-parent, dual earner), mattered most to them. Gerson used feminist theory to explain how "parents developed strategies for breadwinning and caretaking in the face of unexpected economic contingencies and interpersonal crises" (2009, p. 740). When parents exercised gender flexibility, they were better able to meet their children's economic and emotional needs. Gender inflexibility, however, was rough on children, in that they felt unprepared to deal with the problems their parents encountered during parental break-ups, or when financial resources declined.

Gerson also found that 95 percent of her participants wanted a lifelong bond with one partner, and most also wanted an equal partnership. Still, many of these young men and women worried that a dual earner marriage that allowed for personal autonomy would not be possible. They still did not see the signs of broader social change that indicated these ideals were in reach. They faced time-demanding jobs, with few childcare and family-leave options that would support gender equality in marriage. The fallback position, that women opt out of paid work for stay-at-home motherhood, was less and less attractive for many of the women, who were less likely to settle, instead preferring to postpone marriage, and view it as optional and reversible. The men, however, were more likely to fall back on traditional, though somewhat modified, unequal marital relationships. A majority of the men felt that equal sharing in marriage, though appealing, was too costly. These contrasting views of young men and women reveal an emerging gender divide that is challenging the new generation of parents, partners, and employees.

Feminist theory in practice

Feminist theory has been instrumental in several areas of family studies, such as family violence (Yllo and Bograd, 1988), investigating household labor and other forms of unpaid work (Ferree, 1990; Walker, 1999), feminist parenting (Mack-Canty and Wright, 2004), intensive motherhood (Hays, 1996; Newman and Henderson, 2014), social activism, and feminist teaching, among others. Most of what constitutes feminist praxis involves questioning the status quo – or taking a closer look at gendered work policies, educational materials, or even the unspoken routines that we invoke as a part of our daily lives. One of the most important places family scholars can apply feminist theory is in evaluating programming in family life education.

MOPS stands for Mothers of Preschoolers (MOPS, 2016), and is an international Christian organization offered to mothers of young children in an effort to provide support dealing with the new role of mother. During MOPS meetings, women split the cost of childcare and spend time commiserating and discussing motherhood. Over the past 30 years, this organization has grown tremendously and is arguably *the* most popular support group for stay-at-home mothers.

As an organization, MOPS clearly subscribes to the intensive mothering ideology, which Hays defines as the pressure for mothers to be the primary caregivers for their children, which includes "watching, cleaning up after, and playing with their children" (1996, p. 99). This type of child-centered parenting, where a child's every need is attended to at all times, results in what Hays referred to as the "sacred child," who cannot be raised by any other person besides their own mother, including the father/husband.

In order to foster the ideologies of intensive mothering, MOPS sets up curricula that usually involve a guest speaker on a topic related to mothering. Their stated goal is to be supportive of motherhood and reach out to women when they are "most isolated, most lonely, and most looking for outside help."

As a practitioner trained in feminist theory, we might take a closer look at the dominant ideologies inherent in such a group. Is it possible that a group designed to support mothers of young children actually reinforces traditional notions of gender, thereby reinforcing the concept of patriarchy? Should women be troubled by the intensive mothering ideology, which prompts women to stay at home, where they develop the need for outside support? Additionally, if and when women seek support, chances are that they will hear about the most popular group, MOPS, because it is a widespread and well-known support group. Should feminists be troubled by the cycle of disadvantage this creates for women? The intensive mothering ideology creates a deficiency, leading to the need for a support group, and then reinforces that dominant ideology under the guise of a support group. At its core, feminism supports diversity, and therefore groups supporting women's transition into motherhood should also support alternative methods of parenting.

Using our theoretical expertise to analyze the programming of MOPs, we can deconstruct why this institution – filled with seemingly contradictory support for new moms – works so well and is so popular. Part of what makes this support group a powerful place for the reinforcement of intensive mothering has to do with the fact that it is a meso-level institution in society, which means it is a social organization that bridges the gap between structural institutions (e.g., the economy or religion) and individuals (Newman and Henderson, 2014). At the micro-level, women may have encounters with one or two other moms, and disagree with their parenting strategies or ideals about motherhood. It is much easier to disagree with one or two individuals, as opposed to a widely popular national organization for stay-at-home moms that aims to provide support for its members. At the micro-level, it is easier to attribute the other individuals with a character flaw or a personal problem for being "different"; at the meso-level, it is much more difficult to discredit an entire organization, especially when individuals within that organization seem to all subscribe to the same ideology and perform its associated roles seamlessly.

Furthermore, MOPS provides an intimate group where women can forge friendships located within a larger, institutionalized group that is widely acceptable. Subscribing members are likely to view their fellow support group members as their friends and confidants, giving members a sense of solidarity and trust. On the other hand, there is little to no room to question the dominant ideology of working fathers and homemaking mothers. The source of intensive mothering remains anonymous, but omnipresent. This is why studying a meso-level organization like MOPS is an ideal way to connect the macro-level with the micro-level; ideologies are reinforced with very little effort.

Conclusion

Feminist theory has contributed many innovative ideas that allow family researchers and practitioners to utilize its theoretical concepts in the real world. From its beginnings as a way to describe gender oppression and privilege, specifically related to women's rights, feminist theory has evolved to consider how race, class, sexual orientation, age, nationality, and disability, among other social locations, intersect to create different experiences of privilege and oppression. Ultimately, feminist theory offers a critique of the status quo and provides pathways for major social change in the lives of women, men, and families.

Finally, it is important to understand how feminist theory applies to the study of families at the international level. In Box 8.3, we present an example of the fourth wave of feminist activism, in the context of a United Nations campaign to call attention to gender inequality and oppression worldwide. The campaign is being led by a popular celebrity, Emma Watson, whose fame emerged along with the international phenomenon of the *Harry Potter* books and films. Sometimes it takes this type of international renown to raise awareness and instigate social change.

Box 8.3 Global Comparisons: HeForShe Campaign

The HeForShe campaign was launched in 2014, spearheaded by British actress Emma Watson, of *Harry Potter* fame (UN Women, 2014). Aimed at getting men involved as active participants in stopping violence against women, HeForShe is a global effort to end gender inequality. This movement was introduced not long after the National Football League underwent scrutiny for covering up cases of domestic violence among their players.

Emma Watson, Goodwill Ambassador for United Nations Women, addressed the United Nations in 2014 to formally invite men to get involved in the effort to stop gender inequality, speaking from personal experience about her own family:

> Men – I would like to take this opportunity to extend your formal invitation. Gender equality is your issue, too. Because to date, I've seen my father's role as a parent being valued less by society despite my needing his presence as a child as much as my mother's. I've seen young men suffering from mental illness unable to ask for help for fear it would make them look less "macho" – in fact, in the UK, suicide is the biggest killer of men between 20–49 years of age, eclipsing road accidents, cancer and coronary heart disease. I've seen men made fragile and insecure by a distorted sense of what constitutes male success. Men don't have the benefits of equality, either.

She also discussed how feminism is perceived as being "synonymous with man-hating," yet growing up, she still was helped by "inadvertent feminists" – her word for her parents, her teachers, her mentors – who did not limit her just because she was a girl. Watson went on to say that there is not one country in the world where all women have the same rights as men. She also discussed what needs to happen in order for any real change to take place toward real gender inequality, starting with men:

> We don't often talk about men being imprisoned by gender stereotypes but I can see that they are and that when they are free, things will change for women as a natural consequence. If men don't have to be aggressive in order to be accepted, women won't feel compelled to be submissive. If men don't have to control, women won't have to be controlled. Both men and women should feel free to be sensitive. Both men and women should feel free to be strong ... If we stop defining each other by what we are not and start defining ourselves by what we are – we can all be freer and this is what HeForShe is about. It's about freedom. I want men to take up this mantle so that their daughters, sisters and mothers can be free from prejudice but also so that their sons have permission to be vulnerable and human too – reclaim those parts of themselves they abandoned and in doing so, be a more true and complete version of themselves.

She concluded her speech by telling the audience that if they believe in equality, then they might be one of the inadvertent feminists she spoke about.

Multimedia Suggestions

www.hrc.org

This is the website for the Human Rights Campaign (HRC), the most influential civil rights organization for lesbian, gay, bisexual, and transgender equality. The website offers a wealth of information about state-by-state LGBT marriage and parenting rights in the US; the coming out process; religious issues; health and aging; state, federal, and global advocacy; and an ally's guide to LGBT issues. The resources link contains a compilation of facts and maps about all of these issues. Because of the volatile nature of LGBTQ issues, the website is constantly updated to reflect changes in laws and resources.

Activate your theory app: Now that all American citizens have legal access to marriage regardless of sexual orientation, what issues are at the forefront of the HRC? And what issues regarding marriage equality are not yet "over"?

www.socwomen.org

This is the official website for Sociologists for Women in Society, a nonprofit scientific and educational organization of sociologists and others dedicated to issues such as increasing educational and professional opportunities for women, and creating feminist social change. The website provides a number of outstanding fact sheets about feminist social issues, including "Women, poverty, and welfare in the Great Recession"; "Intersectionality in sociology"; "Girls and education: A global approach"; "The menstrual cycle: A feminist lifespan perspective"; "Gender and sport"; and "Gender, sex work, and social justice."

Activate your theory app: Browse this organization's Career Advice section. Sometimes it is useful to really "see" the power of advice by imagining what the advice would sound like if it were directed at someone who already had privilege. As you read through the comments, take note of how reimagining that advice from the perspective of privilege helps point out some of the invisible power of gender inequality.

Frozen (2013)

In this animated Disney movie, princesses and sisters Anna and Elsa are at odds with one another. When

Anna tells Elsa (the eldest sister) she is in love with a man (Hans) she had only just met, Elsa forbids their marriage. In the end, Anna realizes Hans was only after the power of the royal throne; she not only casts him aside, but she punches him in the face, sending him sailing off the side of a ship. Though this film may not be perceived as a "feminist" film, it does still represent a larger cultural shift away from traditional "princess" films where the female character is typically rescued by the male hero.

A scene from *Frozen*, 2013, dir. Chris Buck and Jennifer Lee, Walt Disney Pictures

Activate your theory app: Critique this film using a feminist perspective. Do you think the subtle messages are getting through to young girls, to whom the film is targeted?

The Hunger Games (2012)

This popular film is based on a 2008 novel by Suzanne Collins. There are several examples of feminist theory in the film, especially when applied to Katniss's relationship with her family. Katniss is the eldest daughter and takes on the provider role by bow-hunting wild game in order to feed her widowed mother and sister. Katniss experiences intersectionality because she is poor, female, in a single-parent household, and also the child of a mother with mental illness. She then volunteers to participate in the Hunger Games in the place of her younger sister. Throughout the film, Katniss displays characteristics of hegemonic masculinity, which make the producers of the *Hunger Games* uncomfortable. Therefore, they force her to emphasize her feminine traits and socially construct a love story so that viewers are distracted from her strong personality.

A scene from *Hunger Games*, 2012, dir. Gary Ross, Lionsgate Films

Activate your theory app: Think back to films with similar stories from 10 or 20 years ago. Sometimes it is useful to compare popular films to those from the past to examine whether or not we have really "come as far" as we think with gender inequality. Has feminism been captured in this film, when compared to past films focused on young women?

Further Reading

Calasanti, T., and King, N., "Taking 'women's work' 'like a man': Husbands' experiences of care work," *Gerontologist*, *47* (2007), 516–527 (doi:10.1093/geront/47.4.516). Calasanti and King interviewed husbands caring for their wives during various stages of Alzheimer's disease. In this study, they utilized a feminist structural approach, which means that they not only analyzed how the men constructed masculinity with relation to caregiving, but they took their social class backgrounds (i.e., structured inequality) into account as well. This work is important for family policy and theory development because men's experiences of masculinity vary significantly by race and class, which should inform intervention development and strategies for supporting caregivers.

Collins, P. H., *Black sexual politics: African Americans, gender, and the new racism* (New York: Routledge, 2005).

Collins addressed how the intersections of racism, sexism, and heterosexism are used to reinforce the color line in American culture. She examined the multiple threads that are affecting African American lives and relationships today, including families, education, employment, violence, prison, health, mass media, and popular culture.

Gerson, K., *The unfinished revolution: How a new generation is reshaping family, work, and gender in America* (New York: Oxford University Press, 2009). In this interview study, young men and women who desired egalitarian committed relationships still found that their worlds are based on the traditional distinctions between breadwinning and caretaking. Gerson revealed how gender informs the dilemmas they face and suggested the need for flexible social and economic supports to help new generations realize their goal of equally blending work and family.

Goldberg, A. E., "'Doing' and 'undoing' gender: The meaning and division of housework in same-sex couples," *Journal of Family Theory and Review, 5* (2013), 85–104 (doi:10.1111/jftr.12009). This study revealed how lesbian and gay male couples both do and undo gender through housework. On the one hand, same-sex partners are influenced by heteronormative views of housework as feminine or masculine. At the same time, Goldberg showed how same-sex couples also interpret their household labor as pragmatic and chosen, thus rejecting the idea that their division of labor in the home is based upon gender norms.

Mahalingam, R., Balan, S., and Molina, K. M., "Transnational intersectionality: A critical framework for theorizing motherhood," in S. A. Lloyd, A. L. Few, and K. R. Allen (eds), *Handbook of feminist family studies* (Thousand Oaks, CA: Sage, 2009), pp. 69–80. This chapter provides an in-depth analysis of how the experiences of women of color from around the world challenge the Eurocentric bias about the experience of motherhood. The authors provide a feminist theoretical model of how to examine motherhood from transnational perspectives, particularly when women migrate to a new country. They explain that we should study women's experiences as caretakers and providers by looking at how issues such as cultural narratives, social marginality, the context of migration, and social class impact the well-being of mothers and children. This model provides examples that can inform women from westernized nations about how women in developing countries coordinate complex caring obligations, within their home countries and in the countries to which they migrate.

Questions for Students

Discussion Questions

1 What is a "gender perspective"? How does it differ from the earlier concept of "gender roles as separate spheres"?
2 Describe how status quo definitions of family, gender, and power have challenged the feminist call for social change and family justice.
3 What trends do you notice in the different waves of feminist thinking over time? If we were to have a "fifth wave," what do you think it would involve?
4 Considering Gerson's research, *Children of the Gender Revolution*, do you believe we can finish the gender revolution without turning back the clock? How do *you* deal with resistant institutions and the contradictory pressures facing you as a gendered being today?
5 Define the concept of intersectionality. How do you see it expanding upon a feminist perspective? In what ways is it relevant to women's and men's lives in global perspective?
6 From an international perspective, give examples of how the concept of patriarchy is still relevant today. Give examples of how it may not be relevant.

Your Turn!

Find an article in which the authors have used feminist theory in family studies as a framework for their research. What aspects of feminist theory did the research utilize? How did the researchers locate themselves in the study, if at all? Is there another theory the research could have utilized? What are the strengths and weaknesses of the article? What would YOU do different, if you were in charge of the research?

Personal Reflection Questions

1 How will you manage the gender divide in your own family and work life? What aspects of gender difference do you find useful? What aspects do you find difficult to deal with?
2 In what ways have you been an activist in your own life? What social movements do you follow? What is the difference you want to see and to help create in the world?
3 What versions of feminist theory can you most relate to? What concepts are the hardest for you to relate to?
4 How does the concept of intersectionality play out in your own life? In what ways do gender, race, class, sexual orientation, age, dis/ability and other forms of social stratification structure your opportunities and experiences?
5 When was the first time you noticed gender in your life? How old were you? What were you doing? How did those around you encourage or discourage gender roles?
6 Thinking about the concept of privilege, what are the privileges you are carrying around in your "invisible knapsack"?

References

Acker, J., Barry, K., and Esseveld, J. (1983). Objectivity and truth: Problems in doing feminist research. *Women's Studies International Forum, 6*, 423–435. doi:10/1016/0277-5395(83)90035-3.

Allen, K. R. (2000). A conscious and inclusive family studies. *Journal of Marriage and the Family, 62*, 4–17. doi:10.1111/j.1741-3737.2000.00004.x.

Allen, K. R., Lloyd, S. A., and Few, A. L. (2009). Reclaiming feminist theory, method, and praxis for family studies. In S. A. Lloyd, A. L. Few and K. R. Allen (eds), *Handbook of feminist family studies* (pp. 3–17). Thousand Oaks, CA: Sage.

Allen, K. R., Walker, A. J., and McCann, B. R. (2013). Feminism and families. In G. W. Peterson and K. R. Bush (eds), *Handbook of marriage and the family* (3rd edn, pp. 139–158). New York: Springer.

Baber, K. M. (2009). Postmodern feminist perspectives and families. In S. A. Lloyd, A. L. Few and K. R. Allen (eds), *Handbook of feminist family studies* (pp. 56–68). Thousand Oaks, CA: Sage.

Baber, K. M., and Allen, K. R. (1992). *Women and families: Feminist reconstructions*. New York: Guilford Press.

Baumgardner, J. (2011). *F'em! Goo goo, gaga, and some thoughts on balls.* Berkeley, CA: Seal Press.

Berkowitz, D. (2009). Theorizing lesbian and gay parenting: Past, present, and future scholarship. *Journal of Family Theory and Review, 1*, 117–132. doi:10.1111/j.1756-2589.2009.00017.x.

Bowleg, L. (2008). When Black + lesbian + woman ≠ Black lesbian woman: The methodological challenges of qualitative and quantitative intersectionality research. *Sex Roles, 59*, 312–325. doi:10.1007/s11199-008-9400-z.

Burton, L. M., Bonilla-Silva, E., Ray, V., Buckelew, R., and Freeman, E. H. (2010). Critical race theories, Colorism, and the decade's research on families of color. *Journal of Marriage and Family, 72*, 440–459. doi:10.1111/j.1741-3737.2010.00712.x.

Butler, J. (2004). *Undoing gender.* New York: Routledge.

Christensen, M. C. (2015). New tools: Young feminism in the rural west. *Feminism and Psychology, 25*, 45–49. doi:10.1177/0959353514565219.

Collins, P. H. (1990). *Black feminist thought: Knowledge, consciousness, and the politics of empowerment.* Boston: Unwin Hyman.

Combahee River Collective (1982). The Combahee River Collective statement, 1977. In G. T. Hull, P. B. Scott, and B. Smith (eds), *All the women are White, all the Blacks are men, but some of us are brave: Black women's studies* (pp. 13–22). Old Westbury, NY: Feminist Press.

Connell, R. W., and Messerschmidt, J. W. (2005). Hegemonic masculinity: Rethinking the concept. *Gender and Society, 19*, 829–859. doi:10.1177/0891243205278639.

Coontz, S. (2011). *A strange stirring: The Feminine Mystique and American women at the dawn of the 1960s.* New York, NY: Basic Books.

de Beauvoir, S. (2011). *The second sex*, trans. C. Borde and S. Malovany-Chevallier. New York: Vintage. (Originally published 1949.)

De Reus, L., Few, A. L., and Blume, L. B. (2005). Multicultural and critical race feminisms: Theorizing families in the third wave. In V. L. Bengtson, A. C. Acock, K. R. Allen, P. Dilworth-Anderson, and D. M. Klein (eds), *Sourcebook of family theory and research* (pp. 447–468). Thousand Oaks, CA: Sage.

Dodson, L., and Schmalzbauer, L. (2005). Poor mothers and habits of hiding: Participatory methods in poverty research. *Journal of Marriage and Family*, *67*, 949–959. doi:10.1111/j.1741-3737.2005.00186.x.

Elam, D., and Wiegman, R. (1995). Contingencies. In D. Elam and R. Wiegman (eds), *Feminism beside itself* (pp. 1–8). New York: Routledge.

Ferree, M. M. (1990). Beyond separate spheres: Feminism and family research. *Journal of Marriage and the Family*, *52*, 866–884. doi:10.2307/353307.

Ferree, M. M. (2010). Filling the glass: Gender perspectives on families. *Journal of Marriage and Family*, *72*, 420–439. doi:10.1111/j.1741-3737.2010.00711.x.

Few-Demo, A. L. (2014). Intersectionality as the "new" critical approach in feminist family studies: Evolving racial/ethnic feminisms and critical race theories. *Journal of Family Theory and Review*, *6*, 169–183. doi:10.1111/jftr.12039.

Freedman, E. B. (2002). *No turning back: The history of feminism and the future of women*. New York: Ballantine.

Friedan, B. (1963). *The feminine mystique*. New York: Dell.

Gerson, K. (2009). Changing lives, resistant institutions: A new generation negotiates gender, work, and family change. *Sociological Forum*, *24*, 735–753. doi:10.1111/j.1573-7861.2009.01134.x.

Goldberg, A. E. (2010). Studying complex families in context. *Journal of Marriage and Family*, *72*, 29–34. doi:10.1111/j.1741-3737.2009.00680.x.

Goldberg, A. E. (2012). *Gay dads: Transitions to adoptive fatherhood*. New York: New York University Press.

Hays, S. (1996). *The cultural contradictions of motherhood*. New Haven: Yale University Press.

Lather, P. (2007). *Getting lost: Feminist efforts toward a doubled(d) science*. Albany: State University of New York Press.

Lemert, C. (2008). Charlotte Perkins Gilman. In G. Ritzer (ed.), *The Blackwell companion to major classical social theorists* (pp. 267–289). Oxford: Blackwell.

Lopata, H. Z. (1971). *Occupation: Housewife*. Westport, CT: Greenwood Press.

Lorde, A. (1985). *Sister outsider: Essays and speeches*. Berkeley, CA: Crossing Press.

Lubbe, C. (2013). LGBT parents and their children: Non-Western research and perspectives. In A. E. Goldberg and K. R. Allen (eds), *LGBT-parent families: Innovations in research and implications for practice* (pp. 209–223). New York: Springer.

Mack-Canty, C., and Wright, S. (2004). Family values as practiced by feminist parents: Bridging third-wave feminism and family pluralism. *Journal of Family Issues*, *25*, 851–880. doi:10.1177/0192513X03261337.

MacTavish, K. A. (2007). The wrong side of the tracks: Social inequality and mobile home park residence. *Community Development*, *38*, 74–91. doi:10.1080/15575330709490186.

Magalhães, S. I., and Cerqueira, C. (2015). Our place in history: Young feminists at the margins. *Feminism and Psychology*, *25*, 39–44. doi:10.1177/0959353514563093.

Mahler, S. J., Chaudhuri, M., and Patil, V. (2015). Scaling intersectionality: Advancing feminist analysis of transnational families. *Sex Roles*, *73*, 100–112. doi:10.1007/s11199-015-0506-9.

McCall, L. (2005). The complexity of intersectionality. *Signs*, *30*, 1771–1800. doi:10.1086/426800.

McIntosh, P. (1995). White privilege and male privilege: A personal account of coming to see correspondences through work in women's studies. In M. L. Anderson and P. H. Collins (eds), *Race, class, and gender: An anthology* (2nd edn, pp. 76–87). Belmont, CA: Wadsworth.

Mitchell, J. (1971). *Woman's estate*. New York: Pantheon.

MOPS (Mothers of Preschoolers) (2016). *About MOPS*. MOPS International. At http://www.mops.org/about/about-us/.

Morgan, R. (1970). *Sisterhood is powerful*. New York: Random House.

Naples, N. A. (2002). The challenges and possibilities of transnational feminist praxis. In N. A. Naples and M. Desai (eds), *Women's activism and globalization: Linking local struggles and transnational politics* (pp. 267–281). New York: Routledge.

Nelson, M. K. (2006). Single mothers "do" family. *Journal of Marriage and Family*, *68*, 781–795. doi:10.1111/j.1741-3737.2006.00292.x.

Newman, H. D., and Henderson, A. C. (2014). The modern mystique: Institutional mediation of hegemonic motherhood. *Sociological Inquiry*, *84*, 472–491. doi:10.1111/soin.12037.

Oakley, A. (1974). *The sociology of housework*. London: Martin Robertson.

Okin, S. M. (1989). *Justice, gender and the family*. New York: Basic Books.

Osmond, M. W., and Thorne, B. (1993). Feminist theories. In P. G. Boss, W. J. Doherty, R. LaRossa, W. R. Schumm, and S. K. Steinmetz (eds), *Sourcebook of family theories and methods* (pp. 591–623). New York: Plenum.

Oswald, R. F., Blume, L. B., and Marks, S. R. (2005). Decentering heteronormativity: A model for family studies. In V. L. Bengtson, A. C. Acock, K. R. Allen, P. Dilworth-Anderson, and D. M. Klein (eds), *Sourcebook of family theory and research* (pp. 143–165). Thousand Oaks, CA: Sage.

Perlesz, A., Brown, R., Lindsay, J., McNair, R., deVans, D., and Pitts, M. (2006). Family in transition: Parents, children and grandparents in lesbian families give meaning to "doing family." *Journal of Family Therapy, 28*, 175–199. doi:10.1111/j.1467-6427.2006.00345.x.

Rich, A. (1980). Compulsory heterosexuality and lesbian existence. *Signs, 5*, 631–660. doi:10.1086/493756.

Risman, B. J. (2004). Gender as a social structure: Theory wrestling with activism. *Gender and Society, 18*, 429–450. doi:10.1177/0891243204265349.

Shields, S. A. (2008). Gender: An intersectionality perspective. *Sex Roles, 59*, 301–311. doi:10.1007/s11199-008-9501-8.

Slater, J. (2013). Research with dis/abled youth: Taking a critical disability, "critically young" positionality. In K. Runswick-Cole and T. Curran (eds), *Disabled children's childhood studies: Critical approaches in a global context* (pp. 180–195). Basingstoke, UK: Palgrave.

Stacey, J. (1990). *Brave new families: Stories of domestic upheaval in late twentieth century America.* New York: Basic Books.

Tasker, F. (2013). Lesbian and gay parenting post-heterosexual divorce and separation. In A. E. Goldberg and K. R. Allen (eds), *LGBT-parent families: Innovations in research and implications for practice* (pp. 3–20). New York: Springer.

Thompson, L., and Walker, A. J. (1995). The place of feminism in family studies. *Journal of Marriage and the Family, 57*, 847–865. doi:10.2307/353407.

Thorne, B. (1982). Feminist rethinking of the family: An overview. In B. Thorne with M. Yalom (eds), *Rethinking the family: Some feminist questions* (pp. 1–24). New York: Longman.

UN Women (2014, September 20). Emma Watson: Gender equality is your issue too. Speech by UN Women Goodwill Ambassador Emma Watson at a special event for the HeForShe campaign, UN Headquarters, New York. At http://www.unwomen.org/en/news/stories/2014/9/emma-watson-gender-equality-is-your-issue-too.

van Eeden-Moorefield, B., and Proulx, C. M. (2009). Doing feminist research on gay men in cyberspace. In S. A. Lloyd, A. L. Few, and K. R. Allen (eds), *Handbook of feminist family studies* (pp. 220–233). Thousand Oaks, CA: Sage.

Walker, A. J. (1999). Gender and family relationships. In M. Sussman, S. K. Steinmetz, and G. W. Peterson (eds), *Handbook of marriage and the family* (2nd edn, pp. 439–474). New York: Plenum.

Walker, A. J. (2009). A feminist critique of family studies. In S. A. Lloyd, A. L. Few, and K. R. Allen (eds), *Handbook of feminist family studies* (pp. 18–27). Thousand Oaks, CA: Sage.

Walker, A. J., and Thompson, L. (1984). Feminism and family studies. *Journal of Family Issues, 5*, 545–570. doi:10.1177/019251384005004010.

West, C., and Zimmerman, D. H. (1987). Doing gender. *Gender and Society, 1*, 125–151. doi:10.1177/0891243287001002002.

Wills, J. B., and Risman, B. J. (2006). The visibility of feminist thought in family studies. *Journal of Marriage and Family, 68*, 690–700. doi:10.1111/j.1741-3737.2006.00283.x.

Yllo, K., and Bograd, M. (eds) (1988). *Feminist perspectives on wife abuse.* Newbury Park, CA: Sage.

9

Life Course Theory

Do your grades as a high school student really matter when you are 35 years old? Does being an only child impact your life differently when you are six years old, compared to when you are 60? Does the place where and age at which you lose your virginity play a role in how you experience intimacy and family life when you are age 46? How about age 86?

Questions about how time and culture influence families have plagued social scientists for decades. Life course theory is an exciting integrative theory because with it researchers have developed methods to track the influence of both culture and change over time. Now, we can begin to answer some of these complex questions. For this reason, life course theory is an alternative to functionalist theory (Chapter 2) and family developmental theory (Chapter 5) in that its focus is on the contexts of time, culture, and context. Every family, and every individual, develops within a certain place and time. First we set the stage for the study of life course theory with a story about the diversity and complexity of family life over time.

Case Study

Carrie is at her computer, on the home page of her local community college, trying to decide if she should attempt to finish her degree. She is a 24-year-old single mother to Baylee, her three-year-old little girl. They live with Carrie's grandmother in a small town in rural, mountainous Kentucky. Carrie has about two years' worth of college credits from the University of Kentucky where she had a full scholarship after high school. She dropped out of the university because she was unable to fit in with the other kids there. When she came back home she moved in with her grandmother and mother and got a job at a grocery store, where she met Baylee's father. Since Baylee was born, Carrie's boyfriend has been arrested and sent to prison on drug-related convictions. Later, her mother was killed in a tragic car accident. Carrie knows the name of her biological father, but he has never been involved in her life in any way. She has some friends, but often feels alone and frustrated and wants a different life for Baylee. If it wasn't for her grandmother, Carrie doesn't know what she would do.

What do you notice about Carrie's life course? Who are the important players in her life? How are her experiences linked to theirs? Is Carrie able to make choices that will help her live a life of autonomy and freedom? How does her environment play a role in her life? All these questions point to important principles and assumptions in life course theory, which we describe below.

What Is Life Course Theory?

Life course theory is a theoretical framework researchers use when they want to understand the ways in which time, culture, context, and the interdependence of family relationships influence people's lives. Life course theory is complex, and family scientists can use it in many ways, but a common goal of life course researchers is to look at individual and family development over time and across ever changing and diverse social-historical contexts.

Family Theories: Foundations and Applications, First Edition. Katherine R. Allen and Angela C. Henderson.

History and origins

Before the 1960s, research that took into account both time (longitudinal) and social context did not exist in the social sciences (Elder and Giele, 2009). Most survey research was cross-sectional, and case studies typically looked at individual lives out of the context of broader society or family life. Then beginning in the 1960s, with the advent of federal funding in the US and advanced research methods, social scientists became increasingly interested in ways to capture change over time and change in the context of families and cultures (Elder, Johnson, and Crosnoe, 2003). For example, Norman Ryder's (1965) concept of **cohort** focused on the ways in which groups of people of a similar age experienced or produced social events. We sometimes also refer to this as a **generation**, such as the baby boom generation (born in the post–World War II era). However, it is important to remember that generation and cohort are two very different things when it comes to life course theory: generations span more than one decade, and cohorts are smaller, more specific groups who experience a larger social event at a particular point in time. For example, a cohort of individuals born from 1980 to 1985 no doubt experienced the Iraq War differently than a cohort of individuals born from 1960 to 1965. The 1980–1985 birth cohort was likely to have more members serving in the war or have partners in the war, whereas the 1960–1965 cohort was more likely to include parents of Iraq War soldiers. Further, the concept of cohort is a more precise term for measuring change than generation because generation is so loosely connected to historical time (Elder, Johnson, and Crosnoe, 2003) and often refers to a very wide range of individuals.

Because life course theory developed in conjunction with more sophisticated research methods, researchers have been able to benefit from insights from earlier theories such as family developmental theory (Chapter 5) and symbolic interactionism (Chapter 4). From its very beginning, the life course perspective as applied to families emerged from multiple intellectual traditions and disciplines on individual and family development (e.g., human development, family studies, history, psychology, sociology) (see Bengtson and Allen, 1993; Elder, 1977 and 1981). Early stage models of individual development, particularly Erikson's (1950; 1975) eight stages of psychosocial development that included childhood, adolescence, and young, middle, and late adulthood, proposed normative models of individual change, where one stage emerges naturally from the previous stage, like the unfolding of a flower. However, theories of individual development such as Erikson's did not emphasize the family context of development.

Life course theory also improved on earlier developmental models by showing social-historical variations. For example, rather than mutually exclusive gender roles portrayed in the static life cycle models, where women stayed home and cared for families while men went out to work, social-historical studies revealed much greater variation than a one-size-fits-all model (i.e., the Standard North American Family model (Smith, 1993) described in Chapter 1). Think back to the case study from the beginning of this chapter; could we apply the earlier life cycle model to Carrie? Would Erikson's model of individual development take into account the varying dynamics of Carrie's life? No, they would not; life cycle theory in particular does not "fit" Carrie's experiences because she is not married and cannot fulfill the expectations of that theory (e.g., traditional gender roles). Life course theory makes it possible to take into account all of the forces guiding Carrie's movement through various life course stages, including her cohort, social class expectations and barriers, and her status as a single mother.

Life course theory allows us to take a panoramic view when we gather and analyze data; we are able to see the whole picture and how different disciplines (e.g., sociology, psychology, history, family studies) can contribute to a more complex understanding of what it is we are studying. Because of this, life course theory has been posited as a theory that is emerging from new historical scholarship that has stressed (a) the complexity of social life, and (b) the continued influence of the past. For example, Elder (1981) noted that early theorizing about American family life relied on oversimplified ideas about change. Although many families might have aspired to the SNAF ideal, only a minority of families could afford this arrangement. Likewise, as Elder and others developed life course theory, scholars realized that rather than developing an overarching grand theory of the family, they needed a theory that

Box 9.1 At a Glance: Life Course Theory

Life-span development Human development and aging are lifelong processes.

Agency Individuals construct their own life course through the choices and actions they take within the opportunities and constraints of history and social circumstance.

Time and place The life course of individuals is embedded and shaped by the historical times and places they experience over their lifetime.

Timing The developmental antecedents and consequences of life transitions, events, and behavioral patterns vary according to their timing in a person's life.

Linked lives Lives are lived interdependently and social-historical influences are expressed through this network of shared relationships.

Source: Elder, Johnson, and Crosnoe, 2003.

provided concepts to understand more about family complexity and diversity over time.

Despite their limitations, earlier theories provided a rich intellectual background from which life course theory emerged. Thus, life course theory has benefited by drawing from the core ideas of multidisciplinary perspectives. As Bengtson and Allen (1993) point out, the most influential perspectives in creating a life course theory of human development combine the core contexts from the key disciplines utilized in the family studies field: life course theory draws from psychology to provide perspectives about individuals; sociology to interpret the interplay of social structures and relations; demography to document population trends; anthropology to provide perspectives about cultural distinctions; history to help us understand the meaning of broad scale events; economics to uncover the control and flow of financial capital; and biology to provide perspectives about the role of genetics in human development.

Assumptions of life course theory

Life course theory is built around the ideas of time, context, interdependence, and agency (Demo, Aquilino, and Fine, 2005). One of the major assumptions in life course theory is that there are **multiple timeclocks** affecting families (Bengtson and Allen, 1993). Figure 9.1 provides an illustration of timeclocks. One timeclock is individual time, or the emphasis on the biological and psychological development of particular individuals. A second timeclock is family time, or an emphasis on the familial roles and trajectories in family systems. A third timeclock is historical time, or an emphasis on the events and changes particular birth cohorts (e.g., baby boom, generation X) experience together. Notice that Carrie's individual timeclock for becoming a mother and attending college is different from the standard norm for middle-class young adults who are expected to complete their studies, then marry, and then have children. Because she has a strong family identity, her individual and family timeclocks are closely interlinked. Carrie did not find much satisfaction in having a full scholarship to a major university. She wanted to be close to her family and add to it by finding a partner

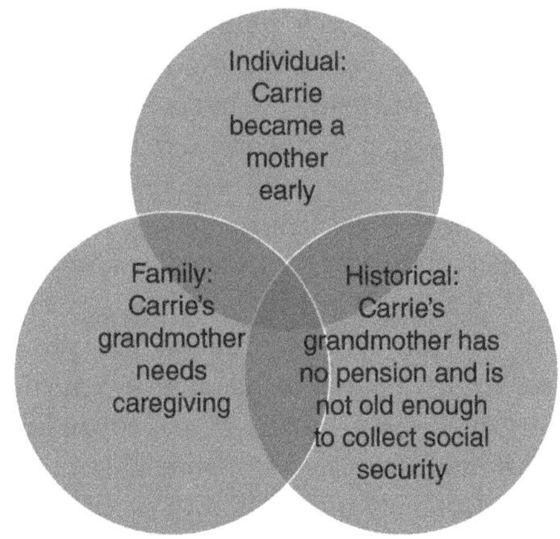

Figure 9.1 Individual, family, and historical timeclocks

and having her own children. As for historical time, Carrie is a part of a cohort from rural America where it is becoming increasingly normative for young people to be involved in the drug trade in order to make extra money. Where once farming and coal mining were enough to sustain families of Carrie's parents' and grandparents' generations, changes in the environment and economy have severely limited her generation's prospects for supporting a family.

Just as there are multiple timeclocks of development, there are also **multiple social contexts** (Bengtson and Allen, 1993). Some scholars refer to this as the social ecology of families, a similar idea to the ones covered in Chapter 10 when we discuss family ecological theory. Social contexts refer to things such as one's social position in terms of gender, race, class, age, sexual orientation, and so on. Carrie is a young, able-bodied, heterosexual, working-class, White mother. In her own rural culture, Carrie is somewhat privileged. She does not have much money, but she has status as a mother and as a woman attached to a man (despite the fact that he is incarcerated). In both her local culture and the larger US culture, she has status as someone who is White, young, and able-bodied. However, in other contexts, Carrie may face stigma and be categorized as a "poor, uneducated, unmarried mother."

A third assumption, similar to symbolic interactionist theory (Chapter 4), is that human beings create meaning within social contexts (Bengtson and Allen, 1993). That is, a fundamental aspect of being human is that we attribute meaning to events in our lives. **Meaning-making** may happen at an individual level, but culture plays a crucial role. Consider for example, that the meaning attributed to and the rituals marking important life events, such as marriage, death, and birth, typically varies between cultures. And in Carrie's case, maintaining her family identity is the most important factor in how she makes meaning about her life.

Key concepts

Life course theory utilizes many concepts to guide both qualitative and quantitative research on families. We review seven of the main concepts used in this theory: (a) timing, (b) social context, (c) linked lives, (d) transitions and turning points, (e) trajectories and pathways, (f) agency, and (g) generations. Note that the concepts are interrelated and often overlap, because individual and family lives, after all, are intertwined. They are also dynamic, in that they must change and adapt to social and historic forces. As we define each of the concepts, we apply them to the case study from the beginning of the chapter to help illustrate the propositions of life course theory.

Timing Timing refers to the temporal distinctions of individual, generational, and social/historical time that segment or divide up the life course. Each individual family member has his or her own unique psychological and physical development. Besides this view of time, they also hold a certain position in the family based on their time of entry into it. That is, each member belongs to a generation in the family, such as the oldest generation, the middle generation, and the youngest generation. Broadening the scope, each individual is also born into a unique social/historical context, or as part of a cohort. Think back to Carrie from earlier in the chapter; Carrie is a member of a cohort that is *expected* to go to college. Her parents and grandparents, on the other hand, came of age in a time when they could secure very good paying jobs without a bachelor's degree. In contrast, Carrie's goal of becoming a manager at the local bank necessitates a college degree. Looking even further down the road, her daughter Baylee may grow up in a time when a master's degree is a required credential for most well-paying jobs. Timing also refers to historical events that can impact life course transitions: Carrie is reconsidering getting her bachelor's degree during an economic recession, which sent many who were left unemployed back to college.

In life course theory, timing also refers to the degree to which people experience major life events as expected, or whether they are "on time" or "off time." When we say that a couple's life turned out as expected, we are referring to many ways of timing as well as historical period. For example, in 1950, it was expected that couples would get married fairly soon after high school. Today, however, it is expected that couples wait until they are finished with not only college, but sometimes graduate school before they marry. After that, they are expected to get stable jobs before they have children; therefore, some may not marry or have children until well into their thirties. In 1950, this would have been considered "off-time."

Social contexts of development As noted above, social contexts refer to the broadest level of social institutions that shape people's opportunities and relationships. The term "social institutions" can have a variety of meanings, but typically refers to entities such as schools, families, religious groups, medical facilities, the economic system, the media, and the military. Laws and cultural norms govern social institutions. This is where social location comes into play: there are norms and laws that regulate the behavior of individuals on the basis of their race, class, gender, sexual orientation, age, and so forth. For example, in the US, people of the same sex have not been able to legally marry until very recently, now that the social context is changing.

Related is the idea of social pathways (Elder, Johnson, and Crosnoe, 2003). Social pathways develop through the intersection of "historical forces" and "social institutions." Think about Carrie's daughter, Baylee. She is being raised in a historical context where same-sex relationships are increasingly accepted (the cultural norm), which has led to legalizing same-sex marriage (the laws that govern us). Because of these changing historical forces, Baylee will most likely have a variety of pathways in front of her as she moves through adolescence into young adulthood. She may have several friends and classmates who are gay, lesbian, bisexual, or transgender. She may see several gay couples at her high school prom, and be invited to just as many gay or lesbian weddings as straight weddings when she is a young adult. Those pathways – gays' and lesbians' legal rights to marry – are opened up because historical forces shifted. Baylee's life course will consist of varying pathways because norms and laws change over time. Therefore, new pathways open with changes in social institutions, particularly with changes in laws and governmental policies.

Linked lives The concept of **linked lives** refers to the way in which significant others' lives are interlocked. When something happens to one member of the family, the lives of other family members are also changed. For example, when Carrie's mother died in the car accident, both Carrie's life and her grandmother's life were affected in significant ways. Carrie lost her mother, and her grandmother lost her adult child. These losses changed the ways in which the two women relate to one another. Carrie's grandmother took on the mothering role, just as Carrie provided the kind of help an adult daughter would give an aging mother.

There is a saying that parents never stop worrying about their children, and research on relationships between aging parents and adult children bears that out. How one's children turn out once they are grown is a source of stress to parents, particularly if the adult children's lives are marked by substance abuse, legal trouble, lack of educational and economic success, and other nonnormative experiences (Greenfield and Marks, 2006). Parents' well-being is greatly tied to the quality of their relationships with their adult children.

Transitions and turning points Transitions and turning points typically involve a change in identity as well as circumstances, and can occur at both the individual and family level. Important individual transitions would be the transition of Carrie taking on the role of mother. Carrie became a mother after she left college, transitioning away from the role of student and into the role of wage earner, and then mother. This influences her view of herself; she no longer is only responsible for just her own needs. She has a commitment to provide for her daughter and a commitment to her place of employment to be able to keep her job. As you might imagine, this transition can be difficult for women who are not necessarily expecting to enter the role of mother, and the transition is unexpected. A change in identity may be a more difficult transition than the actual work involved. When Carrie had Baylee, her normal daily routines changed, but her view of herself changed even more. Her body changed after pregnancy and childbirth, making her feel like she is no longer young and feminine. Instead of going out at night with her friends, she is stuck at home with her daughter. She cannot spend extra money on herself for new clothes; any extra income goes straight to diapers, formula, and baby clothes. Her identity change is much more difficult than the changes in her daily routine.

Typical **family transitions** involve a change in the family system such as entry into school, marriage, parenthood, launching, and widowhood – these are normative family life cycle events that we discussed in Chapter 5 (Duvall, 1957; Hill and Rodgers, 1964). **Turning points** are a type of transition. Typically they are very personal and may not be recognized by an outsider as particularly significant. For instance, consider Carrie's decision to go to college. This decision was a turning point in her relationships with her family of origin, none of whom had gone on past high school. The values she developed as a young adult in the social context of college set her apart from her siblings and her parents. In another example, "coming out" as a lesbian, gay, bisexual, or transgender person also can be seen as both a normative transition and a turning point. It may be that in certain contexts, a person first has to come out to themselves (Savin-Williams, 2001). Think about Carrie's small hometown in rural Kentucky; we could surmise that if one of her male classmates "came out" in a fairly conservative area, he might not only have to first become aware of his sexual orientation, but he would also most likely struggle with self-acceptance in a culture that can be hostile to gay men. On the other hand, coming out to others is a more normative transition for people in less conservative areas, and undoubtedly as legal codes are changing (e.g., marriage equality for same-sex couples) and the process becomes more socially scripted on television and in the news media.

Trajectories and pathways From each new transition emerges a **trajectory** defined as the continuity of roles and identities. For example, when Carrie had Baylee, she began her trajectory as a mother. Trajectories continue throughout our lives. Social pathways are conceptually similar, but typically have longer durations, and are made up of a confluence of trajectories. That is, trajectories flow into one another, creating pathways, just as a river is made up of and shaped by streams along a landscape (see Figure 9.2).

Whereas trajectories are defined by how they begin (i.e., with a transition into a particular role, such as becoming a spouse or a parent), pathways are defined by an outcome (e.g., psychological health in late life; sexual decision-making in early adulthood). For example, to illustrate how trajectories form a particular social pathway, the principle of cumulative (dis)advantage describes how experiences in early life persist across one's lifetime (Willson, Shuey, and Elder, 2007). When considering how some people end up in old age with multiple health problems and

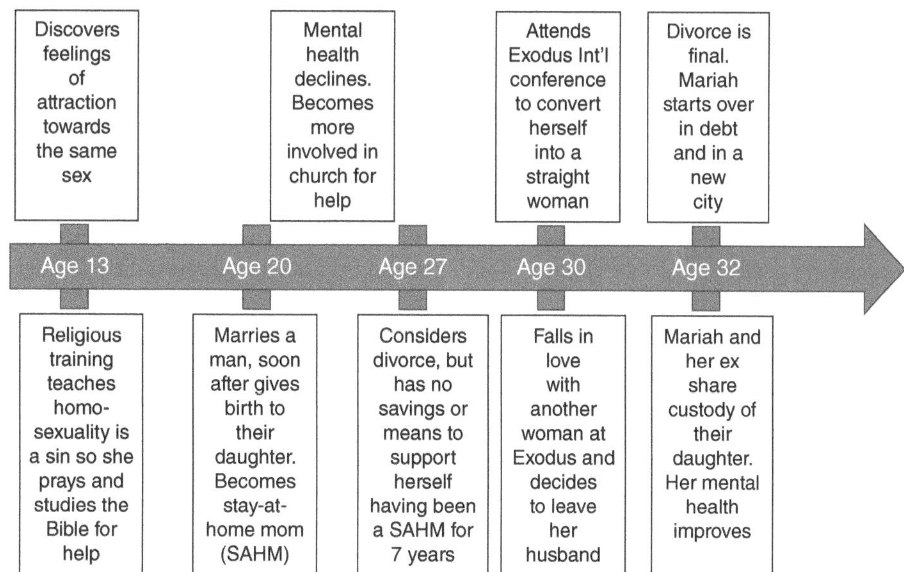

Figure 9.2 A pathway formed by trajectories: Mariah

relatively impoverished, while others come to late life knowledgeable about and able to afford preventive health practices, we see that multiple trajectories over the course of one's life have built a pathway of **cumulative advantage** or **disadvantage** (O'Rand, 2002). Sociologist Robert Merton (1988) first described cumulative disadvantage as "the ways in which initial comparative advantage of trained capacity, structural location, and available resources make for successive increments of advantage such that the gaps between the haves and the have-nots … widen" (1988, p. 606). An example can be seen in Figure 9.2, where Mariah does not accumulate advantage during her marriage, which leaves her restricted when she decides she can no longer stay married. She ends up in debt and without any recent employment history.

In other words, characteristics such as wealth, health, and social status intersect, resulting in either accumulated advantage or disadvantage over time. For example, educational trajectories that begin in early childhood are an obvious confluent factor that shapes opportunities throughout the life course. Getting a high school degree is necessary to enter college; obtaining a college degree increases one's earning potential as an adult. Still another example can be seen using Carrie's circumstances; right now, she is a single mom without a college degree. She is not a homeowner, so she is not building capital to hand down to her daughter like she would if she lived in her own home. Her opportunity to move up the social class ladder is limited by this lack of capital and savings; if she decides to go back to school to finish her degree, she will accumulate student loan debt at the cost of increasing her earning potential with a college degree. Additionally, she will have to find childcare for Baylee so she can go to classes while she continues to work to pay bills. The likelihood that Carrie accumulates disadvantage is higher than it would be for one of her peers coming from a different social class background; that is, someone whose parents are paying for college with an inheritance or savings, who plan on helping their child buy his or her first home and car. This person would be accumulating *advantage* instead of disadvantage.

It is important to keep in mind that cumulative advantage or disadvantage (CAD) is a complex process; on the surface, it appears to be an individualistic problem, as expressed in the adage "the poor get poorer" and "the rich get richer" (Alexander, Entwisle, and Olson, 2001), when in reality, larger, structural forces are at play. What this means is that CAD takes into account the fact that, for example, every choice we make over our life course is tempered by the choices available to us. Carrie's choice to stop attending college and have a baby before both marriage and a steady career is complicated; she grew up in a part of the country where it was not that uncommon to have children earlier than the national average. Taken together, it would be simple to blame Carrie, the individual, for her disadvantages. However, the timing of the series of events is important; she dropped out of college because she did not fit in with her peers. This is probably due to the fact that she grew up in a rural part of Kentucky, where education levels are below the national average (US Census Bureau, 2012). We also do not know if she intended to get pregnant, or if it was accidental. However, research suggests that some women in dire circumstances choose to get pregnant so that they can turn their lives around and have something to live for (Edin and Kefalas, 2011). In addition, two very important life course events occurred completely out of Carrie's control: the tragic death of her mother and the incarceration of her baby's father. To an outsider, Carrie's life course and accumulated disadvantage may appear like an individual-level problem of making the wrong choices. However, CAD would suggest that there are more complex factors contributing to Carrie's trajectories in life.

Another example of the relationship between trajectories and pathways is Carpenter's (2010) theory of gendered sexuality over the life course. Carpenter argues that the intertwining of sexual and gender trajectories creates pathways of gendered sexuality and explains variation in sexual agency over the life course. One example Carpenter gives is how the transition of virginity loss, or conversely, involuntary celibacy, on people's sexual trajectory is linked with people's gender trajectory. Depending on their gender trajectory, Carpenter found that the young people she interviewed may see virginity loss in terms of a gift, a stigma, or a normative transition toward adulthood. Furthermore, people's virginity loss experience shaped their future sexual decision-making, showing that earlier life course decisions have a cumulative effect on later life course experiences.

Agency In life course theory, **agency** is a complex social-psychological process that goes beyond "a vague sense of human freedom or individual volition" (Hitlin and Elder, 2007, p. 171). Although it has been difficult for scholars to define, agency generally refers to one's ability and desire to make choices within the constraints of social institutions.

Life course theorists have said that early social and historical scholarship was focused too much on the structured nature of social life. That is, families were thought to be determined by social structures such as economic and legal constraints. In this view, it was assumed that family life in the past was relatively stable because divorce was not granted except in extreme circumstances. In contrast, Elder contends that new historical scholarship sees families as agents, that is, "actors in structured circumstance" (1981, p. 494). In this view, a new question posed by life course theory is, given that divorce was unavailable for most people (structured circumstance), how did couples (actors with agency) deal with marital conflict, betrayal, and abuse while staying married?

Consider all the choices that Carrie has made and will make over the years. Will she finish college, and increase her earning potential? Will she marry, and have other children? Will she have to care for her grandmother in the near future? Although broader social structures channel the kinds of choices individuals can make, agency means that we do have some control over the direction our lives will take (Hitlin and Elder, 2007). The most important time for exercising agency is at the fork in the road of life – the transition point. Carrie, for example, in considering the community college courses she might take to finish her degree, is in the process of exercising agency. The direction she decides to take regarding her education is in part dependent on how she envisions her future: how does she make meaning of the difference a college education will bring in her life, and in the lives of those she cares about?

Generations One of the advantages of using life course theory is the ability to analyze how different generations of individuals experience life course events. Though researchers have not established universally agreed-upon date cutoffs, there are general characteristics that define each generation. These characteristics are based on similarities in experience and context because members of specific generations move through the life course during similar historical time frames. For example, the Millennial Generation (born between 1979 and1994) experienced adolescence and young adulthood with unprecedented access to technologies like iPhones, YouTube, Facebook, and text messaging. This access to technology and social media fundamentally changes how this generation learned how to communicate – with friends, family, and society in general. Therefore, the combination of generational membership coincides with period, or historical time, to create differential life course experiences.

Understanding generational differences is important to the study of family; after all, members of one generation typically raise members of an entirely different generation. Baby Boomers raised Gen Xers, and Xers raised Millennials. Understanding these generational differences is useful when explaining intrafamily dynamics as well as issues of linked lives, timeclocks, pathways, and trajectories. The different generations, as currently defined (and note that the years may vary depending upon the source), include the following.

First, the *Silent Generation*, born between 1925 and 1942, emphasizes duty, sacrifice, and loyalty to family and work. They are called "silent" because they tend to be quieter and less rebellious than the Baby Boomers. Further, they are not discussed as much, when compared to other generations (Deal, 2007). For the most part, members of this generation experienced family life as male-dominated, with the father as the head of the household, and the mother as a domesticated, stay-at-home parent (as characterized by family developmental theory, Chapter 5). They have great faith in America's institutions (Deal, 2007), view quality over quantity, and willingly follow rules.

Second, the *Baby Boomer Generation*, born between 1943 and 1960, are referred to as "the baby boomers" because of their sheer size – 77 million. They were raised by parents who largely subscribed to "Dr Spock's" approach to parenting Dr. Benjamin Spock was a pediatrician who published a best-selling book on baby and childcare (first published in 1946,

Box 9.2 Life Course Theory in Pop Culture: *Downton Abbey*

A scene from *Downton Abbey*, 2010, cr. Julian Fellowes, ITV Studios

Downton Abbey is a television series about an aristocratic British family set in the early 1900s. Here, we describe the relationships between several main characters and how we can apply concepts from life course theory to the show.

Violet Crawley, Dowager Countess of Grantham, is one of the show's matriarchal characters. She is the grandmother of the three Crawley daughters and tends to have a very stoic attitude, reminiscent of tradition and honor. She often clashes views with another matriarchal character in the show, Isobel Crawley, now connected to Violet by the marriage of Violet's granddaughter, Mary, and Isobel's son, Matthew (a distant cousin and the unexpected heir presumptive to Lord Grantham). Even though Matthew died, the two women remained connected through family gatherings and a shared great-grandson/grandson. Isobel was a trained nurse, so when Violet became very ill, Isobel spent several days by Violet's bedside, caring for her both physically and psychologically. This relationship – though it could have been severed by the death of Matthew – illustrates the concept of linked lives.

Another example of linked lives is Lady Mary Crawley and Tom Branson; both are widowed and are charged with caring for the estate together. Tom is Lady Mary's brother-in-law, and could decide to leave the estate at any time because he was not a member of the aristocratic class before he married Lady Sybil Crawley (Mary's sister). Yet, he and the family's lives are linked because of the emotional bonds forged during his marriage to Lady Sybil and the birth of their daughter. In addition, because he and Lady Sybil married, Tom's trajectory changes dramatically; he went from being a chauffeur to the Crawleys to being a member of their aristocratic family. If he chooses to stay as one of the managers of the estate, this trajectory could lead to a successful pathway of wealth and inheritance.

Life course theory also takes historical time and important events into account, which definitely influence the choices main characters Lady Mary and Lady Edith make. During the early and mid-1900s, women's rights movements were gaining strength, and this opened up new opportunities for the two sisters. Lady Edith broke away from the aristocratic ideals for women, by learning how to drive, becoming a regular writer for a London newspaper, and giving birth to a baby out of wedlock. Lady Mary also benefited from the changing political landscape, having been left in charge of her late husband's share of Downton Abbey. Her father hesitated to let her help make important decisions about the estate, but finally gives in and Lady Mary becomes an active manager of Downton.

There are also several important turning points in this television series. One of the daughters, Lady Sybil, dies after childbirth, leaving Tom Branson feeling like he no longer belongs in this aristocratic world he acquired by marrying her. The series also takes us through World War I, and there are important historical shifts during and after the war. During the war, Downton Abbey was turned into a makeshift hospital, where wounded soldiers came to recover. They were cared for by Lady Sybil and Lady Edith, women of the aristocracy who would never have had to care for anyone before the war, much less wounded soldiers from a very different social class background than their own. This indicates a turning point in the sociohistorical context of the series: what were once well-defined roles based on social class were no longer as relevant because of the shifting needs of members of society.

with many subsequent revised editions), which promoted a more flexible and affectionate style of parenting. His techniques were not critiqued heavily until the 1970s, for allegedly promoting instant gratification. Interestingly, the Baby Boomers are sometimes referred to as one of the first "Me" generations, because cultural trends of the time stressed individuality and developing into a more "whole" person (Strauss and Howe, 1997). Formative events for this generation included the Civil Rights Movement, the assassinations of John F. Kennedy and Martin Luther King, Jr, the Vietnam War, the Woodstock festival, and the Women's Liberation Movement.

Third, *Generation X*, born between 1961 and 1978, are referred to as "latch-key kids," because their mothers went back to work in such large numbers, leaving them home alone after school, until their parents came home from work. As children, Gen Xers experienced divorce and blended families in unprecedented numbers. This generation tends to be very family-oriented, highly educated, and skeptical of social institutions (Miller, 2011). As parents, they are very involved in their children's lives, and have high expectations for their future. They are likely contributing to the "helicopter parenting" trend identified in the 2000s, where parents "hover" too much in their children's lives (LeMoyne and Buchanan, 2011).

Fourth, the *Millennial Generation*, born between 1979 and 1994, emerged at a time when children were recast as special, giving birth to the "Baby on Board" signs seen in cars and a renewed focus on cultivating a child's special talents. This should be no surprise, given the parenting trends of Gen Xers. As a result, Millennials are criticized for being too coddled, and in fact, Twenge and Campbell (2009) have argued that this generation is contributing to a "narcissism epidemic" in our country. Their parents – Gen Xers – are criticized for not letting their children experience disappointment, therefore contributing to a rising sense of entitlement. The technological revolution is also noted for contributing to an increase in narcissism; Facebook, Instagram, MySpace, and Twitter are all contributing to the invention of the "selfie" (taking a self-portrait and posting it on social media).

As we can see, the sociohistorical context in which each generation moves through important life course stages is vital to understanding trends in parenting, partnering, and other dynamics that affect families.

Evaluating Life Course Theory

Strengths of life course theory

Like the other theories in this book, life course theory has several strengths. As we describe next, key strengths include the incorporation of context, the ability to be combined with other theories, and the ability to be useful with both quantitative and qualitative research methods.

A contextual approach As we have described throughout this chapter, some of the most impressive features about life course theory include the use of multiple social timeclocks (individual, family, and social-historical time); the use of multiple disciplines to shed light on individual, social, economic, historical, cultural, and biological experiences; and the importance of understanding lives in context – how what happens to one person has a mutual influence on others in the family (e.g., linked lives). For example, Walker, Allen, and Connidis (2005) conceptualize sibling relationships across central adulthood. In more traditional family theories, such as the family developmental perspective (Chapter 5), with an emphasis on the vertical ties of parents and children (intergenerational) and the horizontal ties of married heterosexual adults (intragenerational), sibling ties are ignored or excluded. But life course theory, with its emphasis on the timing of transitions, experiences, and linked lives, allows us to take the focus away from the static roles of individuals and look, instead, at the social relationships of how kin members relate to one another over time. The sibling relationship is the longest tie that one can have, starting in early childhood (and for younger siblings at birth) and extending for many into old age. Walker and colleagues, however, point out that life course theory in and of itself does not go far enough in conceptualizing the links between aging and social structure; hence it is important to integrate other frameworks to shore up these deficits. The power of an interdisciplinary and flexible life course framework is that it is easily combined with other theories that do shore up any holes. Thus, they integrate a feminist perspective on inequality in social relationships, a social constructionist framework about the partiality of knowledge, and the concept of sociological ambivalence. The concept of sociological ambivalence names the contradiction of expectations for different cohorts that are created by social structures (e.g., legal system; gender relations) and the mixed emotions that it sets up for different family members (Connidis and McMullin, 2002).

An integrative theory Another key strength of life course theory is how well it adapts to integration with other theories. For example, Roberto, McCann, and Blieszner (2013) integrate concepts from life course theory and symbolic interactionist theory (Chapter 4) in their study of care trajectories when one partner is diagnosed with mild cognitive impairment (MCI; nonnormative memory or cognitive problems, but not severe enough to be characterized as dementia). In their research, Roberto and colleagues analyzed how married couples adjusted to changes in their relationships after a diagnosis of MCI for one of the partners. This study is a good example of how life course theory allows researchers to take several theoretical propositions into account; the authors looked at the identity hierarchies of each spouse, and how they changed both over time (i.e., a trajectory) because of the transition of one partner developing MCI. In this analysis, the concept of trajectories from life course theory combined with the concept of identity hierarchies from symbolic interactionist theory (Chapter 4) guided the interpretation of the data. The four trajectories were developed from examining changes in husbands' and wives' spousal identities over time as MCI stabilized or progressed into dementia.

Useful with both quantitative and qualitative research methods Although life course theory was originally developed to be used with quantitative, longitudinal data sets, it has also proven to be useful in **qualitative life history interview studies**. A qualitative approach adds the kind of insider depth from participants that help us to understand how they perceive and experience the major changes that occur throughout their lives. For example, in a qualitative study built upon the key assumptions of life course theory, Allen (1989) found that older women who had never married or had children of their own reflected upon going through family life transitions when they were unexpected. One older woman, for instance, reported that she did not start dating until after her parents died, when she was in her sixties. Her reflections upon life course transitions and trajectories could not be captured in a demographic survey, but they are all the more important because they were described and interpreted from her firsthand insider account.

Weaknesses of life course theory

As we discussed in Chapter 1, no theory holds all the keys. Despite the numerous strengths of life course theory, there are some challenges in applying this perspective in family studies. These challenges include the following.

Difficulty in obtaining and measuring family level data Imagine that you want to study the ways in which families cope when an older family member is diagnosed with cancer. Which individuals in a family would you need to sample? In Carrie's situation, imagine that her grandmother had been diagnosed with cancer. To understand how the family would deal with her needs, whose perspective would you need from the family? Surely you want to talk to Carrie, since she lives with her grandmother. Probably you would want to talk with other close relatives (e.g., siblings; children) who may be helpful in providing care during her grandmother's treatment and recovery. Do you think all these people would agree to speak with you about their family lives? Do you think all these people would agree to speak with you multiple times? Suppose you were able to recruit three key members (for example, Carrie, her grandmother, her grandmother's sister) from 50 families. You would be very fortunate if all three members in each of the families met with you each year over three years to share the changes they were experiencing. In addition to the difficulties of recruitment, the cost of doing the interviews increases exponentially with each additional family member and wave of data collection. At the very least, research that is guided by life course theory is complex, time-consuming, and costly.

Obtaining consistent longitudinal data Many times the questions asked at one point in time may not be relevant decades later as society changes. Moreover, because of funding constraints, it is not possible to know how long a study will continue (Elder, Johnson, and Crosnoe, 2003). For instance, beginning in 1957, the Wisconsin Longitudinal Study began with data from all high school seniors in Wisconsin, with the purpose of tracking the choices students made after high school (Hauser, 2009). Although the researchers planned to collect multiple waves of data, the study has unexpectedly been continued for decades, so that now the participants are entering late life. Questions important now, such as pathways to retirement and health trajectories, were not conceivable during the early years of the study. Thus, some important data related to health and money practices are missing from the early periods of data collection.

Easily confused with other perspectives using family time Students often ask, how does life course theory differ from the family life cycle concept used in family development theory (Chapter 5)? Both family development and life course are interdisciplinary theories, relying on concepts from diverse perspectives, including demography and psychology, among others. But a closer look at the two theories reveals important differences and a shift in how social life is conceptualized. A good example is the way "trajectory" (from life course theory) is defined, compared to the way "career" (from family development theory) is defined. Both of these concepts share a similar origin and meaning, in that they refer to a life pathway over time. The difference, however, is that family developmental theory has a greater focus on normative structure and fixed family roles. As we learned in Chapter 5, by using the concept of career, we are looking at "the marital career," or "the work career," as if there was just one prototype. By using the concept of trajectory from life course theory, however, the focus shifts to process, social context, variation, and complexity in an individual's life (Aldous, 1990; Elder, 1981). Chapter 5 on family developmental theory includes other differences between these two theories.

An alternative theory app: family stress and resilience theory

In this chapter, we have laid out the key concepts, origins, and modern applications as well as the strengths and weaknesses of life course theory. As you have learned, life course theory has the capability to take historical time and agency into account to understand trajectories of families and family members. Family stress and resilience theory (Chapter 11) has similar strengths, giving insight into a family's past, present, and future. Here, we compare these two theories closely so you can easily make the switch between these two perspectives.

Family stress and resilience theory addresses the fact that life is full of risks that threaten both individual and family well-being. At the heart of this theory is an analysis of the ways in which families deal with stressors. At the same time, this theory is built on the assumption that not all stress leads to negative outcomes: thus the focus on both stress *and* resilience. One way to compare this perspective to life course theory is to consider how the two frameworks are complementary. Given how broad life course theory is, as well as how well it focuses on timing, events, and trajectories, we could easily argue that family stress and resilience theory fits well within the scope of life course theory. In fact, a life course theorist may be able to utilize family stress and resilience theory's propositions to repeatedly analyze family life in order to better understand how, for instance, advantage or disadvantage accumulate over time. Family stress and resilience theory provides an in-depth look at how families adapt, and contributes nicely to providing a life course theorist with information that helps provide context for understanding families over a longer period of time, including how family adaptation from one stressor helps predict family (and individual) adaptation later in life as well as across generations.

Working with Life Course Theory: Integrating Research and Practice

Now that we have described the historical background, assumptions, concepts, and strengths and weaknesses of life course theory, we turn to how the theory can be used in practice. First we provide an example of one new direction of life course theorizing, which is the way that the experience of being old has been reconceptualized by life course scholars. We then analyze an empirical study that was guided by life course theory in order to see how scholars put the theory to work in a research project. Finally, we present ideas about how the theory informs the practice of family life education.

Life course theory today

As we have discussed, life course theorists have proposed new ways of understanding young, middle, and old age, particularly in light of the changing demographics of society that we identified in Chapter 1. These demographic changes include the fact that there is greater variability in adult life course trajectories due to the fact that most people are living longer; that lives differ according to gender, race, class, sexual orientation, national origin and the like; and that the occurrence or sequencing of marriage and family roles is not a predictable set of stages, as posited by other family theories.

One current area of life course theorizing is the experience of being old. The older years were once described, in family developmental theory (Chapter 5), as the key transitions of retirement, widowhood, and eventual death. As a result of life course theory, old age has been transformed into early and later phases (e.g., the young old, the old old, the centenarians) (Poon et al., 2000). Changes in the way old age is experienced at the personal and societal levels lead life course theorists to ask new theoretical questions. Now that individuals are living well past their eighth decade, Settersten and Trauten ask, "How are these decades to be filled? Is it that there are no scripts for old age, few scripts, or new scripts that are in the process of being developed?" (2009, p. 457). In the past, there were no, or few scripts for how to live in old age, in part because so few people survived to old age. Yet, today, new scripts are constantly being constructed, as the life course lengthens, and older adults create multiple intimate pathways (e.g., getting a divorce, dating, remaining single, or remarrying following widowhood). Thus, from a life course perspective, we can shed light on how old age is experienced by first considering how older adults lived in their young and middle adult years. That is, the quality and extent of their family relationships, their educational and occupational achievements, their health outcomes and access to care, and the quality of their lives from the past will position them to respond to the opportunities and risks they face in their later years.

Using this example about redefining the later years, life course theory suggests that retirement should no longer be conceived as a destination at which one arrives following the ending of a career (Moen, 2003). A variety of different pathways will bring people through the middle years, and it will no longer be marked by a singular "official" institutional and biographical transition – retirement – at the age of 65 (or, in some cases 62). Instead, depending upon individuals' family, work, health, and other circumstances, how they pass through the fifties, sixties, and seventies into what are now considered the later years will be relatively unscripted, and not characterized by a single event.

Life course theory in research

Life course theory is particularly suited for guiding research as well as for incorporating multiple theoretical perspectives (Giele and Elder, 1998). In her study of how the objective conditions of young adults' lives shape and constrain their orientations to marriage and other intimate relationships, Stephanie Byrd (2009) takes advantage of the flexibility of a life course approach to examine individuals' subjective perceptions of marital commitment. She uses life course as both theory and method (e.g., life history analysis) in order to create a new theory about marital commitment at this social-historical time of what Cherlin (2004) has termed the deinstitutionalization of marriage. The deinstitutionalization of marriage refers to the fact that greater numbers of adults are participating in an array of alternatives to marriage, such as cohabitation, informal unions, permanent singlehood, single parenthood, and gay and lesbian partnerships, than in the past 75 years.

Using life course theory and combining it with concepts from social exchange theory (see Chapter 7) and symbolic interactionist theory (see Chapter 4), Byrd (2009) chose a cohort of men and women aged 28–35 for demographic reasons (e.g., the majority of the population will have married by age 35). She also predicted that decisions regarding family life transitions, such as marriage, family, and childbearing, would be preoccupying young adults during their late twenties and early thirties, especially for those recently married or still single. Byrd interviewed 40 women and 35 men; 59 percent of the participants were married and 41 percent were single. With some exceptions, the majority of the respondents were White, college educated, and heterosexual.

In terms of research method, Byrd departed from the typical use of a quantitative methodology, where participants give answers to predetermined questions, and instead utilized qualitative life history interviews. These interviews lasted an average of three hours. The interviews were structured around open-ended questions about dating (e.g., "What can you tell me about your current dating situation?" or "Why do you think you are not having any relationships or haven't been dating anyone?"), and marital relationships (e.g., "How would you describe your marriage/current relationship at this point in time?"). The interviews also included a semistructured life history organized by key stages in their lives, with questions asked about work, leisure, and relationships at each stage. The use of these broader question areas (e.g., work, leisure), in the logic of a life course approach, is that one area of an individual's life must be understood in relation to other areas of a person's life. Thus, individual time can best be understood by examining the interlocking trajectories of intimate and family relationships, work, leisure, and the other major elements of our existence.

In analyzing marital commitment, Byrd discovered two multifaceted dimensions. First, the value-rational component of marital commitment, which refers to the social exchange aspect of a marital relationship, "captures its relative desirability as a social status and identity resource in relation to alternatives" (Byrd, 2009, p. 323). Individuals held very different expectations for and understandings about what it means to be married or in a committed relationship. Interestingly, very few stated that having a shared religious commitment was needed to ensure marital commitment. Instead, life course issues, such as transitions from school to steady employment, were more responsible for reevaluations of dating and marriage goals. Regarding another life course issue relative to the value-rational component, Byrd also found evidence of a tension between "prioritizing couple identities versus fostering separate identities in marriage" (2009, p. 332) for both single and married participants.

Second, Byrd discovered a practicality component of marital commitment. Marriage is not only a value, but also a status that must be achieved. In her study, the construction of practicality emerged "as a product of two central subjective processes: Perceptions of obstacles to achieving marital commitment and perceptions of the likelihood of overcoming those obstacles" (2009, p. 326). An example of obstacles was found regarding the subjective perceptions of participants whose parents had divorced; sensitive to research that predicted their own marriages would fail, these participants reported being extra cautious in preventing divorce in their own lives.

Finally, Byrd's study is an excellent example of using life course theory to work with the reality that individual life is dynamic and that issues such as marital commitment are contingent upon shifts in other major life commitments, such as work or education. By using a life course framework, with a consistent research methodology, new ideas about individual, family, and social-historical time in contemporary contexts can emerge.

Life course theory in practice

There are several ways in which family science practitioners can apply life course theory in their work with individuals and families. Important roles that practitioners could play include locating and developing educational media for print and the internet, as well as providing intervention within and across cohorts in a family.

Family life educators could be instrumental in applying life course theory in order to help families understand and find resources regarding the complex dynamics associated with change over time. For example, life course theory sheds light on the very practical problem that adult siblings face when their older parents become frail and need formal care. These resources, drawn from life course theory, include the knowledge that sibling relationships can be strained in adulthood just as they were in childhood, and that over the life course, there can be periods of harmony, ambivalence, and conflict (Connidis and McMullin, 2002). Families should be aware that sisters may be closer to one another, but daughters are typically expected to provide more of the emotional and physical care, while sons are exempt from all but financial assistance (Matthews, 2002). A family life educator could help adult siblings understand the need to communicate explicitly with each other about expectations for help from other siblings, inheritance of property, and the like. Individuals and families in such complex intergenerational situations can also benefit from therapeutic intervention.

Website resources are also key. Family life educators can develop fact sheets based on a family perspective regarding topics such as inter- and intragenerational communication, conflict resolution, what to expect when parents become frail, the transition to parenthood, coming out as lesbian, gay, bisexual, transgender, or queer (LGBTQ), health promotion across the life course, and comforting those who have lost a loved one to death.

As the baby boom ages, the needs for services for the various cohorts (e.g., those born in the late 1940s; those born in the 1950s; those born in the early 1960s) will provide opportunities for family life educators and health care practitioners to meet the needs for the swelling numbers of aging individuals. The diverse needs of the aging baby boomers present family educators, health care workers, clinicians, and researchers with a host of issues that will require attention, particularly because research now shows that baby boomers are not as healthy as their parents' generation (King et al., 2013). Differences in their marital status, financial status, number of children, work history, health needs, and the like, all predict a different kind of aging process. Professionals who understand how families function are in a better position to intervene, educate, and help.

Conclusion

In conclusion, life course theory has provided important ideas that allow researchers and practitioners to put the theory to use beyond the conceptual level. Life course theory is easily translated into concepts that can be applied to empirical research, as we have seen in our examples. Further, life course theory, with its emphasis on change over time and multiple individual and family pathways, provides rich resources from which family life practitioners can draw in order to educate and help families.

Additionally, it is important to highlight how this theory is applicable to the study of families across the globe. How individuals move through the life course differs greatly, depending on the country's culture and history. Why do you think this is? How would life course theorists explain the differences between the countries we highlight in Box 9.3? We challenge you to consider these global applications of the theory as you move on to the areas for further study and the discussion and reflection questions in the concluding pages of this chapter.

Box 9.3 Global Comparisons of Emerging Adulthood

One of the life course stages that has recently made its way into the research spotlight is the developmental period between the ages of 18 and 25, referred to as emerging adulthood. This period is an interesting time for researchers because only 60 years ago in the United States, high school graduates typically married and entered into stable, enduring adult roles (Arnett and Eisenberg, 2007). More recently, emerging adulthood has become a time of independent identity explorations and instability (Arnett, 2004). While the concept was first introduced in the US, researchers have also found evidence of young adults experiencing this life course stage around the world in different ways. As we can see from the following examples, this relatively new stage of the life course, emerging adulthood, is highly dependent on culture and social norms.

Sweden is a Nordic country, where overall, young adults leave home the earliest, most likely due to the financial support they receive from the government to encourage them to be autonomous from their families of origin to explore education, jobs, and relationships (Douglass, 2007). The support comes in the forms of housing allowances and unemployment compensation. These young adults finish college later and postpone childbearing. In addition, over half of all births are outside of marriage (usually in a cohabiting relationship).

Spain is characterized by a strong reliance on the family for support. Spanish parents assume that their children will live at home into their thirties or until they get married (Douglass, 2005). In fact, in 2005, 95 percent of Spanish young people between 18 and 25 lived with their parents, as did 63 percent of 25–29 year olds, and 30 percent of 30–35 year olds. Spain has high unemployment rates for this age group as well.

Russia has a cultural bias against women having children after their late twenties, so childbirth usually takes place between 18 and 24 years old (Gabriel, 2005). However, birthrates have declined in recent years, which may be due to transition to a market economy and away from the social safety nets Russians were used to (Douglass, 2005). Therefore, young adults often emigrate in search of better economic and social possibilities.

Chinese culture has ideological roots in Confucianism, which stresses social order and harmony, and suppresses personal needs and desires for the benefit of the entire group (Nelson and Chen, 2007). Fewer than 20 percent of Chinese young people are able to obtain a college education because of competitive college entrance exams. In the 1970s, China instituted a one-child policy to address population control; this policy has contributed to a gender imbalance (120 males to every 100 females) (Hudson and Den Boer, 2002). The policy was in effect until October 2015, when the government announced it would now allow married couples to have two children (Buckley, 2015). The college and university system in China does not allow students to change majors (Nelson and Chen, 2007). Additionally, the sense of obligation to care for aging parents is high in China, so children rarely move far away from their parents.

Multimedia Suggestions

www.ssea.org

This is the homepage of the Society for the Study of Emerging Adulthood, a professional association that sponsors a yearly conference and a scholarly journal, *Emerging Adulthood*. The website provides helpful resources for understanding social and psychological aspects of the post-adolescent period of ages 18–25.

Activate your theory app: Consider this age range as it relates to history. As life expectancy increases in developed countries, will emerging adulthood happen around the same ages as today, or will it extend to accommodate the longer life span?

www.aarp.org

This is the homepage for AARP, begun as the American Association of Retired Persons, founded in 1956. It is the leading organization for those aged 50 and older. With a membership of 37 million members (as of 2015), AARP has a tremendous amount of political clout. They offer a comprehensive array of practical information (e.g., health care, caregiving, employment), discounts on insurance and recreational activities, as well as many other resources and opportunities.

Activate your theory app: Imagine how this website might change to be relevant to your generation when you hit retirement age. What unique characteristics does your generation have that analysts at AARP would have to take into account to better tailor the services offered on the site?

My Sister's Keeper (2009)

This film is based on the 2003 Jodi Picoult novel. In the story, a heterosexual couple gives birth first to a son, and then later a girl. In the daughter's first few years of life, they discover she has leukemia, and neither the brother nor the parents are bone marrow matches. They decide to genetically select one of the mother's eggs and the father's sperm, which creates an embryo that will be a perfect bone marrow match for the girl. They give birth to their third child, Anna, with the sole purpose of keeping her sister alive. Anna is loved and cared for, but because of the need for her to remain healthy so she can be a bone marrow donor, her parents do not allow her to leave home overnight, play sports, or do most of the things adolescent children get to do. Over time, Anna decides she does not want to be a bone marrow donor anymore, and decides to hire a lawyer to represent her in a suit against her parents.

A scene from *My Sisters's Keeper*, 2009, dir. Nick Cassavetes, New Line Cinema

Activate your theory app: How does this story present examples of linked lives, pathways, and trajectories? How does this story reveal the concept of agency, in terms of Anna's choices as well as her parents' choices?

Forrest Gump (1994)

This film follows Forrest Gump over several decades of his life, displaying how some of the important historical events of the late twentieth century define the ways in which Forrest moves through his life course stages. This story also provides a look into Forrest's family relationships, specifically with his mother and his childhood sweetheart, Jenny.

A scene from *Forrest Gump*, 1994, dir. Robert Zemeckis, Paramount Pictures

Activate your theory app: What examples can you see in this film of the importance of historical time and place, as well as linked lives?

Further Reading

Arnett, J. J., *Adolescence and emerging adulthood: A cultural approach*, 4th edn (Boston: Pearson Prentice Hall, 2010). This book is written from a global cultural perspective and extends the developmental period of adolescence into emerging adulthood (ages 18–25). Although a psychologist, Arnett, a leading expert on emerging adulthood, takes an interdisciplinary, sociohistorical approach. This book is especially helpful for college students in exploring the self-discovery context in relation to the scientific literature.

Elder, G. H., Jr, *Children of the Great Depression* (Chicago: University of Chicago Press, 1974). This book contains the seminal life course study that ignited scholarly interest in measuring how social-historical events effect individual development throughout the life span. In this study, Elder traced the impact of relative degrees of economic hardship resulting from different cohorts' experiences in the 1930s from their childhood to middle-age years, examining the impact on their family relationships, careers, and other lifestyle features.

Newman, K., *A different shade of gray: Midlife and beyond in the inner city* (New York: New Press, 2003). Newman gathered qualitative data through in-depth life history interviews with 100 ethnically diverse New Yorkers. Her research paints the picture of growing old in the inner city, and contrasts it to the historical landscape that situated the families in her book on a life course trajectory that often was not of their own making. Families faced White flight, children with serious illnesses, and caregiving for extended kin and grandchildren. Each of these structural forces contributed to the families' accumulating disadvantage over their life courses, in sharp contrast to where they started their lives in the beautiful boroughs of New York in the 1940s and 1950s. This text illustrates nearly every concept of the life course perspective and should be useful to family studies students.

Notter, M. L., MacTavish, K. A., and Shamah, D., "Pathways toward resilience among women in rural trailer parks," *Family Relations, 57* (2008), 613–624 (doi:10.1111/j.1741-3729.2008.00527.x). In this article, the authors describe how resilience is a process that must be negotiated and achieved throughout the life course. Women, and their children, who live in trailer parks in rural areas must deal with, at the very least, hardships derived from the intersection of social class, gender, and geographic location. The authors document the multiple turning points in rural women's lives, in terms of how they live in relative poverty, face many intergenerational risks, and have little or no formal or informal support, but still manage to work toward family survival and strength in often harsh surroundings.

Sharp, E. A., and Ganong, L., "Living in the gray: Women's experiences of missing the marital transition," *Journal of Marriage and Family, 69* (2007), 831–844 (doi:10.1111/j.1741-3737.2007.00408.x). Combining a life course perspective and phenomenological methodology, this study examines the reflections of young adult women (ages 28 to 34) on the life pathway of singlehood. Their stories reveal the uncertainty many felt about the future of their family relationships as well as their reflections on the "missed" transition related to marriage.

Questions for Students

Discussion Questions

1 Think about the "big picture" of life course theory. How has this theory responded to shifts in family realities? How might life course theory be applied if we tried to situate it in 1900? Consider the diversity of families back then, and what this theory might add to the analysis. Would it work?
2 Looking ahead, is life course theory the type of perspective that lends itself to being adapted to adjust to even more changes in the diversity of families, as time goes on? What types of changes might not "fit" into this theory? Which ones would?
3 Compare and contrast the issues of cumulative advantage and cumulative disadvantage. Are they mutually exclusive? Why or why not?
4 What state or federal policies could benefit from an understanding of life course theory? Are there concepts that are more important to point out to policymakers than others?
5 Some researchers suggest that life course theory *needs* to be supplemented by another major theoretical framework. What do you think? Does life course theory stand alone, or is it best used in combination with other theories?
6 What types of research methods have been applied with life course theory? Is it possible to use qualitative, quantitative, and mixed methods to study life course concepts? Which do you think is most appropriate, and why?

Your Turn!

Find an article where the authors have used life course theory as a framework for their empirical research. What aspects of the theory did the research utilize? Is there another theory the research could have utilized? What are the strengths and weaknesses of the article? What would YOU do different, if you were conducting the research?

Personal Reflection Questions

1 To what birth cohort do you belong? What are some of the characteristics of your cohort? In what ways do you, or don't you, identify with your cohort?

2 What birth cohort do your parents and grandparents belong to? Describe the similarities and/or differences you have noticed due to cohort membership.
3 To illustrate the concept of linked lives, give an example of how an event in a family member's life has affected your own life in dramatic ways.
4 How important have broader social-historical events been in shaping your own life course?
5 Give an example of a way in which you, or a member of your family, has experienced a major life event "off time," from a life course perspective.
6 Compose a letter to your local state representative, arguing for a policy change using life course theory. Frame your letter as though you are writing for a specific policy change, and ground your argument in an issue that would be more fully understood if only our state representatives used life course theory when considering policy.

References

Aldous, J. (1990). Family development and the life course: Two perspectives on family change. *Journal of Marriage and the Family, 52*, 571–583. doi:10.2307/352924.

Alexander, K. L., Entwisle, D. R., and Olson, L. S. (2001). Schools, achievement, and inequality: A seasonal perspective. *Educational Evaluation and Policy Analysis, 23*, 171–191. doi: 10.3102/01623737023002171.

Allen, K. R. (1989). *Single women/family ties: Life histories of older women*. Thousand Oaks, CA: Sage.

Arnett, J. J. (2004). *Emerging adulthood: The winding road from the late teens through the twenties*. New York: Oxford University Press.

Arnett, J. J., and Eisenberg, N. (2007). Introduction to the special section: Emerging adulthood around the world. *Child Development Perspectives, 1*, 66–67. doi:10.1111/j.1750-8606.2007.00015.x.

Bengtson, V. L., and Allen, K. R. (1993). The life course perspective applied to families over time. In P. Boss, W. Doherty, R. LaRossa, W. Schumm, and S. Steinmetz (eds), *Sourcebook of family theories and methods: A contextual approach* (pp. 469–499). New York: Plenum.

Buckley, C. (2015, October 30). China ends one-child policy, allowing families two children. *New York Times*. At www.nytimes.com/2015/10/30/world/asia/china-end-one-child-policy.html.

Byrd, S. E. (2009). The social construction of marital commitment. *Journal of Marriage and Family, 71*, 318–336. doi:10.1111/j.1741-3737.2008.00601.x.

Carpenter, L. M. (2010). Gendered sexuality over the life course: A conceptual framework. *Sociological Perspective, 53*, 155–178. doi:10.1525/sop.2010.53.2.155.

Cherlin, A. J. (2004). The deinstitutionalization of marriage. *Journal of Marriage and Family, 66*, 848–861. doi:10.1111/j.0022-2445.2004.00058.x.

Connidis, I. A., and McMullin, J. A. (2002). Sociological ambivalence and family ties: A critical perspective. *Journal of Marriage and Family, 64*, 558–567. doi:10.1111/j.1741-3737.2002.00558.x.

Deal, J. (2007). *Retiring the generation gap. How employees young and old can find common ground*. San Francisco: Jossey-Bass.

Demo, D. H., Aquilino, W. S. and Fine, M. A. (2005). Family compositions and family transitions. In V. Bengtson, A. C. Acock, K. R. Allen, P. Dilworth-Anderson, and D. M. Klein (eds), *Sourcebook of family theory and research* (pp. 119–142). Thousand Oaks, CA: Sage.

Douglass, C. B. (2005). "We're fine at home": Young people, family and low fertility in Spain. In C. B. Douglass (ed.), *Barren states: The population "implosion" in Europe* (pp. 183–206). Oxford: Berg.

Douglass, C. B. (2007). From duty to desire: Emerging adulthood in Europe and its consequences. *Child Development Perspectives, 1*, 101–108. doi:10.1111/j.1750-8606.2007.00023.x.

Duvall, E. (1957). *Family development*. Philadelphia: J. B. Lippincott.

Edin, K., and Kefalas, M. (2011). *Promises I can keep: Why poor women put motherhood before marriage*. Berkeley: University of California Press.

Elder, G. H., Jr (1977). Family history and the life course. *Journal of Family History, 2*, 279–304. doi:10.1177/036319907700200402.

Elder, G. H., Jr (1981). History and the family: The discovery of complexity. *Journal of Marriage and the Family, 43*, 489–519. doi:10.2307/351752.

Elder, G. H., Jr, and Giele, J. Z. (2009). Life course studies: An evolving field. In G. H. Elder, Jr and J. Z. Giele (eds), *The craft of life course research* (pp. 1–24). New York: Guilford Press.

Elder, G. H., Jr, Johnson, M. K., and Crosnoe, R. (2003). The emergence and development of life course theory. In J. T. Mortimer and M. J. Shanahan (eds), *Handbook of the life course* (pp. 3–19). New York: Kluwer.

Erikson, E. H. (1950). *Childhood and society*. New York: Norton.

Erikson, E. H. (1975). *Life history and the historical moment.* New York: Norton.

Gabriel, C. (2005). "Our nation is dying": Interpreting patterns of childbearing in post-Soviet Russia. In C. Douglass (ed.), *Barren states: The population "implosion" in Europe* (pp. 73–92). Oxford: Berg.

Giele, J. Z., and Elder, G. H., Jr (eds) (1998). *Methods of life course research: Qualitative and quantitative approaches*. Thousand Oaks, CA: Sage.

Greenfield, E. A., and Marks, N. F. (2006). Linked lives: Adult children's problems and their parents' psychological and relational well-being. *Journal of Marriage and Family, 68*, 442–454. doi:10.1111/j.1741-3737.2006.00263x.

Hauser, R. M. (2009). The Wisconsin Longitudinal Study: Designing a study of the life course. In G. H. Elder, Jr and J. Z. Giele (eds), *The craft of life course research* (pp. 1–24). New York: Guilford Press.

Hill, R., and Rodgers, R. H. (1964). The developmental approach. In H. T. Christensen (ed.), *Handbook of marriage and the family* (pp. 171–211). Chicago: Rand McNally.

Hitlin, S., and Elder, G. H., Jr (2007). Time, self, and the curiously abstract concept of agency. *Sociological Theory, 25*, 170–191. doi:10.1111/j.1467-9558.2007.00303.x.

Hudson, V. M., and Den Boer, A. (2002). A surplus of men, a deficit of peace: Security and sex ratios in Asia's largest states. *International Security, 26*, 5–39. doi:10.1162/016228802753696753.

King, D. E., Matheson, E., Chirina, S., Shankar, A., and Broman-Fulks, J. (2013). The status of baby boomers' health in the United States: The healthiest generation? *JAMA Internal Medicine, 173*, 385–386. doi:10.1001/jamainternmed.2013.2006.

LeMoyne, T., and Buchanan, T. (2011). Does "hovering" matter? Helicopter parenting and its effect on well-being. *Sociological Spectrum, 31*, 399–418. doi:10.1080/02732173.2011.574038.

Matthews, S. H. (2002). *Sisters and brothers/daughters and sons: Meeting the needs of old parents*. Bloomington, IN: Unlimited.

Merton, R. K. (1988). The Matthew effect in science, II: Cumulative advantage and the symbolism of intellectual property. *Isis, 79*, 606–623. doi:10.1086/354848.

Miller, J. D. (2011, fall) Active, balanced and happy: These young Americans are not bowling alone. In *The Generation X report: A quarterly research report from the longitudinal study of American youth*. Ann Arbor: University of Michigan.

Moen, P. (2003). Midcourse: Navigating retirement and a new life stage. In J. T. Mortimer and M. J. Shanahan (eds), *Handbook of the life course* (pp. 269–291). New York: Kluwer.

Nelson, L. J., and Chen, X. (2007). Emerging adulthood in China: The role of social and cultural factors. *Child Development Perspectives, 1*, 86–91. doi:10.1111/j.1750-8606.2007.00020.x.

O'Rand, A. M. (2002). Cumulative advantages theory in life course research. In S. Crystal and D. Shea (eds), *Annual Review of Gerontology and Geriatrics* (vol. 22, pp. 14–30). New York: Springer.

Poon, L. W., Johnson, M. A., Davey, A., Dawson, D. V., Siegler, I. C., and Martin, P. (2000). Psycho-social predictors of survival among centenarians. In P. Martin, C. Rott, B. Hagberg, and K. Morgan (eds), *Centenarians: Autonomy versus dependence in the oldest old* (pp. 77–89). New York: Springer.

Roberto, K. A., McCann, B. R., and Blieszner, R. (2013). Trajectories of care: Spouses coping with changes related to MCI. *Dementia: International Journal of Social Research and Practice, 12*, 45–62. doi:10.1177/1471301211421233.

Ryder, N. B. (1965). The cohort as a concept in the study of social change. *American Sociological Review, 30*, 843–861. doi:10.2307/2090964.

Savin-Williams, R. C. (2001). *Mom, Dad, I'm gay: How families negotiate coming out*. Washington, DC: American Psychological Association.

Settersten, R. A., Jr, and Trauten, M. E. (2009). The new terrain of old age: Hallmarks, freedoms, and risks. In V. L. Bengtson, D. Gans, N. M. Putney, and M. Silverstein (eds), *Handbook of theories of aging* (2nd edn, pp. 455–469). New York: Springer.

Smith, D. E. (1993). The Standard North American Family: SNAF as an ideological code: *Journal of Family Issues, 14*, 50–65. doi:10.1177/0192513X93014001005.

Spock, B. (1946). *The common sense book of baby and child care.* New York: Dutton.

Strauss, W., and Howe, N. (1997). *The fourth turning: An American prophecy. What the cycles of history tell us about America's next rendezvous with destiny.* New York: Broadway.

Twenge, J. M., and Campbell, W. K. (2009). *The narcissism epidemic: Living in the age of entitlement*. New York: Free Press.

US Census Bureau (2012). *Selected social characteristics in the United States: 2012 American Community Survey 1-year estimates.* At http://factfinder.census.gov/.

Walker, A. J., Allen, K. R., and Connidis, I. A. (2005). Theorizing and studying sibling ties in adulthood. In V. Bengtson, A. C. Acock, K. R. Allen, P. Dilworth-Anderson, and D. M. Klein (eds), *Sourcebook of family theory and research* (pp. 167–190). Thousand Oaks, CA: Sage.

Willson, A. E., Shuey, K. M., and Elder, G. H., Jr (2007). Cumulative advantage processes as mechanisms of inequality in life course health. *American Journal of Sociology, 112*, 1886–1924. doi:10.1086/512712.

10

Family Ecological Theory

Have you ever been in a relationship with someone, and after several months, you discover something about them that is both surprising and yet makes so much sense? Perhaps the person you have been dating revealed that they had been sexually assaulted previously, but never reported it to law enforcement or sought out help from counseling professionals or support groups. As a loved one, you might feel conflicted – both angry and compassionate at the same time. Angry at the perpetrator of the assault, and angry because you wish your loved one had reported it and served justice. Yet, you feel sad and want to be comforting and supportive of your loved one in whatever way they need.

Imagine the complexities associated with a sexual assault; a case like this can be examined on multiple levels, each one important in different ways to understanding families and their members. First, you imagine your loved one's family – what prevented her from telling her parents? You know the family does not have very good health insurance, and your loved one mentioned that by calling 911, she feared she would have to pay for expensive ambulance services and transportation, as well as costly hospital examinations and tests, and draw attention to her family's home with all the police and emergency vehicles that would arrive. She also has seen how law enforcement officials treat rape victims on TV: the fear of the same thing happening to her felt overwhelming. As long as she avoided the perpetrator, she could protect herself without involving anyone else. Given how close she was to graduating high school and heading off to college, she figured starting a new chapter in life would provide a chance to start over anyway.

Each of the layers to this story represents a different level of system that family ecological theory addresses. As we explain in this chapter, there are several levels of analysis that family ecological theory uses to understand families, including the microsystem, mesosystem, exosystem, macrosystem, and chronosystem. Each of these levels represents a different way of examining the interaction that families and their members have with their larger communities (e.g., neighborhoods, peers, school), social institutions (e.g., religion, the criminal justice system), and cultural ideals (e.g., dominant values and norms), and how these change over time. Each of these systems will be described in detail later in this chapter, but given the comprehensiveness of this framework, it should be no surprise that this theory, though unique, has ties to many other theories, in particular family developmental (Chapter 5), family systems (Chapter 6), and life course (Chapter 9). This theory allows researchers and practitioners the chance to take into account all the forces that contribute to family interactions both internally and externally. This provides scholars and practitioners with a more complex understanding of families, including the roles that larger social institutions play in family life, as well as larger cultural forces that determine what is "right," "wrong," or even "normal" for families. Further, this theory is perhaps the most committed to ensuring the well-being of individuals and their families. Below, we elaborate on the topic of sexual assault to provide a multifaceted look at how such an event can impact

Family Theories: Foundations and Applications, First Edition. Katherine R. Allen and Angela C. Henderson.

not only the woman, but also her family, long after it happened.

Case Study

Nina and James have been married for 12 years and have two children together. About two months after they married, James took a job 1,000 miles away and had to relocate before Nina was able to follow, leaving them living in separate states for about a month. One night after James had moved, a serial rapist broke into Nina and James's home and raped Nina, who was one of three women attacked in a three-month span. All three women reported the assaults, which provided police with DNA and the arrest of the perpetrator who was already in "the system" for similar crimes. After a jury trial, the perpetrator was sentenced to 317 years in prison.

As a result of this event, Nina and James began a long journey of interacting with social institutions on several levels. First, Nina sought out medical treatment immediately, getting tested for sexually transmitted diseases and possible pregnancy, and she also was prescribed medication to help her sleep at night and manage recurring panic attacks. She also received long-term medication to deal with her diagnosis of posttraumatic stress disorder. She immediately connected with psychological services by establishing weekly appointments with a professional counselor, a psychiatrist, and a support group of survivors. In addition, she and James began couples counseling to help them navigate the murky complexities associated with sexual assault, marital communication, and healthy relationship building.

Over the three years following the attack, James and Nina became very familiar with how the criminal justice system processes cases like this. Nina had weekly interactions with the victim's assistance advocate, the district attorney, and investigators on the case. She testified at both the jury trial and at the sentencing hearing. In processing each step with her own counselor and her support group, she also was exposed to aspects of the larger culture that she never really had to think about before, such as the stigma associated with rape, the perception of victims who have been assaulted by strangers versus relatives or acquaintances, and the barriers women face when deciding whether or not to report sexual assault. Additionally, these experiences impacted Nina's view of herself and her sexuality, as well as the relationship she built with her children, who came along after the conviction and imprisonment of the perpetrator. How would she explain what happened to her to her children? Would she raise her son differently than her daughter, given the experiences she had as a result of the sexual assault? How does the ever changing cultural discussion of sexual assault and the oppression of women inform both Nina's parenting decisions as well as her relationship with her spouse? Furthermore, what were the rippling effects that reached back to her own nuclear family, particularly her relationships with her mother, father, and two brothers? Undoubtedly, their own well-being and perceptions of these issues are also affected.

Finally, think about how women's rights have changed significantly even in the last 50 years, making discussions of sexual victimization more prominent than they were in the past. This aspect – time – made it possible for Nina not only to report the crime, but to also seek professional psychological assistance because society has evolved to include positions such as a "victim's advocate" within the district attorney's office. The sociohistorical context played a huge role in the choices available to Nina and her family. Family ecological theory captures these complexities, including how they affect and are affected by systems outside families, as well as how they change over time.

What Is Family Ecological Theory?

Family ecological theory helps us understand the ways in which these experiences intersect for Nina on the individual, familial, social, and cultural levels, which allows us to bring in multiple sources of information when explaining family life. This theory thoroughly captures the intersectionality of the multiple layers and how they influence and are influenced by families and their members. It takes into account complexities that families experience in their daily lives *because of* their interactions with various social systems. Think about family ecological theory in this way: imagine a traditional wedding cake, but without a couple at the top. The figure at the top is just one person; imagine it being you! The very top of the cake, where you stand, represents the individual characteristics of the family member. By examining the figure at the top, you can identify age, race and/or ethnicity, and gender, among a host of other individual-level characteristics. The layer you stand on represents the **microsystem**, or the immediate family or peers that you rely closely on and come in contact with regularly. The next layer, the **mesosystem**, has tiny plastic stairs that lead to the wider layers below; this represents how the microsystem interconnects with the two outer layers of the cake – the exosystem and macrosystem. Think about how the economy (an exosystem), for instance, affects families differently. How does an economic recession affect families in the working class, middle class, or upper class? The mesosystem is like a channel through which the two outer systems reach the inner microsystems. The important thing to remember is that meso separates families from systems *external* to them; forces that, for the most part, are outside of their control.

The next layer is the first of the three external systems. The **exosystem** can include social institutions such as the economy, the media, industry, or the criminal justice system. How did Nina's interactions with the criminal justice system differ from that of the perpetrator? The perpetrator and his family had very different interactions with the system than Nina and her family. He had previously been "in the system" for similar crimes, and was estranged from his mother and immediate nuclear family. He had extended family that had also been incarcerated and inevitably this affects his view of the system. Nina, on the other hand, hopes that her interactions with the criminal justice system are long behind her; she had never been in trouble with the law or victimized prior to the rape. She hopes that the three years through the assault, arrest, investigation, trial, and sentencing represent the entirety of her interactions with the criminal justice system for the rest of her life.

The largest layer, the **macrosystem**, represents cultural ideologies, ways of thinking, and attitudes that exist at a broader level. How do the societal expectations guide what you think, believe, or perceive in life? Nina had no idea how stigmatized rape victims are until she had to experience it firsthand and also hear her support group members talk about it. She is now hyper-aware of cultural beliefs surrounding rape, gender inequality, and victim blaming. Given the seriousness of this event in Nina's life, her interactions with the macrosystem will undoubtedly affect members of her family of origin as well as her nuclear family for generations to come.

Finally, the "invisible" system, the **chronosystem,** represents the influence of time on each layer. Imagine you are sitting atop the aforementioned wedding cake as a toddler, then as an adolescent, a young adult, and then as an older adult. Clearly, age and historical time are going to influence not only the individual, but also the composition of the layers of the cake surrounding you. Exosystems and macrosystems change over time: the economy is always subject to upturns and recessions, and cultural ideals not only about family life but also about broader ideologies are constantly in flux at the macro level. As such, each layer of the cake is dependent on the other, and together, they build a foundation for you to stand on. If you look too closely at the person at the top, you are missing the entirety of the cake and all the layers that are holding it up. Family ecological theory allows us to really cut into each of those layers and examine the foundation of individuals and their families, from the large bottom layer all the way up to the top. Thus, family ecological theory is one of the most comprehensive frameworks currently in use today.

History and origins

As we have pointed out throughout this book, it is important to examine the historical context in which a theory was developed in order to appreciate the ways in which the theory can help us to understand the issues that we study. As we will see, family ecological theory has ties to many other theories, in particular, family developmental (Chapter 5), family systems (Chapter 6), and life course (Chapter 9). Further, it lends itself to creative pairings, such as social exchange theory (Sabatelli and Ripoll, 2004). The theory has roots in two primary disciplines, human ecology (formerly called home economics) and developmental psychology.

Family ecology Let's start by discussing how the family ecology movement evolved out of the discipline of home economics (Faust et al., 2014; Hook and

Box 10.1 At a Glance: Family Ecological Theory

Family ecology An adaptation of human ecology theory to the family as an ecosystem, in which family is defined as an energy transformation system. The components of the family ecosystem are the human-built environment, the social-cultural environment, and the natural physical-biological environment.

Microsystem Events, developmental processes, and family relationships experienced in an individual's immediate surroundings.

Mesosystem How the microsystem interconnects the individual and family to events that may not be experienced directly in the broader institutions associated with the outer layers of the nested system (e.g., the exosystem and macrosystem).

Exosystem The broader social institutions which structure society, such as the economic, educational, legal, mass media, military, and political systems.

Macrosystem The ideologies, organization, values, attitudes, and ways of thinking evident in a culture, which may vary by subculture within the society (e.g., social classes, ethnic and religious groups).

Chronosystem The layer of time, in which an individual's age and the ordering of events, context, and historical sequence identify the impact of prior experiences upon subsequent development.

Process-person-context-time (PPCT) model The four components in the bioecological model that influence the developmental outcomes and interaction among the nested systems.

Paolucci, 1970). Home economics, now called family and consumer sciences, was the original discipline employing female scholars in the early twentieth century, when women were almost exclusively barred from academic appointments in the male-dominated disciplines of sociology, psychology, biology, chemistry, and others, and most male scholars ignored issues of home and family (Thompson, 1988). Though a German biologist named Ernst Haeckel first coined the term *ecology* in 1873, it was Ellen Swallow Richards who adapted more general ideas about ecological science to a "science of the environment focused on home and family" (Bubolz and Sontag, 1993, p. 420). Richards, the first woman admitted to the Massachusetts Institute of Technology (MIT), used her training as an industrial and environmental chemist to study the family's interaction with the natural, biological environment. Early in her career as a scientist, Richards studied the effects of industrialization on water quality, which eventually led to the establishment of water quality standards across the United States. As she uncovered the impact of environment on families and well-being, she began to acknowledge the importance of educating the largest group of consumers: women. She envisioned a science of household management, referred to as "oekology" early on. This term stems from the Greek *oikos*, which means "place of residence." Richards viewed the family as the primary location for the foundation of life and thus developed a theory linking the physical environment with the social context of individual and family development. Her studies of how families operated within their environments laid the groundwork for what we know as family ecological theory today.

These foundational ideas in the field of home economics were concerned with the intersection of human beings in their natural/physical and human-built environments. Thus, this model considered the broader social context in which families lived and interacted every day (Bubolz and Sontag, 1993). The family ecological framework elaborated upon key ideas about context, environment, interdependence, adaptation, and ecosystem. Figure 10.1 presents an ecological model from the family environmental perspective.

You can see in the figure that the family is the central focal point of the model. Thus, families must be understood in the context of other, nonhuman groups

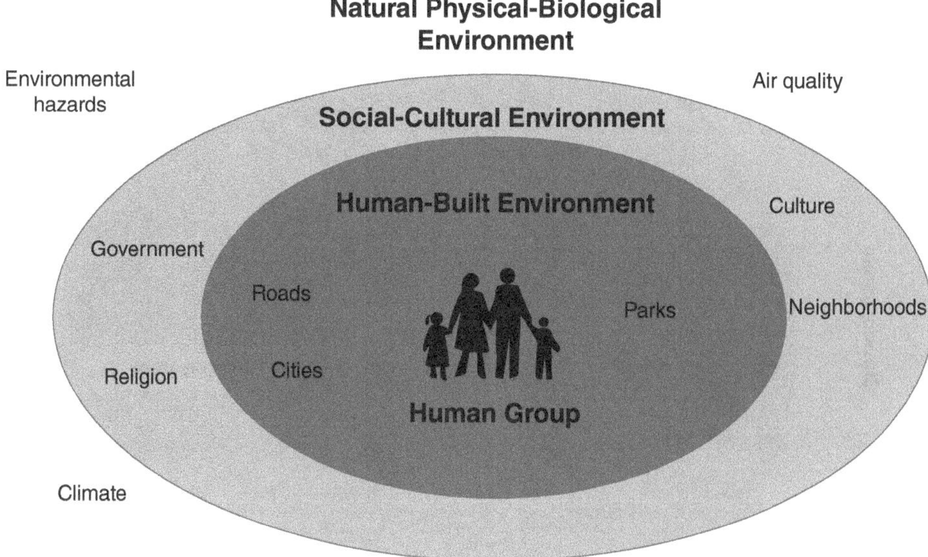

Figure 10.1 A family ecosystem

that surround it. The environments are nested, or embedded, within one another. The natural physical-biological environment represents the largest force that encompasses every other environment. It should be easy to see why this was the first model of family ecology, given Richards's emphasis on the importance of the link between a family and its physical environment. Using this early model of family ecology, theorists, researchers, and practitioners could identify, for instance, the importance of the availability of nutritious foods, clean water, and clean air where families live. The quality of the outermost environment is directly related to the social-cultural environment, which includes social institutions like schools. Let's look at this issue in more depth to illustrate this model of family ecology.

First, it is important to consider that not all families include children. However, for families with children, the presence of children contributes to the likelihood that a family will interact with certain social institutions. Would a family without children be as concerned about the air quality near the local school, compared to a family with school-aged kids? It is important to consider these differences when taking a family ecological approach because, as you can see in Figure 10.2, the two-directional arrows suggest that the human group influences the outer environment and vice versa. Depending on family structure, some institutions may or may not be integral to a family's well-being.

Now, thinking back to what you learned from conflict theory (Chapter 3), you should remember that schools are often directly impacted by the immediate environment and economic well-being of one's community. If poor communities have low air quality, low water quality, and limited access to nutritious foods, this inevitably affects the quality of the schools, which in turn affects the children and families who interact with the schools. Will schoolchildren be able to play outside at recess if an industrial waste site is nearby, compromising the air quality? Will that same school have regular access to clean water? Further, what human-built environments will serve as a buffer between the outer environments and the human group, or family? Consider schools that are situated in middle- or upper-class neighborhoods; the buildings and roads leading to schools are likely safe, attractive, and well-maintained. On the other hand, schools in lower-income communities are not only directly impacted by the air and water,

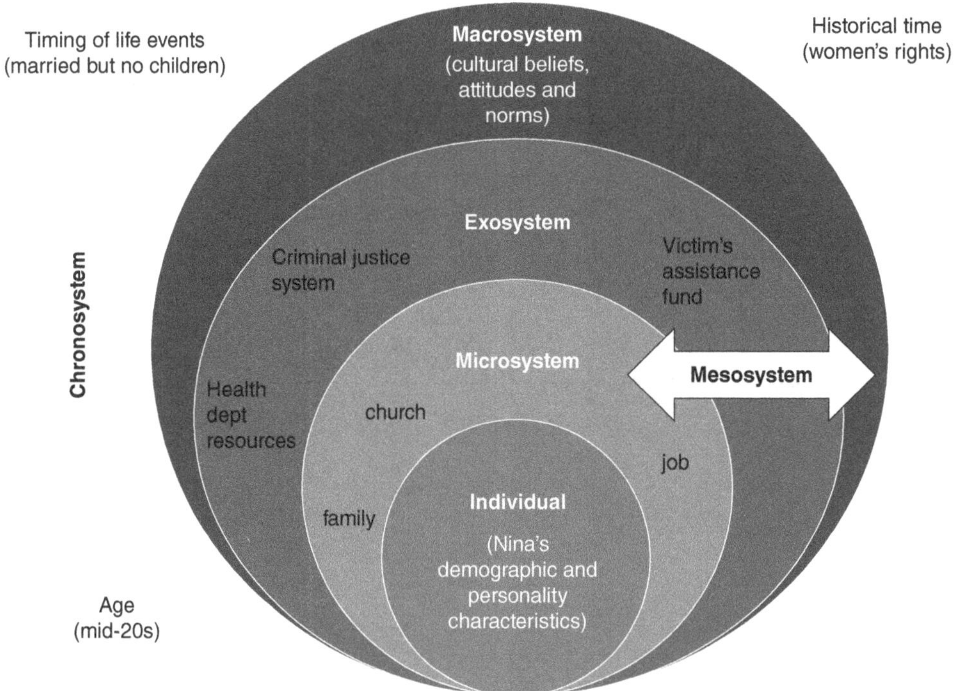

Figure 10.2 Bronfenbrenner's ecological model applied to Nina

but also the safety and security surrounding the buildings and routes to school. Consider whether or not children have to cross busy highways to get to school from residential areas; in some communities, there may be a "buffer" that protects the family (and children) from the external environments. Each of these factors can be taken into account using this family environmental model.

Human ecology As the other major influence on an ecological model, we turn now to the field of psychology. From the perspective of ecological psychology, Barker (1968) examined the impact of the environment on individual behavior. Later, Urie Bronfenbrenner (1979), from Cornell University, articulated an individual perspective on human development by positing that nested systems of the biological, psychological, and social spheres influenced the development of the individual. His ecological theory of human development was highly influenced by the German American psychologist Kurt Lewin, who is considered a pioneer of social, organizational, and applied psychology (Bronfenbrenner, 1978). Lewin is credited with the classic statement, "there is nothing so practical as a good theory" (Bronfenbrenner, 2005, p. 43).

Bronfenbrenner's (2005) ecological theory portrays development as an interconnected system of ever widening layers, much like that of nested Russian dolls. This is similar to the model put forth by Bubolz and Sontag (1993) in that the layers are nested, but the two models differ in terms of the primary unit of analysis: Bubolz and Sontag's model begins by theorizing about the family, whereas Bronfenbrenner's model begins by theorizing about the individual. Bronfenbrenner's ecological theory includes (a) the individual family members in the microsystem; (b) the connections between microsystems, such as between families and schools, in the mesosystem; (c) the influences from larger social systems that provide the immediate context for families, such as neighborhoods, in the exosystem; (d) the largest social contexts and levels of influence, such as politics, religion, cultural, and legal institutions in the macrosystem; and (e) the timing and patterning of events over the life course in the chronosystem (Bush and Peterson, 2013, p. 277).

More recent adaptations of the theory include a combination of prior versions, which, as we have seen throughout this text, is very common when it comes to theoretical development. In the field of family sociology, prior versions of family ecological theory have evolved with the influence of life course theorists (Chapter 9). In particular, Glen Elder (1974) worked with Bronfenbrenner at Cornell University, and their perspectives on individual, family, and social development over time were mutually influential. In conceptualizing various dimensions of time over the individual's life (e.g., the chronosystem), the life course framework was helpful in showing the dynamic ways that different dimensions of time (individual, family, and historical) shape developmental change. Thus, the combination of human ecology and developmental theories into family ecological theory has allowed us to go beyond individual development and toward the interactions of families with their near and external environments. Figure 10.2 illustrates a contemporary version of family ecological theory that includes the chronosystem, applied to our case study involving Nina.

Further, the family ecological perspective has been a forerunner in understanding family diversity, with variations in family structure, ethnicity, life stage, and socioeconomic status (Bubolz and Sontag, 1993; McAdoo, Martinez, and Hughes, 2005). Harriette McAdoo (1993; 1999) and John McAdoo (1988), who were professors in the Department of Family Ecology at Michigan State University, were among the major theorists who expanded the family ecology model to include more diversity, particularly to the ecology of Black families. This framework was among the first to address the intersections of race, ethnicity, and family in an overt way. Harriette McAdoo explained that "persons of color often have a greater reliance on the social network than families who are more readily accepted within the context of our society or who have greater resources within their control" (1993, p. 299). A more comprehensive understanding of the ecological contexts of minority families requires a stronger look at the mesosystemic layer which helps us see that the differential treatment and reliance upon kin is necessary given the unequal access to opportunities and resources available to members of society who experience greater prejudice and discrimination overall. In this regard, family ecological theory has ties to the description of added stressors faced by minority families (Chapter 11, on family stress and resilience theory), and the resilience that can result (Peters and Massey, 1983).

Key concepts

Now that we have described some of the history of the development of family ecological theory, we turn to definitions of key concepts that are used in this theory. These concepts are increasingly used in the social and behavioral sciences, including psychology, sociology, studies of public and community health, and family science, because they cover the interconnections across individuals, families, institutions, and time.

Ecosystem This concept is used in various biological and environmental sciences. It can be commonly defined as a community of living organisms that interacts with its surrounding environment (Bubolz and Sontag, 1993). Therefore, the term ecosystem can be used in almost any discipline that studies living organisms that affect and are affected by their environments; examples could be a marine ecosystem or a desert ecosystem. A human ecosystem is a type of living system comprised of humans interactive with their environment. A **family ecosystem** is a subset of a human ecosystem that involves the interaction between families and their environment. As identified by Bubolz and Sontag, some of the major assumptions about human–environment relations are:

> (1) Social and physical environments are interdependent and influence human behavior, development, and quality of life; (2) Environment is a source of available resources; (3) We can choose, design, or modify resources and environments to improve life and well-being, and we should do so. Implicit in these assumptions is the worldview that humans can exert some control over their lives and the environment. (1993, p. 421)

As seen in this description, it is clear that the ecological perspective is a very dynamic one, and has an activist component: it is not enough to describe the biological–environmental connection, it is also important to protect and improve it.

Nested ecological levels One of the major assumptions family ecological theory rests on is that the family is a system that is nested within larger systems (Bronfenbrenner 1979; Bubolz and Sontag, 1993). Each system operates on a specific level, ranging from the smallest (microsystem) to the largest (macrosystem). The smallest systems are nested within the larger systems, and each level can be determined by the proximity to the individual psychologically, physically, or socially. As we move outward from the individual at the center of each model of family ecology, there is a corresponding increase in distance. That is, individuals are closer to and interact more with family members regularly than they do with laws or government.

Think back to the case study; for 24 years of her life before the assault, Nina did not have to interact with the legal or criminal justice system. She also did not have to consider cultural ideologies surrounding the objectification of women or the socialization of boys and men in society. Now, her son and daughter will be raised with unique views on power, sex, sexual assault, and what some researchers refer to as a "crisis of masculinity" in the US (see Chapter 8, feminist theory, for a more detailed discussion of issues associated with masculinity). Nina, as an individual, is nested within (a) her nuclear family as well as her family of origin; (b) larger social institutions which contribute to socialization of boys and men (e.g., education, mass media); and (c) the larger cultural system that perpetuates ideologies about the hypersexualization of women, and the hypermasculinity and dominance of men.

Adaptation The concept of adaptation which emerged from systems theories refers to the fact that individuals and families are dynamic and capable of changing their beliefs and behaviors in order to adapt to their environments. There is a give and take in how **adaptation** occurs. Humans are affected and changed by their environments, but given the feedback and communication processes that we studied in Chapter 6 (family systems theory), humans also directly modify their environments. Adapting to inevitable changes from their near and far environments, families must learn to replace one set of rules with another (Bubolz and Sontag, 1993). In a recent study on the quality of the relationships of lesbian, gay, and heterosexual couples across the transition to adoptive parenthood, Goldberg, Smith, and Kashy (2010) showed that the process of adoption was linked to intersecting ecological layers. These layers included the ways that parents adjusted in light of intrapersonal factors (e.g., experiencing depression), relationship quality (e.g., experiencing friction and other negative emotions related to one's partner), and the broader social contexts (e.g., satisfaction with the adoption agency).

Values Values are present on every level of the ecological model; all families have values that guide their decisions and actions. Understanding the values of individuals and their families (whether they are compatible or not) is vital to family ecological theory: "When studying a family ecosystem, one must make explicit the values and goals that each individual holds, those that are shared by the family as a unit, as well as those operative in the social-cultural environment" (Bubolz and Sontag, 1993, p. 436). A **value** reflects the belief systems of the individual, family, and society about important ideals such as what is pragmatically useful, economically profitable, and morally correct.

Family ecological theory ascribes to the value of **human betterment**, which is the goal to which humans should individually and collectively strive. In this model, there are four "great virtues" that contribute to the common good. The first is economic adequacy, to ensure adequate nourishment, housing, health care, and other essentials of life. The second is justice, to ensure equality in work, education, and health. The third is freedom, in contrast to coercion and confinement. And the fourth is peacefulness, in contrast to conflict and warfare (Bubolz and Sontag, 1993, p. 426).

Bioecology of human development As we discuss throughout this chapter, Bronfenbrenner developed a theory that identifies the complex interactions among several layers of experience. Consider his definition:

> Development is defined as the phenomenon of continuity and change in the biopsychological characteristics of human beings both as individuals and

> as groups. The phenomenon extends over the life course across successive generations and through historical time, both past and present. (2005, p. 3)

There are five layers, or systems, in this model that locate individual and family development at the micro, meso, exo, macro, and chrono levels. For example, the microsystem begins with the developing child and the setting into which he or she is born. The overall circumstance of a child's birth is the first context in which life chances are formed, but it is by no means a "life sentence." Given the subsequent outer layering of other systems, individual lives are constantly changing and taking new directions. For example, the neighborhood in which a child grows up impacts the kind of social and material resources available to the child and his or her family. Neighborhoods with convenient shopping centers, public transportation, adequate housing, local doctors, and good schools provide an adaptive environment in which children and families are supported. Yet, neighborhoods with few grocery stores, inadequate schools, lack of transportation, and entrenched crime set up extra hurdles and limitations that impact family well-being. On the basis of such neighborhood deficits, Bronfenbrenner was one of the leaders in creating Head Start (2016), a federally funded program started in 1965 to provide a support system for children in disadvantaged communities at the local level. Head Start is a good example of bolstering the mesosystem through the involvement of children, parents, teachers, and the whole community in order to turn around the effects of poverty and poor resources to give young children a better beginning.

Another key aspect of Bronfenbrenner's theory is the macrosystem. Bogenschneider (1996) has developed and analyzed programs and policies that affect families, for better or worse. At the macro-level, public policies reflect and also influence a society's cultural values. In the US and other countries around the world, attitudes and practices regarding what constitutes a family, as well as which families "deserve" financial, health care, and other support that is underwritten by the government, are constantly changing. For example, The Defense of Marriage Act was instituted in the US in 1996 to define marriage as a union between one man and one woman, barring same-sex marriage and all of its entitlements at state and federal levels (Bogenschneider, 2000). Yet, in 2015, this Act was overturned, in light of vast and rapid changes in the public attitudes toward marriage rights for members of the lesbian, gay, bisexual, transgender or queer (LGBTQ) population. Society, then, must adapt to these social shifts, and institute new laws, institutions, and policies to accommodate broad institutional changes.

Process-person-context-time (PPCT) model One of Bronfenbrenner's enduring concerns has been with creating a theory and method dynamic enough to analyze individuals and families as they interact with their multiple intersecting environments – the **process-person-context-time model**. The PPCT model is the result of many decades of work in trying to specify the most comprehensive way of studying human development in an environmental context. Bronfenbrenner and colleagues identified and critiqued the **social address model** as the most simplistic way of understanding human and family development. "Social address" means that we look at only one influence from a person's environment. An example of the social address model is reducing the complexity of life to whether a child lives in a rural versus an urban environment. The social address model only captures one environmental label, with no attention to "what the environment is like, what people are living there, what they are doing, or how the activities taking place could affect the child" (Bronfenbrenner, 1986, p. 724).

To advance beyond the social address model, Bronfenbrenner and colleagues proposed a more rigorous model for understanding the dynamic and comprehensive nature of human development. The PPCT model is based on the premise that all persons in a family respond differently to outside environmental influences. It is important to take into account the various spheres of influence: (a) the context in which development is taking place, (b) the personal characteristics of the individuals present in that context, and (c) the process through which their development is elicited. Further, the interaction among at least two of these spheres must be considered (e.g., the person-context, the process-context) as well as the influence of past and present time.

Box 10.2 Family Ecological Theory in Pop Culture: *Divergent*

A scene from *Divergent*, 2014, dir. Neil Burger, Lionsgate Films

Divergent is the first novel of a trilogy by Veronica Roth, and was adapted as a film in 2014. In the story, we can see evidence of family ecological theory throughout many of the main characters' lives. The story is set in post-apocalyptic Chicago, where individuals are divided into five "factions" based on their psychological dispositions: Abnegation (for the selfless), Amity (for the peaceful), Candor (for the honest), Dauntless (for the brave), and Erudite (for the intellectual). When society members turn 16 years old, they are psychologically tested in order to determine what faction they are best suited for. This process of dividing people by their individual attributes into factions of similar-minded people is a prime example of family ecological theory's micro-level systems. Each faction's immediate peers, families, and day-to-day lives are impacted by an individual's aptitude for fitting into that particular group. The overarching culture of the society is such that the aptitude test determines to which faction children will go after they turn 16; individuals rarely deviate from this norm. This pressure to "go where you are best suited" is a part of the macro-level system, or the cultural ideologies and expectations for all societal members. This becomes evident when Tris, one of the main characters, gets inconclusive results on her aptitude test. Her parents expect her to select Abnegation (where she was raised), but she chooses Dauntless, which is arguably the polar opposite of her home faction.

The majority of the film is set within the Dauntless faction, where the two main characters, Four and Tris, develop a close relationship as Tris goes through the initiation process. Viewers learn that Four's background – particularly the physical and verbal abuse he suffered at the hand of his father – plays a huge role in his connections between his micro- and exosystems. He has four fears he cannot overcome, which is why he earned the nickname "Four." Throughout the film, viewers see how these fears and his microsystems affect his interactions with the exosystem, or his place as a leader within Dauntless, as well as his attitudes toward the overarching social structure. Tris goes through similar struggles, as she witnesses her mother's murder during an uprising toward the end of the film. Throughout the rest of the film and subsequent novels, Tris's loss of her mother as well as the loss of her brother to Erudite, situate her on a pathway to actively try to change not only the exosystem (the factions), but also the cultural ideologies which present factions as the only way for a society to function.

Evaluating Family Ecological Theory

Strengths of family ecological theory

Like all of the theories we describe in this book, family ecological theory has both strengths and weaknesses. The strengths include the wide popularity and utility of this comprehensive theory of individual development in the context of family and society.

Comprehensive view of individuals, families, communities, and societies Family ecological theory is one of the most comprehensive in use today because it weds the genetic and psychological development of the individual with the ever widening social environments to which the individual must adapt. This theory also takes family into account as a set of relationships *and* also as a social institution, which enhances the original understanding of children as being influenced by biology and psychology. Although many family theories examine the individual, relational, and societal levels of influence on families (e.g., family developmental in Chapter 5 and life course in Chapter 9), family ecological theory is very useful in zeroing in on how the microsystem and the macrosystem interact via the mesosystem. The mesosystem describes the processes that operate between two or more of the person's behavior systems in mediating the biological, familial, and social. This comprehensive view gets at the mechanisms of how individuals and families function and change, and allows us to analyze how the biological, familial, and social aspects of a person's life are always interacting.

Addresses the nature versus nurture question One of the greatest contributions of family ecological theory is that it links the genetic heritage of individuals with multiple social and cultural environmental contexts. In doing so, it reveals that biology (nature) *and* environment (nurture) are both important, and that nature/nurture is not an either/or question. This theory says that it is the interaction of nature and nurture that influences an individual's life, and the interaction between the individual and the family is especially important in the process of how humans develop and the circumstances of their lives.

Highly applicable to practice Family ecological theory is very useful across multiple health and social services practices. This theory is especially useful for researchers and educators who want to translate theory into practice in order to work with and improve the lives of clients. For example, Bronfenbrenner originally developed this theory in order to address the need for enhancing formal and informal support for children at risk for educational delays, as in the Head Start program. In another example, Ann Hartman (1979), a family therapist and social worker, adapted ecological theory for use with clients in family therapy. She developed the concept of the ecomap, which works similarly to the genogram that we described in Chapter 6 (family systems theory). The ecomap consists of the family unit in the center circle, with outer circles connected by various types of solid or dotted lines. Each line represents the energy flow to and from the client's micro to macro contexts. In a third example, Karimi, Jarrott, and O'Hora (2014) utilized an ecological approach to address the therapeutic value of intergenerational relationships between older adults and youth who are not related to one another. Later in this chapter, we discuss a fourth example of how family ecological theory has been applied to working with children who have a disability and their families.

Weaknesses of family ecological theory

Despite its strengths, family ecological theory is not without its weaknesses. As we have found in most of the family theories, some of its strengths also reflect its weaknesses. For example, the adaptability of family ecological theory to multiple fields of study can also be viewed as a weakness, as well as other ideas we describe next.

Difficulty of translating such a comprehensive theory into experimental research A theory with such wide appeal and applicability to many different contexts remains difficult to translate into empirical research. Indeed, Bronfenbrenner and Ceci (1993) set out to develop propositions, hypotheses, and experimental methods that would address this issue of advancing the science of ecological theory by testing it quantitatively. They sought to go beyond the typical question asked in ecological theory of "how much do heredity and environment contribute to development," which is only descriptive, and thus to expand it to a question that allows the study of process, such as "How do they contribute? What are the proximal mechanisms through which genotypes are transformed into phenotypes?" (Bronfenbrenner and Ceci, 1993, p. 313).

The experimental approach, with its benefit of predicting behavior rather than reflecting on the outcomes post hoc (White, Klein, and Martin, 2015), has been slow to develop, despite recent scientific progress in fields of behavioral genetics and human development (Bronfenbrenner and Ceci, 1993). Thus, it is difficult to implement the conceptual benefits of the interaction among the multiple environments that impact individual and family lives. In their analysis of theories of child maltreatment, Del Vecchio, Erlanger, and Slep (2013) stated that although ecological theory has been popular for many years, it remains limited because researchers have not found many ways to test hypotheses derived from the theory as a whole. Family ecological theory is a good example of how challenging it is to merge multiple fields and so many broad concepts into a theoretical whole.

Too much focus on the developing child rather than the family A major critique of ecological theory, in general, is that its focus is primarily on the developing child at the individual level, while the focus on the *family* lags behind. This is, in part, because of the difficulty of studying families as more than just a singular unit, without attention to all of the variability that comes from studying the interaction among family members. This is a unit of analysis problem: when the model was developed with the individual child in the center of analysis, the ability to deal with the intersecting lives of family members was compromised. Perhaps other theories, such as family developmental theory (Chapter 5) and life course theory (Chapter 9) do a better job of moving beyond the child in handling multiple family members at various family stages.

Inattention to the social inequalities of race and gender systems The ecological model, as proposed by Bronfenbrenner (1979) and advanced within many disciplines, addresses the individual's connections to the economic system, because it was originally developed to address the inadequacies of education, health, and housing for children and their families that accompany poverty. Yet, the theory does not identify racism and sexism as matters that also affect individual and family life (Uttal, 2009). In other words, merely addressing social class issues does not get at the intersectionality that structures all life chances. We need to look to both conflict theory (Chapter 3) and feminist theory (Chapter 8) in order to address the intersections of race, class, gender, sexual orientation, age, and other systems of social stratification.

An alternative theory app: conflict theory

In this chapter, we have laid out the key concepts, origins, modern applications, and strengths and weaknesses of family ecological theory. As you have learned, family ecological theory addresses the complexities associated with both individual-level and cultural-level forces that affect families. As we pointed out above, it is useful to consider how conflict theory (Chapter 3) can pick up where family ecological theory leaves off.

Conflict theory assesses the ways in which access to power and conflict over resources affect family dynamics. Think back to the inequality track described in Chapter 3; how would family ecological theory explain the complexities associated with each lane, including the barriers, advantages, and unequal access to resources that exist for each competitor? Conflict theory allows researchers to examine the sometimes invisible privileges that situate some families onto very different trajectories than other families. Conflict theory directly examines access to wealth and social capital that can cushion the blow of job loss or a failed investment. Other families that do not have access to invisible privileges not only lack those buffers, but they also could face additional stressors, such as discrimination based on race, ethnicity, or sexual orientation. Conflict theory better addresses these struggles by zeroing in on how conflict over resources affects families on both a micro- and a macro-level.

Working with Family Ecological Theory: Integrating Research and Practice

Now that we have described family ecological theory, we turn to how the theory can be used in theory, research, and practice. We provide an example of current theorizing, analyze an empirical study that was guided by family ecological theory, and describe how the theory informs the practice of violence prevention.

Family ecological theory today

Focusing on a cultural perspective of ecological theory, Garcia Coll and colleagues (1996) developed a model to understand identity formation among monoethnic minority youth (that is, those whose parents are both from the same ethnic background). Melinda Gonzales-Backen (2013) expanded the model to ethnic identity formation among biethnic adolescents. The cultural ecological model has commonalities with theoretical perspectives we note in family stress and resilience theory (Chapter 11), regarding Meyer's (2003) minority stress theory and its applications to LGBTQ individuals and families, and Peters and Massey's (1983) theory of double socialization for Black children. These perspectives have shed light on how families that experience some marginalization and discrimination must prepare their children for both challenges and successes. Gonzales-Backen's theory, then, is another attempt to guide scholars in understanding even more complex identity formations. Biethnic youth have parents from different ethnic backgrounds, typically where one parent is a member of the White ethnic majority, and the other parent is a member of an ethnic minority (e.g., Asian American, Latino, African American, and others).

In her theoretical expansion, Gonzales-Backen (2013) based her ideas on the rapidly increasing size of the biethnic population, in the US and internationally. For example, in the US Census of 2010, 8 million people identified as being from more than one race, compared to the 5 million people who did so in the 2000 Census. The author takes into account the ecological nests of individual development in multicultural family contexts and the interactions with the broader social contexts and climates of ethnicity, peer influence, racism, and the like.

As we are seeing in many family theories, scholars must be cognizant of the fact that our society is increasingly multiethnic, multiracial, and multicultural, yet few family theories are equipped to deal with such complexity. Although, as Uttal (2009) pointed out, one of the weaknesses of the original ecological theory is that it did not take an intersectional approach, now we are seeing a change in how society is increasingly recognizing and accepting the diversity of individuals and families. For example, it is no longer accurate to speak exclusively in the binaries of Black/White, male/female, gay/straight, rich/poor. As we point out in regard to feminist theory (Chapter 8), we must account for difference and intersectionality. The Gonzales-Backen (2013) study offers a way into this diversity by understanding the genetic and social-environmental factors associated with mixed racial and ethnic experiences. In this way, scholars are beginning to refine and update ecological theory in light of current thinking about unique individual experiences, both within and outside their families.

Gonzales-Backen (2013) theorizes how several cultural ecological concepts can be extended to examine issues faced by biethnic youth. These concepts include social position; discrimination; segregation; promoting/inhibiting environments; child characteristics (e.g., physical appearance and child's cognitive development); and the family context (e.g., familial ethnic socialization and parent–adolescent relationship quality). Let's consider how the first concept, social position, can be used to expand family ecological theory to consider biracial identity. Social position refers to the impact of having one ethnic minority and one ethnic majority parent on a child's ethnic identity development, where the individual belongs to two different kinds of groups: one with a marginalized status and the other with greater social power. Their mixed social positions are reduced, however, to a monoethnic identity, as explained by the one-drop rule. US society has a history of reducing individuals with any ethnic or racial minority background, regardless of White heritage, to being non-White, and thus biracial or biethnic individuals are often forced to ignore their other racial identity and heritage (Root, 1999). Living in a society that is still "not there yet" in terms of recognizing mixed heritages (in ecological terms, it is the most distal, or far-reaching, factor) can make accepting and integrating their biethnic backgrounds into their identity more difficult. Thus, the expansion of an ecological framework is helpful to scholars to gain a more complete look at the processes associated with diversity in adolescent identity formation.

Family ecological theory in research

It is clear that family ecological theory is very useful across many fields of study. Physical therapists and other allied health professionals have applied the theory to their understanding of families of children with disabilities. By doing so, they have been able to go beyond the individualistic, social address level (e.g., the child with a disability) to account for the multiple systems that interact across the biological-ecological spectrum. In an example of research utilizing family ecological theory, Alyssa Fiss and colleagues (2014) studied the parents of young children from diverse backgrounds who had cerebral palsy (CP) and whose average age was 3.7 years. Typically, children with CP have only been studied at the level of their individual functioning or in the context of the kind of therapy and services they require from professionals. Hypothesizing that the family environment is also highly influential for the child's physical, cognitive, and emotional development, Fiss and her colleagues created a multidisciplinary research and educational program, Move & PLAY, associated with the Centre for Childhood Disability Research at McMaster University in Canada (CanChild, 2016).

Fiss et al. (2014) surveyed 398 parents (mostly mothers) from Canada and the US using four measures related to the family as an ecological system. The first measure was the Family Environment Scale (FES). The FES was developed by Moos and Moos (2009) and is widely used in studies of family processes. Researchers use it to measure three dimensions of family functioning: (a) relationships (including the dimensions of cohesion, expressiveness, and conflict); (b) personal growth (including the dimensions of independence, achievement orientation, intellectual/cultural orientation, active/recreational orientation, and moral/religious emphasis); and (c) system maintenance (including the dimensions of organization and control). The second measure, the Family Expectations of Child (FEC), includes five items that parents report regarding their expectations for their child: (a) to do the best that they can, (b) assist in taking care of themselves; (c) try everything; (d) do activities recommended by their child's therapists; and (e) do all regular activities. The third measure was the Family Support to Child (FSC), which measured the kinds of supports families give to their child to enhance their growth: (a) encouraging independence; (b) encouraging risk taking; (c) offering encouragement and recognizing accomplishments; (d) engaging in enjoyable and energetic physical play; (e) involving many people who regularly interact with the child in therapy activities throughout the day; and (f) responding positively to the child's interests. The fourth measure was the Family Support Scale (FSS), and it assessed parents' "perceptions of the helpfulness of the people and groups who are often helpful to parents raising a young child with a disability" (Fiss et al., 2014, p. 565). Drawing from family ecological theory, the FSS provides a parent's view of support from family members, friends, coworkers, members of the community, and service providers.

In addition to the family level scales, the researchers utilized the Gross Motor Function Classification System (GMFCS) to assess the range of physical functioning of children with CP. This measure classifies gross motor function on five levels, based on the child's abilities in sitting, transfers, walking, need for caregiver assistance, and need for assistive devices such as wheelchairs (Fiss et al., 2014, p. 565). In Level I, children with CP had the highest levels of motor functioning, whereas children in Level V needed the most support as they had the least amount of physical functioning.

The findings of this study showed the importance of taking this perspective, because in doing so, family strengths and high expectations for their child, and their positive influence on their child's development and functioning, could be examined. This is an improvement over simply looking at children's disabilities and self-mobility limitations. Finally, having extended family members and friends who supported the parents helped to improve parental satisfaction and emotional well-being. The authors provided practical suggestions for physical therapists and other health care professionals regarding the importance of looking at family strengths and the need to invite families to talk about the people in their wider kinship and friendship circles who support them and their children in daily life.

Family ecological theory in practice

There are several areas where family ecological theory can be applied in practice; in fact, this theoretical perspective may be one of the most versatile when it comes to its application across disciplines. Below, we elaborate on how this model can be used to understand issues surrounding public health in neighborhoods and communities.

Public health policymakers, researchers, and practitioners remain interested in ways to promote healthy, active living in communities. In the 1990s, public health professionals began to reconceptualize these goals with a broader scope. Instead of focusing attention on invoking change only at the individual or family level, public health officials began to focus on social and physical environments and public policies in order to achieve population change. This approach not only considers the multiple levels where healthy, active living can be promoted, but it also includes a call for a transdisciplinary approach which brings in experts from across disciplines to combine concepts and methods to provide a more inclusive model of change (Sallis et al., 2006).

At the heart of these models of public and community health is the family microsystem. Families are vital to the process of creating active living communities, because family members can both model and support healthy beliefs and behaviors. Of course, factors external to the family such as the safety of the surrounding neighborhood and access to reliable walking, biking trails, and park systems are important to creating change as well. Remember that it is the mesosystem that connects the microsystem (family) to the exo- and macrosystems. According to family ecological theory, if family members have access to safe spaces for active living, and healthy choices are readily available (e.g., farmers' markets, community gardens), they are more likely to model healthy, active behavior to their family members because the opportunities exist to actually enact such changes. Even in extremely harsh conditions (e.g., refugee camps), children can receive support and gain hope through programs that encourage their engagement with healthy activities such as the arts (Yohani, 2008).

Another interesting way to think about how culture directly impacts our attitudes about healthy activity is to consider the cultural phenomenon of the very popular 5K race, where individuals run for 5 kilometers. Have you ever participated in a 5K race, a "fun run," or an obstacle course? Did your parents run in these types of races when you were growing up? Chances are, they did not; since 1990, the number of participants in 5K races has increased threefold, from around 5 million to over 15 million (Running USA, 2013). The cultural ideal of being active and healthy emerges from the macrosystem, which clearly has adapted over time to the point that we now are more interested in running for leisure and recreation than we were even 20 years ago. If the culture adopts a new "normal," and the opportunities are available (financially or otherwise) for families to choose to live a healthy, active lifestyle, they may be likely to do it.

Another example of how the family ecological model applies to public and community health is the 5-2-1-0 health campaign. The 5-2-1-0 message promotes five servings of fruits and vegetables a day, two hours of screen time, one hour of physical activity, and no sugary drinks. This messaging has primarily been directed toward children and schools with the ultimate goal of infiltrating families' food choices and monitoring children's activities. Distributed as part of a "childhood obesity prevention program" through schools, health care providers, and day care centers, these messages are ideally communicated from the exosystemic level to the family microsystem level. Public health professionals are increasingly tuned in to the effectiveness of the ecological model of promoting change via multiple levels (Sallis et al., 2006). Again, translating family ecological theory into practice requires examining each level of the "wedding cake" and understanding that only looking at just one level, or only one solution, is shortsighted.

Conclusion

Since its origination in the field of home economics and its elaboration in the field of developmental psychology, family ecological theory continues to evolve. Now, it is one of the primary theories used to guide research in the family, social, behavioral, and health sciences. Indeed, the Centers for Disease Control (CDC, 2015) provides a social-ecological model as a framework for prevention of violence. This ecological model was developed by researchers associated with the World Health Organization and is applied to violence occurrence and prevention around the globe.

Family ecological theory, like family developmental theory (Chapter 5), offers a rich metaphor for understanding the complex interconnections among the ever widening layers of the individual, family, community, and society, over time. Yet there are still many challenges, as in most theories, for expanding upon this theoretical foundation in order to investigate how these multiple layers influence one another. Given the track record of scholars and practitioners to date, we have every confidence that this theory will continue to have a strong influence in studying and helping diverse families. Now, let's consider how family ecological theory is applicable to the study of families across the globe. In Box 10.3, we present information from three very different countries regarding their ages of compulsory education. Each country has its own macrosystem, which contributes to the laws and norms that govern expectations for educating children.

Box 10.3 Global Comparisons of Family–School Interface: Ages of Compulsory Education

Most countries require some kind of education for children; however, the ages of compulsory, or required, education varies significantly between countries (UNESCO, 2009, table 2, pp. 74–82). This affects the relationship between families (the microsystem) and the educational system (the exosystem). In Singapore, for instance, children with special needs are excluded from compulsory education. In other countries (e.g., the US), parents are allowed to home-school their children. Imagine how these requirements – undoubtedly a part of the macrosystem that includes the value societies place on education and the norms associated with it – affect both the social institutions of education as well as families in society. Here, we describe various national policies regarding compulsory education to illustrate how each of the systems in family ecological theory might be affected, depending on the broader context.

Spain Children in Spain are required to attend school from ages 6 to 16. The school day lasts from 9 a.m. to noon, then 3 p.m. to 5 p.m. The midday siesta (an afternoon rest or nap) is typical in Spanish culture. Schools care for children younger than age 12 during the siesta. There is no siesta break for secondary students.

Germany Children in Germany attend elementary school, and after fourth grade, they enter one of three "tracks": (a) Hauptschule (similar to a vocational school) generally attracts students with average grades or below, and goes to grade 9; (b) Realschule (has strict entrance requirements; all students learn one foreign language and choose between extended education in technology, home economics, and a second foreign language) and goes to grade 10; (c) Gymnasium (students learn classical language, modern language, mathematics, and natural science), which lasts until grades 12 or 13 and ends with a qualifying examination for admission to the university. One other option is for children to attend Gesamtschule, which is only found in some states in Germany, has no entrance requirements and goes to grade 10. This school is comprehensive and includes students from all backgrounds. In terms of prestige, the "best" students complete Gymnasium, followed by Realschule and Hauptschule.

India Children in India are required to attend school from ages 6 to 14. India also has a large private school system, where approximately a third of students receive their education (Joshua, 2014). Since India has been separated by a caste system of prestige and status, some affirmative action policies have secured spots in the school system for historically disadvantaged groups.

Multimedia Suggestions

www.acf.hhs.gov/programs/ohs

This is the official website of the Office of Head Start, funded through the Administration for Children and Families of the US Department of Health and Human Services. Head Start was established in 1965 as part of President Lyndon Johnson's War on Poverty campaign. The aim of this program was to provide comprehensive community-based child development services and education for disadvantaged preschool children. Among the many innovative features of Head Start was that from the beginning, it has included bilingual and bicultural programs. The official Head Start website provides continuously updated information for parents and teachers, technical assistance to Head Start centers, implications for policies, and governmental funding opportunities. Their motto is "Head Start: Educating kids, empowering families, changing communities." Clearly, Head Start is grounded in a family ecological perspective.

Activate your theory app: What other theories of family could we use to apply to the Head Start program? Choose at least two other theories from this text and see if other theories "fit" this program and the families it serves.

http://www.ajol.info/index.php/jfecs

The *Journal of Family Ecology and Consumer Sciences* is the official publication of the South African Association of Family Ecology and Consumer Sciences (SAAFECS). The journal publishes scholarly papers, in both English and Afrikaans, related to the natural and built environment for individuals and families across the life cycle, including individual, social, and economic resources in small and large households and in the community. Also addressed are consumer behavior and professional practice, particularly in economic and educational settings. Recent articles include "Female Muslim students' dress practices in a South African campus context" and "Coping strategies of households in the Timane community of Idutywa, Eastern Cape, South Africa."

Activate your theory app: Browse any of the recent articles and look for both implicit and explicit applications of family ecological theory.

Winter's Bone (2010)

This film won actress Jennifer Lawrence her first Oscar and Golden Globe nominations. She stars as Ree Dolly, a 17-year-old girl from an impoverished family living in the Ozark Mountains in Arkansas. After her father's disappearance, she is left to care for her two younger siblings, Sonny and Ashlee, and deal with the looming threat of being evicted from their home. As she tries to track down her father, she encounters brutality at the hands of her extended family, the effects of methamphetamine use and distribution on her family and community, and the local crime boss who threatens to take her home away. This is a gritty story of the interactions among an individual, her nuclear family and extended kin, the impoverished rural community in which she lives, and the macrosystem that condones violence, brutality, drug abuse, and hardship for the poor. Yet, above it all, Ree is a survivor; she is determined and committed to caring for her siblings by providing stability to their lives.

A scene from *Winter's Bone*, 2010, dir. Debra Granik, Roadside Attractions

Activate your theory app: How does the main character in this film access exosystems to bring stability to her family?

Game of Thrones (2011–present)

This HBO television series is based on three storylines from *A Song of Ice and Fire* by George R. R. Martin. The show is fantasy-based, and the setting for the series is thousands of years ago. It features the violent struggle between the realm's noble families for control of the Iron Throne. One of the most important themes early in the series is the motto of the Stark family: "Winter is coming." This phrase is both literal and metaphorical. The literal meaning of the phrase refers to the winter season, which lasts for years and is extremely harsh, so the phrase is one of warning. The metaphorical meaning foreshadows the dark period that falls upon the Stark family as they are torn between the family's duty to serve the king, protecting their own, and doing what is right. There are layers upon layers involved in the storyline of both the television show and the books, and family ecological theory can be applied to almost any aspect of this story.

A scene from *Game of Thrones*, 2011, cr. David Benioff and D. B. Weiss, HBO

Activate your theory app: What examples of the different levels of family ecological theory can you find in this series? How does the early storyline in the series differ from the later storylines? Do the systems and levels change as the storyline changes?

Further Reading

Bronfenbrenner, U., and Weiss, H., "Beyond polices without people: An ecological perspective on child and family policy," in E. F. Zigler, S. L. Kagan, and E. Klugman (eds), *Children, families, and government* (New York: Cambridge University Press, 1983), pp. 393–414. This important paper about Urie Bronfenbrenner's research with 276 families, each with a preschool child, in Syracuse, New York describes the ways in which environmental stresses and supports associated with mass societal changes have impacted children's lives and public policies. In this article, the authors offer two environmental principles of development, both of which undergirded Bronfenbrenner's emerging ecological paradigm. Proposition 1 states that for a child to develop well, he or she needs the enduring involvement of one or more adults in their care. In other words, "somebody has to be crazy about that kid," meaning that "someone has to *be there,* and to be *doing something* – not alone, but together *with* the child" (p. 398). Proposition 2 is that public policies and practices must provide "Opportunity, status, resources, encouragement, stability, example, and above all, time for parenthood ... both within and outside the home" (p. 398). Though seemingly self-evident, this advice is even more relevant today, as the nature of parenting and family life continues to change dramatically, and the amount of public support for disadvantaged children and families continues to shrink.

Garbarino, J., *See Jane hit: Why girls are growing more violent and what we can do about it* (New York: Penguin, 2007). This book, about the increasing incidence of physical aggression among girls, is one of many by James Garbarino, a renowned scholar of the social ecology of child and adolescent development. Garbarino received his doctorate from Cornell University, working with his advisor and mentor, Urie Bronfenbrenner. He has studied issues of violence and trauma in children's lives and is also the author of *Lost boys: Why our sons turn violent and how we can save them* (1999). In *See Jane hit,* he explains that girls are just as likely as boys to "get physical," by participating in physically demanding activities such as martial arts and competitive sports. Garbarino says that girls are moving away from the cultural dictate that "girls don't hit" and embracing the new cultural dictate, that "girls kick ass." Female aggression is increasingly portrayed in movies, books, and television as heroic, competitive, and even violent, such as the time when Ree Dolly's female kin brutally beat her, in the movie *Winter's Bone*, described above. Examples of aggressive females include the confident and heroic female character, Hermione, who punched Malfoy in the movie *Harry Potter and the Prisoner of Azkaban*, to the deceitful and cruel teens in the film *Mean Girls* who play a vicious game of lacrosse.

Rosenfeld, L. B., Caye, J. S., Mooli, L., and Gurwitch, R. H., *When their worlds fall apart: Helping families and children manage the effects of disasters*, 2nd edn (Washington, DC: NASW Press, 2004). This book offers multiple perspectives on the real world of natural and technological disasters as well as the trauma of terrorist acts suffered by children, families, and communities. Many theories are integrated with an ecological approach, including cognitive and behavioral, developmental, resiliency, and family systems theories. The book is written primarily from the perspective of the social work profession, but is applicable to other helping professionals, including teachers, nurses, doctors, and mental health practitioners.

Samuels, G. M., "'Being raised by White people': Navigating racial difference among adopted multiracial adults," *Journal of Marriage and Family, 71* (2009), 80–94 (doi:10.1111/j.1741-3737.2008.00581.x). This article addresses the normative ecological context of racial discrimination in which children of color develop. When a child of mixed race is adopted, the child must be socialized from both the perspective of their adoptive family and the perspective of their own racial backgrounds. Navigating racial differences is a growing issue, because multiracial children comprise a dominant (though hidden) group of transracially adopted children in the United Kingdom and the US. One of the major experiences transracially adopted children must deal with is constantly being asked questions such as "Who are you? and "Is that your mother?" In this qualitative interview study of 22 young adults with Black and White heritage, who were adopted as infants by White families, Samuels found that they often dealt with difficult issues such as their parents endorsing colorblindness and thus not preparing them for the racism they would face as children of color. This made it difficult for them to manage societal perceptions of multiracial adoption and the reinforcement of difference in being both adopted and of "mixed" race. The participants and the author emphasize the importance of families building connections with the members of the broader community of those who share their racial heritage, as a way to "experience their multiracial family systems and heritages as both unique and shared" (p. 93).

Song, J., Mailick, M. R., and Greenberg, J. S., "Work and health of parents of adult children with serious mental illness," *Family Relations, 63* (2014), 122–134 (doi:10.1111/fare.12043). This article deals with the mesosystemic context of the interface between several family microsystems. The authors are researchers at the University of Wisconsin-Madison's Waisman Center, which is "dedicated to the advancement of knowledge about human development, developmental disabilities, and neurodegenerative diseases" (www.waisman.wisc.edu). In this paper, they focus on the negative spillover from work to family and how it affects the health of mothers and fathers who have adult children with a serious mental illness (SMI). They found that work stress and the lack of work schedule flexibility could lead to greater work–family conflict. They suggest that practitioners should offer parents psychoeducation about the nature of their child's illness and ways to cope with and manage their stress over their child's behavior problems and need for assistance. At the level of public policy, they suggest the need for flexibility over one's time at work, particularly for parents of a dependent adult child with SMI.

Questions for Students

Discussion Questions

1 What is the main difference between Bronfenbrenner's ecology of human development model and Bubolz and Sontag's human ecology model?
2 Compare and contrast family ecological theory with life course theory (Chapter 9). How do these two theories address human development, families, time, and social context?
3 Now that you have read about ecological theory, how do you understand the "nature–nurture" debate about how humans develop and are socialized?
4 In addition to biethnic identity formation, what are other important individual and family contexts to which family ecological theory can be adapted?
5 Investigate other applications of ecological theory. How is this theory applied in disciplines such as biology and earth science?
6 Choose another theory described in this book, and show how it complements family ecological theory. Describe how these two theories can work together to explain a wider range of family behavior and process.

Your Turn!

Bogenschneider (1996) describes a promising new approach, ecological risk/protective theory, to propose a more supportive model for creating prevention programs and public policies to help youth at risk for substance abuse, dropping out of school, criminal behavior, and early unprotected sexual activity. Take this model and apply it to another population often at risk, such as victims of elder abuse, or veterans returning from war. How can you use the components of risk and protective factors at each of the ecological levels to promote more positive prevention programs and policies to support the population you choose?

Personal Reflection Questions

1 Thinking about your life today in relation to family ecological theory, describe events and relationships in your life that are reflected in the interrelated layers of micro-, meso-, macro-, exo-, and chronosystems.
2 If you plan to enter into an educational or health related career, how do you think you can apply an ecological perspective to your work?
3 How do the values expressed in your family reflect those values held by the various groups with whom you identify (e.g., religious, economic, ethnic, and the like)?
4 What do you believe about the relative importance of the individual, family, or social environment in terms of a person's ability to succeed and thrive in the world?
5 Draw your own ecomap by placing yourself and your family in the center circle. Now draw the outer circles and assess the energy flows among all the parts of your ecological family system.
6 Think about your own "digital ecologies." Read the article by Bjork-James (2015) and consider the relationships and communities you have developed online. In which of the ecological layers would you place your online communities? For example, do you position them at the micro-level, macro-level, or both?

References

Barker, R. G. (1968). *Ecological psychology: Concepts and methods for studying the environment of human behavior*. Stanford, CA: Stanford University Press.

Bjork-James, S. (2015). Feminist ethnography in cyberspace: Imagining families in the cloud. *Sex Roles*, *73*, 113–124. doi:10.1007/s11199-015-0507-8.

Bogenschneider, K. (1996). An ecological risk/protective theory for building prevention programs, policies, and community capacity to support youth. *Family Relations*, *45*, 127–138. doi:10.2307/585283.

Bogenschneider, K. (2000). Has family policy come of age? A decade review of the state of U.S. family policy in the

1990s. *Journal of Marriage and the Family*, *62*, 1136–1159. doi:10.1111/j.1741-3737.2000.01136.x.

Bronfenbrenner, U. (1978). Lewinian space and ecological substance. *Journal of Social Issues*, *33*, 199–212. doi:10.1111/j.1540-4560.1977.tb02533.x.

Bronfenbrenner, U. (1979). *The ecology of human development: Experiments by nature and design*. Cambridge, MA: Harvard University Press.

Bronfenbrenner, U. (1986). Ecology of the family as a context for human development: Research perspectives. *Developmental Psychology*, *22*, 723–742. doi:10.1037/0012-1649.22.6.723.

Bronfenbrenner, U. (1988). Interacting systems in human development. Research paradigms: Present and future. In N. Bolger, A. Caspi, G. Downey, Y. M. Moorehouse (eds), *Persons in context: Developmental processes* (pp. 25–49). New York: Cambridge University Press.

Bronfenbrenner, U. (ed.) (2005). *Making human beings human: Bioecological perspectives on human development*. Thousand Oaks, CA: Sage.

Bronfenbrenner, U., and Ceci, S. J. (1993). Heredity, environment and the question "how": A first approximation. In R. Plomin and G. E. McClearn (eds), *Nature, nurture, and psychology* (pp. 313–323). Washington, DC: American Psychological Association.

Bubolz, M. M., and Sontag, M. S. (1993). Human ecology theory. In P. Boss, W. Doherty, R. LaRossa, W. Schumm, and S. Steinmetz (eds), *Sourcebook of family theories and methods: A contextual approach* (pp. 419–448). New York: Plenum.

Bush, K. R., and Peterson, G. W. (2013). Parent–child relationships in diverse contexts. In G. W. Peterson and K. R. Bush (eds), *Handbook of marriage and the family* (3rd edn., pp. 275–302). New York: Springer.

CanChild (2016). Move & PLAY Study (Understanding determinants of motor abilities, self-care, and play of young children with cerebral palsy). CanChild research centre, McMaster University, Hamilton, Ontario. At https://canchild.ca/en/research-in-practice/current-studies/move-play-study-understanding-determinants-of-motor-abilities-self-care-and-play-of-young-children-with-cerebral-palsy.

CDC (Centers for Disease Control and Prevention) (2015). *The social-ecological model: A framework for prevention*. At http://www.cdc.gov/ViolencePrevention/overview/social-ecologicalmodel.html.

Del Vecchio, T., Erlanger, A. C., and Slep, A. M. S. (2013). Theories of child abuse. In M. A. Fine and F. D. Fincham (eds), *Handbook of family theories: A content-based approach* (pp. 208–227). New York: Routledge.

Elder, G. H., Jr. (1974). *Children of the Great Depression: Social change in life experience*. Chicago: University of Chicago Press.

Faust, V., Jasper, C. R., Kaufman, A., and Nellis, M. J. (2014). Cooperative inquiry in human ecology: Historical roots and future applications. *Family and Consumer Sciences Research Journal*, *42*, 267–277. doi:10.1111/fcsr.12060.

Fiss, A. L., Chiarello, L. A., Bartlett, D., Palisano, R. J., Jeffries, L., Almasri, N., and Chang, H.-J. (2014). Family ecology of young children with cerebral palsy. *Child: Care, Health and Development*, *40*, 562–571. doi:10.1111/cch.12062.

Garcia Coll, C., Lamberty, G., Jenkins, R., McAdoo, H. P., Crnic, K., Wasik, B. H., and Garcia, H. V. (1996). An integrative model for the study of developmental competences in minority children. *Child Development*, *67*, 1891–1914. doi:10.2307/1131600.

Goldberg, A. E., Smith, J. Z., and Kashy, D. A. (2010). Preadoptive factors predicting lesbian, gay, and heterosexual couples' relationship quality across the transition to adoptive parenthood. *Journal of Family Psychology*, *24*, 221–232. doi:10.1037/a0019615.

Gonzales-Backen, M. A. (2013). An application of ecological theory to ethnic identity formation among biethnic adolescents. *Family Relations*, *62*, 92–108. doi:10.1111/j.1741-3729.2012.00749.x.

Hartman, A. (1979). *Finding families: An ecological approach to family assessment in adoption*. Beverly Hills, CA: Sage

Head Start (2016). Office of Head Start: An Office of the Administration for Children and Families. At www.acf.hhs.gov/programs/ohs.

Hook, N., and Paolucci, B. (1970). The family as an ecosystem. *Journal of Home Economics*, *62*, 315–318.

Joshua, A. (2014, January 16). Over a quarter of enrolments in rural India are in private schools. *The Hindu*. At www.thehindu.com/features/education/school/over-a-quarter-of-enrolments-in-rural-india-are-in-private-schools/article5580441.ece.

Karimi, H., Jarrott, S. E., and O'Hora, K. (2014). Therapists working in new *and* old ways: An integrative ecological framework for non-familial intergenerational relationships. *Australian and New Zealand Journal of Family Therapy*, *35*, 207–222. doi:10.1002/anzf.1061.

McAdoo, H. P. (1993). The social cultural contexts of ecological developmental family models. In P. Boss, W. Doherty, R. LaRossa, W. Schumm, and S. Steinmetz (eds), *Sourcebook of family theories and methods: A contextual approach* (pp. 298–301). New York: Plenum.

McAdoo, H. P. (ed.) (1999). *Family ethnicity: Strength in diversity* (2nd edn). Thousand Oaks, CA: Sage.

McAdoo, H. P., Martinez, E. A., and Hughes, H. (2005). Ecological changes in ethnic families of color. In V. Bengtson, A. Acock, K. Allen, P. Dilworth-Anderson, and D. Klein (eds), *Sourcebook of family theory and research* (pp. 191–212). Thousand Oaks, CA: Sage.

McAdoo, J. L. (1988). The roles of Black fathers in the socialization of Black children. In H. P. McAdoo (ed.), *Black families* (2nd edn). Newbury Park, CA: Sage.

Meyer, I. H. (2003). Prejudice, social stress, and mental health in lesbian, gay, and bisexual populations: Conceptual issues and research evidence. *Psychological Bulletin, 129*, 674–697. doi:10.1037/0033-2909.129.5.674.

Moos, B., and Moos, R. (2009). *Family environment scale: Manual* (4th edn). Menlo Park, CA: Mind Garden. At www.mindgarden.com/family-environment-scale/150-fes-manual.html.

Peters, M. F., and Massey, G. (1983). Mundane extreme environmental stress in family stress theories: The case of Black families in White America. *Marriage and Family Review, 6*(1–2), 193–218. doi:10.1300/J002v06n01_10.

Root, M. P. P. (1999). The biracial baby boom: Understanding ecological constructions of racial identity in the 21st century. In M. H. Sheets (eds), *Racial and ethnic identity in school practices: Aspects of human development* (pp. 67–89). Mahwah, NJ: Erlbaum.

Running USA (2013). *2013 State of the sport: Part III: U.S. race trends.* At http://www.runningusa.org/state-of-sport-2013-part-III.

Sabatelli, R. M., and Ripoll, K. (2004). Variations in marriage over time: An ecological/exchange perspective. In M. Coleman and L. H. Ganong (eds), *Handbook of contemporary families: Considering the past, contemplating the future* (pp. 79–95). Thousand Oaks, CA: Sage.

Sallis, J. F., Cervero, R. B., Ascher, W., Henderson, K. A., Kraft, M. K., and Kerr, J. (2006). An ecological approach to creating active living communities. *Annual Review of Public Health, 27*, 297–322. doi:10.1146/annurev.publhealth.27.021405.102100.

Thompson, P. J. (1988). *Home economics and feminism: The Hestian synthesis*. Charlottetown, Prince Edward Island, Canada: UPEI Publishing Collective.

UNESCO (2009). *Global education digest 2009: Comparing education statistics across the world.* UNESCO Institute for Statistics. At http://unesdoc.unesco.org/images/0018/001832/183249e.pdf.

Uttal, L. (2009). (Re) visioning family ties to communities and contexts. In S. A. Lloyd, A. L. Few, and K. R. Allen (eds), *Handbook of feminist family studies* (pp. 134–146). Thousand Oaks, CA: Sage.

White, J. M., Klein, D. M., and Martin, T. F. (2015). *Family theories: An introduction* (4th edn). Thousand Oaks, CA: Sage.

Yohani, S. C. (2008). Creating an ecology of hope: Arts-based interventions with refugee children. *Child and Adolescent Social Work Journal, 25*, 309–323. doi:10.1007/s10560-008-0129-x.

11

Family Stress and Resilience Theory

You may be familiar with the one phone call people who are arrested are allowed once they are taken to jail. Have you ever had to use that one phone call? If not, who *would* you call, if you were ever arrested? Would it be a family member, or someone else? The one answer to this very simple question can tell us so much about how you manage stress and resilience, and by extension, how your family deals with stress and resilience. Think about how your answer to the phone call question relates to your family. If you choose to call a family member, which one would it be? A sibling, an aunt or uncle, or a parent or guardian? Why? Some may choose to avoid calling a parent, for fear of retribution or punishment. Others may automatically default to calling one parent over the other, because their relationship with one is closer than the other. Or, perhaps you have seen your brother go through the same thing, and you remember what happened to him, and how his arrest put the entire family dynamic in jeopardy. Sometimes you think the family never truly recovered from that, and it would be much worse if you were to repeat his same mistakes.

What is also interesting to think about is if you imagine that *you* are the one receiving the phone call. How do you deal with it? Does it matter who the person is on the other end? Would you view it differently if it were your mother, your sibling, your own adult child, or your roommate? How would you react to the stress of being "the one" who was called?

Family stress and resilience theory is actually a combination of several theories that address the fact that all individuals experience vulnerabilities, stressors, and crises that challenge their ability to cope (Boss, 1987). From a family sciences perspective, the family unit itself is a resource that can help us stay healthy and grow even in the face of adversity (Patterson, 2002). This theory builds upon earlier work in family stress theory (ABCX model) by Hill (1958), where *A* is the stressful event, *B* is the family resources or strengths, and *C* is the family's perception of the event, or how they define or attribute meaning to the event. If the event or stressor is such that the family cannot immediately figure out how to solve the problem, this will lead to crisis, the *X* component of the model (McCubbin et al., 1980). The other contributing perspective to family stress and resilience theory as it is used in family studies today is risk and resilience (Demo, Aquilino, and Fine, 2005). This added perspective brings into focus how families react to experiences that can produce negative outcomes (risks), as well as the ability to overcome life challenges and grow stronger (resilience). Taken together, family stress and resilience theory addresses the "whole picture" of how families are prepared for, deal with, and learn from stressful events. To put it into perspective, think about your own family. How well is your family prepared to deal with external stressors? How closely integrated are you, as a family? How adaptable are family members who would be affected by the stressor? Imagine how your family would deal with your arrest, depending on how serious the offense is. Would you need to hire a lawyer, or possibly face a jury trial? Will your family be able to afford such an expense? Perhaps your family relies on shared spiritual beliefs that would provide a source of strength during such an event. Or, would the family's social support network help the family adapt and make itself stronger because of it?

Family Theories: Foundations and Applications, First Edition. Katherine R. Allen and Angela C. Henderson.

As you consider those questions, keep in mind that family stress and resilience theory takes into account the type of stressor (e.g., internal or external), and qualities like family closeness, history, and adaptability. Each of these factors helps to set the stage for interactions that can lead to positive or negative outcomes. Families provide a sense of history and understanding that help them heal, particularly through the use of shared rituals, spirituality, and cultural and ethnic traditions (Walsh, 2007). Each of these factors makes up a family's "repertoire" for coping with problems and crises; they can provide protection against negative outcomes, leading to family resilience. Strong families are a protective factor in the face of adversity and risk. How strong is your own family? What about your friends' families? Below, we provide a case study to help you understand how the theory can apply to very complex, interrelated issues that families face in their daily lives.

Case Study

Eliza's father, Joe, has just lost his driver's license because of repeated driving under the influence (DUI) offenses. Joe was facing a jail sentence, but the family decided to pay a lawyer to get his sentence suspended. The lawyer was very expensive, and the money that went to pay for her father's legal fees was the money earmarked for Eliza's second semester tuition at college. Because of that, Eliza had to take a leave of absence from school and get a job to once again save money for college. Her mother also took on another job to help support the family financially.

Because Joe had lost his license, he could not drive to work, so he ended up losing his job. Fortunately, the 500 hours of community service he was assigned was done at the local library, which was within walking distance. Eliza and her mother sought out support by attending Al-Anon, a self-help organization that provides support and information about living with a family member who has an addiction. One of the issues they worked on in the group was the shame that every member in the family felt about the addict's chronic alcoholism. Over time, the social support provided by this group and the move toward financial stability, along with the social capital Joe built by working at the local library, all helped the family to get back on their feet. Their ability to talk with one another about the father's addiction, his willingness to get help, and the mother's and daughter's willingness to face their own feelings all contributed to the family pulling together. Shame, fear, and anger are strong feelings that can accompany addiction in families; but these feelings often coexist with the sense of hope about how individuals can change and families can restabilize, creating new rituals and positive experiences to help deal with difficulty.

What were some of the stressors Eliza and her family faced? How did they experience stress in relation to their own lives, and in terms of the family as a system? What relationship processes did family members activate in order to help the family as a whole cope with the devastating causes and consequences of a serious and chronic condition such as an addiction? How did Eliza, in particular, balance both risk and resilience in order to accept and act for positive change in the face of such adversity? What does this family's past tell us about their future? Family stress and resilience theory helps us understand the multiplicity of stressors, including how one stress can and often does lead to another, like what happened to Eliza and her family. However, this theory does not stop at just examining how stress affects individuals and families; it also takes a look at the whole picture, examining how families can become more resilient in the face of stressors, which inevitably affects how they deal with similar situations in the future. Conversely, this theory also takes into account how families may ignore or avoid challenges, which may lead to the family or its members never learning how to deal with difficulties. In this sense, family stress and resilience theory provides a unique look at families, allowing us to focus on the past, present, and future within one framework.

What Is Family Stress and Resilience Theory?

Family stress and resilience theory addresses the fact that life is full of risks that threaten both individual and family well-being. As you have learned throughout other chapters, when something happens to one individual, their family members are inevitably affected, and vice versa. Stressors are a natural occurrence in daily life, and as such, they can pile up and intensify. Stressors can also be traumatic, and involve multiple losses, such as those that occur through devastating or catastrophic events. Whatever its origin, family stress disrupts how individuals and families function and adapt over time. However, stress is not the only side of the story; individuals and families also have strengths and are resilient. Resilience is the "capacity to overcome adversity, or to thrive despite challenges or trauma" (Power et al., 2016).

One of the ways that families demonstrate resilience is in their ability to mobilize personal and community resources and thus cope with everyday stress and unanticipated trauma. Indeed, family resilience refers to the fact that families become stronger by coping and learning from whatever life throws their way. Family stress and resilience theory allows family scholars and practitioners to analyze reactions to present stressors by accounting for how the family has dealt with stress in the past, either making the family stronger or perhaps weaker. Each of these factors helps predict how the family will adapt (or not) in the present and even the future. Think back to your "one phone call" – if you considered how your arrest would impinge upon the family, you are taking history into account because you may have an idea of how an event like this was received by your family in the past. Perhaps your family is exceptionally skilled at pretending things do not happen, and brushing difficulties "under the rug," so to speak. This knowledge would inform your decision to call your favorite aunt, who you can trust not to tell your parents and disrupt the family dynamic. Right there, in that moment when you are deciding who to call, we can catch a glimpse of your family's history, how that impacts your present-day decision, and perhaps what you (and your family) will do again in the future. In the words of family therapist Froma Walsh (2012), family stress and resilience theory shows us how family strength is forged (or not) through adversity.

As we will see in this chapter, there is an infinite supply of stressors that impinge on families. In addition to the everyday hassles (Patterson, 2002), such as a flat tire, or an unwanted bird flying around your house, or oversleeping and thus missing a parent–teacher conference at a child's school, some stressors are more unexpected, prolonged, and severe. Examples of more

Box 11.1 At a Glance: Family Stress and Resilience Theory

Family stress An upset in the family system; the pressures placed on a family system due to the interaction of family stressors, resources, and perceptions (ABCX model).

Stressor events Life events that are potentially strong enough to force change in the family system. Stressor events can be classified by type (e.g., from normative to disaster); source (inside or outside the family), and severity (chronic to acute; mild to severe).

Family resilience The pathways, processes, and outcomes associated with family reorganization and growth in the face of significant stress and vulnerability.

Family protective processes The qualities that moderate the relationship between a family's exposure to hardship and risk and their ability to demonstrate competence in accomplishing family functions and stability.

Family coping resources The individual and collective family strengths at the time the stressor event occurs. These are the assets upon which the family can draw in order to respond to the stress or crisis that occurs.

Crisis A time of major disruption and disorganization in a family which may lead to major changes in family structure and process.

Minority stress The uniquely stressful events and crises linked to systems of social stratification that perpetuate disadvantages for racial, sexual, ethnic, and other minority individuals and families.

severe stressors include growing up with a parent who has a mental illness (Power et al., 2016), major disruptions and losses to life and home such as a fire (Jones et al., 2012), the legacy of child physical and sexual abuse on intimate partner violence in adulthood (Flemke, Underwood, and Allen, 2014), and the effects of parental incarceration on child outcomes (Dallaire, 2007). Stressors can also include chronic poverty (Edin and Kissane, 2010), periodic separation from parents due to military deployment (Hill, 1949), and the social stigmas associated with having a minority status (Meyer, 2003; Oswald, 2002; Russell et al., 2014). Severe stressors also include major catastrophes, such as war, terrorism, and natural disasters that can shatter even the most invulnerable families (Walsh, 2007).

History and origins

Family stress and resilience theory began with a question about why some families, when compared to others, are able to make it through a crisis despite going through an event that they perceive as very stressful. That is, how are some families relatively invulnerable to stress, but others unable to cope?

Since its inception, theorists have tried to explain the ways that families marshal their resources to cope with stress. One of the key strategies used has been to join individual level theories, typically developed by psychologists, of resilience in the face of hardship, such as how a child survives and thrives in the face of parental abandonment (Rutter, 1987), with family stress theory, initially developed by sociologists (Hill, 1949 and 1958), in order to come up with a more complex and nuanced perspective on family resilience in the context of adversity. Henry, Morris, and Harrist (2015) describe these developments in terms of waves, with Wave 1 dealing with the origination of family stress theory, and Wave 2 expanding the theory and incorporating time, multiple pile-ups, and the family's sense of meaning and cohesion. Wave 3 is emerging, and further develops the ideas of family resilience that integrate multilevel systems and a multidisciplinary approach. Thus, the combining of family stress theory and family resilience theory has progressed over time into a comprehensive framework that allows us to understand the role of individual members, the family unit as an entity, and various community processes affecting how families deal with everyday and traumatic stressors and crises.

ABCX model A founding father of the field of family studies, Reuben Hill (1949; 1958) originally developed family stress theory to explain family adjustment after a crisis. His original formulation of the theory was based on the "dismemberment of a family through conscription of the husband-father into the armed services" during World War II (Hill, 1958, p. 140). He termed this theory the **ABCX model**, by conceptualizing family stress as a process that consisted of three main variables and a crisis:

a The A factor is the **stressor**, which is the crisis-precipitating event. A stressor becomes a crisis when the family has little or no prior preparation for dealing with it.
b The B factor is the psychosocial **resources** or strengths the family has at the time of the event.
c The C factor is the definition of the event as stressful. This refers to the **meaning of the event** that the family (individually and collectively) attaches to it. This is also referred to as the family's perception of the situation to which they must respond.
d The X factor is the stress or **crisis** that causes the disruption in family dynamics and leads to the family's reorganization.

Pauline Boss (1987) further developed the ABCX model as a way to help therapists and other practitioners intervene in stressful situations and to help researchers measure the ways that families define their perceptions of the crisis situation. Boss combined research on stress from medical, sociological, and psychological research and devised a definition of family stress as "Pressure or tension in the family system – a disturbance in the steady state of the family" (2002, p. 16). The reason for this revision was that a family's definition of a situation (the C factor) is the most important factor in their recovery from stress. And, as Hill (1958) originally noted, no stressor event, or its interpretation, is the same for every family. You probably remember that the "definition of the situation" is also a concept developed first in symbolic interactionist theory (Chapter 4).

A crisis perspective on family stress and adaptation has been likened to a roller coaster (Boss, 1987; Hill 1958). The roller coaster begins with the family being at a particular level of functioning. Then, the stressor occurs, and the family experiences a **period of disorganization**, where their prior ways of coping and interacting with one another are inadequate or blocked. In other words, their usual ways of dealing with family issues no longer apply because those coping mechanisms cannot meet the demands of the new stressor in addition to the other aspects of family life. Third, depending on the family's varying vulnerability to stress, they reverse this process of disorganization, and activate their ability to reorganize, which is referred to as the **period of recovery**. Finally, they reach a new level of **reorganization** that is characterized by the ability, or inability, to develop new ways of interacting with each other and handling stress. One of three levels of organization usually occurs following this process: families can reach a new level of organization that is (a) below the previous level of functioning prior to the stressor event; (b) equal to the previous level of functioning prior to the stressor event; or (c) at a higher level of functioning than prior to the stressor event (Boss, 1987, p. 697). The reorganization level can be an outcome that increases, decreases, or does not affect the family's ability to cope with stress. To help illustrate how this works, Figure 11.1 presents Hill's ABCX model.

Although Hill (1949) originally developed the ABCX model to account for men leaving for war and then reuniting with their families as a major stressor event, there are countless other contexts for which this model applies. For example, in a more recent study of nine wives of Israeli veterans with posttraumatic stress disorder (PTSD), Dekel et al. (2005) used family stress theory to understand how women married to men with a chronic emotional illness stay in their marriages despite living with a husband who is no longer like the one they married. This study extended family stress theory by finding ways in which the women tried to deal with their suffering and that of their husbands. Through therapeutic change they reframed the meaning of the most negative situation in their married life as something positive. One of the major challenges the women faced was that they felt they were losing their own sense of self, as they had to cope with their husbands' ongoing symptoms of trauma. The women lost their personal space because they had to attend to the emotional and physical needs of their husbands. Their own loss included having to deal with the physical presence of their husbands in the face of their husband's psychological absence, what we described in family systems theory (Chapter 6) as the concept of ambiguous loss (Boss, 2006). Further, although the women considered separation and divorce, they defined it as "the impossible path," saying that their husbands threatened suicide if their wives left them. Finally, all of the women found ways to move away from seeing their situations in strictly negative terms; they purposely sought out the positive aspects of their situations, and found ways to view

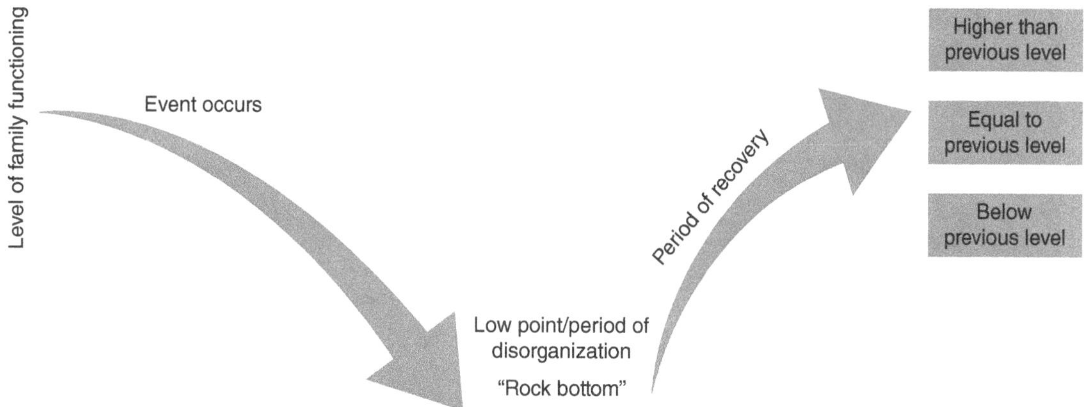

Figure 11.1 Hill's ABCX model

their husbands as strong and empowering, despite the new demands that PTSD placed on the marriage.

Double ABCX model Given the enduring value of the ABCX model, other scholars have offered important additions and revisions. One of the major revisions is the **Double ABCX model**, in which McCubbin and Patterson (1983) devised a way to account for how families deal with multiple stressors over time (see Figure 11.2 for an illustration). The factor of family transformation over time explored in Chapter 5 about family developmental theory helps us to understand the cumulative **pile-up of stressors** and the ability of families to effectively reorganize. The Double ABCX model became a way to address the fact that there can be multiple stressors happening in the life of the family (McCubbin et al., 1980). This addition to the theory is very relevant when we think back to Eliza's experience. Stressors in her life inevitably piled up: (a) her father's legal fees ate up her college savings; (b) he lost his driver's license and thus his job; (c) her mother had to take on an additional job to help pay bills; and (d) her father had to complete 500 hours of community service as a part of his court-mandated arrangement. Therefore, the Double ABCX model attempts to account for the multiple contributing factors that can add to and exacerbate the stress. As Lavee, McCubbin, and Patterson explain, the Double ABCX model of family stress and adaptation

> redefines precrisis variables and adds postcrisis variables in an effort to describe (a) the additional life stressors and strains, prior to or following the crisis-producing event, which result in a pile-up of demands; (b) the range of outcome of family processes in response to this pile-up of stressors (maladaptation to bonadaptation); and (c) the intervening factors that shape the course of adaptation: family resources, coherence and meaning, and the related coping strategies. (1985, p. 812)

In this model, theorists added the additional variables right into the model, identifying them with "aA," "bB," "cC," and "xX." An aA factor is the pile-up of demands and their cumulative effect over time. In the case of Eliza's family, this could describe the practical demands of transportation independence, the financial demands of paying legal fees and losing an income, and the emotional demands of living with a family member struggling with addiction.

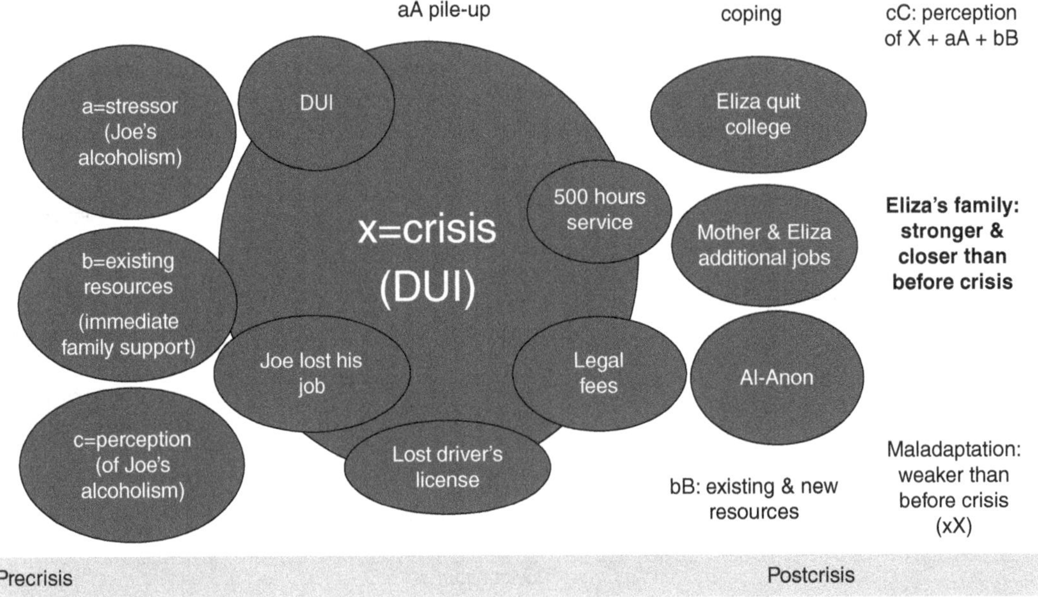

Figure 11.2 Double ABCX model applied to Eliza

The bB factor refers to the family adaptive resources that exist and then are expanded upon or changed when the crisis occurs. There are three types of resources that can be accessed: personal, as in family members' self-esteem and skills that are available to the family system; systemic, which include family unit cohesion and communication skills; and social support, which are the institutions and people that the family can draw upon to help them deal with their situation. For example, Eliza and her mother were able to access social support through Al-Anon, and use that support to adapt to the stress.

The cC factor refers to the family's perception of the stressor that led to the crisis, or cC = perception of X + aA + bB. When the cC factor is positive, family members are better able to cope. As an example, some families swear by the adage "what does not kill us only makes us stronger." If that perception holds true for families experiencing crisis, they will likely have a positive perception of the crisis, and adapt accordingly. Thinking back to Eliza, her family could have perceived the crisis as a blessing that her father lost his license and his job so that he could go to rehab and get better, making the family stronger. Perhaps some families view similar situations as a perfect opportunity to address the problem and move forward as a unit, stronger for having gone through it.

Finally, the xX factor refers to the postcrisis variables, such as the pile-up of stressors on the initial stressor. Thus, there is more to deal with after the crisis because factors throughout were multiplied. This is a major contribution to the original ABCX model, because it accounts for the interconnected aspects of the Double ABCX model. That is, the family cannot return to the way it was before the crisis. Eliza's family has adapted to the crisis, but their lives are inevitably different now compared to before, which makes returning to "business as usual" impossible. In postcrisis, families must make new meanings of their lives to help them adapt to difficult circumstances.

It is also important to note that how the family adapts to stressful situations depends upon a number of factors. These factors include: (a) the severity of the crisis; (b) the severity of the pile-up of stressors; (c) the amount of personal and family resources and social support; and (d) the level of the family's sense of coherence of the total situation; that is, how they utilize their capabilities and strengths to handle the demands of the crisis (Lavee, McCubbin, and Patterson, 1985; McCubbin and Patterson, 1983).

FAAR model An important addition to the Double ABCX model is the **family adjustment and adaptation response (FAAR) model** (Patterson and Garwick, 1994). This model further develops the adaptive part of the stress process, and focuses on how families make meaning of the stressful situation. There are two levels of meaning. The first level, situational meanings, deals with the family members' subjective definitions of their needs and capacities in dealing with the stress. The second level, global meanings, refers to the ways families transcend a situation and develop more stable cognitive beliefs about their relationships both within the family and in relation to the larger community. As Boss (1987) noted, the level of meaning is the most difficult to understand and measure. Boss (2002) went on to develop the concept of boundary ambiguity in the contextual model of family stress. Boundary ambiguity refers to the psychological limbo when family members are uncertain about who is in their family and who is not. This concept, developed as the theory of ambiguous loss (Boss, 2006), is very useful in helping families come to terms with the various combinations of psychological and physical presence or absence of members. Boundary ambiguity can produce a great deal of stress, and its management and resolution is necessary for healing and moving forward in life.

McCubbin and McCubbin (1988) also emphasized the nature of family strengths. They borrowed from individual resiliency theory and combined it with family stress and coping theory to develop the definition of resilient families as hardy, adaptable, and able to find meaning in adversity. Thus, they acknowledged that although a family stressor is not perceived or experienced in the same way by every family, there are some characteristics of families who are strong and resilient that are common across families.

Toward a consolidated theory of family resilience Henry, Morris, and Harrist (2015) explain that the second wave of family stress and resilience theory began with recognition of multiple ways to conceptualize how families face hardships, express strengths, and continue to grow and change. The concept of family resilience grew out of several individual and family theories that include individual resilience theories (see Masten and Monn, 2015 for an updated version), family stress theory, family systems theory (Chapter 6), and family ecological theory (Chapter 10).

Major conceptual advances have led to a more refined view of family resilience, what Henry, Morris, and Harrist (2015) refer to as Wave 3. Patterson (2002) elaborated upon the nature of life as a risky venture, placing families in vulnerable positions, but thereby giving families the ability to protect themselves against such risk and to make further adaptations. Another advance was the introduction of family protective factors that can be applied to any family stressor, from the ordinary hassles of daily living (e.g., being late to pick up your child at day care) to situations that involve significant risk (e.g., driving while intoxicated). Family protective factors include basic needs such as adequate housing, nutrition, and health care, and strong interpersonal relationships between parents and children, adult partners, and their extended support networks.

Creating a balance in life, through practices such as family rituals that allow family members to rely on one another and build cohesion, helps families to cope with the stress of chronic problems. For example, in an Australian study of 11 adults who grew up with a parent with a mental illness, the stress accompanying having a parent with a chronic illness such as depression or bipolar disorder had a severe impact on children as they grew to adulthood, yet they also found ways to cope. Power et al. (2016) examined this situation from a resilience perspective, in which families create a balance between stress/distress and optimism/strength. They found that these adult children were able to balance hope against hopelessness, even in the face of family turmoil and uncertainty.

Key concepts

Now that we have described some of the key features of the development of family stress and resilience theory, we turn to definitions of key concepts that are used in this theory. These concepts include some that have been used since its inception (e.g., stressor events) and others have that developed over time and continue to show potential today (resilience).

Stress As noted earlier in the chapter, Hill (1949; 1958) provided the seminal definition and description of family stress as the process of dealing with crisis as (A) an event and related hardships; interacting with (B), the family's crisis-meeting resources; interacting with (C), the definition the family makes of the event; that may combine to produce the crisis (X). Boss also described stress as "An upset in the steady state of the family. It may be as mild as a bat flying around the house or as severe as a holocaust; it includes anything that may disturb the family, cause uneasiness, or exert pressure on the family system" (1987, p. 695).

Coping Coping refers to the fact that not all families become stressed when a crisis occurs. Many families are able to avoid a stressor becoming a crisis by holding the degree of stress to a tolerable level, thereby demonstrating their ability to cope with stress (Boss, 1987). A major way that families cope is by relying on their kinship and friendship networks. Traditionally, it was very helpful when families lived in close proximity to one another. For example, imagine that Eliza's older sister, Esther, just gave birth to a baby prematurely, and the baby needs to stay in the neonatal unit at the hospital until he is stronger. Esther also has two other young children at home, and her husband works two jobs to support the family. Esther has no choice but to rely upon relatives and neighbors to take care of the other children while she goes back and forth to the hospital. Eliza and her mother take shifts, to help Esther and her family cope with the current crisis. They are able to tolerate the level of stress they are experiencing, but it takes the whole family pulling together, in spite of the many adversities they face.

Family resilience As we noted earlier, the concept of family resilience places a stronger emphasis on the ways that a family positively adapts to and rebounds from stressful situations. Hawley and DeHaan combine the various strands in the individual and family resilience literatures, described above, and offer an integrated definition:

> Family resilience describes the path a family follows as it adapts and prospers in the face of stress, both in the present and over time. Resilient families respond positively to these conditions in unique ways,

> depending on the context, developmental level, the interactive combination of risk and protective factors, and the family's shared outlook. (1996, p. 293)

Family resilience is not the same for every family, but there are common characteristics that some families demonstrate that allow them to confront, cope, and rebound from what might hinder other families who are unable to regroup after a major stressor occurs. Consider again Eliza's family. One of their strengths is the ability to seek out social support during a crisis. Another factor is that they live near each other and can rely on one another for physical care and transportation. Yet, what if Esther lived in another city or away from her family of origin and was unable to rely on them for daily help in caring for her other children? Esther and her family could still have the resources to cope with the situation—perhaps they already provide emotional support daily through telephone calls, Skyping, and Facebook. Another resource is Caring Bridge, one of the many online support systems in which you can post updates about your loved one's illness and recovery, and receive words of comfort and encouragement from friends, family, and even acquaintances. There may be neighbors and church members who fill in when family are not in close physical proximity. And, even if Eliza didn't live near Esther, she could still organize a website to keep track of offers from Esther's local support group members who have volunteered to provide meals, babysitting, and other kinds of support. In all of these ways, Eliza and Esther and their wider support networks show the strength of emotional bonds that help families stay strong in the face of a crisis, or multiple crises.

Trauma Walsh explains that "The word trauma comes from the Latin word for wound. With traumatic experiences, the body, mind, spirit, and relationships with others can be wounded" (2007, p. 207). **Trauma** is associated with extreme stress, often coming from major disasters and other types of catastrophic events which individuals, families, and communities are ill prepared to deal with or deter. Some of the extremely traumatic events affecting families are (a) untimely, sudden, or violent deaths; (b) physical illness, harm or disability; (c) abduction, torture, incarceration, or persecution; (d) relationship dissolution; (e) job loss; (f) migration/relocation; (g) violence and/or sexual abuse; (h) terrorism, war, genocide, and refugee experience (Walsh, 2007).

Complex trauma is a relatively new concept in which it is recognized that past and present traumas that occur in a family context can intersect to revictimize individuals. In particular, complex trauma goes beyond the concept of posttraumatic stress disorder by including the role of interpersonal trauma linked to child abuse (van der Kolk, 2002). Flemke, Underwood, and Allen (2014) reviewed the emerging research on complex trauma and intimate partner violence (IPV), and found that women's use of IPV was linked to having a history of experiencing one or more forms of child abuse, particularly physical abuse, sexual abuse, or observing another family member being abused. The complex trauma lens reveals that there is a critical interpersonal factor that must be taken into account when examining the intersection between individual and family stress. This concept helps us understand women's violent actions against their own partner by linking them to the family context, suggesting that when women commit acts of IPV, their earlier childhood traumas may have been triggered by some interaction with their current intimate partner. Trauma doesn't simply occur to one individual; it has a family context that in some cases has lasting or intergenerational consequences. The concept of complex trauma provides a bridge between individual-level and family-level theories of stress and resilience, particularly in an area (child abuse and IPV in the family) that is so difficult to understand, prevent, and intervene in.

Evaluating Family Stress and Resilience Theory

Strengths of family stress and resilience theory

Like all of the theories we describe in this book, family stress and resilience theory has both strengths and weaknesses. This theory is highly adaptable, gives insight into a family's past, present, and future, and addresses the very real problems and stressors families face on a daily basis, no matter how big or small. We elaborate on these strengths here.

Box 11.2 Family Stress and Resilience Theory in Pop Culture: *The Theory of Everything*

A scene from *The Theory of Everything*, 2014, dir. James Marsh, Universal Pictures

In this Academy Award winning film, the concepts of family stress, coping, and resilience forged through adversity are dramatically revealed. The main characters are Stephen Hawking, the world-renowned physicist, and his former wife Jane Hawking, the author of the book *Travelling to infinity: My life with Stephen* (2007), from which the movie was adapted. In the beginning of the film, Stephen's life is shown as one of great promise and accomplishment. He came from a loving and supportive family, his brilliant career was unfolding, and he found the perfect partner in Jane. However, he discovers he has motor neurone disease, which will affect his ability to walk, talk, swallow, and move most of the other parts of his body. He is also told that he has only two years to live. Despite his challenging circumstances, Jane is determined to stay by his side. They marry, begin their family, and appear to be the perfect couple. As Stephen's ability to care for himself or contribute to raising his children worsens, the stress on their relationship takes its toll. Yet, over and over again, Stephen and Jane find ways to reinvest in their marriage and family life. One of the ways they keep their family on track is to enlist the help of a young widower, Jonathan, who becomes a close friend of everyone in the family. Their relationships are all tested, however, when Jonathan and Jane become close and fall in love.

Over time, Stephen goes from using canes to wheelchairs to losing his ability to speak. Yet, given his own individual determination and his family's strength, he continues to study, write, and thrive as a scientist. His books are international bestsellers, particularly *A Brief History of Time* (1998 [1988]). By the end of the story, Stephen receives an honor bestowed by Queen Elizabeth II and his whole family attends. Stephen and Jane divorce, but continue to remain steadfast in their support of one another and their children. Both remarry and seem to find renewal and happiness.

In sum, this is a story about a couple and their children who continually face challenges, but each time, they find ways to reorganize, rebound, and recover. Stephen and Jane are hardy and able to bounce back from adversity. Ultimately, this film is about a family who, individually and collectively, show strength and resilience through the unexpected losses and challenges that are associated with living with a debilitating illness and disabilities. These challenges impact the family's dynamics and often bring great pain and suffering, even betrayal and forgiveness. One of the main messages of the film is that people are strong and can maintain their ties in the face of ongoing trauma. They can also experience divorce, find new partners, reorganize family boundaries and relationships, and reestablish stability. With concerted effort, their family unit can survive and thrive throughout all of these stressors, crises, traumas, and changes.

Positive perspective on family change and growth By incorporating the concept of resilience, family stress theory now includes a necessary corrective to the original focus on loss and crisis. In addition, there are positive aspects to coping, even to the extent that people can grow and even thrive in the face of such challenges to well-being and daily functioning. Family bonds can also be strengthened by the processes of communication and caring that are needed to get on the other side of a stressful event or a family transition. By taking a salutary (positive) approach, family strengths are also emphasized (McCubbin et al., 1980).

Extends earlier family theories by "normalizing" the inevitability of stress Family stress and resilience theory is grounded in family developmental theory (Chapter 5), which makes sense, as Reuben Hill is also the founder of that theory. Family stress and resilience theory is also grounded in a family systems approach (Chapter 6) that emphasizes boundaries, communication, and process. Each of these theories can be considered traditional theories of the family, and thus have roots in functionalist theory (Chapter 2), with the emphasis on normative family processes. But, family stress and resilience theory does not stop at the door of the negative or the deviant; it emphasizes that stress is a normal, naturally occurring dynamic in any family, and it can lead to positive outcomes. Stress and coping, crisis and reorganization, among other concepts, are important to consider and to keep in balance as we examine the inner workings of families. Families inevitably deal with the things that make them grow: both problems and their solutions. Family stress and resilience theory, then, builds upon and extends other theories we have described in this book.

Conceptualizing family stressors according to severity The concept of putting family stress, coping, and resilience into perspective as a continuum of severity is important for understanding different layers of stressor events and different levels of family resources to cope with family stress. There is quite a difference in being late for a meeting because you cannot find a parking space, compared to losing your home in a disaster like a flood or fire. Further, having one's house burn down is a catastrophic event for any family, but it still may be more devastating to some families than others (Jones et al., 2012). Compare, for example, the varying circumstances of a family dealing with the aftermath of a fire. How might a family's circumstances differ if they have extended kin or friends who offer their home temporarily, or if they own another property that they can move into while their damaged home is being rebuilt? What about a family that lacks resources and must turn to their car or a homeless shelter for housing? How the family makes meaning of the stressor, in the context of their available resources, affects and is affected by the severity of the precipitating event.

Weaknesses of family stress and resilience theory

Despite its strengths, family stress and resilience theory is not without its weaknesses. As with other theories, we could argue that its very strengths – adaptability, for instance – can also be viewed as a weakness. We outline each of these arguments.

Difficulty of simultaneously focusing on both stress and resilience As Power et al. (2016) point out, emphasizing resilience alone cannot capture the ways that people also experience the stress and difficulties of family life. This is one of the reasons that the concept of family stress must be combined with the concept of family resilience. Family stress theorists say that resilience is what results from the family's ability to cope with stress. Remember Walsh's (2012) insight that resilience is forged through adversity. Thus, both are essential to understanding families. As family stress theory has evolved into family resilience theory (see the waves identified by Henry, Morris, and Harrist, 2015), it is important not to forget that how they deal with stress and the pile-up of stressors is what makes a family become resilient. This is why we position family stress and resilience theory together; the movement toward resilience theory does not capture the whole picture or process of how stress and resilience work together.

Do normative family stressors and catastrophic traumas simply differ by severity? On the one hand, as we noted under the strengths of this theory, the concept of "severity" is helpful to putting into context differences in degrees of stress in terms of what happens to a family. But, is stress and its severity really the same thing, with the differences in stressful events merely running from bad to worse along a severity continuum? That is, how similar are the following events: a car accident, the devastating losses that come from war, refugee status, and the death of many family members? Do these extremes, from bad to worse, simply represent a quantitative difference between stressors, or are they qualitatively different, and thus not really comparable? This question is important in terms of helping families cope with stress and trauma. Does the same theory of stress, such as the ABCX model, work in the same way when one is dealing with the normative transition to parenthood outlined in family developmental theory (Chapter 5), as when one is dealing with a devastating loss such as the sudden death of a child? In the first instance, families can expect that the birth of a child is part of the expected family life cycle, whereas no one expects or yearns for the early death of a child. Society treats the first instance with celebration, gifts, and hope, but often stigmatizes the second instance. What is important to consider is that sometimes there is more at stake than simply where a stressor falls on a continuum; birth, death, catastrophe, or trauma each are accompanied by specific societal expectations, and perhaps gendered expectations. For example, suffering from PTSD as a rape survivor is not the same as suffering as a war veteran; untangling gender from such experiences is difficult to do, even when a theory is as adaptable as family stress and resilience.

Can individual stressors be resolved if the family is the cause? The origins of family stress theory come from perspectives on the traumatic events that happen to individuals. As is sometimes the case when a traumatic event occurs to an individual, the family can react with denial or scapegoating (Boss, 2002), taking on an attitude that "if only Dad wasn't an alcoholic, we would all be fine." Or, "if my son didn't get arrested and sentenced to prison, our family wouldn't have to cope with such stress, shame, and stigma." Thus, most family stressors occur at the individual level but families are not always equipped to cope with these challenges by addressing them at the family level. Can the individual level and the family level really be combined, or are we always just dealing with the so-called family stressor as if it was just an individual one?

An alternative theory app: family developmental theory

In this chapter, we have laid out the key concepts, origins, modern applications, and the strengths and weaknesses of family stress and resilience theory. As you have learned, this theory addresses the complexities associated with facing experiences that can result in negative outcomes as well as positive outcomes (resilience) in families. As a result, this theoretical perspective allows a very close look at how families respond to external experiences, in order to predict how they might respond again if faced with another crisis in the future.

Another theory that complements this perspective is family developmental theory (Chapter 5). You may recall from that chapter how family developmental theory suggests that each family progresses through specific "stages" with accompanying developmental milestones. Similarly, family stress and resilience theory looks at how families move through the stages of dealing with stressors that they face. This theoretical perspective only enhances family developmental theory. Consider how a married or partnered couple deals with the new addition of a family member; this is an often stressful and life-changing event. Family developmental theorists suggest that families will experience struggles (e.g., sleep deprivation, anxiety) similar to other families in the same stage. However, what family stress and resilience theory adds to this understanding is a more specific *family-level* understanding of how the couple has addressed similar transitions in the past. Do they have one or more children? Did they transition from one to two children smoothly? How does that knowledge help us understand the shift from two to three children? While family developmental theory provides a general understanding of what "most" families may experience during times of transition, family stress and resilience theory gives more information about the family itself, which provides much more family-specific context when trying to understand and explain why we do what we do.

Working with Family Stress and Resilience Theory: Integrating Research and Practice

Now that we have defined family stress and resilience theory, described the historical origins and key concepts, and pointed out its strengths and weaknesses, we turn to how the theory can be used in research and practice. We provide an example of current theorizing, analyze an empirical study that was guided by family stress and resilience theory, and describe how the theory informs the practice of family therapy and family policy.

Family stress and resilience theory today

Meyer (2003) developed minority stress theory in order to recognize that there are specific forms of social prejudice that impact individuals and families from minority groups. Although this framework is rooted in an individualistic, psychological perspective, it is highly adaptable to studies of family stress. Minority stress theory explains how "stigma, prejudice, and discrimination create a hostile and stressful social environment that causes mental health problems" (Meyer, 2003, p. 674). Being a member of a minority group is linked to alienation and problems with self-acceptance (e.g., internalized homophobia, racism, sexism).

Versions of minority stress theory have a strong history in family studies. For example, Peters and Massey (1983) identified a theory of racial discrimination against Black families, addressing the added stressors put upon those coping with the daily stressors of prejudice and institutionalized racism. They found that one of the ways Black families coped with this chronic stress was to socialize their children with a double consciousness about race. Children needed to understand the values and pressures associated with minority status, as well as the expectations associated with living in the broader society. This theory helps to explain both the strengths of Black families and the unique stressors that impinge on their lives.

Minority stress theory has been further adapted to deal with the stress that older lesbian, gay, bisexual, transgender, or queer (LGBTQ) adults experience (Allen and Roberto, 2016). Older LGBTQ individuals experience a unique form of minority stress, through the pile-ups of micro-aggressions associated with ageism and homophobia, often compounded by racism, sexism, and classism, among others. A study by Wight and colleagues (2012) was guided by minority stress theory to examine if same-sex marriage is a protective factor against the combined effects of sexual minority stress and aging-related stress. These authors analyzed a sample of gay married men (age range of 44–75 years, with a mean age of 57 years) to examine the intersection of minority stress and aging related stress on their lives. They found that legal marriage among HIV-negative and HIV-positive older gay men was a protective factor that may offset the mental health issues associated with being gay and growing old. In these studies, then, minority stress theory was applied to the family context in order to incorporate the intersections of gender, race, class, sexual orientation, age, and other systems of stratification, a topic that we addressed as part of feminist theory (Chapter 8).

Family stress and resilience theory in research

Yoon, Newkirk, and Perry-Jenkins (2015) examined the role of dinnertime rituals as a protective factor for parents and children when a family is under financial and parenting stress. Building on Fiese's (2006) definition of family ritual as a regular routine that contributes to predictability in family life for the benefit of children's well-being, the authors specifically examined the importance of establishing the routine of eating together at dinnertime. Family stress is especially likely to happen when both parents work outside the home, and even more so for parents who hold working-class jobs. Working-class jobs, such as factory work, often involve low wages, mandatory overtime, inflexible work hours, stressful working conditions, and minimal sick leave – and the absence of the kinds of paid family leave that are offered by more middle-class professions.

Yesel Yoon and her colleagues conducted family interviews with 93 families, consisting of mothers, fathers, and children. These families were part of a longitudinal study that began during the transition to parenthood, and then followed them through the oldest child's transition to first grade. The parents were employed in working class positions, and their challenges included both financial stress as well as having limited resources to help them manage family life transitions. Yoon, Newkirk, and Perry-Jenkins describe how the transition to school is a "developmentally sensitive period when children may have positive or negative transitional experiences" (2015, p. 95). Family routines are often disrupted during such transition periods, and it is increasingly difficult to maintain them.

One of the most intriguing findings of this study was the gender-specific affects. Fathers and daughters benefited the most from dinnertime rituals. The authors suggest that perhaps fathers are compensating for the fact that they tend to spend more time doing things with their sons, and that dinnertime is an opportunity for fathers to connect with their daughters. Both fathers and daughters in this study found that family rituals were especially meaningful as a context in which positive emotional interactions occurred. The authors also explain why family mealtime is not as effective in buffering daily parenting stress for mothers. Mothers are typically the parents who organize, prepare, and facilitate meals, so that there is nothing that makes dinnertime unique for mothers compared to any other activity of parenting. Instead, mothers typically seek the opportunity to have positive interactions with their children whenever and wherever they can. As such, dinnertime rituals may be more stressful for mothers than fathers. Nevertheless, the enhanced interaction and connection between fathers and daughters can be "a protective and stabilizing mechanism in family life" (Yoon, Newkirk, and Perry-Jenkins, 2015, p. 105) that can benefit the family unit as a whole.

Family stress and resilience theory in practice

There are several ways in which educators, therapists, practitioners, and family policy makers can apply family stress and resilience theory in their work with individuals, families, and communities, particularly when families are faced with a catastrophe that pushes them beyond the brink of their resources and ability to cope.

When families are faced with extreme trauma and disaster, family practitioners need to utilize "multisystemic approaches to recovery and resilience" in order to support individuals, families, and communities in dealing with such difficulties (Walsh, 2007, p. 219). Situations such as the World Trade Center terrorism attack on the US in 2001, Hurricane Katrina in 2005, and the displacement of refugee communities and societies through war that is rampant today, require a comprehensive approach to addressing adjustment, bereavement, and inevitable losses. Family practitioners, social workers, and aid workers must understand that such catastrophic events shatter the very foundations of our lives. Families could be faced with the loss of their homes, their economic livelihood, and their faith in the future, all of which inevitably affect mental health (Walsh, 2003). Rather than expect families to "get over it" and "move on," it is important to recognize that grief in the face of such traumatic loss will be an ongoing aspect of life; remember that resilience does not mean "closure" (Walsh, 2007, p. 210).

Walsh and McGoldrick (2004) describe four tasks that are required for individuals, families, and communities to facilitate healing and resilience in the face of major trauma. Clinicians and family practitioners can help the healing process by guiding families through these tasks. First, the reality of the traumatic event and losses must be acknowledged. Practitioners can help families clarify facts, circumstances, and ambiguities. Second, it is important to help families share their experience of loss and survivorship. Practitioners can guide families in establishing memorial rituals, tributes, and rites of passage. This also involves the use of spirituality, expressing emotions, and constructing shared meanings. Third, the family and community require restabilizing and reorganizing. This literally means rebuilding homes, kinship, and livelihood. Finally, families must be helped to reinvest in their relationships and life goals. Key issues at this point involve helping them revise their life plans, and construct new hopes and dreams. As Walsh points out, one of the tasks is "finding new purpose from the tragic loss and the spirit of loved one(s) lost" (2007, p. 210).

Conclusion

Family stress and resilience theory has contributed major ideas to the understanding of how families experience and possibly recover from difficult circumstances, whether they involve the loss of a family member through divorce or death, or the loss of a family's entire way of life through disaster and catastrophe. This theory has brought to our vocabulary necessary descriptions of stressors, crises, pile-ups, and resilience. It has also helped us understand that not all families can be viewed as perceiving and responding to stress and disaster in the same way. Family perspectives differ according to the history of trauma in their past, the nature of resources available to them, and the community support that they can muster to help them cope with and reorganize in the face of change.

Now, let's consider how family stress and resilience theory is applicable to the study of families across the globe. Recently, the National Council on Family Relations (NCFR) provided a series of articles that feature a strengths-based approach to intimate partner violence worldwide, which we summarize in Box 11.3. In the introductory article, Asay and colleagues (2014) describe how violence against women is now regarded as a worldwide human rights issue, and not just a personal issue. They describe various strengths that can be used to deal with and understand family violence from an international perspective. Individual strengths include women's ability to think through the options available to them and seek help. Family strengths include ways that family members protect and care for one another in the face of a violent member or intergenerational patterns of violence that involve multiple members. Community strengths include the coordinated efforts of public and private agencies to inform the public and push for social change. Cultural strengths are linked to the national context in which family violence and intimate partner violence occur. Global awareness helps to modify and change cultures where violence is considered a private affair and is justified by male dominance. Global women's groups, as well, are helpful in changing cultures by using an international platform to raise awareness and seek legal sanction against countries that tolerate IPV.

Box 11.3 Global Comparisons of Intimate Partner Violence

Intimate partner violence is not just a private family affair. Today, it is considered a crime in many countries and a serious threat to human rights worldwide. Despite important cultural differences, many of the same issues can lead to IPV, including generational violence, alcoholism and substance abuse, and male dominance. Increasingly, many countries are finding culturally sensitive ways to prevent and intervene in this traumatic issue.

Kenya Kenya is a society in transition. International calls to action have led to new programs, social policies, and legal advances. However, the incidence of women experiencing IPV is on the rise. Njue (2014) reports that about 45% of Kenyan women (aged 15–49) have experienced some form of physical or sexual violence. Efforts are underway to educate Kenyans about the illegality of IPV, and to empower women and girls and help them achieve economic independence so that they can leave abusive relationships.

Mexico Esteinou (2014) reports that, as in other countries, IPV is both the most common and the most traumatic for the women who experience it. A 2006 survey found that among women in marital or cohabiting relationships that had lasted 15 years or more, 10% of women experienced physical violence, 6% sexual violence, 27% emotional violence, and 20% economic violence. The survey also found that "greater decision-making power in women, increased autonomy, and an ideology of gender equality" are protective factors against physical and sexual violence, but increase the risk for emotional and economic violence (2014, p. 7). These results indicate the need to deal with IPV in Mexico from a multifaceted, legal, and family strengths approach.

Turkey A 2008 survey found that 40% of women in Turkey reported being subjected to physical violence by a spouse or partner (Balkanliojlu and Seward, 2014). Of these, 12% reported serious injuries. In addition, 44% of women reported emotional violence. In the past few years, both public and private organizations have emerged to curtail IPV. Among the new services provided are violence prevention, monitoring, and counseling; national campaigns to raise awareness about domestic violence; and manuals with information about patterns of IPV.

United States In citing the World Health Organization's survey of violence against women, it was found that urban Japan showed the lowest rates, at 15%, and countries such as Bangladesh, Ethiopia, and Peru ranged from 60% to 70%. In contrast, the figures for the United States were about 25%. One of the major reasons for IPV in the US, according to Whiting and Merchant (2014), is the tendency among victims, perpetrators, and professional practitioners to deny or minimize the incidence and extent of violence. Despite the relative advantages of a more wealthy society, IPV is still a severe problem in the US and in need of public and governmental support for prevention and intervention programs.

Multimedia Suggestions

https://www.mfri.purdue.edu/about/mission.aspx

The Military Family Research Institute (MFRI) at Purdue University provides research and outreach with the goal of improving the lives of individuals in military service and their families. MFRI lists five strategic goals that guide their work: (a) support the military infrastructure that supports families; (b) strengthen the motivation and capacity of civilian communities to support military families; (c) generate important new knowledge about military families; (d) influence policies, programs, and practices supporting military families; and (e) create and sustain a vibrant learning organization.

Activate your theory app: How could family stress and resilience theory be used to study military families? Are there other theories in the text that would be useful as well?

www.soccerwithoutborders.org

Soccer without Borders (SWB, 2015) was formed in 2006 as an international nonprofit organization dedicated to using soccer as a vehicle for positive change and providing underserved youth with "a toolkit to overcome obstacles to growth, inclusion and personal success." While the organization is open to serve all marginalized populations, its main participants are refugee children who have recently relocated to new countries. SWB aims to provide "an accessible, familiar space to build friendships and social capital, gain confidence, experience success, acclimate to new surroundings, and heal." SWB directly addresses the stress facing many refugee families and offers them opportunities to build their coping skills, hopefully resulting in resilience and growth.

Activate your theory app: While family stress and resilience theory focuses on the family as the unit of analysis, how does the SWB program step in and provide social support for refugee families dealing with crises?

Transparent (2014–present)

This television show is an Amazon series original, and won the Golden Globe Award for Best Television Series in 2014. It is centered on a Los Angeles family as they discover that their father, Mort, is transgender. As the characters' stories unfold, we begin to see how the family deals with multiple stressors, including how their father's trans-identity is related to their own underlying coping skills. We also see how the family's closeness, or solidarity, helps predict how they deal with stressors, and what helps predict resilience or maladaptive outcomes.

A scene from *Transparent*, 2014, cr. Jill Soloway, Amazon Studios

Activate your theory app: How does the experience of resilience interact with this family's ability to deal with stress? Would it differ if the children were younger, or much older?

Wild (2014)

This film was based on Cheryl Strayed's memoir titled *Wild: From Lost to Found on the Pacific Crest Trail* (2012). In the film, we learn about Cheryl's chaotic life leading up to her journey hiking over 1,000 miles of the Pacific Crest Trail. Scenes of Cheryl hiking the trail are paralleled with flashbacks to Cheryl's earlier life, as a child, teenager, and young adult, interacting with her mother, brother, and ex-husband. Stressors in Cheryl's life could easily fit into the ABCX or Double ABCX model; her mother left a physically abusive relationship when Cheryl and her siblings were young. Cheryl married young, and admits to having affairs throughout her marriage. When Cheryl's mother was diagnosed with cancer, Cheryl's crumbling marriage soon fell apart. Each of these events, including her stint with heroin leading up to her hike, can be linked to family stress and resilience theory and the way Cheryl's past coping skills predict her present, and future. Hiking the Pacific Crest Trail was a major turning point in her life, when she truly began to face the reality of her past life of devastation. The long, grueling hike helped Cheryl move beyond her former life of destruction, arming her with coping skills, strength, and resilience.

A scene from *Wild*, 2014, dir. Jean-Marc Vallée, Fox Searchlight Pictures

Activate your theory app: Which of the models described in this chapter could be used to describe how Cheryl Strayed dealt with life's stressors?

Further Reading

Arditti, J. A. (ed.), *Family problems: Stress, risk, and resilience* (Hoboken, NJ: Wiley, 2014). This edited collection of interdisciplinary research on family stressors examines multiple perspectives on the complex circumstances many families face. Stress and trauma are balanced by a social justice perspective in which broader issues of legal and social reform are incorporated, as well as therapy and interpersonal changes at the individual and family level. In the first chapter, Arditti offers a comprehensive overview of family stress, risk, and resilience theories. Additional chapters focus on micro and macro stressors and traumas that challenge individual and family well-being yet also draw upon resilience and coping. The authors examine important contemporary issues such as parental incarceration, military families, same-sex marriage, war, substance abuse, family violence, intergenerational caregiving, and social inequality.

Feigelman, W., Jordan, J. R., McIntosh, J. L., and Feigelman, B., *Devastating losses: How parents cope with the death of a child to suicide or drugs* (New York: Springer, 2012). Written by a sociologist, a psychologist, a suicidologist, and a social worker, respectively, these authors studied 575 parents who are living in the wake of their own child's traumatic death. Although 80 percent of the parents lost their child to suicide, other traumatic deaths of children included drug overdose deaths, accidental deaths (such as drowning and auto accidents), natural deaths, and death by homicide. The book offers a guide for parents and practitioners who have been down the "most treacherous area of bereavement, the loss of a child to suicide" (p. xiii). Following the death of their son, Jesse, by suicide, William and Beverly Feigelman participated in survivor support groups as both participants and facilitators. They and their colleagues examine the experiences of parents who have dealt with the despair and other intense emotions that parents feel, and that ultimately affect their relationships with one another. Parents reported not only debilitating and overwhelming grief and marital discord, but also shame, guilt, depression, blame, and the ongoing trauma of stigmatization and insensitivity of others regarding the loss of a child in a violent or taboo way. Through therapeutic intervention, in-person and internet support groups, spirituality, social activism on behalf of educating the public about suicide, and a commitment to personal posttraumatic growth, many parents were able to cope with the loss, and move forward with their lives.

Helms, H. M., Walls, J. K., and Demo, D. H., "Everyday hassles and family stress," in S. J. Price, C. A. Price, and P. C. McKenry (eds), *Families and change: Coping with stressful events and transitions* (Thousand Oaks, CA: Sage, 2010), pp. 357–379. This chapter expands upon the vulnerability-stress-adaptation (VSA) model developed by Karney and Bradbury (1995) to examine everyday hassles that cause family stress. Departing from a focus on major life crises and trauma, everyday hassles refer to the common, yet unexpected annoyances of life. These daily hassles are distinct from major life events such as divorce, job loss, and death of a loved one. Instead, everyday hassles include commuting to work, chauffeuring children, working extended hours over holidays, and arguing with a spouse. Such hassles also include getting a phone call in the midst of a busy workday that one's child is sick and has to be picked up at day care. Over time, these seemingly minor issues pile up, creating tensions and vulnerabilities that affect individual well-being and the family's cohesion. Family-friendly workplace policies and practices (e.g., giving workers more control over their time to address family needs; increasing worker benefits; and creating a more supportive and egalitarian workplace culture) are one of the major "fixes" the authors recommend for alleviating the influence of daily hassles.

Huebner, A. J., Mancini, J. A., Wilcox, R. M., Grass, S. R., and Grass, G. A., "Parental deployment and youth in military families: Exploring uncertainty and ambiguous loss," *Family Relations, 56* (2007), 112–122 (doi:10.1111/j.1741-3729.2007.00445.x). In this qualitative study, the authors conducted 14 focus groups consisting 107 different boys and girls (ages ranged from 12 to 18). These youth had a parent who was a member of one of the armed services (e.g., Army Navy, Air Force, Marines, National Guard, and Reserves) and currently deployed to Iraq or Afghanistan. The adolescents were recruited through the National Military Family Association and State 4-H Military Liaisons. The study was guided by the Double ABCX framework, and the concept of boundary ambiguity in the ambiguous loss framework. According to Boss (2006), boundary ambiguity refers to uncertainty about who is in or out of one's family, and is especially an issue when a parent is away for work for long periods of time. Parental deployment in war is a type of family crisis that is associated with emotional risks (e.g., outbursts, depression, anxiety) to a child's well-being, as well as difficulty when the deployed parent comes home and rejoins the family. But this crisis is also softened by the presence of supportive adults and practitioners in other military families, and civilian and military community associations.

Marks, L. D., Hopkins, K., Chaney, C., Monroe, P. A., Nesteruk, O., and Sasser, D. D., "'Together, we are strong': A qualitative study of happy, enduring African American marriages," *Family Relations, 57* (2008), 172–185 (doi:10.1111/j.1741-3729.2008.00492.x). This study was inspired by college students who wanted to read research on Black families that did not take a deficit view. This research used a qualitative interview method of 30 African American couples (30 wives and 30 husbands) and was guided by a "salutogenic approach to examine some of the strengths of happy, enduring African American marriages" (p. 173). The findings reveal several themes that characterize how these couples cope with the family and work-life challenges they face, that are often brought about by racism. In addition to dealing with the challenges, these couples developed resilient strategies to enable them to pull together and find tremendous satisfaction with their marriage. They leaned on each other and their faith when problems arose. They resolved marital conflicts as they arose, rather than allowing tension and anger to fester. They believed in unity and teamwork, and practiced this through their commitment to the biblical concept of being "equally yoked" in the eyes of God.

Questions for Students

Discussion Questions

1 In what ways has Hill's original conceptualization of stress theory changed over time?
2 Compare and contrast family stress and resilience theory with conflict theory (Chapter 3). How do these two theories address crisis, change, and growth?
3 Describe some of the ways that you believe young children are resilient. What about older adults?
4 Considering all of the stressors and traumas presented in this chapter, is it possible to rank them according to severity? Why or why not?
5 What is the grieving process for those who have lost a family member or close friend to death? Research some of the grieving practices in other countries and see how they are similar to or different from those in the US.
6 Consider the needs of refugee families and children from around the world. How should family practitioners prepare to work with refugee families? Would family stress and resilience theory be applicable, or might the combination of two or more theories be better?

Your Turn!

Research best practices for helping refugee families assimilate and adapt to their new country. Are there refugee communities nearby where you live? Where is the closest refugee community, and what community resources are in place? Research more than one ethnic or cultural group and consider how community resources should be adapted to meet the needs of such unique populations.

Personal Reflection Questions

1 In what ways are you a resilient person? In what ways is your family resilient?
2 What are the most difficult challenges you and your family have faced? What resources did you rely upon in order to deal with the changes that these challenges brought?
3 What are the protective factors in your family background that have helped you stay in college?
4 Aside from college, have you ever lived apart (e.g., study abroad, long-term hospitalization, foster care) from your family of origin (e.g., your parents, your siblings) for a significant length of time? What was difficult about being "away from home"? What were strengths you discovered in yourself as a result of this experience?
5 What "everyday hassles" are you currently experiencing? How are they affecting your ability to cope with your responsibilities? What do you do to ease the tension they bring?
6 Who is your role model for dealing with life's stressors and challenges?

References

Allen, K. R., and Roberto, K. A. (2016). Family relationships of older LGBT adults. In D. A. Harley and P. B. Teaster (eds), *Handbook of LGBT elders: An interdisciplinary approach to principles, practices, and policies* (pp. 43–64). New York: Springer.

Asay, S. M., DeFrain, J., Metzger, M., and Moyer, B. (2014). Intimate partner violence worldwide: A strengths-based approach. *NCFR Report: International Intimate Partner Violence, FF61*, 1–4.

Balkanliojlu, M. A., and Seward, R. R. (2014). Perceptions of domestic violence by Turkish couples in long-lasting marriages: An exploratory study. *NCFR Report: International Intimate Partner Violence, FF61*, 12–14.

Boss, P. (1987). Family stress. In M. B. Sussman and S. K. Steinmetz (eds), *Handbook of marriage and the family* (pp. 695–723). New York: Plenum.

Boss, P. (2002). *Family stress management: A contextual approach* (2nd edn). Thousand Oaks, CA: Sage.

Boss, P. (2006). *Loss, trauma, and resilience: Therapeutic work with ambiguous loss*. New York: Norton.

Dallaire, D. H. (2007). Incarcerated mothers and fathers: A comparison of risks for children and families. *Family Relations, 56*, 440–453. doi:10.1111/j.1741-3729.2007.00472.x.

Dekel, R., Goldblatt, H., Keidar, M., Solomon, Z., and Polliack, M. (2005). Being a wife of a veteran with posttraumatic stress disorder. *Family Relations, 54*, 24–36. doi:10.1111/j.0197-6664.2005.00003.x.

Demo, D. H., Aquilino, W. S., and Fine, M. A. (2005). Family composition and family transitions. In V. L. Bengtson, A. C. Acock, K. R. Allen, P. Dilworth-Anderson, and D. M. Klein (eds), *Sourcebook of family theory and research* (pp. 119–142). Thousand Oaks, CA: Sage.

Edin, K., and Kissane, R. J. (2010). Poverty and the American family: A decade in review. *Journal of Marriage and Family, 72*, 460–479. doi:10.1111/j.1741-3737.2010.00713.x.

Esteinou, R. (2014). Intimate partner violence in Mexico. *NCFR Report: International Intimate Partner Violence, FF61*, 6–7.

Fiese, B. H. (2006). *Family routines and rituals.* New Haven: Yale University Press.

Flemke, K. R., Underwood, J., and Allen, K. R. (2014). Childhood abuse and women's use of intimate partner violence: Exploring the role of complex trauma. *Partner Abuse: New Directions in Research, Intervention, and Policy, 5*, 98–112. doi:10.1891/1946-6560.5.1.98.

Hawking, J. (2007). *Travelling to infinity: My life with Stephen.* Richmond, UK: Alma.

Hawking, S. (1998). *A brief history of time* (updated, 10th anniversary edn). New York: Bantam. (Originally published 1988.)

Hawley, D. R., and DeHaan, L. (1996). Toward a definition of family resilience: Integrating life-span and family perspectives. *Family Process, 35*, 283–298. doi:10.1111/j.1545-5300.1996.00283.x.

Henry, C. S., Morris, A. H., and Harrist, A. W. (2015). Family resilience: Moving into the third wave. *Family Relations, 64*, 22–43. doi:10.1111/fare.12106.

Hill, R. (1949). *Families under stress: Adjustment to the crises of war separation and reunion.* New York: Harper.

Hill, R. (1958). Generic features of families under stress. *Social Casework, 49*, 139–150.

Jones, R. T., Ollendick, T. H., Mathai, C. M., Allen, K. R., Hadder, J. M., Chapman, S., and Woods, O. (2012). "When I came home ... everything was gone." The impact of residential fires on children. *Fire Technology, 48*, 927–943. doi:10.1007/s10694-012-0252-2.

Karney, B. R., and Bradbury, T. N. (1995). The longitudinal course of marital quality and stability: A review of theory, method, and research. *Psychological Bulletin, 118*, 3–34. doi:10.1037/0033-2909.118.1.3.

Lavee, Y., McCubbin, H. I., and Patterson, J. M. (1985). The double ABCX model of family stress and adaptation: An empirical test by analysis of structural equations with latent variables. *Journal of Marriage and the Family, 47*, 811–825. doi:10.2307/352326.

Masten, A. S., and Monn, A. R. (2015). Child and family resilience: A call for integrated science, practice, and professional training. *Family Relations, 64*, 5–21. doi:10.1111/fare.12103.

McCubbin, H., and McCubbin, M. (1988). Typologies of resilient families: Emerging roles of social class and ethnicity. *Family Relations, 37*, 247–254. doi:10.2307/584557.

McCubbin, H. I., and Patterson, J. M. (1983). The family stress process: The Double ABCX model of adjustment and adaptation. *Marriage and Family Review, 6*(1–2), 7–37. doi:10.1300/j002v06n01_02.

McCubbin, H. I., Joy, C. B., Cauble, A. E., Comeau, J. K., Patterson, J. M., and Needle, R. H. (1980). Family stress and coping: A decade review. *Journal of Marriage and the Family, 42*, 855–871. doi:10.2307/351829.

Meyer, I. H. (2003). Prejudice, social stress, and mental health in lesbian, gay, and bisexual populations: Conceptual issues and research evidence. *Psychological Bulletin, 129*, 674–697. doi:10.1037/0033-2909.129.5.674.

Njue, J. R. (2014). Intimate partner violence: The case for Kenya. *NCFR Report: International Intimate Partner Violence, FF61*, 2–4.

Oswald, R. F. (2002). Resilience within the family networks of lesbians and gay men: Intentionality and redefinition. *Journal of Marriage and Family, 64*, 374–383. doi:10.1111/j.1741-3737.2002.00374.x.

Patterson, J. M. (2002). Integrating family resilience and family stress theory. *Journal of Marriage and Family, 64*, 349–360. doi:10.1111/j.1741-3737.2002.00349.x.

Patterson, J. M., and Garwick, A. (1994). Levels of meaning in family stress theory. *Family Process, 33*, 287–304. doi:10.1111/j.1545-5300.1994.00287.x.

Peters, M. F., and Massey, G. (1983). Mundane extreme environmental stress in family stress theories: The case of Black families in White America. *Marriage and Family Review, 6*(1–2), 193–218. doi:10.1300/J002v06n01_10.

Power, J., Goodyear, M., Maybery, D., Reupert, A., O'Hanlon, B., Cuff, R., and Perlesz, A. (2016). Family resilience in families where a parent has a mental illness. *Journal of Social Work, 16*, 66–82.

Russell, S. T., Toomey, R. B., Ryan, C., and Diaz, R. M. (2014). Being out at school: The implications of school victimization and young adult adjustment. *American Journal of Orthopsychiatry, 84*, 635–643. doi:10.1037/ort0000037.

Rutter, M. (1987). Psychosocial resilience and protective mechanisms. *American Journal of Orthopsychiatry, 57*, 316–331. doi:10.1111/j.1939-0025.1987.tb03541.x.

Strayed, C. (2010). *Wild: From lost to found on the Pacific Crest Trail*. New York: Knopf.

SWB (Soccer without Borders) (2015). *Mission and values*. At www.soccerwithoutborders.org/#!mission/c1fd4.

van der Kolk, B. A. (2002). The assessment and treatment of complex PTSD. In R. Yehuda (ed.), *Traumatic stress* (pp. 1–29). Washington, DC: American Psychiatric Press.

Walsh, F. (2003). Family resilience: A framework for clinical practice. *Family Process, 42*, 1–18. doi:10.1111/j.1545-5300.2003.00001.x.

Walsh, F. (2007). Traumatic loss and major disasters: Strengthening family and community resilience. *Family Process, 46*, 207–227. doi:10.1111/j.1545-5300.2007.00205.x.

Walsh, F. (2012). Family resilience: Strengths forged through adversity. In F. Walsh (ed.), *Normal family processes: Growing diversity and complexity* (4th edn, pp. 399–427). New York: Guilford Press.

Walsh, F., and McGoldrick, M. (2004). Loss and the family: A systemic perspective. In F. Walsh and M. McGoldrick (eds), *Living beyond loss: Death in the family* (2nd edn, pp. 3–26). New York: Norton.

Whiting, J. B., and Merchant, L. V. (2014). Intimate partner violence in the United States: The role of distortion and desistance. *NCFR Report: International Intimate Partner Violence, FF61*, pp. 9–11.

Wight, R. G., LeBlanc, A. J., de Vries, B., and Detels, R. (2012). Stress and mental health among midlife and older gay-identified men. *American Journal of Public Health, 102*, 503–510. doi:10.2105/AJPH.2011.300384.

Yoon, Y., Newkirk, K., and Perry-Jenkins, M. (2015). Parenting stress, dinnertime rituals, and child well-being in working-class families. *Family Relations, 64*, 93–107. doi:10.1111/fare.12107.

12

Conclusion

We started this book with a discussion of theory as an application that you can use to problem solve as a family researcher and practitioner. By now, your theoretical mind should be actively engaged as you move through both your personal life and academic studies. One of the goals of theory is to fundamentally change the way you see the world around you. When you interact with loved ones, family members, or classmates, you should be seeing theory. When you watch a movie, a YouTube video, or scroll through Instagram, Twitter or Facebook, you should notice concepts from this book that you cannot ignore. Your theoretical mind has been ignited, and theorizing about the world around you should be second nature by now.

Even more importantly, your theoretical insights have likely provided you with the academic toolkit you will need to pursue your professional goals, whether it is furthering your education, working directly with families and children, or even in a health care or business setting. The case study we present in this final chapter asks you to consider what life beyond this class will look like: What will you take away from a more thorough understanding of theories? How will you use what you have learned beyond the classroom, when you are working as a professional in your chosen field? A.J., the subject of our case study, is reviewing applications for a guidance counselor position in his school district serving several small schools in the area. We understand that not all of our readers may be interested in pursuing this type of career, but the case study should illustrate ways in which you can utilize your newly acquired theoretical "app" in any profession you seek.

Case Study

A.J., the principal at a local school, has been reviewing applicants' resumes, cover letters, and references for a guidance counselor position in his school district. Many of the applicants have similar qualifications, with the requisite bachelor's and master's degrees. Some have completed internships in places like group homes, and others have experience working in health care settings. A.J. and his search committee have whittled the applicant pool from 55 applicants down to two final candidates. The committee gathered together to conduct telephone interviews in one afternoon, with eight questions prepared for the interviewees:

1. How did you get interested in this profession?
2. What do you think is the most important aspect of your formal education that will help you in this position?
3. What is the counseling theory or approach that you most closely follow?
4. What is the role of the school counselor in relation to teachers, parents, administrators, and other counselors?
5. What is the most difficult situation you have been faced with in your current position? How did you address it?
6. How would you handle an irate parent?
7. What is your strongest asset?
8. What is something new you could bring to this program?

The first applicant, Shawna, held a bachelor's degree in Human Development and Family Studies and a

Family Theories: Foundations and Applications, First Edition. Katherine R. Allen and Angela C. Henderson.

master's in School Psychology from a prestigious university with a strong reputation for producing well-trained students. She also had relevant work experience and an impressive list of work-related references. However, Shawna answered the interview questions tentatively, and based her answers on her experiences growing up in her own family and dealing with conflict across generations, between siblings, and distant relatives. The committee felt lukewarm about Shawna's responses, sensing that her experiences working at a group home – a private residence for children or young people who cannot live with their families – might have skewed her responses. Her responses, for the most part, included reference to her work experience at a group home and were based solidly on her perspective that boundaries are important between clients and counselors. The theory she said she most closely followed was conflict theory (Chapter 3), based on the fact that her entire workday at her current job was spent "putting out fires." One of the committee members shook her head during the interview, knowing full well that Shawna's interpretation of conflict theory was inaccurate. Given her misapplication of the theory early on in her interview, the rest of her answers to the questions unfortunately kept referring back to this mistake, and she missed opportunities to show the committee that she was able to think outside the box, or look at a problem from several different angles. She made the mistake of basing her answers on anecdotes as opposed to documented trends and research in the field. In response to the question about difficult situations, Shawna said that bullying is an issue on all school campuses and the best way to handle it is to escalate punishment for the bully and expel him or her from school. She said that she dealt with bullying in her role at the group home, and that she learned quickly that the most effective way to handle it was to remove the bully from the premises permanently. Committee members were surprised that Shawna did not outline the major differences between group homes and elementary and secondary school campuses. When one committee member asked a follow-up question about how this policy would work in a school, Shawna quickly said that she was confident she could do it, no matter what the barriers.

The second applicant, Kendrick, has the same degrees as Shawna but from a university that the committee was not as familiar with. He had strong letters of recommendation from his professors, who commented on his intellect, work ethic, and ability to synthesize material at a much higher level than most of his classmates. In the telephone interview, Kendrick was very impressive to the committee. He addressed the question about how his formal education would help him in the position by saying that his coursework taught him to rely on researching an issue – including what others have established works and *does not* work – before analyzing a problem. He said he feels it is of utmost importance to work together as a team when serving the needs of families of children, and that he envisioned his role as a school counselor as being just one piece in a complex puzzle that students and families navigate within the school system. When asked about how to deal with an irate parent, he cited both family ecological theory (Chapter 10) and family systems theory (Chapter 6), stressing the importance of understanding the "big picture" before developing a plan to put the student's needs first to help students grow and thrive in the best possible way. One of the most important jobs of a school counselor, he said, was to listen. By listening, he said, he can identify the heart of the problem and work together to come up with an exchange that is mutually beneficial to both parties. As an example, he discussed a conversation he had with his father during his freshman year of college. Kendrick was complaining about a coworker's poor attitude, and he just could not believe people could be so negative all the time. His dad's response was to the point: "Kendrick, there are jerks everywhere. They will have different faces and different names. You will come across them for the rest of your life. You just need to learn how to deal with it." Kendrick cited that conversation as one of his most memorable because it taught him a very important lesson in adaptation and diplomacy. When difficult interactions arise, he feels it is best to wait until emotions have simmered, so that productive communication can occur.

While Kendrick had limited work experience in a counseling setting, he made up for it with his thoughtful answers. He also said that he viewed his role as a school counselor as that of a "facilitator of success," which to him meant meeting students on whatever level they were on, and helping them achieve their goals. This involves helping students from varying social class backgrounds, those who may struggle with societal gender expectations or gender identity, and how students can be resilient, by changing and growing over the course of their careers in school. Clearly, Kendrick answered the interview questions with a thorough understanding of the importance of using multiple angles to problem solve.

While the two candidates presented in this case study are not meant to be representative of all hiring scenarios, there are several important aspects to note as you think about preparing for your own career. First, consider why these two candidates were chosen for telephone interviews. For Shawna, her cultural capital set her above the rest of the applicants because she had a degree from a prestigious university with a solid reputation. Kendrick also had social capital working in his favor, but in a very different way: his professors raved about his academic abilities, strongly supported his application, and felt he would make an outstanding school counselor. On paper, both candidates were impressive and brought different qualities to the table.

When it came to the interview, Shawna did not have nearly as much depth to her answers as Kendrick. In addition, her work experience actually worked against her; she incorrectly described conflict theory and came off as inflexible when answering questions about how to deal with difficult situations. To use the analogy we have carried throughout this book, she was not able to rely on her theory "app" to think on her toes and answer with insight and thoughtful theoretical consideration. She did not mention precedent set by researchers in the area of school bullying, and she was unable to see outside of her own immediate experiences working in a group home. This alarmed the committee members because they all feel it is imperative to work as a team in a school setting; Shawna's answers made it seem like she was already set in her ways and thus, she may not be the most adaptable coworker.

Kendrick, on the other hand, used his theory "app" like it was second nature. His answers were thoughtful, grounded in research and practice, and showed maturity and dedication to the field. When he discussed his epistemological orientation to the field of school counseling, he presented himself as firm in his beliefs, but also flexible to be able to work as a team member. He made it clear that he saw the "bigger picture" – even without having experience in a counseling setting – by discussing issues on both a macro-level (e.g., gendered cultural norms and social class backgrounds) and a micro-level (e.g., gender identity and resiliency). Many of the committee members identified with Kendrick because he was humble, yet knowledgeable and well-informed.

By now it is probably clear who the committee chose to hire for this position. While both candidates had assets and liabilities, Kendrick was able to "think theoretically" and bring a level of intellectual maturity to the position that the committee felt was very important. As the principal, A.J. also felt strongly about finding a candidate who would be adaptable and able to see things from multiple perspectives, and utilize his resources to make well-informed decisions.

Having your theory "app" activated and well-tuned can only help you as you traverse the rest of your academic journey and begin your professional career. Before you move to the next section in this chapter, go back to the list of questions we posed in the case study, and consider the career path you are seeking. For instance, edit the question about the role of a school counselor with a similar question about a social worker, program director, therapist, or health educator; in addition, exchange the word "student" with "client." How would you answer these questions? Even if the hiring committee may not ask specifically about your "theoretical approach," how might your theory app be used in a more subtle way? To use theoretical terms, how might your app develop with you as you move through the life course and add more experience to your repertoire? Are you gravitating toward one theory over the other, because it resonates with your own personal experience? How do you think that might change over time?

Clearly, your theoretical app can be engaged on a micro-level, helping you select and identify which framework best matches your own epistemology as you move forward through the life course. However, it is also important as a professional to keep the other frameworks close at hand because just one theory may not fit all the problems you will face in the workforce. Later in this chapter, we outline ways you can utilize several theoretical lenses at once to address issues facing families in the local community. But first, let's consider *all* of the differences and similarities between the theories we have covered in this text. We have presented the 10 theories in the chronological order in which they emerged within the disciplines of human development and family studies, psychology, and sociology. In each chapter, we also highlighted each theory's unique perspective when it comes to explaining family dynamics. While it may be challenging to keep the complexities of each perspective in mind at all times, we hope Figure 12.1 can serve as a handy reference when you need to quickly compare and contrast the theories and their basic propositions.

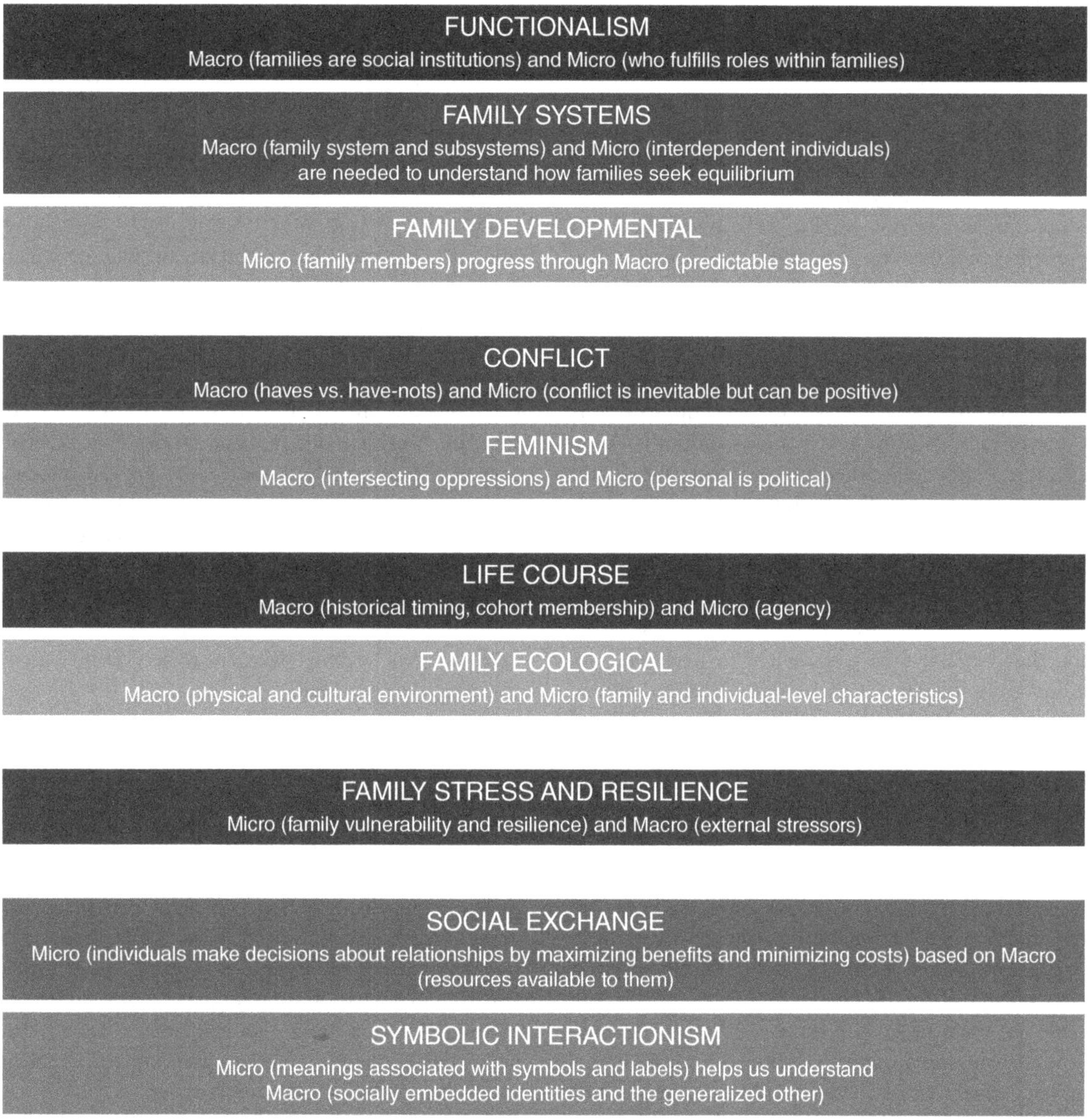

FUNCTIONALISM
Macro (families are social institutions) and Micro (who fulfills roles within families)

FAMILY SYSTEMS
Macro (family system and subsystems) and Micro (interdependent individuals) are needed to understand how families seek equilibrium

FAMILY DEVELOPMENTAL
Micro (family members) progress through Macro (predictable stages)

CONFLICT
Macro (haves vs. have-nots) and Micro (conflict is inevitable but can be positive)

FEMINISM
Macro (intersecting oppressions) and Micro (personal is political)

LIFE COURSE
Macro (historical timing, cohort membership) and Micro (agency)

FAMILY ECOLOGICAL
Macro (physical and cultural environment) and Micro (family and individual-level characteristics)

FAMILY STRESS AND RESILIENCE
Micro (family vulnerability and resilience) and Macro (external stressors)

SOCIAL EXCHANGE
Micro (individuals make decisions about relationships by maximizing benefits and minimizing costs) based on Macro (resources available to them)

SYMBOLIC INTERACTIONISM
Micro (meanings associated with symbols and labels) helps us understand Macro (socially embedded identities and the generalized other)

Figure 12.1 A theory map for your theory app!

As you can see, we do not categorize any theory as strictly micro- or macro-level. In fact, all of the theories covered in this book can be adapted to include both micro- and macro-level analyses. While we covered the theories chronologically in this text, we group them in this "theory map" in a way that illustrates that there are similarities and differences in how each theory conceptualizes individuals, families, and society.

As an example, notice the first group of three. Functionalism, family systems, and family developmental theories are near to each other because they are similar in orientation: they examine family behavior as it relates to norms, systems, and institutions surrounding families in society. Functionalist theorists and family systems theorists may approach studying the family in similar ways; they may analyze what part of a system is not functioning as it should. Similarly, family developmental theorists would analyze the progression of family members through predictable "stages" in life, and analyze family issues in the context of those developmental norms.

Conflict and feminist theorists are also similar in orientation to each other because they approach the study of families from a structural standpoint. As an example, both conflict theorists and feminist theorists critique the unequal distribution of power in society. They would ask: how can we explain family dynamics by examining who has access to power, and who does not? Thus, these two theories are grouped together.

Life course theory and family ecological theory are together because they take aspects of both the previous groupings into account. It should be no surprise that such contemporary perspectives have had the opportunity to build on earlier theories, resulting in the opportunity to analyze complex relationships over time. Both of these theories allows researchers to account for individual-level factors (e.g., agency in decision-making) as well broad social forces such as historical time, cultural norms, and even environmental influences that may impact families.

Family stress and resilience theory, another relatively new perspective to family studies, is on its own to represent its focus on the family as the unit of analysis, as well as this theory's ability to look at a family's response to past stressors to predict future outcomes (similar to life course theory). Family stress and resilience theorists are able to capture micro-level processes in response to both stressors. This theory contrasts with other theories that are primarily macro-level in analysis, however, because it allows researchers to study diverse family forms, such as LGBT families, families or color, and blended families. This theory also posits that stress is a normal part of family life, and that positive change can result. It all depends on how family members respond.

Finally, social exchange theory and symbolic interactionism are together because they offer primarily micro-level perspectives, though each takes macro-level forces into account. Social exchange theory analyzes how individuals calculate costs and benefits when, for instance, deciding whether or not to become involved in a relationship. Macro-level forces are at play during this decision-making process, especially when considering what available alternatives one may have and what resources exist when calculating an important decision. Similarly, symbolic interactionism argues that individual actors are undoubtedly influenced by symbols, labels, and preexisting generalizations when deciphering meaning from individual-level interactions. In fact, this perspective suggests that the meaning derived out of those individual-level interactions is both dependent on and interacts with larger, more macro-level forces like culturally embedded stereotypes and expectations about family and relationships. Thus, while this theory focuses on micro-processes that some other theories overlook, it is still in the same "family" (pun intended) as macro-level theories because structure is very important to this perspective as well.

Using the Theories

Now that you have learned the ins and outs of all the theories presented in this book, you are most likely finding yourself preferring one or two theories over others. Below, we outline how to use multiple perspectives at once to come to a solution you or others may face in your profession someday. The scenario we present asks you to bring your theoretical app "to the table" to help partners in the community address the needs of local individuals and families.

Representatives from the United Way (a non-profit community service organization), the County

Box 12.1 A Theoretical Analysis of Families and Social Media

Using social media is one of the most common ways that people communicate in modern society. As a family researcher and practitioner, it is important to consider how social media has affected family life, for better or for worse. Here, we theoretically analyze family use of social media using a few of the theories we have presented in this text. Let's begin with more macro-level theories.

From a functionalist perspective (Chapter 2), social media can serve an important purpose for families. Parents and children can communicate and keep updated on life events both big and small via social media, and this is especially important when families are separated by geographical distance. Thus, the manifest function of social media, which keeps people connected, is relevant for families. At the same time, there could be several latent functions; Facebook has been shown to increase feelings of jealousy in romantic relationships (Muise, Christofides, and Desmarais, 2009) and also increase rates of depression among teens (Melville, 2010; Selfhout et al., 2009).

In addition, life course theorists (Chapter 9) might be interested in how the posts of preadolescents and adolescents on social media affect them later on in their adult lives (Palfrey, Gasser, and Boyd, 2010). Inappropriate posts, messages, videos, or pictures can often pop up later in life and put reputations at risk, even if one has outgrown immature behaviors. These issues are important for families to consider as parents help children navigate social media.

From a conflict perspective (Chapter 3), social media can increase (or decrease) families' social capital. Parents often post on social media to ask for parenting advice, or advice related to purchases for their families. This is called crowdsourcing: "asking for advice on social media provides a quick way of getting a lot of opinions and ideas at one time" (Wallace, 2015). By capturing these responses, Facebook users are able to literally capitalize on their social networks and make a more informed decision about what approach might work best. Social *and* cultural capital can both be strengthened on social media.

In a similar way, social media give us insights into how families operate using more micro-level theories as well. Symbolic interactionist theory (Chapter 4), particularly Goffman's (1959) concepts of "presentation of self," can be applied to various social media sites like Facebook, Instagram, Twitter, and Pinterest. Pinterest is a website where members can save "pins" to categorized boards, ranging from craft ideas for children to recipes and ideas for hairstyles, outfits, and travel destinations. It should be no surprise that women outnumber men as Pinterest users 18 to 1 (Ottoni et al., 2013), which provides a tool for women to surveil themselves, as well as other women, by following what women post and save on the site. Recent research has examined mothers' use of Pinterest and the so-called "mompetition" that can occur on such sites (Griffin, 2014). Pins that mothers choose to save to their boards can serve as a presentation of self that mothers idealize and aspire to, reminiscent of Hays's (1996) conceptualization of intensive motherhood. At the same time, behavior on sites like this contributes easily to studying Goffman's presentation of self and impression management, because pins are often based on how people want others to perceive them (Griffin, 2014).

From a family stress and resilience perspective (Chapter 11), any of the social media sites – Facebook, Pinterest, Twitter, or Instagram – can be used to communicate to friends and followers that a family crisis or stressor is occurring. On Twitter and Facebook, users can choose an emotion when they update their status, such as feeling pained, drained, emotional, sad or broken, to name a few. This alerts friends and family members to a stressful

Box 12.1 A Theoretical Analysis of Families and Social Media (*Continued*)

time or crisis in someone's life, which can serve the purpose of drawing on potential resources for dealing with the crisis as well as initiating the coping process. The Double ABCX model (McCubbin and Patterson, 1983) can be useful in understanding these seemingly public accounts of individuals' private lives, including how one develops postcrisis as a result of sharing with other Facebook users.

There are endless possibilities for applying the theories presented in this book to social media. Consider your own experiences with social media, and think about ways in which you have witnessed one or more theories "in action" on Facebook, Pinterest, YouTube, Instagram, or any other medium worth analyzing. How do you think theories of family will adapt to these new forms of communication in the future? What other aspects of social media should be considered when applying theory to a very complex (and new!) set of social norms and expectations about how to use social media?

Department of Public Health, the community services board, the local school district, the local university, a local behavioral health organization, and the city's neighborhood resource office manager have all come together at a meeting to address how to best support low-income families in need of affordable child care so they can manage working the 12-hour day shifts at a local factory. The purpose of their meeting is to gather information about available resources in the community and come up with a plan to disseminate the information to families in need.

From a family ecological standpoint (Chapter 10), there are several considerations that need to be made when pooling together a list of solutions. First, the macrosystem should be analyzed in order to account for the diversity of the families who are in need of childcare. The neighborhood resource office manager presents a map of the city to outline where the majority of plant workers and their families live, the available public transportation, and schools and childcare centers that are open before and after the 12-hour day shift. By doing this, she is factoring in the mesosystem (connections between the micro family system and greater society) as well. From this map and discussion, the group identifies several social institutions that should be included in the "network of help" they have begun to outline for families and children in the area.

Several nonprofit organizations in the area have been known to offer services that may have been helpful in the past, but the group is not sure if those services are presently available. The group decides to reach out to employees at the city-operated community center to see if they could transport children after school to their facility to provide programming free of charge like they do for residents in nearby neighborhoods. You begin to notice that the conversation surrounding this issue sounds a lot like social exchange theory (Chapter 7); someone mentions that the community center may be eligible for an increase in both grant money and city funding if they can prove that the needs of children in the surrounding areas outweigh the available resources. The school district official volunteers to contact the community center to see if they might be willing to front a few resources to help this cause, in exchange for the documentation of need to increase the resources they receive. Together, it is hoped these two community partners can pool their resources to improve both the services offered and families reached by this one organization.

Finally, the university researcher present at the meeting suggests gathering data on the families in the targeted area to establish exactly what developmental stage they are in. For instance, some of the workers at the factory may be in the preschool family stage, and therefore may not need afterschool care; they may just need childcare with an emphasis on early childhood education. Conversely, it could be that a sizable proportion of families are in the middle years, and perhaps part of the "sandwich generation," where they are caught between caring for teenage or young adult children and their own parents, who need caregiving (Miller, 1981). It is important to know exactly what the needs are of this group of workers so that the community partners can come together with solutions that make sense for the families in need. During this discussion, you hear aspects of both family developmental theory (Chapter 5) and life course theory (Chapter 9). You are also quick to make the link between theory and research, noting that both are equally important as you try to assess the needs of families and come up with solutions that can be flexible and pragmatic.

As you can see throughout this chapter, we are constantly connecting theories we covered throughout the book to help fine-tune your "app." Now that we have addressed what that might look like during a job interview and in the workforce, we move to another

Box 12.2 Family Theory in Pop Culture: *Big Hero 6*

A scene from *Big Hero 6*, 2014, dir. Don Hall and Chris Williams, Walt Disney Pictures

Big Hero 6 is an animated superhero action movie that tells the story of a 14-year-old boy named Hiro Hamada and his older brother's robot named Baymax. Hiro's parents died when he was very young, and during the film, his older brother Tadashi dies in a tragic fire. Hiro's only remaining family is his Aunt Cass, who serves as his guardian.

Several relationships in the film can be analyzed using any theoretical perspective presented in this book. The main character, Hiro, wrestles with the loss of his older brother as well as the emotional difficulties associated with adolescence. Another character in the film, Professor Callaghan, also has to deal with the loss of his own daughter due to an accident during a simulation in a robotics lab. Both of these characters deal with the grief in different ways. Callaghan channels his anger into evil and becomes the villain of the film, trying to avenge the loss of his daughter. Hiro, on the other hand, utilizes his intelligence, interest in robotics, and his social network of his late brother's classmates to form a "family" of superheroes. One of the most appropriate theoretical frameworks to apply to this film is family stress and resilience theory (Chapter 11), because it specifically addresses ways in which children "bounce back" from stressful events. Functionalist theory (Chapter 2) could also be applied to this film to better understand how when one part of a system stops functioning, it affects other systems as well (i.e., Hiro's Aunt Cass has to step in and be the guardian for him and his brother when their parents die). Even theories that may not seem immediately applicable to this film can be utilized. For example, life course theorists (Chapter 9) might analyze the timing of Hiro's parents' death (when he was three), and the timing of his brother's death (during adolescence), and how Hiro transitions through life course stages differently than his peers because of these two tragedies. Feminist theorists (Chapter 8) would examine the gendered expectations that are present in the film, including some characters' display of hegemonic masculinity (Professor Callaghan) and emphasized femininity (Honey Lemon).

Consider how conflict theory (Chapter 3), symbolic interactionist theory (Chapter 4), family developmental theory (Chapter 5), family systems theory (Chapter 6), social exchange theory (Chapter 7), and family ecological theory (Chapter 10) might be applied as well. There are countless possibilities for applying theory to this film!

pop culture example in Box 12.2 to remind you that theories – whether you like it or not – are everywhere!

Future of Family Theories

In Chapter 1 on "What Is Theory?" we described several assumptions that all family theories make about the inner workings of families and the broader structures that constrain and support them: (a) the *developmental* assumption that families change over time; (b) the *diversity* assumption that families vary in their composition and structure; (c) the *systemic* assumption that families are systems; and (d) the *processual* assumption that families are dynamic. As we reflect back on these core ideas of change, diversity, systems, and dynamics that all family theories address, we cannot ignore the role that technology will play in the future development of family theories. Family mobility, communication, stress and resilience, development, and relationships have all been revolutionized by technology. Now all family theories must also incorporate the assumption that *technology* is infused throughout family life, regardless of social location and nationality. Therefore, we hope that we have connected you with theories of family in the same way that your technologies

Box 12.3 Global Comparisons of Cell Phone and Social Media Use

Consider the use of cell phones, the internet, and social media as ways that families now communicate and stay connected. How does this trend apply to various destinations around the world? A 2014 report from the Pew Research Center found that 91 percent of Americans have a cell phone, and many developing nations (such as Turkey, Lebanon, and Chile) are rapidly catching up to cell phone use patterns similar to the US. Other countries, such as Pakistan and Mexico, however, lag behind the US with approximately 50–60 percent of their populations having a cell phone. On balance, though, the trend for the vast majority of citizens of most countries to own a cell phone is likely to rise, because many developing nations have "skipped landline technology and moved straight to mobile" (Rainie and Poushter, 2014).

Another interesting feature of the Pew Research Center's report on technology use reveals global trends in social media use. Americans are most likely to have access to and use the internet (84 percent), and a large proportion of Americans use it at least daily (71 percent). A different pattern has been found in some other countries, particularly emerging nations. Although emerging countries include a smaller share of adults who actually use the internet, those who do are very active social media users. Compared to the US, where 73 percent of internet users are also social networking site users, figures are much higher in Turkey (79 percent), Russia (86 percent), and Egypt (88 percent). To explain this trend, the authors suggest that one of the reasons that some Americans lag behind those in other countries in terms of using the social media platforms that have emerged since 2008 is because they may be more comfortable with earlier social platforms such as email. Again, developing countries may be skipping the older forms of electronic communications as new platforms and opportunities arise.

Consider how access to and use of new technologies affects family mobility; we could argue by using functionalist theory (Chapter 2) that some family members may outsource their needs – such as romance, affection, and love – by using (or abusing) the internet to form extramarital relationships. At the same time, technology keeps families connected across a distance like never before. How have your own family and relationships with loved ones benefited from technology? On the flip side, what have the downsides been? Keep tuned in to your theoretical app as you work through these personal experiences to help name some of the pros and cons of technology use in families.

connect you with ways of thinking, knowing, doing, and learning. Additionally, while technology does change rapidly, we hope we have communicated that the family is an enduring institution that has proven capable of adaptation and transformation over time, and you are now armed with the ability to follow these changes with your theoretical app! We look forward to observing, and explaining, how technological innovation will intersect with the original assumptions we have identified in continuing to change the nature of family theory and family theorizing in the future.

Multimedia Suggestions

The websites listed are presented here to familiarize you with the occupations that family studies students are most likely to pursue after graduation. While this list is not exhaustive, it should provide an overview of what fields you could consider for yourself, as a budding family theorist!

- School counselors: https://www.schoolcounselor.org/
- International Association for Counseling: http://www.iac-irtac.org/
- World Federation of Occupational Therapists: http://www.wfot.org/
- Social work: https://www.socialworkers.org/nasw/default.asp
- Nonprofit work: http://www.idealist.org/
- Community health workers/educators: http://explorehealthcareers.org/en/home
- Adoption work: http://thenationalcenterforadoption.org

Activate your theory app: Rank the occupations above in terms of your level of interest, and map out how your experiences both inside and outside the classroom will help prepare you for each field. Have at least one "backup" plan in mind.

Harry Potter (1997–2007)

Harry Potter is arguably an "empire" based on seven novels written by British author J. K. Rowling. The books were first turned into films, then video games, and even an amusement park owned by Universal Studios and Warner Brothers, opened in 2014. The premise of the story is centered on a young boy, Harry, as he develops into a wizard at Hogwarts School of Witchcraft and Wizardry. Harry is orphaned as a baby because the dark wizard Voldemort murdered his parents. The adventures of the series pit Harry against Voldemort and several themes and plots can be analyzed using *any* theory presented in this book. To list a few: (a) family stress and resilience (Chapter 11), Harry's relationship with his guardians, the Dursleys; (b) symbolic interactionist theory (Chapter 4), the meaning associated with the four houses of Hogwarts; (c) feminist theory (Chapter 8), the role Hermione plays in the fight against evil; and (d) family systems theory (Chapter 6), as it applies to the Weasleys.

A scene from *Harry Potter and the Sorcerer's Stone*, 2001, dir. Chris Columbus, Warner Bros. Pictures

Activate your theory app: Compare the *Harry Potter* series to another popular trilogy/film series that has been produced during an older family member's lifetime. Apply theory to the two and contrast them, paying attention to how cultural and social expectations affect each.

The Wizard of Oz (1939)

Though this film was made nearly 80 years ago, it remains one of the best known musicals of all time.

It is also a great movie to apply theories of family to! The main character, Dorothy, "dreams" of visiting the "Land of Oz," arguably because she was experiencing considerable stress after an interaction with a mean neighbor, a fortune teller, and then a tornado on her family's farm in Kansas. Social exchange theory (Chapter 7) is evident when Dorothy needs to present the Wizard of Oz with the Wicked Witch of the West's broom in exchange for a brain (for Scarecrow), a heart (for Tin Man), courage (for Lion), and a return trip home for Dorothy. From a family systems perspective (Chapter 6), we could also analyze the subsystems in Dorothy's family: she has close kin-like relationships with the farmhands as well as her guardians. The power surrounding the Wizard of Oz could also be analyzed through the lens of conflict theory (Chapter 3), as the fantasy world seemingly operates with one individual (Oz) profiting off the backs of many (the Munchkins).

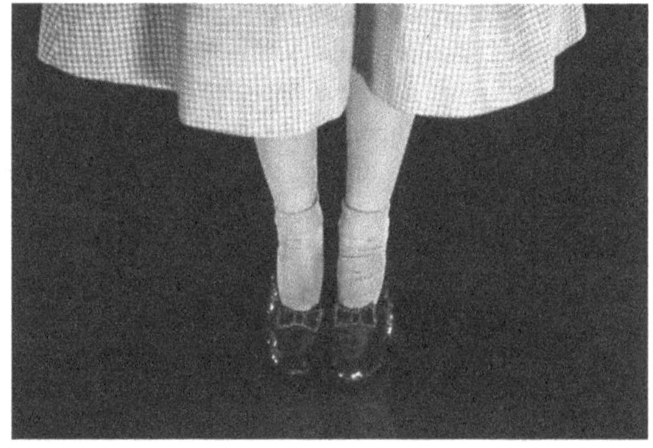

A scene from *The Wizard of Oz*, 1939, dir. Victor Fleming, Metro-Goldwyn-Mayer

Activate your theory app: You may also be familiar with the story *Wicked*, which is a "prequel" to the *Wizard of Oz* that includes both a novel and Broadway musical. Consider how we could theoretically analyze the story of Elphaba as it relates to the *Wizard of Oz*.

Further Reading

Lorde, A., *Sister outsider: Essays and speeches by Audre Lorde* (Berkeley, CA: Crossing Press, 2007; originally published 1984). Audre Lorde was a Black lesbian poet and feminist writer/activist. In this collection of her inspirational essays, Lorde articulates a perspective on intersectionality that served as a forerunner of contemporary feminist work on the theory of intersectionality. In particular, her essay "The master's tools will never dismantle the master's house" is a compelling critique of feminist thought that excludes differences of race, sexuality, class, and age. She powerfully encourages all women to work together to turn their differences into strengths in order to dismantle the existing patriarchal, homophobic, racist, and ageist foundations of society. Countless scholars and activists have been inspired and changed by the theoretical framework she put into words.

Mills, C. W., *The sociological imagination* (Oxford: Oxford University Press, 1959). This book by C. Wright Mills is a sociological classic. No doubt this is assigned in many theory classes because it provides the grounding on which scholars learn, often as students, how to begin and hone the process of thinking theoretically. The book also teaches about the process of critique. For example, Mills provided a critique of the grand theories at the time (e.g., Parsons's structural functionalism) for attempting to be abstract and value-free. Mills's insights have inspired generations of scholars to think outside the box, be creative in their theorizing, and take bold steps in conducting research that matters to those we seek to understand and assist.

Newman, B. M., and Newman, P. R., *Theories of human development* (Mahwah, NJ: Lawrence Erlbaum, 2007). This book is written for students interested in understanding the kinds of theories that are used by psychologists and human development scholars. The authors describe nine theories from three major perspectives: (a) those that emphasize biological systems (i.e., evolutionary, psychosexual, and cognitive developmental); (b) those that emphasize environmental factors (i.e., learning, social role, and life course); and (c) those that emphasize a dynamic interaction between biological and environmental factors (i.e., psychosocial, cognitive social-historical, and dynamic systems). This book is a good complement to the current text on family theories, especially for gaining insight into how family and human development theories overlap and differ.

Wacker, R. R., and Roberto, K. A., *Community resources for older adults: Programs and services in an era of change*, 4th edn (Thousand Oaks, CA: Sage, 2014). In this comprehensive book, gerontologists Robbyn Wacker and Karen Roberto combine theory, research, policy, and practice to help students and practitioners understand the needs of older adults, from the aging babyboomers to the oldest-old. The book is applicable to social workers, gerontologists, family practitioners, health care providers, adult services administrators, just to name a few disciplinary backgrounds, who work in private, nonprofit, and public agencies and organizations. The authors offer many practical suggestions that are grounded in a variety of theoretical frameworks that build upon and extend the theories we address in this book.

Questions for Students

Discussion Questions

1 We have presented theories of family in this book as emerging from different disciplines, such as sociology, psychology, family studies, history, and economics. Compare how two of these disciplines (e.g., family studies and economics) approach studying the family. What are the main differences and similarities?
2 Consider the following research question: What predicts whether or not a couple engaged to be married *will actually* get married? Think about which theoretical framework would be best suited to answer this question, and why. In contrast, which theoretical framework might not be the best to explain this research question?
3 We have described four main assumptions (development, diversity, system, and process) that all family theories seek to make, and then, added a fifth, technology. Now that you have read every chapter in this book (we hope!), can you think of any other assumptions that run through all or most of the theories?
4 How would you explain the ways that theory, research, and practical application work together to help family scholars intervene into family life and family problems?
5 Which of the theories you have read about seems to be the most applicable to everyday life? That is, which of these theories translates best into practices and policies that can improve family life?
6 Next time you go on a job interview, do you think you will incorporate any of these family theories into the questions your prospective employer might ask about how you work with families? Why or why not?

Your Turn!

Using one of the theoretical frameworks from this textbook as a starting point, construct *your own* theoretical framework to be used to study families. Identify whether or not your theory will be micro, macro, or a combination of both. Create and define at least two concepts that are unique to your theory, and give examples of how those concepts are different from the theory you are starting from, and what new considerations they bring to the theoretical canon.

Personal Reflection Questions

1 Revisit those five reasons that people get divorced that you identified in the first personal reflection question when you read Chapter 1. Which theory or theories align with your answers? Or, have your answers changed after reading this book? Try to pair a theoretical framework with where you stand.
2 Which family theory, or theories, can explain most of the way you see the world? Which theoretical framework from this text do you most

identify with? Which one do you least identify with? Why?

3 If the authors asked you to help them revise this book, which of the theories would you suggest they "throw out"? Are there other theories you would like to know more about?

4 Thinking about all of the case studies we have described in this book, write up a case study, based on your own life, and show how at least two of the theories can help explain the circumstances you describe.

5 On a scale of 1 to 10, with 1 being low and 10 being high, how would you rate your understanding of theories now, compared to when you first opened this book? Why?

6 What is the last TV show or film that you saw to which you found yourself applying some of the theoretical concepts in this book? In what ways?

References

Goffman, E. (1959). *The presentation of self in everyday life.* New York: Doubleday.

Griffin, K. M. (2014). *Pinning motherhood: The construction of mothering identities on Pinterest* (Doctoral dissertation). University of Central Florida, Orlando.

Hays, S. (1996). *The cultural contradictions of motherhood.* New Haven: Yale University Press.

McCubbin, H. I., and Patterson, J. M. (1983). The family stress process: The Double ABCX model of adjustment and adaptation. *Marriage and Family Review, 6*(1–2), 7–37. doi:10.1300/j002v06n01_02.

Melville, K. (2010, February 3). Facebook use associated with depression. *Sci GoGo.* Retrieved from http://www.scienceagogo.com/news/20100102231001data_trunc_sys.shtml.

Miller, D. (1981). The "sandwich generation": Adult children of the aging. *Social Work, 26,* 419–423. doi:10.1093/sw/26.5.419.

Muise, A., Christofides, E., and Desmarais, S. (2009). More information than you ever wanted: Does Facebook bring out the green-eyed monster of jealousy? *CyberPsychology and Behavior, 12,* 441–444. doi:10.1089/cpb.2008.0263

Ottoni, R., Pesce, J. P., Las Casas, D. B., Franciscani, G., Jr, Meira, W., Jr, Kumaraguru, P., and Almeida, V. (2013). *Ladies first: Analyzing gender roles and behaviors in Pinterest.* At http://homepages.dcc.ufmg.br/~jpesce/wp-content/plugins/papercite/pdf/icwsm13_pinterest.pdf.

Palfrey, J. G., Gasser, U., and Boyd, D. (2010). *Response to FCC notice of inquiry 09-94: Empowering parents and protecting children in an evolving media landscape.* Berkman Center Research Publication, 2010–02; Harvard Public Law Working Paper 10–19.

Rainie, L., and Poushter, J. (2014, February 13). *Emerging nations catching up to U.S. on technology adoption, especially mobile and social media use.* Pew Research Center. At www.pewresearch.org/fact-tank/2014/02/13/emerging-nations-catching-up-to-u-s-on-technology-adoption-especially-mobile-and-social-media-use/.

Selfhout, M. H., Branje, S. J., Delsing, M., ter Bogt, T. F., and Meeus, W. H. (2009). Different types of internet use, depression, and social anxiety: The role of perceived friendship quality. *Journal of Adolescence, 32,* 819–833. doi:10.1016/j.adolescence.2008.10.011.

Wallace, K. (2015, January 13). *Why Facebook parenting can backfire.* CNN. At http://www.cnn.com/2015/01/13/living/feat-facebook-crowdsourced-parenting/.

Glossary

ABCX model A is the stressful event, B is the family resources or strengths, and C is the family's perception of the event. X is a crisis, when the family cannot figure out how to solve the problem.

adaptation Individuals and families are dynamic and capable of changing their beliefs and behaviors in order to adapt to their environments.

agency A complex social-psychological process referring to one's ability and desire to make choices within the constraints of social institutions.

alienation When workers are removed from the product of their labor, from fellow workers, or from reaching their full human potential.

assumptions Ideas that scholars take to be true about families.

back stage Where social actors retreat from the performance.

behavioral psychological approach A psychological exchange model that uses principles of learning and reinforcement that occur between a dyad of two individuals.

blended family The family form that includes children from a previous marriage.

boundary The various parts of a system are divided into discrete boundaries that are either permeable or impermeable.

bourgeoisie The ruling class which owns the means of production (e.g., landowners and capitalists).

capitalists Profit off of the labor of the working class.

chronosystem An "invisible" system that represents the influence of time on each layer.

classes Groups of people in competition for scarce resources.

cohort Groups of people who experienced or produced social events at a specific point in time.

collective conscience Common sense of morality that all members of the community believe in and uphold.

comparison level (CL) A measure of relationship satisfaction by which people evaluate the rewards and costs of a relationship in terms of what they feel is deserved or obtainable.

comparison level for alternatives (CLalt) A measure of relationship stability that refers to the lowest level of relational rewards a person is willing to accept given available rewards from alternative relationships or being alone.

concepts Terms and definitions used to explain a theory's framework based on the assumptions. The building blocks used to create the theory.

conflict management Occurs when the conflict is addressed, but does not disappear.

conflict resolution When the conflict ends because a solution has been reached.

consciousness When individuals start to become aware of the differential treatment and unearned privileges operating at the personal, familial, and societal levels.

consensus The stable state needed to reach either conflict resolution or management.

Family Theories: Foundations and Applications, First Edition. Katherine R. Allen and Angela C. Henderson.

conversation of gestures Humans engage in social interaction and interpretation in order to make sense of the world around them.

cost-benefit analysis Calculating the potential rewards or benefits and the costs in a relationship to decide whether or not the relationship is worth investing in.

costs The potentially negative things about a relationship that we seek to avoid or minimize.

crisis, the X factor The event that causes the disruption in family dynamics and leads to the family's reorganization

critical epistemology What gets to count as knowledge is defined by those who are in power, and thus, the powerful members of society impose their definitions onto others.

cultural capital Nonmaterial forms of capital such as aesthetic preferences, verbal skills, and levels of education, knowledge, or expertise.

cultural lag When society evolves but aspects of culture, such as beliefs and values, take longer to change.

cultural system The overarching system of values, norms, and symbols that guide the choices individuals make, limiting the type of interaction that could occur.

cumulative advantage or disadvantage The ways in which structural location, available resources, and opportunities accumulate over time.

cybernetics A model for understanding the forms and patterns that steer a system and allow that system to self-regulate.

deprivation-satiation When a reward loses value because it has been given too much in the recent past to hold high value.

differentiation of self One's sense of being an individual compared to being related to others.

disengagement When there is low cohesion among family members; they tend to operate independently of one another.

distributive justice Based on equity theory, the expectation that a person in an exchange relation will expect their rewards will be proportional to their costs.

Double ABCX model How families deal with multiple stressors over time. The model includes precrisis and postcrisis variables.

double bind When a person is given two commands that contradict each other.

dramaturgy Life is acted out like a stage drama or play.

dynamic density The number of people living in any given place, as well as the number of people interacting.

dysfunction The part of a system that has broken down.

economic capital The material resources, such as wealth, land, and money that one controls or possesses.

economic-utilitarian framework A sociological exchange model that examines broader institutions dealing with power and inequality.

emotion work When we attempt to change an emotion or feeling so that it is appropriate for the situation.

emotional cut-off The extreme distancing that family members can experience as a way of coping with heightened anxiety.

emotional labor The idea of extending emotion work into the paid labor force, existing to "sell" emotions to customers.

enmeshment When there is high cohesion among family members, who are highly dependent upon one another and closed off to others outside the family system.

epistemology One's orientation to answering questions about the world.

equilibrium Seeking a balance between change (positive feedback loops) and stability (negative feedback loops).

exosystem Social institutions such as the economy, the media, industry, or criminal justice system.

expressive roles Showing love, care, concern, and support for the system.

extrinsic rewards When the outcome of a relationship is more important than the emotional value (intrinsic reward) of the relationship.

family adjustment and adaptation response (FAAR) model How families make meaning of the stressful situation including family members' subjective definitions of needs and capacities and how families transcend the situation to develop more stable cognitive beliefs about their relationships within the family and in relation to the larger community.

family career Family dynamics over time that includes individual members, the family as a system, and the family within broader society.

family development A longitudinal process of going through a hierarchical system of age and stage related changes, such as birth, death, marriage, and divorce.

family developmental tasks Individuals and family units have normative goals that they must accomplish in order to move forward to the next level of development.

family ecosystem The human-built environment, the social-cultural environment, and the natural physical-biological environment.

family life cycle Beginning with marriage, the normative stages and shared experiences in families as they progress over time.

family of origin The family one is born into.

family of procreation The family that is started when partners marry and have children.

family stages Predictable phases across the family life cycle, marked by marriage, procreation, parenthood, empty nest, grandparents, and widowhood.

family system A unit of interdependent individuals.

family transitions A change in the family system when major changes occur in the lives of individual family members.

feedback A way of capturing the interdependence function of systems, where individuals in a family system influence one another; feedback can be either negative or positive.

front stage Social actors tailor their role performance for an audience.

function The purpose each part of a system serves to contribute to the overall operation.

generalized other An organized set of attitudes that are common in the group to which an individual belongs.

generation Similar to a cohort, when a group of people experienced or produced social events, but spanning more than one decade.

glass ceiling The invisible barrier that keeps women and members of minority groups in lower-level positions by denying them the same opportunities for career advancement as White, privileged men.

hegemonic masculinity Socially mandated ideas of how men should behave; can refer to strength, power, wealth, virility, aggression, and being emotionless.

holism The idea that the whole family should be studied in order to understand family dynamics.

homeplace A self-supporting safe space where minority individuals can experience the safety, affection, and full acceptance not available in the wider society.

human betterment The goal toward which humans should individually and collectively strive.

identity Internalized expectations and meaning.

identity salience Our identities are arranged in a hierarchy by order of importance.

imbalanced exchange When one individual becomes dependent on the person with more power because they have few rewards to offer and few alternatives to turn to.

impression management Social actors try to control or guide the impression others form.

index person The person whose life is featured in a genogram.

institutionalization When a part of the larger cultural system becomes part of a standard in society; a long-standing tradition that is embedded and identifiable.

instrumental roles Being a leader, making important decisions, and providing material needs for the system.

internalization When individuals adhere to the cultural norms in such a way that they become part of need-dispositions and our patterns of communication and ways of thinking.

interpretive epistemology The view that knowledge is subjective, with the goal of understanding how families make meaning of their own experiences. Explains the why of family dynamics.

intersectionality How multiple systems of oppression, such as race, class, gender, sexuality, religion, age, and nationality, intersect to create advantage or disadvantage; the politics of location.

intrinsic rewards The tangible and intangible things that give us pleasure in and of themselves, not because they provide the means for obtaining other benefits.

latent functions Unintended consequences of the system.

lesbian feminism Combined sexual orientation with gender theory, by critiquing the concept of compulsory heterosexuality.

liberal feminism The push for women's equality with men.

linked lives The ways in which a person's life is changed when something happens to another family member.

locational intersectionality The identities of social positions of disadvantaged groups, such as those who are poor, members of an ethnic minority group, LGBTQ, old, or disabled.

looking-glass self How an individual's sense of self develops based on beliefs about how he or she is perceived by significant others.

macro-level The analysis of the larger patterns in society that influence individual and family life.

macrosystem The largest layer represents cultural ideologies, ways of thinking, and attitudes that exist at a broader level.

manifest functions The intended purpose of a system.

Marxists Sociologists who utilize Marx's theories to critique the effects of capitalism on various aspects of society.

meaning of the event, the C factor Perception of the event or situation to which a family must respond.

meaning-making Attributing meaning to events in our lives.

mechanical solidarity Societies held together by commonalities, where members are generalists and perform similar tasks with similar responsibilities.

mesosystem The connection between the microsystem and the exosystem.

micro-level Analyzing phenomena more closely, in smaller doses, to explore meanings and experiences for individuals.

microsystem Your immediate family or peers that you rely on closely and come in contact with regularly.

moral individualism An outlook on life based on what is good for oneself.

multiple social contexts One has multiple social positions in terms of gender, race, class, age, sexual orientation, and so on.

multiple timeclocks Individual time, family time, and historical time that are interrelated over the life course.

need-dispositions Types of action guided by emotion and individual drive, or representations of individuals' personal uniqueness.

negative spaces Aspects of everyday family life that are hidden from view.

norms Societal expectations.

norms of reciprocity The history of fairness in a relationship that strengthens feelings of trust between both parties in an exchange relationship.

object Ideas, roles, social norms, behaviors, or actions.

ontogenic change How an organism, such as a family or individual family members, changes and matures over time.

organic solidarity Societies held together by difference.

patriarchy A political system of male dominance.

period of disorganization The previous ways a family coped or interacted with one another are inadequate or blocked and cannot meet the demands of the new stressor.

period of recovery Reversing the process of disorganization and activating the ability to reorganize.

personality system Takes individual characteristics into account while still being embedded in the social structure.

pile-up of stressors When stressors accumulate over time and affect the family's ability to reorganize.

pluralistic A heterogeneous population made up of different genders, racial-ethnic groups, religions, sexual orientations, and social classes.

position The location of a family member in the family system.

positivist epistemology The view that guides the scientific method and presumes there is an objective, value-free truth that can be discovered about families through systematic research procedures.

postmodern feminism A feminist approach that deconstructs gender systems and the practices that uphold them, primarily through challenging and exposing what has come to be seen and accepted as normal and natural.

power In exchange theory, the probability that one actor in a relationship will carry out his or her own will despite resistance from the other actor in the dyad.

pragmatism The meaning of objects lies in their practical use.

praxis The part of feminist theory that guides the practical or activist part of feminism.

privilege Power differences in society create social institutions and interactions that value and advantage the elite group and create disadvantages for minority groups.

process-person-context-time (PPCT) model The four components in the bioecological model that influence the developmental outcome and interaction among nested systems.

proletariat The working class who sell their labor to the capitalist class in return for a wage.

propositions Statements that make theories testable and are based on both assumptions and concepts that we use when we "apply" theory to the study of families.

qualitative life history interview studies In-depth interviews conducted between the researcher and the participant that address an individual's experiences over time.

queer theory Calls attention to the construction of sexual orientation as a social phenomenon, rather than a mental illness or medical issue.

radical feminism A feminist approach that seeks to uncover the root cause of mechanisms of women's oppression and men's privilege with the goal of creating massive social change.

rational choice The assumption that individuals will act on the desire to maximize their own personal advantage by making decisions based on a cost-benefit analysis of the situation.

reflexivity An explicit and comfortable use of self-reflection in research and writing.

relational intersectionality A type of feminist theory that explains how intersectionality affects every individual, not just the most oppressed and marginalized.

reorganization The ability or inability to develop new ways of interacting with each other and handling stress.

resources The tangible and intangible forms of capital that individuals have to exchange in a relationship; capital can be physical, human, and social.

resources, the B factor Strengths to help a family be resilient. Assets the family can draw on to respond to the stress or crisis.

rewards The potentially positive benefits about a relationship that we seek to maximize.

rhetoric Messages that are aimed at persuading the audience.

role The dynamic aspect of a position; a detailed set of obligations for interaction; behavioral expectations and meanings that are attached to positions located in the social structure.

self The individual's emergence through social interaction.

self-interest One of the driving forces that motivate individuals in an interdependent relationship for exchanging something of value with one another.

significant other Greater priority is given to the perspectives of individuals who are most important to you.

social address model A simplistic way of understanding human and family development, based upon only one influence from a person's environment.

social capital An individual's or family's network of contacts and acquaintances that can be used to secure or advance one's position.

social construction of reality The belief in what is real that arises out of social interaction; typically considered important and valuable if seen that way by powerful members of society.

social integration The degree to which people are tied to their social groups.

social system The level of interactions between two or more actors, where actors are aware of one another's ideas and intentions, and their interactions are governed by shared norms or expectations.

socialist feminism An approach to feminism that is rooted in Marxist class theory, where capitalism and its relation to patriarchy are responsible for women's second-class citizenship.

socialization When individuals come to regard specific norms as binding; it occurs during the interaction of the personality and the social systems.

Standard North American Family (SNAF) The normative model of White, middle-class Americans with married, heterosexual parents.

stimulus proposition When an individual responds to a stimulus that provided a reward in the past.

strain theory Posits that societies have a set of cultural goals that all societal members are pressured to achieve, or live up to, which results in strain.

stressor, the A factor Internal or external and a natural occurrence in daily life; can be traumatic, and/or involve multiple losses; the crisis-precipitating event.

structural functionalism A variation of functionalist theory that emphasizes how social systems produce shared moral codes and norms that trickle down to individuals.

subjective The experiences we have with objects and how we make meaning of those experiences through social interaction.

subsystems Smaller subcultures that are under the umbrella of a social system; also, units within the family that can be examined on their own in relation to the larger unit.

success proposition When individuals are rewarded for their actions, they repeat them.

symbolic capital Prestige, honor, reputation, or charisma.

symbolic interactionism A micro-level theory that considers processes at the individual level.

The Family A term that implies there is one "normative" family, rather than an acknowledgment that families are very diverse.

theorize The process that we work through in creating or refining a theory.

theory A set of ideas that serves as a framework for understanding the world around us.

trajectory Emerging from each new transition, such as becoming a spouse or a parent, and marked by the continuity of roles and identities.

transnational carework When migrant women work as live-in or live-out domestic workers for families in wealthy nations.

trauma Associated with extreme stress, often coming from major disasters or other types of catastrophic events that people are ill prepared to deal with or deter.

triangulation When a three-person relationship occurs and two of the members of the relationship exclude the third.

turning points A type of transition that is very personal and may not be recognized by an outsider as significant.

value The individual, family, and society's belief system about important ideals.

waves of feminism A way to think about and characterize the history of feminist theory and activism over the past two centuries.

womanist feminism A feminist approach developed by women of color to challenge the liberal paradigm, arguing that race, gender, and class cannot be separated.

zero-sum game Family dynamics are dependent on one another to the point that when one member of the family gains, other family members lose.

Index

Family Theories: Foundations and Applications, First Edition. Katherine R. Allen and Angela C. Henderson.